Development Theory

WITHDRAWN

Theory, Culture & Society

Theory, Culture & Society caters for the resurgence of interest in culture within contemporary social science and the humanities. Building on the heritage of classical social theory, the book series examines ways in which this tradition has been reshaped by a new generation of theorists. It also publishes theoretically informed analyses of everyday life, popular culture, and new intellectual movements.

EDITOR: Mike Featherstone, *Nottingham Trent University*

SERIES EDITORIAL BOARD
Roy Boyne, *University of Durham*
Nicholas Gane, *University of York*
Scott Lash, *Goldsmiths College, University of London*
Roland Robertson, *University of Aberdeen*
Couze Venn, *Nottingham Trent University*

THE TCS CENTRE
The Theory, Culture & Society book series, the journals *Theory, Culture & Society* and *Body & Society*, and related conference, seminar and postgraduate programmes operate from the TCS Centre at Nottingham Trent University. For further details of the TCS Centre's activities please contact:

The TCS Centre, Room 175
Faculty of Humanities
Nottingham Trent University
Clifton Lane, Nottingham, NG11 8NS, UK
e-mail: tcs@ntu.ac.uk
web: http://sagepub.net/tcs/

Recent volumes include:

Sociology of Intellectual Life: The Career of the mind in and around Academy
Steve Fuller

Globalization and Football: A Critical Sociology
Richard Giulianotti and Roland Robertson

Saturated Society: Regulating Lifestyles in Consumer Capitalism
Pekka Sulkunen

Changing Bodies: Habitat, Crisis and Creativity
Chris Shilling

The Media City: Media, Architecture and Urban Space
Scott McQuire

Development Theory

Deconstructions/Reconstructions

Second Edition

Jan Nederveen Pieterse

Los Angeles | London | New Delhi
Singapore | Washington DC

© Jan Nederveen Pieterse 2010

First published 2001
Second edition 2010
Reprinted 2010, 2012, 2013

Published in association with Theory, Culture & Society,
Nottingham Trent University

SAGE Publications Ltd
1 Oliver's Yard
55 City Road
London EC1Y 1SP

SAGE Publications Inc.
2455 Teller Road
Thousand Oaks, California 91320

SAGE Publications India Pvt Ltd
B 1/I 1 Mohan Cooperative Industrial Area
Mathura Road, Post Bag 7
New Delhi 110 044

SAGE Publications Asia-Pacific Pte Ltd
3 Church Street
#10–04 Samsung Hub
Singapore 049483

Library of Congress Control Number: 2009921642

British Library Cataloguing in Publication data

A catalogue record for this book is available from
the British Library

ISBN 978-1-4129-4514-1
ISBN 978-1-4129-4515-8 (pbk)

Typeset by C&M Digitals (P) Ltd, Chennai, India
Printed in Great Britain by MPG Printgroup, UK
Printed on paper from sustainable resources

MIX
Paper from
responsible sources
FSC
www.fsc.org   FSC® C018575

In memory of W.F. Wertheim, Gerrit Huizer,
Vincent Tucker and Ranjit Dwivedi

Contents

List of Tables and Figures

Tables

Figures

Acknowledgements

Most chapters in this book have appeared earlier as articles in journals and books and they have all been revised for this volume. I acknowledge the kind permission of the following publishers and copyright holders:

Institute of Social Studies: 'Dilemmas of development discourse: the crisis of developmentalism and the comparative method', *Development and Change* (22, 1, 1991); 'My paradigm or yours? Alternative development, post development, reflexive development', *Development and Change* (29, 2, 1998). A newly added section in Chapter 5 draws on my review article 'Tough Liberalism: the Human Development Report and cultural liberty', *Development and Change* (36, 6, 2005).

Routledge: 'The development of development theory: towards critical globalism', *Review of International Political Economy* (3, 4, 1996); 'Trends in development theory', in Ronen Palan (ed.), *Global Political Economy* (London, 2000); 'After post-development', *Third World Quarterly* (20, 1, 2000).

Frank Cass: 'The cultural turn in development: questions of power', *European Journal of Development Research* (7, 1, 1995). 'Growth and equity revisited: a supply-side approach to social development', *European Journal of Development Research* (9, 1, 1997) and in Cristóbal Kay (ed.), *Globalisation, Competitiveness and Human Security* (London, 1997). 'Critical holism and the Tao of development', *European Journal of Development Research* (11, 1, 1999).

Zed Books: A short version of 'Critical holism and the Tao of development' appears in Ronaldo Munck and Denis O'Hearn (eds), *Critical Development Theory: Contributions to a New Paradigm* (London, Zed, 1999).

'Delinking or globalization?' appeared earlier in *Economic and Political Weekly* (29, 5, 1994).

An early version of 'Digital capitalism and development' appeared in the *Incommunicado Reader*, edited by Geert Lovink and Soenke Zehle (Nederveen Pieterse, 2005a). This chapter has benefited from being presented at a Communication and Development workshop in Malmö (www.k3.mah.se/comdev, www.thirdspaceseminar.org) and at the Incommunicado conference on Information for Development in Amsterdam 2005 (www.incommunicado.info/conference). I thank Linda Aitio for research assistance and Sanjay Gupta, Oscar Hemer and Dan Schiller for comments.

Amsterdam University Press: An early version of Chapter 12 appeared in *Doing Good or Doing Better: Development policies in a globalising world*, edited by Peter van Lieshout, Monique Kremer and Robert Went and published by Amsterdam University Press for the Dutch Scientific Council for Government Policy (Nederveen Pieterse, 2009b). I thank Robert Went and other editors for their comments.

I am indebted to many more friends and sources of inspiration than I can acknowledge. Friends and colleagues have commented on different chapters. I cordially thank Thomas Blom Hansen, Lisa Chason, Ranjit Dwivedi, Aurora Galindo, Des Gasper, Ananta Giri, Frank Hirtz, Gerrit Huizer, Sudipto Kaviraj, Cristóbal Kay, W.D. Lakshman, Lily Ling, Gilbert Rist, Henk van Roosmalen, Jan Aart Scholte, David Slater, Thanh-dam Truong, Vincent Tucker, Peter Waterman, W.F. Wertheim and Chris Williams. Most chapters were written while I was at the Institute of Social Studies, an international graduate school in development studies in The Hague, and I am grateful to the Institute for many lessons learnt. I have been inspired by several generations of ISS students, particularly in the Politics of Alternative Development Strategies MA programme. To name only a few, my thanks go to Hanan and Wafa Abdel Rahman, Michael Chai, Daniel Chavez, Tony Chiejina, Mike Demel, Fiona Dove, Azza Karam, Sergio Lenci, Wangu Mwangi, Edgar Pieterse, Melania Portilla Rodriguez, Jeff Powell, Imad Sabi, Ali Salman, Kim Scipes, Albana Shala, Nahda Sh'hada Younis, P.L. de Silva, Mukta Srivastava, Ignatius Swart, Stuart Todd, Reaz Uddin and Hasmet Uluorta.

For the second edition, I would like express my appreciation to graduate students at the University of Illinois Urbana-Champaign and all those who commented on its theses, among others, Emin Adas, Chandler Armstrong, Serife Genis, Ravi Ghadge, Jin-Ho Jang, Jae Kim, Jongtae Kim, Amit Prasad, Ben Smith and Daniel Tessema. My perspective has been influenced by research trips to Asia, Africa and Latin America and friends and colleagues to whom I am indebted are too many to mention. I have appreciated probing questions by Tila Kumar and Amiya Das of Delhi University. I thank Chris Rojek at Sage for proposing the second edition. I thank Sharada Srinivasan for commenting on a draft. The usual disclaimer of course applies.

Preface to the second edition

Since the first edition of this book appeared in 2001 there have been momentous changes in the field of development policy and studies. Some are the deepening of trends that have long been in motion—in particular the rise of Asia and newly industrialized countries—and some have been radical ruptures. Among the latter, two major trend breaks are the weakening of neoliberalism and of American hegemony. Neither has left the stage but they have been on the losing side, face mounting problems and gather no new adherents. Neoliberalism—essentially the style of Anglo-American capitalism turned into doctrine—is crumbling from its own excesses and swerves from crisis to bubble to crisis. The weakening of American hegemony has been on the cards for some time but has been hastened by neoconservative overreach, particularly in Iraq and Afghanistan.

Originally the book outlined three main eras of development. First, the preludes to development in the 1800s and the catch-up policies from the mid-nineteenth to the mid-twentieth century; second, the postwar Keynesian consensus, broadly 1950-1980; and third, the neoliberal era of the Washington consensus, 1980-2000. In the book's first edition, the main thrust was the tension between the Keynesian approach and the Washington consensus—in brief, the state-centred and the market-led approach, rippling and echoing through the development field in many ways. Thus, Chapter 11 (the then closing chapter) argues that the main tension in contemporary development policy and thinking is the rift between the Washington institutions (the International Monetary Fund (IMF) and World Bank, aligned with the World Trade Organization (WTO)) and the human development approach (represented by the United Nations Development Programme (UNDP) and other UN agencies, development ministries in developing countries and some agencies of development cooperation).

Now the twenty-first century brings another phase of globalization and another era of development. It has only just begun. So far we know that neoliberalism is passé and the Washington consensus is no more; we know there are trend breaks and new trends, but it may be too early as yet to discern a new pattern. Among the new trends are the rise of the south, the growth of south–south relations in trade, energy and politics, and the growing role of leading emerging societies (including BRIC or Brazil Russia India China) and sovereign wealth funds from the global south. A further variable is economic instability in the United States, culminating in the economic crisis of 2008 and spreading outwards. The pendulum shifts toward greater state regulation, both in the west ('we are all Keynesians now') and as part of the rising influence of developmental states in the south. The BRIC economies are typically economies with large public sectors.

Of the contours of this era we know, so far, that the major target of criticism of the previous period (and this book's first edition) is becoming a background issue, still pertinent, but now on the backburner. The imbalances in the world economy are so profound and structural that a major rebalancing is on the cards, although it is difficult to identify the specifics of a new development paradigm. Chapter 12, a new chapter, focuses on the emerging trends in the development field.

Let me briefly indicate the main changes in this revised edition. I have updated and fine-tuned the entire text by streamlining formulations and refining arguments, adding some references. In Chapters 1 and 2, I have updated the closing section. Chapters 3, 5, 8 and 11 have undergone significant changes. I have revised Chapter 3 because its original keynote, critical globalism, is now a common platform and the literature on globalization and development has grown exponentially. I have expanded Chapter 5 on culture and development with a discussion of new literature such as the Human Development Report on *Cultural Liberty in Today's Diverse World*. In Chapter 8 I have fine-tuned and expanded the argument on social development.

I have added a new chapter on digital capitalism and development (Chapter 10). This argues that information-for-development (ICT4D) is primarily driven by market expansion and market deepening. As the latest accumulation wave, digital capitalism generates information technology boosterism and cyber utopianism with the digital divide as a refrain. This chapter criticizes the discourses and policies of 'bridging the digital divide' and views information-for-development as part of a package deal in which cyber utopianism is associated, not exclusively but primarily, with marketing digital capitalism. The actual task of information-for-development is to disaggregate ICT4D. Less emphasis on the internet and more on telephone, radio and television would normalize and ground the discussion. I conclude by arguing that the ICT4D discussion should move away from development aid, NGOs and externally funded projects, to the central question of disembedding technology from capital.

Chapter 11 on futures of development has undergone many changes, understandably because it was a forward-looking chapter. A new closing chapter discusses the main challenges of twenty-first-century globalization and development (Chapter 12).

During the years when the book was written, and since then, several close friends passed away. Wim Wertheim, my teacher at the University of Amsterdam whose work on emancipation has continued to inspire me throughout the years, was a dear friend. Wim Wertheim's teaching on Southeast Asia and Indonesia and his views on emancipation and the importance of the peasant hinterland influenced me greatly and his long friendship meant a lot to me. Wim Wertheim died in 1998. Gerrit Huizer, director of the Third World Centre at Nijmegen University and a close friend and companion, passed away not long after Wim Wertheim. Gerrit's work on peasant movements also followed in the lines of emancipation studies. My dear friend Vincent Tucker died in a car accident near Cork, Ireland. Chapter 9 in this book is inspired by his work on the sociology of health; it was also the Inaugural Vincent Tucker Memorial Lecture at the University College of Cork, February 1998. Ranjit Dwivedi was a close friend at the Institute of Social Studies. We left the Institute around the same time. Shortly after defending his dissertation on the Narmada Valley protest movements, he left to take up a position at the Open University in England and I left for the University of Illinois. Less than a year later Ranjit died. I dedicate the second edition of this book with great affection and warmth to the memory of these dear friends and profound scholars.

When the first edition of the book came out in 2001 I moved jobs from the Institute of Social Studies in The Hague to the University of Illinois at Urbana-Champaign. From 2009 I am to be at the University of California, Santa Barbara, as Mellichamp Professor of Global Studies and Sociology.

Jan Nederveen Pieterse, 2009

Introduction

This book represents my engagement with development studies over many years. To guide the reader here is a brief overview of the treatment and arguments in the different chapters.

Chapter 1 is the substantive introduction to the book. It problematizes development knowledge and offers a stock taking of major trends in development thinking. Chapter 1 (Trends) and Chapters 11 (Futures) and 12 (Twenty-first century globalization) tie a ribbon around the book.

Chapters 2–7 mainly consist of critical treatments of different approaches to development. Chapters 2 and 3 discuss the career of development thinking in the mode of discourse analysis. Chapter 2 focuses on the deep legacies of Eurocentrism in developmentalism. Chapter 3 addresses the zigzag character of development thinking and its inconsistencies over time. Its closing argument on critical globalism is both analytic and programmatic. One of the limitations of discourse analysis (taken up in Chapters 1 and 7) is that it fails to engage the specifics of political economy. Chapter 4 revisits the political economy approach by way of a critique of Samir Amin's work. His thesis in favour of delinking is contrasted to globalization processes, continuing the argument of critical globalism in the previous chapter. Another theme is Amin's political economy approach to 'culture'. Chapter 5 takes up various ways in which 'culture' has been incorporated into development discourse and policy.

While alternative development is a critique of mainstream development, Chapter 6 subjects alternative development claims to a critical treatment, in particular the claim for an alternative development paradigm. Chapter 7 is a critique of post-development arguments and, I plead guilty here, a deconstruction of deconstruction. Chapters 4–7 address four critical approaches in development: prioritizing structures (political economy), prioritizing culture (culture and development), prioritizing social forces (alternative development) and prioritizing discourse (post-development).

A book with just criticisms and goodbyes to paradigms would be too easy and not quite satisfactory, although this has long been the common fare in development studies. Lengthy analyses or critiques often conclude with just a brief note on ways forward and I would like to be more constructive and affirmative. Thus, Chapters 8–11 consist of programmatic treatments or reconstructions in the sense of affirmative and innovative turns and forward options for development. On balance these treatments argue more 'for' than 'against'. Chapter 8 argues for extending the human development

Table I.1   *Précis of book treatment*

Approaches	Keywords	Chapters
Development thinking	Overview	1
	Deconstructions	
Discourse analysis	Developmentalism	2
	History of development thinking	3
Political economy	Dependency theory and delinking	4
Culture and development	Cultural turn, anthropology	5
Alternative development	Social forces	6
Post-development	Discourse analysis as ideology	7
Human development	Capacitation	8
ICT and development	Disembedding technology from capital	10
International development cooperation	Compartmentalizing macroeconomics and foreign aid	12
	Reconstructions	
Globalization and development	Critical globalism, global development	3, 11, 12
Intercultural development	Cultural difference as a catalyst	4
Social development	Supply-side	8
Critical holism	Tao of development	9
Reflexive development	Collective learning, reform platform	11
	Development pluralism	12

approach to social development and for a supply-side approach to social development, including taking on questions such as social capital. Chapter 9 is a philosophical and methodological reflection; it takes the arguments on Eurocentrism in Chapter 2 further and argues for critical holism as the Tao of development. Chapter 11 on futures of development takes the opening arguments on trends in development thinking and policy into the future tense, redefines development in light of the overall discussion, and concludes with reconstructions in development. A précis of the treatment is above (Table I.1). Chapter 12, new in the second edition, reflects on twenty-first century developments.

Any of these approaches—discourse analysis, anthropology, cultural studies, alternative development, political economy, etc.—is a vantage point from which to probe the complexities of development. Any approach handled with depth and subtlety can be fruitful if it becomes an instrument and avenue of reflexivity. This is the lesson I arrive at in the closing two chapters. Development is too complex to allow partial approaches to have their way—although these lend themselves to technical finesse and managerial intervention, the managerial fiction of knowledge and mastery itself is part of the problem. Combining different angles and approaches yields an holistic assessment of development. Fallibility and open-endedness are necessary features of development thinking and what matters in relation to any of these approaches is reflexivity; what matters is not merely what but also how. This also applies to holism itself: hence critical holism, lest holism become an all-purpose way out of the perplexities of development. These critical treatments are not dogmatic closures but contributions to reflexivity. And it applies to reflexivity lest it become snake oil: reflexivity must be politically enabling and serve an emancipatory interest.

From the combination of terms in the title – deconstructions/ reconstructions – it is obvious that this is not an exercise in deconstruction in the classic sense (cf. Willett 1999: 2-3) for then reconstructions would not belong. Reconstructions are ways ahead, forward options, contextual and time bound. In time they will yield other deconstructions and then other reconstructions will emerge, which is the way of things. Chapter 1 argues that development is a struggle. To be precise, development is a struggle over the shape of futures, a dramatic and complex struggle.

1

Trends in Development Theory

Development in question

Globalization and regionalization are overtaking the standard unit of development, the nation. International institutions and market forces are overtaking the role of the state, the conventional agent of development. The classic aim of development, modernization or catching up with advanced countries, is in question because modernization is no longer an obvious ambition. Modernity no longer seems so attractive in view of ecological problems, the consequences of technological change and many other problems. Westernization no longer seems compelling in a time of revaluing local culture and cultural diversity. In view of the idea of multiple modernities, the question is modernization towards *which* modernity? Several development decades have not measured up to expectations, especially in Africa and parts of Latin America and South Asia. The universalist claims of neoclassical economics and structural adjustment policies have undermined the foundation of development studies, the notion that developing countries form a special case.

Doesn't all this mean the end of development? Everything that development used to represent appears to be in question, in crisis. There are various views of what this crisis means. One is that since development is in crisis, let's close the shop and think of something entirely different – 'beyond development'. This is the position associated with post-development thinking. A different response is to qualify the crisis, acknowledging the failures of the development record but also its achievements, avoiding simplistic, one-sided assessments. Thus health care and education have improved even in the poorest countries and in countries where growth has been stagnant. Another reaction is to acknowledge crisis and to argue that crisis is intrinsic to development, that development knowledge is crisis knowledge. From its nineteenth-century beginnings, development thinking was a reaction to the crises of progress, such as the social dislocations caused by industrialization. Hence questioning, rethinking and crisis are part of development and not external to it. A related view is not merely to acknowledge questioning as part of development but to consider it as its spearhead – viewing development thinking as ongoing questioning critique and probing alternative options. Development then is a field in flux, with a rapid change and turnover of alternatives. Precisely because of its crisis predicament, development is a high-energy field.

This chapter maps major trends in development thinking. The subsequent chapters examine these trends in detail, building up to an inventory of current and future directions in the closing chapter. Trends in this discussion refer to long-term and ongoing as well as plausible future directions in the development field. The focus is on development theories, that is, organized reflections on development, rather than on development *tout court* and in its entirety. Since the major development theories are also policy frameworks, this approach includes development strategies; but actual policies are informed by many other considerations so this discussion emphasizes development theories. Trend-spotting is not exactly an intellectually neutral activity so it needs to be contextualized. This treatment opens with general observations on the character of development thinking and the status of development theory. The argument then turns to the different meanings of 'development' over time, which places the discussion of contemporary trends in a historical context. The next section juxtaposes these different understandings of development to changing patterns of global hegemony. Zeroing in on the contemporary setting, I map out different stakeholders and institutions in the development. Against this backdrop we turn to development trends over time, first long-term trends in theory and methodology and then policy changes.

The status of development theory

What is the contribution of development theory to this situation? Theory is the critique, revision and summation of past knowledge in the form of general propositions and the fusion of diverse views and partial knowledges in general frameworks of explanation. What is referred to as 'development theory' largely belongs to the level of grand theories, broad explanatory frameworks. This is part of its limited character. There is a lot that development theory does not talk about. Many development problems are addressed by mid-range or micro theories – questions of rural development, industrialization, urbanization, trade policy, etc. Development theory as such concerns the larger explanatory frames. In addition, 'development theory' usually refers to the leading theories and many rival and subsidiary theories do not quite make it to the limelight.

In social science it is now widely assumed that realities are socially constructed. The way people think and talk about social realities affects agendas, policies, laws and the ways laws are interpreted. Just as perception does not merely register but shaping reality, knowledge does not simply reflect but constructs reality. Knowledge is political, shaping perceptions, agendas, policies. If this were not the case then why bother, why research, why hold conferences? Theory is a meeting place of ideology, politics and explanation. Framing, defining the field, the rank order of questions, are the business of theory.

Theory is a distillation of reflections on practice in conceptual language so as to connect with past knowledge. The relationship between theory and practice is uneven: theory tends to lag behind practice, behind innovations on the ground, and practice tends to lag behind theory (since policy makers and activists lack time for reflection). A careful look at practice can generate new theory, and theory or theoretical praxis can inspire new practice. Theories are contextual. While theories react to other theories and often emphasize differences rather than complementarities, the complexities encountered in reality are such that we usually need several analytics in combination.

Is development theory a matter of social science or of politics? Writers have different views on the degree of autonomy of development theory. Some treat development theory primarily as part of social science and thus emphasize the influence of classical economic and social thought (e.g. Preston 1996, Martinussen 1997). Others implicitly view development theory mainly as ideology – like a ship rocked in a sea of political pressures and shifting tides. They consider political leanings, in a broad sense, as more important in shaping development theory than theoretical considerations (e.g. Frank 1971). The advantage of this view is that it draws attention to the ideological role of development theory – in setting agendas, framing priorities, building coalitions, justifying policies. Its limitation is that it treats development theory as a by-product of political processes and not as an intellectual process as well. Some cynicism in relation to theory is appropriate. How often is a theory in effect a political gesture? What is the politics of theory? Whom does discourse serve? In between these views is a middle position that recognizes the intellectual as well as the political elements in development theory. It doesn't make sense to isolate development theory from political processes and treat it as an ivory-tower intellectual exercise; but neither can we simply reduce it to ideology or propaganda. In the contextual approach to development theory both political contexts and influences from social science count (as in Corbridge 1995, Leys 1996). This is the approach – we can term it the sociology of development knowledge – that this book adopts.

For a development theory to be significant, social forces must carry it. To be carried by social forces it must match their worldview and articulate their interests; it must serve an ideological function. However, to serve their interests it must make sense and be able to explain things. By the same token, explanation is not a neutral function. There are as many ways of explaining things as there are positions from which to view realities. The explanation that satisfies a peasant is not the same as one that satisfies a landlord, a banker or an IMF official.

According to Björn Hettne, 'Development in the modern sense implies intentional social change in accordance with societal objectives' (2008a: 6). Since not all societal objectives are developmental (some are simply concerned with establishing authority, etc.) I would insert the criterion of *improvement* and define development as *the organized intervention in collective affairs according to a standard of improvement*. What constitutes improvement and what is an appropriate intervention obviously varies according to class, culture, historical context and relations of power. Development theory is the negotiation of these issues.

The strength and the weakness of development thinking is its policy-oriented character. This is part of its vitality and inventiveness. It is problem-driven rather than theory-driven. It is worldly, grounded, street-smart, driven by field knowledge, not just book knowledge. In part for the same reasons, development thinking ranks fairly low on the totem pole of social science. As applied social science, development thinking has a derivative status. It has more often been a follower of frameworks developed in other sciences than a trendsetter. It has been a net importer of social science theories and has been influenced by other social sciences more often than it has influenced them. Evolutionism, Marxism, Neo-Marxism, Keynesianism, structural functionalism, neoclassical economics and poststructuralism are among the social science paradigms imported by development theories at different times. A major area in which development theory influenced social science generally is dependency theory. Studies in dependency theory were widely read outside development studies and inspired, for instance, world-system theory.

Arguably, development theory is underestimated in social science. The notion that development theory counts for less because it concerns 'merely the south' while major developments in social theory are spearheaded by the west reflects a deep-seated prejudice. It reflects a (neo)colonial division of labour in the production of knowledge according to which theory is generated in the north and data, like raw materials, are produced in the south (Pletsch 1981, Slater 2004). In this schema the advanced societies are supposed to be the mirror and guide for less-developed societies. This cognitive colonialism is passé on several counts. This kind of unilinear thinking is no longer plausible. Besides, development knowledge is increasingly relevant also in the north. The conventional distinction between developing and developed societies is less and less relevant – the 'south' is in the 'north' and vice versa. With the decline of welfare economies there is increasing polarization within countries on account of shrinking public services. In the United States and the UK there is mention of 'two-thirds societies'. Social exclusion nowadays is a problem that is common to north and south, east and west.

Knowledge production in the south has been influential not merely in the past but also under the shadow of western hegemony. A case in point is Gandhi and his influence on the Civil Rights Movement (Nederveen Pieterse 1989). Dependency thinking, Maoism, Guevarism and the Delhi school of development thought (Dallmayr 1996) are other examples. Japanese perspectives on management, production and development have been profoundly influential and so has the Asian developmental state (Iwasaki et al. 1992; Wade 1996).

Development is a strange field. Development practice, policy and studies are all flourishing. Universities are opening new development schools (particularly in the UK). Yet for quite some time the field has been said to be in crisis, impasse, or passé. Part of this is a crisis of ideologies, which reflects a wider paradigm crisis – of Neo-Marxism and dependency theory as well as Keynesianism and welfare politics. There have been plenty of critical positions but no coherent ideological response to the neoliberal turn. The crisis is further due to changing circumstances including development failures, the growing role of international financial institutions, and conflicts in developing countries.

According to Marx's eleventh thesis on Feuerbach, 'Philosophers have only interpreted the world in various ways. The time has come to change it'. Arguably, the actual power of development is the power of thesis eleven. Nowadays the ambition to 'change the world' meets with cynicism – because of the dismal record of several development decades, doubts about modernism and its utopian belief that society can be engineered – how about social engineering if we look at Bosnia, Rwanda, Somalia, Sierra Leone, Liberia – and media triviality ('We are the world')?

The status of development theory reflects the theory-lag between development studies and social science generally, a 'colonial legacy' in knowledge and a recurring impasse in the development field. The decolonization of knowledge is a matter of ongoing contestation (Apffel-Marglin and Marglin 1996, Dahl 2008, Nederveen Pieterse and Parekh 1995). As part of accelerated globalization, neoliberal policies impose neoclassical economics on the south, applying western standards of policy and systems of accounting to align economies and financial and credit regimes. It is appropriate to consider this episode as part of the wider historical relations between north and south. In tandem with changing geopolitical relations, 'development' has been changing its meaning over time.

Meanings of 'development' over time

Over time 'development' has carried very different meanings. The term 'development' in its present sense dates from the postwar era of modern development thinking. In hindsight, earlier practices have been viewed as antecedents of development policy, though the term 'development' was not necessarily used at the time. Thus Kurt Martin (1991) regards the classic political economists, from Ricardo to Marx, as development thinkers for they addressed similar problems of economic development. The turn-of-the-century latecomers to industrialization in central and eastern Europe faced basic development questions such as the appropriate relationship between agriculture and industry. In central planning the Soviets found a novel instrument to achieve industrialization. During the Cold War years of rivalry between capitalism and communism, the two competing development strategies were western development economics and central planning (in the Soviet, Chinese or Cuban varieties). In this general context, the core meaning of development was catching up with the advanced industrialized countries.

Cowen and Shenton uncovered yet another meaning of development. In nineteenth-century England, 'development', they argued, referred to remedies for the shortcomings and maladies of progress. This involves questions such as population (according to Malthus), job loss (for the Luddites), the social question (according to Marx and others) and urban squalor. In this argument, *progress and development* (which are often viewed as a seamless web) are contrasted, and development differs from and complements progress. Thus, for Hegel, progress is linear and development curvilinear (Cowen and Shenton 1996: 130). Accordingly twentieth-century development thinking in Europe and the colonies had already traversed many terrains and positions and was a reaction to nineteenth-century progress and policy failures, where industrialization left people uprooted and out of work, and social relations dislocated.

The immediate predecessor of modern development economics was colonial economics. Economics in the European colonies and dependencies had gone through several stages. In brief, these were an early stage of commerce by chartered companies, followed by plantations and mining. In a later phase, colonialism took on the form of *trusteeship*: the management of colonial economies not merely with a view to their exploitation for metropolitan benefit but also allegedly with a view to the interests of the native population. Development, if the term was used at all, in effect referred mainly to colonial resource management, first to make the colonies cost-effective and later to build up economic resources with a view to national independence. Industrialization was not part of colonial economics because the comparative advantage of the colonies was held to be the export of raw materials for the industries in the metropolitan countries. Indeed there are many amply documented episodes when European or colonial interests destroyed native manufacturers (textile manufacturing in India is the classic case) or sabotaged industrialization efforts in the periphery (as in Egypt, Turkey and Persia; see Stavrianos 1981). This is a significant difference between the colonial economies and the latecomers in central and eastern Europe.

In modern development thinking and economics, the core meaning of development was *economic growth*, as in growth theory and Big Push theory. In the course of time mechanization and industrialization became part of this, as in Rostow's *Stages of Economic Growth* (1960). When development thinking broadened to encompass *modernization*, economic growth was combined with political modernization, that is, nation building, and social modernization such as fostering entrepreneurship and 'achievement orientation'. In dependency theory, the core meaning of development likewise was economic growth or capital accumulation. Its distorted form was dependent accumulation which led to the 'development of underdevelopment', and an intermediate form was 'associated dependent development'. The positive goal was national accumulation (or autocentric development). Alternative development thinking introduced new understandings of development focused on social and community development and 'human flourishing'

Table 1.1 *Meanings of development over time*

Period	Perspectives	Meanings of development
1800s	Classical political economy	Remedy for progress, catching up
1870 >	Latecomers	Industrialization, catching-up
1850 >	Colonial economics	Resource management, trusteeship
1940 >	Development economics	Economic growth – industrialization
1950 >	Modernization theory	Growth, political and social modernization
1960 >	Dependency theory	Accumulation – national, autocentric
1970 >	Alternative development	Human flourishing
1980 >	Human development	Capacitation, enlargement of people's choices
1980 >	Neoliberalism	Economic growth – structural reform, deregulation, liberalization, privatization
1990 >	Post-development	Authoritarian engineering, disaster
2000	Millennium Development Goals	Structural reforms

(Friedmann 1992). With human development in the mid-1980s came the understanding of development as *capacitation*, following Amartya Sen's work on capacities and entitlements. In this view the point of development, above all, is that it is enabling. The core definition of development in the Human Development Reports of UNDP is 'the enlargement of people's choices'.

Two radically different perspectives on development came to the fore around the same time. *Neoliberalism*, in returning to neoclassical economics, eliminates the foundation of development economics: the notion that developing economies represent a 'special case'. According to the neoliberal view, there is no special case. What matters is to 'get the prices right' and let market forces do their work. Development in the sense of government intervention is anathema for it means market distortion. The central objective, economic growth, is to be achieved through deregulation, liberalization, privatization – which are to roll back government and reduce market-distorting interventions and in effect annul 'development'. In other words, this retains one of the conventional core meanings of 'development', economic growth, while the 'how to' and agency of development switch from state to market. Accordingly, neoliberalism is an anti-development perspective, not in terms of goals but in terms of means. *Post-development* thinking also puts forth an anti-development position. This is still more radical for it applies not merely to the means (the state is accused of authoritarian engineering) but also to the goals (economic growth is repudiated) and the results (which are deemed a failure or disaster for the majority of the population) (Rahnema and Bawtree 1997; also discussed in Chapter 7 below). An overview is shown in Table 1.1.

Thus the lineages of development are quite mixed. They include the application of science and technology to collective organization, but also managing the changes that arise from the application of technology. Virtually from the outset development includes an element of *reflexivity*. It ranges from infrastructure works (roads, railways, dams, canals, ports) to industrial policy, the welfare state, new economic policy, colonial economics and Keynesian demand management.

There are several ways of making sense of the shift of meanings of development over time. One is to view this kind of archaeology of development discourse as a deconstruction of development and as part of a development critique. Another is to treat it as part of an historical context: it's quite sensible for development to change meaning in relation to changing circumstances and sensibilities. 'Development' then serves as a mirror of changing economic and social capacities, priorities and choices. A third option is to recombine these different views as dimensions of development, that is, to fit them all together as part of a development mosaic and thus to reconstruct development as a synthesis of components (e.g. Martinussen 1997). A limitation of this perspective is that it takes the history out of development. If we consider each theory as offering a Gestalt of development, a total picture from a particular angle, then the array of successive and rival theories offers a kaleidoscopic view into the collective mirror. By any account, the different meanings of development relate to changing relations of power and hegemony, which is part of the view in the collective mirror.

Development is struggle

Besides different meanings of development over time, there are different dimensions to 'development' at any one time. To each development theory there are, implicitly or explicitly, various dimensions or layers. First, the historical context and political circumstances. Each perspective unfolds in a particular historical setting. Understanding development theory in context means understanding it as a response to problems and arguments at the time. Another dimension is explanations or assumptions about causal relationships. This implies epistemology or rules of what constitutes knowledge. In addition, it involves methodology, or indicators and research methods. Development thinking also performs a role of representation, of articulating and privileging particular political and class interests and cultural preferences. Besides different meanings of development, another register is 'perceptions of development' or how different stakeholders perceive and represent their interests (e.g. Wallman 1977). Development theories also reflect images of improvement or desirable change. A further element is the agenda-setting role of theory, as a set of policy implications and a future project.

Understanding development theory means being aware of these multiple layers (see Figure 1.1). Each development theory can be read on multiple levels and in terms of the ongoing and shifting relations among the following components: practice→ research→ policy→ ideology→ image→ theory→ ideology→ policy→ practice→ theory→ ideology→ image→ policy ...

- *context* – historical context and political circumstances
- *explanation* – assumptions about causal relationships
- *epistemology* – rules of what constitutes knowledge
- *methodology* – indicators and research methods
- *representation* – articulating or privileging particular interests and cultural preferences
- *imagination* – images, evocations, symbols of development, desire
- *future* – policy, agenda, future project

Figure 1.1   *Dimensions of development theories*

A central issue is the relationship between knowledge and power. That every truth is a claim to power and every power is a centre of truth is the point of discourse analysis and part of postmodern understandings of knowledge. This involves more or less subtle considerations. For instance, one can argue for a relationship between technological capacities and epistemology and politics. 'Heavy technology' such as the steam engine then correlates with an epistemology of determinism and a politics of hierarchy; whereas soft or light technology, such as touch-button and ambient tech, implies subtler epistemologies and more horizontal relations (Mulgan 1994).

Broadly speaking, each development theory can be read as a hegemony or a challenge to hegemony. Explanation, then, is not always the most important function of theory – others are agenda setting, mobilization and coalition building.

In line with the neocolonial intellectual division of labour in which 'theory' is generated in the west and data are supplied by the south, grand theories have typically been fashioned in the west and therefore articulate western political interests and western intellectual styles and priorities. Reading development theory then is also reading a history of hegemony and political and intellectual Eurocentrism (Amin 1989; Mehmet 1995; and see Chapter 2 below). Notable exceptions are dependency theory (which was also informed by Marxism, that is, a western counter-hegemony), alternative development and human development thinking, which largely originate outside the west.

We can map the main contours of development thinking in different periods alongside the patterns of international hegemony and the structures of explanation that were prevalent at the time (Table 1.2). Thus we relate global relations of power or international hegemony to intellectual patterns of hegemony (in line with the Gramscian approach to international relations; see Cox 1991). The assumption in this schema is that the paradigms that are available in the intellectual market at the time shape the explanatory frameworks that inform development thinking.

The development field

Development thinking and policy, then, is a terrain of hegemony and counter-hegemony. In this contestation of interests there are many stakeholders and

Table 1.2 *Global hegemony and development theories*

Historical context	Hegemony	Explanation	Development thinking
Nineteenth century	British Empire	Colonial anthropology, social Darwinism	Progress, evolutionism
1890–1930s	Latecomers, colonialism	Classical political economy	Catching up
Postwar boom	US hegemony	Growth theory, structural functionalism	Modernization
Decolonization	Third World nationalism, NAM, G77	Neo-Marxism	Dependency
1980s >	Globalization, finance and corporate capital	Neoliberalism, monetarism	Structural adjustment
1990s >	Rise of Asia, big emerging economies, BRIC	Capabilities, developmental state	Human development

Table 1.3 *Actors in the development field: different stakeholders, different development*

Institutional	State	IFIs	UN system	Civil society
Structure	Governments, ministries south and north	IMF, World Bank	UN agencies	(I) NGOs
Infrastructure	Bureaucracies, interest groups, parties, factions, citizens	WTO, G7, central, international and development banks, TNCs	UN General Assembly, governments, ILO, WHO, etc.	People, social movements, trade unions, parties, firms, churches, etc.
Locations	Capitals, etc.	Washington DC	New York, Geneva, Paris, Nairobi, etc.	Dispersed
Development thinking	Economics (neoclassical to Keynesian) and human development	Neoclassical economics, neoliberalism	Human development	Alternative development (and post-development)
Disciplines	Economics, political science, public administration, demography	Economics	Economics, political economy, IR, political science	Sociology, anthropology, ecology, gender and cultural studies

multiple centres of power and influence. Taking a closer look at the contemporary development field, we can schematically map the main actors and forces as shown in Table 1.3.

To the surface structure of dispersed centres of influence we can add the *infrastructure* of forces behind the scenes, that is, those on whom the overt centres of influence depend. Thus what matters are not simply the World

Bank or IMF but their boards of trustees and other forces that shape policy parameters. Thus the 'Treasury–Wall Street–IMF complex' (Wade and Veneroso 1998) identifies two forces behind the scenes, to which we can add the US Congress, the Federal Reserve, the G7 central banks and the Bank for International Settlements in Basel. Further, at some remove (because these relations are not always clear-cut and straightforward) we can add the development thinking that would be congenial to these circles and the disciplines that typically inform their angle of vision. The dispersal of stakeholders in development roughly correlates with the disciplinary sprawl of development studies, so this fragmentation may have not only an intellectual basis in the academic division of labour but also an institutional basis.

This is only a schematic representation. Some provisos are that in the infrastructures of power different ideologies may prevail; NGOs need to be differentiated in various types, etc. From this mapping of the development field several points follow. (1) It isn't really possible to generalize about development – the question is, whose development? Different stakeholders have different takes on what development means and how to achieve it. This is not a minor point but a fundamental circumstance. Development is intrinsically a field of multi-level negotiation and struggle among different stakeholders. (2) Though it is schematic this outline may enable us to fine-tune our thinking about the relationship between power and knowledge in development. The field is in flux. Thus the World Bank has been shifting position repeatedly in view of policy failures and political pressures and trends. (3) New concerns and priorities that are broadly shared by development stakeholders – such as globalization, sustainability, gender, diversity, poverty alleviation – prompt new combinations and partnerships that crosscut 'boxes'. Emergencies, such as humanitarian action, conflict prevention and post-conflict reconstruction, also make for crosscutting combinations. In this light this kind of map is already overtaken on the ground, which is a reminder that the map should not be mistaken for the territory.

Trends in development theory

Obviously, the selection and representation of trends are tricky issues. If it is true that development is a mirror of the times, then a development trend report is to look in the collective mirror – and there are many angles to take and arguments to fit the occasion. There is no methodology to achieve this in a neat and clean fashion. The format adopted here is a concise profile of trends, by way of introduction to later discussion in the book. Limitations to this kind of discussion are the absence of magnitudes or relative values and the fact that everything is contextual. Certain trends may well be significant but without a quantitative analysis this remains inevitably impressionistic. First we will discuss long-term trends in development theory. Because they are long-term changes (over fifty years or more) they have a certain degree of plausibility but, on the other hand, they are also rather general and of a high level of abstraction. Even so a long-term perspective in a field dominated by short-termism may be welcome. Next we will look at current trends in development thinking and policy.

Arguably, the long-term trends in development theory parallel general shifts in social science. They may be characterized as a gradual shift from nineteenth-century to late twentieth-century epistemologies. In the first place this involves a shift from structuralist perspectives that emphasize the role of macro-structures towards more agency-oriented views. Classical and modern development thinking were fundamentally structuralist: the emphasis was on the large-scale patterning of social realities by structural changes in the economy, the state and the social system. This also applies to critical development thinking of the time, which was informed by Marxism, which in its orthodox forms is basically structuralist. It further applies to the structuralist school associated with Raúl Prebisch, which preceded the emergence of dependency theory in Latin America, and to Neo-Marxism, dependency theory, modes of production analysis, structuralist Althusserian Marxism and the regulation school.

In social science generally this outlook began to change with the growing influence of phenomenology (dating back to nineteenth-century antecedents) and a variety of orientations such as existentialism (and its emphasis on individual responsibility), hermeneutics (involving a more complex epistemology), symbolic interactionism and ethnomethodology (in anthropology), new institutional economics and rational choice, public choice and capability (in economics) and feminism (e.g. standpoint theory). In Marxism, it began to change with the influence of Gramscian Marxism. In different ways, these orientations all imply a shift in emphasis from structuralist toward institutional and agency-oriented views. This can also be described as a change from deterministic to interpretative views (cf. Bauman 1992 on the changing role of the intellectual from legislator to interpreter) and from materialist and reductionist views to multidimensional and holistic views. A different account of this shift is from structuralism to constructivism, that is, from an account of social realities as determined and patterned by macro-structures, to an account of social realities as being socially constructed. The lineage of constructivism includes phenomenology – as in Schutz (1972), Berger and Luckmann (1967), and Max Weber – indeed much of Weber's work is constructivist in outlook. A familiar turning point is Giddens's (1984) structuration theory. Poststructuralism and postmodernism, taken in a methodological sense, are further expressions of this reorientation (Rosenau 1992).

In development studies, these broad changes involve various implications. One of the consequences of the emphasis on agency is that development thinking becomes spatialized and more local or regional. Another implication is the concern for differentiation and diversity. Early and modern development thinking were generalizing and homogenizing; structuralism is intrinsically essentialist. By contrast, the post-impasse trend in development thinking highlights diversity and differentiation (Booth 1994b, Schuurman 1993). Along with this comes a movement away from grand overall theories and big schema policies. There are no more general recipes, no development policies that are relevant across countries and regions. The singular makes way for the plural generally – not simply development but what kind of development, not simply growth but what kind of growth? Thus new qualifiers and attributes proliferate, such as sustainable development, people-friendly growth, pro-poor growth, etc. Such qualifiers had always figured in the critical literature; now they enter mainstream discourse. Among the concrete expressions of the agency orientation in development thinking are work on strategic groups, the actor-oriented approach (Long 1994) and the general emphasis on a participatory approach (e.g. Oommen 1998).

The concern with diversity and agency introduces a new kind of tension: what then is the relationship between the local and the global, between the internal and the external, the endogenous and exogenous, between micro- and macro-policies? The shift from structuralism to constructivism and from structure to agency refers to a shift in emphasis and perspective; one does not replace the other but complements it. Structural changes and macro-policies obviously matter, such as structural adjustment lending and the World Trade Organization. What has changed is that these no longer constitute the field but are perceived as only part of the field. Many stakeholders actively negotiate them politically and analytically and feel they can do something about them. The impact of these actors on public debate and policy making can be measured (e.g. Clarke 1998). This is a step towards the democratization of development politics. Constructivism, in this sense, is the methodological expression of a political transformation.

This perspective offers one angle on current trends in development studies. Several trends are linked to these general changes (as outlined in Figure 1.2), or follow on from it, without being reducible to it. Current trends are discussed further with a view to changes in different spheres. In methodology, what stands out is the trend towards interdisciplinarity and the role of discourse analysis. In general sensibilities, the cultural turn is significant. In development policy, significant themes are intersectoral cooperation, social diversity, human security, gender and environment, and changes in development cooperation and structural reform.

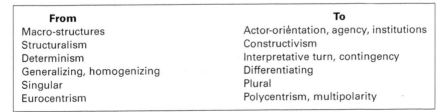

From	To
Macro-structures	Actor-oriéntation, agency, institutions
Structuralism	Constructivism
Determinism	Interpretative turn, contingency
Generalizing, homogenizing	Differentiating
Singular	Plural
Eurocentrism	Polycentrism, multipolarity

Figure 1.2   *General trends in development theory over time*

Interdisciplinarity

A significant methodological change is the gradual trend toward interdisciplinarity. Traditionally sectoral theories have dominated development studies. They have been marked by a gap between economic development and social and political development, although in grand theories (such as modernization and dependency theory) these were somehow articulated. A transitional phase has been the shift from disciplinary case studies and policies towards multidisciplinary approaches. Increasingly we can now see – although fragmented development economics, politics, etc., also continue as usual – more attention to cross- or transdisciplinary work. Several developments contribute to this: failures in development policies; new problems that require combined approaches; crises and emergencies that prompt new combinations of efforts. Novel disciplinary combinations and themes include, for instance, new institutional economics, the sociology of economics, the social economy, development as social process or as public action. Notions such as the embeddedness of economic and market activities in political institutions, social capital, cultural practices and social relations, imply new combinations of disciplinary sensibilities. New methodologies, such as social accounting, require such new combinations. Accordingly there is a new awareness that development demands a multidimensional, holistic approach (Chapter 9).

Discourse analysis

The origins of this methodology are in linguistics and literature studies, while it owes its influence to the general impact of poststructuralism. Here development studies follow a general trend in social science. The upshot is to treat development as story, as narrative, text. This has generated a wave of deconstructions and critiques of development texts (cf. Chapter 2). According to this literature, the power of development is the power of storytelling – development is a narrative, a myth (Crush 1996a, Rist 1997), which has since become a standard genre (Grillo and Stirrat 1997).

Discourse analysis in development involves a medley of motifs. At a general methodological level it no doubt represents a gain. This is not remarkable; it is simply the 'linguistic turn' applied to development studies. It is the awareness that development is not simply theory or policy but in either form is *discourse*. This means a step beyond treating development as ideology, or interest articulation, because it involves meticulous attention to development texts and utterances, not merely as ideology but as epistemology. Thus it involves the sociology of knowledge not only in terms of class interests (as in ideology critique) but also in terms of what makes up an underlying 'common sense'.

An effective use of discourse analysis is as an analytical instrument applied for example to development policy (e.g. Apthorpe and Gasper 1996, Rew 1997). A different application is to argue that since development is discourse it is therefore fictional, untrue, bogus, deceptive. It is a form of western modernism and scientific distortion that sets illusory goals of material achievement and in its pursuit wreaks havoc upon

Third World people. In this mode, discourse analysis turns into anti- or post-development thinking (e.g. Escobar 1992b, Sachs 1992a). In the process methodology turns into ideology – an instrument of analysis becomes an ideological platform, a political position; politics of knowledge turns into knowledge of politics. There have been similar agnostic moves in Foucault's and Derrida's work. In development studies this shift from methodology to ideology likewise involves the admixture of outside elements: an *esprit* of anti-modernism with romantic overtones (as in Ivan Illich), or post-Gandhian utopianism (as in Nandy 1989). Development as a discourse that is alien to the Third World (western), authoritarian (state, the IMF), engineering (modern), controlling and steamrolling and perverting local culture, grassroots interests and perceptions: this development critique is the newest critical populism.

A slightly different current is to apply discourse analysis in the sense of 'unmasking' development as 'myth' or 'fairy tale' (Rist 1997); that is, development is 'only a story', only a narrative, only a grand narrative. In a methodological sense this is a contradictory move: the very point of discourse analysis is that discourse matters, talk and representation matter; representation is a form of power, it constructs social realities. Some analysts seem to want to have it both ways: development is a story *and* it is 'only a story'. This confuses two different methodological dispositions: that of ideology critique (which measures ideology, taken as masked interests or false consciousness, against some yardstick of 'truth') and discourse analysis.

The methodological gain of discourse analysis is to add a level of reflexivity, theoretical refinement and sophistication to development studies, and thus to open up the politics of development to a more profound engagement. Its weakness and limitation – in development studies just as in literature criticism and cultural studies – is that it may skirt around the actual issues of power. It may divert attention from relations 'on the ground'. In that case, from determinism we risk slipping into *discursivism*, that is, reading too much into texts, or textualism, and overrating the importance of discourse analysis, as if by rearranging texts one changes power relations. This comes down to an alternative structuralism: from economic and political macro-structures to linguistic and epistemic structures; or, the order of language as a stand-in and code for the order of social relations.

The emergence of new fields of interest also shapes development studies. Gender, ecology, democratization, good governance, empowerment, culture, communication and globalization now figure prominently in development agendas. Ecology involves not just resource economics but also novel syntheses such as ecological economics and ecological politics. Gender plays a fundamental role in development practice and discourse. 'Empowerment' and 'participation' are also ubiquitous in development management. Besides more effective public administration, accountability, democracy and citizenship figure prominently. Globalization is also a major vortex of change in the development arena. These fields of interest generate new theoretical and policy angles but so far not necessarily new overall theoretical frameworks.

Several themes are not new in themselves but the emphasis they receive is novel. Or, some themes acquire a new significance over time. Thus, corruption has been a familiar theme in development work but at each turn of the wheel it takes on a different meaning. In the context of modernization it was taken as a residue of premodern, particularist leanings. In the dependency framework corruption was a symptom of dependent development and of the *comprador* politics of the lumpen bourgeoisie. Kleptocracy, crony capitalism and 'money politics' are variations on this theme. In the context of neoliberalism corruption becomes rent seeking, an ominous sign of state failure and market distortion and 'a hazard to free trade and investment' (Leiken 1996: 55) and the remedy is transparency. From a political angle, corruption is a matter of public accountability and democracy.

Culture and development

Conventionally development has been a monocultural project. Modernization and Westernization were virtually synonyms. As part of 'nation building' development was taken as a homogenizing project. In the context of decolonization struggles this began to change: along with the indigenization of politics and administration, indigenous culture and knowledge became an additional topos. Thus, culture was incorporated into development studies but in a subsidiary fashion ('add culture and stir'). The critique of Eurocentrism generated a concern with polycentrism, cultural multipolarity (Amin 1989) and pluralism. The UNESCO-sponsored World Decade on Culture and Development also resulted in a growing regard for cultural dimensions of development. In the wake of the cultural turn in development, culture represents another dimension of development, which is no longer ignored or viewed as just an obstacle, as in orthodox modernization thinking (see Chapter 5 below). 'Culture' now figures in several ways. One is a regard for cultural diversity – which in an age of ethnicity and religious resurgence is not an entirely innocent theme. A second concern is cultural capital, both as a form of human capital and capability and as political currency (in ethnic and religious mobilization and as an asset in economic relations). A further step is to view cultural diversity as an engine of economic growth (see Chapter 5).

The unit of development

In development thinking from the classics to dependency theory the conventional unit of development was the nation. The key development statistics and measures used by the international institutions are still country statistics. However, while the nation remains the central domain of development it is no longer the only game in town. Gradually development is becoming a multilevel, multiscalar series of efforts, simultaneously taking place at levels lower than the nation, at the national level and at levels beyond the nation.

Below the national level are community development, local economic development (LED) and microregional development. Community development, a subsidiary theme in colonial times and during the era of modernization, received a new emphasis with alternative development. Local development in its various forms connects with questions of rural/urban disparities, urban development, regional inequality, new regionalism, ethnic mobilization ('ethnodevelopment') and new localism, with a view to endogenous development and in reaction to globalization. Beyond the nation are questions of macroregional cooperation and global macroeconomic policies. Macroregional cooperation concerns the conventional issues of economies of scale, the increase of market size, regional standardization and interfirm cooperation, as well as the horizons of the regional Development Banks. Besides country statistics, other development statistics are regional, concerning 'Latin America', 'Africa', 'Asia', 'the Caribbean', etc. The region, in other words, is becoming almost as familiar a unit of development as the nation. A third scale of development action is the world: local, national and macroregional decision making interfaces with global macro-policies on the part of international institutions and the UN system.

Hence, development policy is increasingly a matter of decision making dispersed over a wide terrain of actors, institutions and frameworks. Development theorizing, which is habitually centred on the state, needs to accommodate this widening radius. It needs to be renewed by reconceptualizing development as multiscalar public action. Contemporary development policy is incoherent because the different levels of development action – local, microregional, national, macroregional, international, global – are not adequately articulated. Thus a comprehensive, holistic approach to development is not only multidimensional but also multiscalar, such that development efforts at different levels are cumulative and interconnect.

Intersectoral cooperation

After development thinking has been, more or less successively, state-led (classical political economy, modernization, dependency), market-led (neoliberalism) and society-led (alternative development), it is increasingly understood that development action needs *all* of these in new combinations. New perspectives and problems (such as complex emergencies, humanitarian action) increasingly involve cooperation among government, civic and international organizations, and market forces. Human development, social choice, public action, urban development and LED all involve such intersectoral partnerships. For government at local and national levels, this increasingly involves a coordinating role as facilitator and enabler of intersectoral cooperation.

The theme of development partnership at present serves an ideological role as part of a neoliberal new policy framework which papers over contradictions and the rollback of government (e.g. Hearn 1998). However, the underlying significance is much more profound: just as sectoral approaches and disciplinary boundaries have been losing their relevance, sectoral agendas are now too narrow. The ideological use that is being made of this conjuncture should not obscure the significance of the trend itself.

International development cooperation has been changing in several ways. The emphasis has shifted from projects to programmes and from bilateral to multilateral cooperation. The trend is towards, on the one hand, formal channels (particularly multilateral cooperation through international and regional institutions) and, on the other, informal channels (NGOs) (Bernard et al. 1998). A précis of current trends is presented in Table 1.4.

These themes are elaborated in the chapters that follow. These changes in development thinking, such as interdisciplinarity and discourse analysis, and in policy, such as the changing unit of development and intersectoral cooperation, don't add up to a single pattern, but they do significantly change the Gestalt of development. Their overall significance is taken up in Chapter 11 on futures of development.

Table 1.4   *Current trends in development theory*

Conventional and recent views	Trend	New themes
Grand theories	Differentiation	Middle-range theories, local knowledge
(1) Unreflexive use of language, indicators, models; (2) discourse analysis	Reflexivity, self-questioning	Development as social learning, social feedbacks, reflexive development
Sectoral theories. Gap between economic and social/political development. (Multi)disciplinary case studies, policies.	Interdisciplinarity	Bridging approaches (new institutional economics, sociology of economics) and themes (embedded ness, social capital, social economy, holism)
State-, market- or society-led development	Intersectoral cooperation	Intersectoral synergies. Public action
Homogenization, essentialism	Diversity	Politics of difference
(1) Betting on the strong; (2) humanitarian assistance, from relief to development	Human security	Risks of polarization, global social policy, global social contract
(1) Gender blind; (2) WID (Women in Development) (add women and stir)	Gender awareness	Gender interests, gendering development
(1) Mastery over nature; (2) sustainable development (add environment and stir)	Environment	Green GDP, political ecology
(1) Westernization; (2) homogenization vs. indigenization (add culture and stir)	Cultural turn	Diversity and cultural capital as political currency, (3) as growth pole
(1) Nation; (2) local	Unit of development	Regional and world development and multiscalar partnerships

2

Dilemmas of Development Discourse: The Crisis of Developmentalism and the Comparative Method

In the holograms of hegemony panoramas of power subtly fade into theories of history. Evolutionism was an imperial vision, modernization theory bears witness to the American century, and development theory translates contemporary relations of power. In the discourses of history produced by western hegemony, knowledge and power are intricately interwoven.

In his analysis of what he calls the post-totalitarian system, Václav Havel observes: 'the principle involved here is that the centre of power is identical with the centre of truth' (Havel 1985: 25). This also applies to the centres of power and leading truths in the western world. The central thesis of developmentalism is that social change occurs according to a pre-established pattern, the logic and direction of which are known. Those who deem themselves furthest advanced along its course claim privileged knowledge of the direction of change. Developmentalism is the truth from the point of view of the centre of power; it is the theorization (or rather, ideologization) of its own path of development and the comparative method usually serves to elaborate this perspective.

From evolutionism to development

Herodotus's *Histories* are replete with cross-cultural comparisons phrased in terms of correspondences as well as differences (Hodgen 1964: 25). From the outset in the western tradition, intercultural comparisons interacted with conceptions of history. Aristotle made comparisons not simply between types but within a presumed order of growth and development of types, that is, according to a comparative-developmental perspective. 'When Aristotle compared his own polity to that of the Cyclopes in Homer, and then adduced "barbarous" people living even in his time, he was pointing to a presumed line of development from kinship through the community to the polis. Contemporary barbaric peoples seemed to Aristotle fit evidence of what the Greeks themselves had once been like' (Nisbet 1969: 193).

Thus comparisons establish boundaries of inclusion and exclusion, identifying others in a mirror of similarity and difference and deploying alterity as part of the discourse of identity. In addition, in the Athenian empire of

Aristotle's time cross-cultural comparisons were not culturally neutral. Comparison established boundaries of inclusion and exclusion, identifying others in a mirror of similarity and difference, defining alterity as part of the discourse of identity. Accordingly, the comparative-developmental discourse of nineteenth-century evolutionism followed a pattern with classical antecedents. Victorian anthropology, race science and evolutionism formed part of the discourse of the British Empire. The comparative method served as an adjunct to evolutionism, for instance in the hands of Herbert Spencer, where it consisted of 'the accumulation of customs and ideas gathered from many places and periods, to substantiate developmental schemes arrived at through speculation' (Mair 1965: 42).

During the nineteenth century, race science served as the nexus between natural history and social history, between biological and social evolutionism. Alongside evolutionism it explained and justified European supremacy: identifying the Caucasian, Nordic and in particular the Anglo-Saxon race as superior in its endowments, with Europe leading the way in the trajectory of evolution and exhibiting the most advanced stage in the progress towards human perfectibility. Thus imperial history was assimilated into natural history.

Nineteenth-century social science was profoundly preoccupied with mapping and conceptualizing Europe's Great Transition, which was variously associated with the Enlightenment industrialization, capitalism, urbanization. The main types of conceptualization to emerge have been stages theories, dichotomous theories and critical variable theories. Comte's social dynamics, Marx's 'economic law of motion of modern society', Morgan's reflections on the development of kinship systems, Maine's views on the family and property, and Tylor's ideas about culture were *stages theories*. They all share the Enlightenment depiction of social evolution as a succession of stages: primitivism, savagery, barbarism, civilization.

Dichotomous theories conceptualize social change as a bipolar process – from status to contract, from mechanical to organic solidarity (Durkheim), *Gemeinschaft* to *Gesellschaft* (Tönnies). Stages theories may be interpreted as dichotomous theories 'spelled out' or extended. A different type of theory conceptualizes social change in terms of a single critical variable such as differentiation, an increase in complexity, or rationalization (Weber).

Central to the general understanding of social change was the biological metaphor of growth. Social change, as Nisbet (1969) points out, was regarded as natural, directional, immanent, continuous, necessary and proceeding from uniform causes. Social evolution was unilinear, its direction the same for societies the world over. Peoples at earlier stages of evolution were viewed as 'contemporary ancestors', a perspective that the anthropologist Johannes Fabian refers to as 'coevalness denied' (1983). Evolution sorted history, producing an imperial panorama that dehistoricized non-western peoples, or, rather, granted them a history only from the perspective of the imperial lighthouse.

From the point of view of the centre, global *space* appeared transformed into a *time* sequence, with Europeans as the only contemporaries, the sole inhabitants of modernity. Empire, then, was a time machine in which one moved backward or forward along the axis of progress. This Eurocentric perspective also served as a manual for the imperial management of societies at different evolutionary stages.

Europe defined the world. Like Adam in an earlier script she gave names to phenomena in the genesis of the new world brought forth in the wake of European expansion and conquest, the spread of the world market and the Industrial Revolution. The naming process was an extension and function of the process of conquest. In political studies too this had been the standard discursive practice. To a considerable extent political science is a comparative science. From the classical authors onward, from Aristotle to Montesquieu, the comparative method in political studies served as a substitute for experiment. John Stuart Mill reformulated the comparative approach with the methodology of concomitant variables. With the onset of evolutionism the comparative method became an adjunct to evolutionist speculation.

Twentieth-century social science, from the 1930s on, rejected race science and social evolutionism. Two western world wars undermined the faith in progress. Cyclical theories of history of a pessimistic cast prevailed, in the imagery of rise, decline and fall, as in the work of Oswald Spengler, Pitrim Sorokin, Vilfredo Pareto, Arnold Toynbee. In anthropology, cultural relativism seemed appropriate amidst the social realities of the interbellum. German critical theory contemplated the 'dialectics of Enlightenment'. After the Second World War there were attempts to reformulate evolutionary perspectives (Sahlins and Service 1960) as a subtext of modernization theory and the emerging (and in several respects interchangeable) discourse of development.

What Victorian anthropology was to the British Empire, modernization theory is to American States hegemony – its justification, rationale and agenda. It arose as the theoretical corollary of American globalism in the context of the cold war and decolonization. Initially it took shape as a substitute for knowledge; the conceptual schemes of modernization served as surrogates for a tradition of inquiry into African and Asian societies which was lacking almost entirely in the United States and was only later filled in by 'area studies'.

Modernization theory evolved from a marriage of evolutionism and functionalism, with modernization conceptualized either as a critical variable or a dichotomous theory. Examples of *critical variables* – which are not the most common form of modernization theory – are rationalization and industrialization. Advantages of this conceptualization are that modernization is regarded as an open-ended rather than a goal-directed process and the defining terms are narrow. On the other hand, 'when defined in relation to a single variable which is already identified by its own unique term, the term "modernization" functions not as a theoretical term but simply as a synonym' (Tipps 1973: 205).

Another option is to interpret modernization in terms of a set of critical variables: rationalization and industrialization. This may be an open-ended perspective as well, but here the problem is one of boundaries: which variables to include. What about adding to the profile of modernity, market relations, urbanization, the nuclear family, individualization, democratization, or, for that matter, anomie, alienation and so forth? Each additional variable would mean defining modernity in terms of another, implied theory, and a combination of variables is but an amalgam of theories.

Most concepts of modernization are of the dichotomous type and follow some version of the tradition–modernity contrast. The scenario laid out in Talcott Parsons' 'pattern variables' is a familiar example: modernization is defined as a movement from particularism to universalism, from ascription to achievement, from functional diffuseness to functional specificity, and from affective roles to affective-neutrality.

In this context the meaning of modernity changed again. When the term *modernus* was first used in seventh-century Europe it referred to Christians; by the sixteenth century it served to distinguish between moderns and ancients, with the 'middle ages' as the middling term (Jones 1961). By the nineteenth century it had come to mean contemporaneity and by the twentieth it had acquired a distinctly positive ring and was identified with improvement and efficiency (Williams 1976). In American discourse, however, modernity is contrasted with 'tradition' (frequently operationalized as 'resistance to change'). Feudalism, which in European discourse would belong to the middle or transitional stage, the precursor to modernity, from the American viewpoint, appears as part of the general morphology of backwardness.

Europe and North America followed different paths of modernization. In the European context modernity was originally a Renaissance concept, whereas in the American context it is an Enlightenment concept. European societies are layered and composite including tribal, peasant, feudal, monarchical, urban mercantile and industrial identities; more composite and complex than North American society, where industrialization came upon rural settlements (colonies termed 'plantations' in the seventeenth century) which adopted an Enlightenment political structure (alongside Christian culture). Accordingly European understandings of modernity tend to be more layered and complex than American views. Modernity is a European theme but modernization theory as such is an American discourse.

Intrinsic to the tradition–modernity dichotomy is the idea that 'tradition' is a residual and diffuse concept, denoting everything 'unmodern', so the terms in the dichotomy are not symmetrical, not of equivalent conceptual status. The same applies to the notion of 'non-western' societies (cf. Huntington 1976). As Frank notes: 'This entire approach to economic development and cultural change attributes a history to the developed countries but denies all history to the underdeveloped ones' (1969: 40).

In the fine print of modernization theory the evaluation of 'tradition' is usually not so diffuse. As Edward Said points out, the fictions of modernization theory rhyme well with Orientalism. With respect to the Islamic world, for instance, it holds 'that before the advent of the United States, Islam existed in a kind of timeless childhood, shielded from true development by an archaic set of superstitions, prevented by its strange priests and scribes from moving out of the Middle Ages into the modern world. At this point, Orientalism and modernization theory dovetail nicely' (1981: 28). Dichotomous conceptualizations of modernization are teleological – the destination is assumed to be known. They are normative, universalizing 'western values', and ethnocentric, with the United States (the American way of life) as the epitome of modernity. Modernization theory differs from evolutionism in that modernization is no longer regarded as immanent and inevitable; change is not always progressive. Outside stimuli, help from more advanced societies, may be necessary. Besides, there are multiple roads towards modernity – democratic or totalitarian.

Modernization theory competed with communism in a world split via the Cold War. The open door of 'free enterprise' economics and the neo-mercantilism of centrally planned economies were the two main avenues of modernization. The aim of comparative politics was to assess which way the 'preindustrial countries' would go. All the same, modernization was virtually synonymous with westernization. In the words of Edward Shils:

> Modern means being Western without the onus of dependence on the West ... The image of the Western countries, and the partial incorporation and transformation of that image in the Soviet Union, provide the standards or models in the light of which the elites of the unmodern new states of Asia and Africa seek to reshape their countries. (Shils 1966: 10)

Indeed, politics was by no means of marginal concern in American modernization theory. This understanding of politics was essentially the politics of the American Revolution. Walt Rostow, the author of the classic of modernization theory, *The Stages of Economic Growth* (subtitled *An Anti-Communist Manifesto*), later devoted a study to *Politics and the Stages of Growth*. Even as he equated modernization with economic growth, its motive, Rostow declared, was generally non-economic. Indeed, 'the glory of America has been not its relative material wealth but the sense of its transcendent political mission in reconciling liberty and order' (Rostow 1971: 6). Here a pure Enlightenment argument (liberty, order) mingles with Christian metaphors (glory, transcendence, mission).

Political modernization the American way means a programme of eighteenth-century political rationalism with an icing of Jeffersonian democracy, which can be summed up in the following principles: the legitimacy of the state is derived not from supernatural but from secular sanctions inhering in the people; the continual widening of citizenship, or incorporation into a consensual moral order, ultimately including all adults; and the growing scope and reach of the power of state agencies (Eisenstadt 1966).

Modernization meant the adoption of 'western' political institutions. How this worked out in the 'unmodern' countries depended on the character of 'traditional' institutions and the manner of 'westernization'. This was the thrust of comparative politics (e.g. Almond 1964). In reality this programme was not that of 'the west' but only that of the American and

French Revolutions, updated in American discourse such that the United States emerges as the culmination of 'the west'.

Generally, accounts of political modernization have been careful not to conflate modernization and *democratization*. Political modernization theories, whether following functionalist or market models, define democracy as formal democracy, in effect the exercise of citizenship rights by the propertied class. It is significant that the key American theories of political modernization make democracy contingent upon economic growth – read: the formation of a propertied class. This is middle-class democracy. It is the theory and practice of the White revolution bitterly resisting the Red revolution, the bourgeois revolution of the rights of the propertied classes resisting the proletarian revolution of the dispossessed: for the latter is regarded not as the fulfilment and completion of the former but as its negation. Accordingly, modernization is essentially social engineering from above and an operation of political containment rather than democratization. American modernization projects such as community development and the Green Revolution exemplify this character of the White revolution.[1]

Stages theories of political modernization could accommodate any form of authoritarianism as a 'necessary' stage towards transcendence – provided they were not communist; hence the crucial distinction between authoritarian and totalitarian political systems. Modernization theory has been emphatic in distancing itself from Marxism, the main source of bourgeois angst. Time and again modernization has been defined as a way of class compromise and not class struggle. In the European context, this cleavage reproduced the nineteenth-century dispute between right and left Hegelians.

The deepest disputes in western social science have not been between developmentalism and an alternative but between strands of developmentalist thought. Developmentalism comes in multiple varieties, liberal and radical, with Marxism as the quintessential radical evolutionism. Marx formulated developmentalism in a nutshell in the preface to the first edition of *Capital*: 'The country that is more developed industrially only shows, to the less developed, the image of its own future'. Marxist stages theory (primitive communism, slavery, feudalism, capitalism, socialism) and the 'iron necessity' with which social changes ensue according to historical materialist determinism exemplify unilinear evolutionism.

These features of classical Marxism have been abandoned in western Marxism. Gramsci rejected the thesis that there are objective laws of historical development similar in kind to natural laws and the belief in a predetermined teleology. Gramsci's historicism and his concern with the 'ethico-political realm' and the spiritual and moral character of hegemony broadened the terrain conceptually and politically. Still, Gramsci's thought follows the format of radical modernization theory, conceived more broadly and less mechanically. Gramsci's fondness of Fordism and his views on futurism and Americanism parallel Lenin's interest in Taylorism. Gramsci did not share German critical theory's *Kulturkritik* and reservations against technology. The concept of 'passive revolution', which Gramsci used to characterize the Risorgimento, may be read as a notion of modernization and, in effect, a concept of the White revolution.[2]

In Marxist perspectives, modernization is equivalent to capitalist development and the role of the state is to facilitate this process. In postcolonial society, according to Alavi (1973), the state mediates the competing interests of the three propertied classes – the metropolitan bourgeoisie, the indigenous bourgeoisie, and the landed classes.

With the waning of United States' hegemony, the war in Vietnam, the upheavals of 1968 and the end of the postwar boom, and in the context of social theory, the mounting criticism of functionalism and Parsonian sociology, modernization theory lost its appeal. In general discourse the keyword became 'development', which was generally short for economic development. Thus from a broad, sociological and ethnocentric concept of modernization the discourse shifted to a narrow, economic and ethnocentric concept.

Underwritten by the international community, encoded in the Development Decades of the United Nations, the discourse of development appears more neutral than previous formulations of social change. Development is primarily economic development and as such is measurable. It is basic to the discourse of international institutions such as the IMF, the World Bank, development banks and the combines of donor countries. Conventional development theory reflects a mixture of discourses, primarily neoclassical economics with affinities to modernization theory and evolutionism. If modernization theory is steeped in eighteenth-century political rationalism, development is steeped in nineteenth-century economic rationalism, oscillating between neoliberal and neomercantilist perspectives, between the self-regulating market and state intervention. The categories used in the UN system of highly developed, developed, less developed and least developed countries structurally resemble the stages of evolutionism; they replicate similar underlying developmental assumptions in a 'modern', 'affectively neutral' language. The terminology of centre and periphery – derived from nineteenth-century political geography – replicates the centrist logic of the diffusionist school of evolutionism.

'Development' tends to be short for the western development model. The perspective remains linear, teleological, ethnocentric. On the other hand, development theory is nowhere nearly as 'optimistic' as previous developmentalist perspectives and the nineteenth-century faith in perfectibility and progress. The faith in Progress applied principally to the metropolitan, imperial world. Now neo-Malthusian notions – overpopulation, 'basket cases', triage, lifeboat ethics, ecological constraints – cloud the horizon of development.

The state in development discourse is attributed a role as conductor and conduit of development, the executive agency of development policy. Initially boundless optimism prevailed: following a concept of state capitalism, the state was the prime mover of development. Increasingly this has turned into scepticism about the capacities of Third World states for social engineering. In the west this is paralleled in generalized doubts concerning state capacities and the possibility of social engineering (Migdal 1988). In the 1980s the notion of the state as obstacle emerged (Lal 1983). The neoliberal creed opted for market-led development. The twentieth-century seesaw between liberalism and state intervention parallels the nineteenth-century zigzags in economic theory and policy.

Dependency theory criticized development thinking for being a historical, for concealing historical relationships and denying the relationship between development and underdevelopment – in other words, for denying the role of imperialist exploitation in European modernization, as if modernization occurred independent of the stream of world history. In Frank's words (1969: 46): 'If the now underdeveloped were really to follow the stages of growth of the now developed ones, they would have to find still other peoples to exploit into underdevelopment, as the now developed countries did before them'.

Dependency theory accounts for the limited capacities of Third World states with the concept of the dependent state. The role of the state in this perspective is to facilitate world market access into society. 'The state in the periphery has the function again to remove economically as far as possible the political border between the world market and the national economic area that this same state brings into existence' (Tilman Evers, quoted in Frank 1981: 234). Thus, in effect, the interests of the metropolitan bourgeoisie are viewed as being preponderant over indigenous interests.

Dependency theory and other critiques of development thinking generated ideas of 'alternative development'. Whether we are talking about development alternatives or alternatives to development is one of the questions that present themselves (e.g. Apter 1987, Kothari 1988, Chapter 7 below).

What these pairs of perspectives – modernization theory and Marxism, development thinking and dependency theory – have in common is economism, centrism and teleology. Economism because economic growth is the centrepiece of social change, teleology in that the common assumption is goal-oriented development, centrism because development (or underdevelopment, according to the dependency view) is led from where it is furthest advanced – the metropolitan world. As such they are variations on a theme. This testifies to the strength and complexity of developmentalism as a paradigm. Part of this strength is that developmentalism is a layered, composite discourse that combines several discourses: liberal and radical, secular and religious.

Development as redemption

What sets western universalism apart from other, non-western universalisms, according to Rajni Kothari (1988: 192), is its secular character. Generally developmentalism is cast, according to its self-definition and the way it is perceived, as a rationalization process, the advance of enlightenment. As such it carries the appeal of secular utopianism. However, developmentalism is also a secularized version of the Christian perspective:

'throughout its history the idea [of progress] has been closely linked with, has depended upon, religion or upon intellectual constructs derived from religion' (Nisbet 1980: 352).

Developmentalism conforms to a Christian format and logic in viewing history as a salvific process. Thus it merges Christian and Enlightenment discourses so the momentum of faith corresponds with the logic of reason – reason and rationalization operating toward the fulfilment of the expectations of faith. Providence recast as Progress. Predestination reformulated as Determinism. The basic scenario of the scripture, Paradise–Fall–Redemption, comes replicated in evolutionary schemes. Primeval simplicity and innocence (the pastoral past and the good savage), followed by the fall from grace (corruption, decay, capitalism, urbanism, varying according to the discourse), which is in turn to be followed by a redeeming change (modernity, technology or revolution). This transmutation and secularization of scriptural utopianism had begun to take place in the seventeenth and eighteenth centuries, while some of the first steps were taken in the context of the Reformation. A fusion of scientific and Christian futurisms, of biology and faith, is the work of the palaeontologist Teilhard de Chardin (1955).

As European states emancipated from clerical authority while taking over the Church bureaucracy, likewise in social philosophy emancipation from the dogmas of faith took place both through emulation of biblical scenarios and promises and by their substitution and transcendence by different methods and symbols, as in Robespierre's altar of Reason and Comte's Civilization in the role of the Supreme Being. Developmentalism arose from a rejection of religious explanations and clerical claims while following parallel cognitive tracks.

In the age of empire, the English and the Germans looked to India to take the place of Eden, and the Hebrews and the French looked to Egypt. Sanskrit was regarded as the *fons et origo* of everything, or alternatively Egypt appeared as the source of all civilization (Said 1985: 137). The horizon broadened but the lens was unchanged.

Enlightenment discourse followed the same star as Judaeo-Christianity though the manner of redemption was different. David Livingstone passionately believed that what was missing in the African interior was the light of the gospel. Henry Morton Stanley in his footsteps called out in the heart of the Congo jungle that there should be light – except that he meant electricity.

Hence the western ambivalence vis-à-vis non-western cultures – primitivism betokens purity, reminiscent of paradise, development brings corruption and decay, and redemption lies only in the completion of development, the full achievement of modernity. The latter, also for western societies, can only be achieved through further technological development. Hence the missionary zeal frequently associated with modernization and development, comparable to earlier missionary passions of conversion, improvement and reform. Developmentalism and its master plan is not merely a matter of reason and logic, it is also, at heart, the performance of a religious duty, the quest for a utopian rendezvous, the pursuit of a messianic course. That this passion has been secularized does indeed make a difference – although the attitude toward reason and science tends to be as totalizing as in the previous overtly religious outlook.

This convergence of discourses is one explanation of the inner strength of the developmentalist paradigm, but not the only one. There are yet other reasons why it is difficult to think outside of this conceptual frame, some of which may be found in the context of language.

Spatial metaphors are deeply embedded in everyday English and in the language of social theory. Anne Salmond's (1982) inquiry into the semantics of social theory shows that knowledge is a landscape, that is, knowledge has a spatial existence, and that intellectual activity is a journey. Related notions, that knowledge is territory and argument is war, are the basis of accusations of intellectual 'imperialism' in theoretical texts. Understanding as 'seeing' and explanations as light sources ('illuminating') are related to the notion of intellectual activity as a journey. That theoretical systems are buildings is a metaphor related to structuralist discourse. Spatial distinctions of levels and of high and low further structure discourse. Notions of intellectual advancement and the progress of science follow likewise. So the general conception of knowledge and social theory itself tends to be structured in terms of spatial or organic metaphors and of (linear) motion in space. Knowledge itself 'develops'. Developmentalism 'grows' out of these semantics of space/time.

The crisis of developmentalism

The crisis of developmentalism as a paradigm manifests itself as a crisis of modernism in the west and a crisis of development in the south. The awareness of ecological limits to growth is a significant part of the crisis of modernism. New social movements in the west enunciate the end of linear progress (Melucci 1988: 254). Modernity is viewed increasingly as a theory and practice that is more exclusive than inclusive. The charmed circle of achievement and success, glamorized in media and advertisements, exacts a high toll and excludes and marginalizes many. There are other writings on the wall. The United States, the postwar epitome of modernity, claims the largest underclass of any western country and a growing number of homeless people. In terms of infrastructure and public and private investments it is in dire need of rebuilding. It has become the world's largest debtor nation and teeters on the brink of decline (Nederveen Pieterse 2008a). Japan, fairly new in the annals of developmentalism, boasts high productivity but doesn't set an example the way previous centres of developmentalism did. It doesn't serve as a cultural role model but largely follows western footsteps. East Asian tiger economies, recent arrivals to modernity, do serve as development models but not in terms of democracy or ecological sustainability. Similar limitations apply to the emerging societies of the BRIC (Brazil Russia India China) (Nederveen Pieterse 2008b).

In the south, the crisis of development takes multiple forms. Failures of development policies correlate with a profound impasse in development thinking. The rhetorical character of developmentalism stands exposed in several ways. Development discourse in its ahistorical and apolitical character is incapable of coming to terms with the realities of world power and global interests, as is evidenced in the question of third world debt. The metropolitan logic in development thinking is enshrined in the conditionalities of the IMF. Resistance to development in the south is an affirmation of autonomy and an expression of cultural resistance to western ethnocentrism.

The critique of development is associated with a critique of science. As Maurice Bazin (1987) observes: 'Third World peoples were first made to believe in God, now they have to believe in science ... first comes Salvation, then Progress; first through spiritual confessors, then through presidents' science advisers'. Shiv Visvanathan (1988: 285) remarks: 'what we are witnessing today is a civil rights movement against development-as-terrorism, based on the recognition that the modern state committed to science has become the prime anti-ecological force in the world'. The critique of science also has a western tradition (e.g. Aronowitz 1989; see also Chapter 9 below).

Universalizing from western experiences, developmentalism created an ahistorical model of change which created a 'Third World' that was but an historical construct and constructed 'the west', which had no basis in historical reality either. The actual modernization paths of western countries diverged (e.g. early, late industrializers) and deviated from the ideology of 'development'. Different countries applied diverse combinations of mercantilism and free trade, varying according to periods and contexts. Thus to characterize the bias of developmentalism, ethnocentrism is not even a correct term, for the divergence among western countries is much larger than the ideology of modernity and development suggests.

Development is also a neocolonial discourse – 'where colonialism left off, development took over' (Kothari 1988: 143). Thus, its premises began to come apart even as its policies were still being formulated. The comparative-developmental paradigm could not withstand the momentum of decolonization. The assumption that the western concepts of the nation, state, civil society and representative government are universal increasingly proved invalid, as political developments in Africa and Asia showed. The crisis of Orientalism, diagnosed by Anouar Abdel-Malek (1963) and examined by Edward Said (1985), is a case in point. Universalism is an adjunct of hegemony and as hegemony shrinks so does truth.

Options

The comparative method in social science has followed the tracks laid by developmentalism and, accordingly, the crisis of developmentalism is also a crisis of the comparative method. In comparative politics this has given rise, according to Bertrand Badie (1989), to a threefold crisis of universalism, of explanation, and of the relationship between history and comparative political analysis. A crisis of universalism because, since the end of the 1970s, the transcultural nature of concepts derived from western discourse is increasingly in doubt. A crisis of explanation because the assumption of a unitary, transcultural logic is not tenable: comparative analysis, therefore, cannot be causal; it can only be interpretative. The prioritization of economic development in development and modernization thinking assumes that economic factors are equally important everywhere and that the relationship between economics and politics is perceived in similar terms everywhere.

Accordingly, the present direction in political studies tends to be away from grand theory and a general model of history towards more modest aims. Badie, in a drastic departure from developmentalism and the comparative method, advocates the reconstruction of political science as a cultural science, that is, the return of anthropology to political science. Semiotics would assume an important place in political studies, to compare social actors' different meaning systems; linguistics, to examine the social history of political vocabularies; and history, to problematize the historical autonomy of the unit of analysis. This approach, according to Badie, cannot be of the same theoretical status as the classical comparative approach. The limitation of the cultural analysis approach is that it can produce description and interpretation but not explanation. To address this he seeks recourse to an interpretative Weberian sociology of action that would address action in terms of its meaning to the actors themselves.

Another shift in the direction toward cultural specificity is the plea for the indigenization of sociological theory. This follows an from the critique of universalism and seeks to be a remedy for intellectual dependence and imperialism in social science.[3] Scepticism also speaks out in the words of Partha Chatterjee with regard to the future of third world nationalism: 'A historical discourse, unfortunately, can only struggle with its own terms. Its evolution will be determined by history itself' (Chatterjee 1986: 162). Here also the assumption is the absence of a general model of history, the absence of a universal discourse.

The general current in comparative studies, however, particularly in historical studies, continues to follow different methodological options. Theda Skocpol defends the approach of comparative historical analysis, a method for examining large historical questions by comparing different societies. Causal associations are tested by comparing positive cases (in terms of the hypothesis tested), and positive with negative cases, which are otherwise similar in relevant respects. This approach would be 'generalisable across cases and historically sensitive' and 'an ideal strategy for mediating between theory and history'. This method is followed in Barrington Moore's work and in her own comparative study of social revolutions (Skocpol 1979: 35–40; 1984; Moore 1969).

A similar intermediary position of methodological caution and theoretical aspiration is found in Charles Tilly's (1984) work. In its rejection of grand theory this is a partial criticism of universalism but does not exclude the possibility of universal explanatory hypotheses. It matters whether one's comparisons tend to be mainly within a single zone of world society (as in Tilly's work which is concerned with European politics) or whether the comparisons are also across cultural zones, notably north–south (as in the case of Badie and advocates of the indigenization of social science); in the latter case greater methodological caution is warranted.

These options raise a number of questions. While the crisis of developmentalism and the comparative method is beyond repair, a complete U-turn toward 'methodological individualism' and cultural specificity is an overreaction. There are limits to cultural specificity because societies the world over are part of a globalizing momentum – the inroads made by the world market, media, industrial and postindustrial technologies, the homogenizing influence of the interstate system, the expanding galaxy of international bodies and conventions and growing human mobility (migration and tourism). When globalization is advancing and barriers are broken down, is it the time for a retreat into theoretical provincialism?

In world-system theory, globalism itself is made the single overarching dynamic. The argument of globalism is taken to the point where nation states are not units of development; only the world system develops. Here the problem of comparative analysis does not and cannot arise: as a single system without an exit the world by definition is governed by a single logic. Thematizing the economic logic of world market extension, world-system theory treats culture as an epiphenomenon (Robertson and Lechner 1985). What is not acknowledged in world-system theory, however, is that economism itself is a cultural precept.

So neither universalism nor relativism globalism nor provincialism can provide adequate answers. This leads to further questions. When we discard evolutionism, should we also discard evolution? When we reject developmentalism, should we also drop development? The discourse of western hegemony belongs to the past and is epistemologically and politically untenable. Yet the other extreme, relativism, leaves us without a common human discourse. If five hundred years of western expansion and hegemony have, even in adverse and perverse ways, contributed to the unification of the world and humanity, relativism would make it impossible for us to harvest what fruits there are from this globalizing momentum. If universalism in contemporary social theory is a veil of western ethnocentrism, does it mean there are no universals at all? Does it mean that everything diffuses in cultural specifics and perspectives without the possibility of a common human discourse? Or, rather, does it mean that the question of what is universal is to be posed anew, not in Eurocentric but in polycentric ways?

From bipolarity to polycentrism

> It's not a matter of emancipating truth from every system of power (which would be a chimera, for truth is already power) but of detaching the power of truth from the forms of social, economic and cultural hegemony within which it presently operates. (Foucault 1980: 133)
>
> You do not stand in one place to watch a masquerade. (An Igbo saying, quoted in Clifford 1988: 189)

I come back to the observation of Václav Havel quoted earlier: the identity of the centre of power and the centre of truth. In terms of the balance of power, the world of colonialism involved multipolar competition among the western powers, that is, among countries that shared the same civilizational framework. This changed when Japan joined the great powers in the early 1900s and changed again with the Bolshevik revolution. Yalta and the Cold War produced a bipolar world, with two centres of power and two centres of truth. Both discourses have been developmentalist, though they subscribed to different varieties of modernization – 'forging ahead' (or 'muddling through') and 'catching up'.

For a while it seemed that the bipolar world gave way to a unipolar world dominated by the United States. In the twenty-first century it is clear, however, that the United States is nowhere near its previous position of leadership, economically and financially, although it may retain a military and political lead. The larger transition we are experiencing at present is from the bipolar world of superpower rivalry, of capitalism and communism, to a world of multipolar competition again, except this time the centres of power, or potential centres of power, belong to multiple civilizational frameworks. These centres of power need not be identified here – though some can readily be imagined. In some spheres of international affairs, geopolitics and the world economy, polycentrism is operative already. Trilateralism may be regarded as a stage of polycentrism. The transition we are in now concerns its further unfolding in political discourse and culture.

This relates to what we might term, with Manoranjan Mohanty (1989), in analogy with the terms of trade, the question of the 'changing terms of discourse'. Previously, the main counter-discourse to western hegemony was Marxism, another western and developmentalist discourse from the same civilizational family. Now cross-civilizational questions may become more important.

Indian thinkers have been leading the way in the critique of modernity (e.g. Desai 1971). Another line of approach has been to separate modernization from westernization. There are examples of this in the Arab world (e.g. Abdel-Malek 1980/1983). Alternative conceptualizations of modernization have been formulated in Japan (Kishimoto 1963). This line of reasoning is presently being followed in China as well (Li Lulu 1989). A related approach is a dialogue of paradigms of rationality among different cultures (Kang 1985, Park 1985).

With bipolarity, ideological, military, political and economic cleavages accumulated to create clear and distinct lines of demarcation. Polycentrism cannot be expected to unfold in this fashion. This also accounts for the peculiar, uncertain and fuzzy character of the period we are in. Structurally, culturally and ideologically, the momentum of globalization – the impact of western hegemony, the world market, and technologies of production and communication – shapes the emerging centres of power. Nationalism does not have an ideological autonomy comparable to communism.

The transition from bipolarity to polycentrism affects the terms of discourse in contradictory ways. On the one hand, the field of debate is opened wide; the focal point is no longer confined to the bipolar confrontation of capitalism and Marxism. On the other, the transition is taking place in the context of globalization: it's a question of cultural multipolarization in conjunction with globalization. So might both tendencies be meaningful and complementary – globalism and localism, an increase in scale and segmentation?

The deconstruction of the west

Developments such as the opening of eastern Europe have stimulated attempts to revive modernization theory. It is difficult to view neo-modernization analysis (Tiryakian 1991) other than as an expression of western triumphalism. Samir Amin's analysis of Eurocentrism restates the *fin de siècle* dilemma in familiar terms: 'socialist universalism or Eurocentric capitalist barbarism' (1989: 152). Both perspectives remain well within the developmentalist paradigm. At another pole of the debate, Rajni Kothari (1988: 216) perceives a different dilemma: 'If "development" itself has become a problem, and has sowed the seeds of discontent and ethnic conflict, a corrective to development can only come from other worldviews, other visions'.

In the west, as mentioned before, the paradigm of modernity is increasingly contested. It appears hazardous in view of ecological limits to growth and limits to well-being. It is questioned by new social movements that challenge the notion of a universal historical master plan (e.g. Melucci 1989). The Enlightenment promise and programme appear questionable in view of twentieth-century tragedies, the Shoah, Gulag and Hiroshima. Epistemologically, modernism and its simple positivism no longer measure up to contemporary standards of the critique of knowledge. Out of the implosion of linear, futurist discourses postmodernism has emerged. Initially a movement in art, architecture and literature, postmodernism stresses ambiguity, indeterminacy, irreverence and deconstruction and indicates historical and semantic instability. As a social philosophy it is a cultural expression of postindustrial or information society.

Several authors (Anderson 1998, Giri 1998, Lee 1994, Slater 1992) explore the relevance of postmodernism to the global south. But to the extent that the south is regarded as still being in the throes of modernization, as either preindustrial or industrializing, postmodernist perspectives tend to be dismissive of the south. Rather than exploding developmentalism, postmodernism merely recapitulates it (as it implicitly follows a sequence of preindustrial, industrial, postindustrial stages) on a different plane.

Postmodernism is a western deconstruction of western modernism and to address the problem of developmentalism more is required. What matters most and comes across least in many analyses of development discourse is the complexity and 'holism' of western developmentalism. Developmentalism is not merely a policy of economic and social change, or a philosophy of history. It reflects the ethos of western culture and is intimately intertwined with western history and culture. Ultimately the problem of developmentalism cannot be settled in terms of political economy, or in terms of social philosophy, the critique of ideas or unpacking discourse; it requires a profound historical and cultural review of the western project, a task we might term the deconstruction of the west.

The deconstruction of the west is about returning the west to world history. This follows on from the logic of decolonization. It also follows on from the crisis of the western development model, not least in the west itself, and may yield a basis for reopening the debate on rationality and values. Here I will indicate only briefly what directions this might take.

The deconstruction of the west is a historical as well as a conceptual project. A key historical question is to what extent what we call 'western civilization' is actually a universal human heritage that comes to us, for historical and geographical reasons, in the guise of a western synthesis? In this context certain forms of being 'anti-western' are as irrelevant as, say, being anti-algebra, which in the first place is not western but Arabic in origin and in the second place doesn't make sense. A conceptual question is what in 'western' contributions is particularistic and what is universal, what is culture-specific and what is general or generalizable?

Martin Bernal's *Black Athena: Afroasiatic Roots of Classical Civilization* (1987) and the research programme indicated in the title, is part of what needs to be done. The 'separate history' of the west goes back a long way but has also been retrospectively invented and continues to be invented. In fabricating the past to suit their imperial frames, western elites have obfuscated western history and, in the process, world history.

The analysis of western discourses is important but a wider cultural engagement is also required: the analysis of cognitive patterns underlying discourse, of western iconography, art and popular culture (Nederveen Pieterse 1994, 2006). Here we approach the point of reversal: the erstwhile model examined as a problem. Part of the deconstruction of the west is anthropology in reverse: the analysis of the west in terms formerly reserved for history's backwaters; the analysis of western fetishism as an act of therapy. This is where the significance emerges of Gandhi and other nonwestern critics of the west who cared enough and carried cultural weight enough to vocalize their critiques.

These inquiries pave the way for a more specific project: the deconstruction of 'development', which can be taken in several modes. It can be taken in the sense of the deconstruction of development discourse, which this chapter has done in a historical-interpretative fashion; or in a stricter sense of deconstructing development discourse in Foucauldian fashion (DuBois 1991, Escobar 1985) or in the fashion of Derrida (Johnston 1991). In addition, the deconstruction of development can apply to development policies and take the form of the disaggregation of policy formulations, for example, between those that are (a) inevitable, (b) necessary, (c) desirable or acceptable under certain specified conditions, and (d) nonsensical and reflecting western biases and ethnocentrism. Accordingly, the deconstruction of development is the prerequisite for its reconstruction. This cannot be a single reconstruction but should be polycentric reconstructions, given the varying itineraries and circumstances in different countries.

It is obvious that carrying out this agenda would require filling in many blank spots and that this would both settle and raise a number of problems. But it also means changing the terms of the debate. The predominance of developmentalism structures the debate in terms of either 'westernization'/modernization or 'anti-development' positions, while other registers remain beyond earshot. The deconstruction of the west is a poser. It is a way to reopen a discussion that has so far been conducted in universalist terms. The middle way between universalism and relativism is pluralism.

Notes

1 Henry Kissinger 1970, among others, elaborates on the concept of the White Revolution.
2 For example, 'a process of modernization presided over by the established élites, who used the "revolutionary" changes to maintain their supremacy' (Femia 1981: 48).
3 On universalism and indigenization see Akiwowo 1988, 1999; cf. Ake 1979.

The Development of Development Theory: Towards Critical Globalism

The prevalent note in development thinking has long been saying goodbye to paradigms. Many articles open by saying goodbye to modernization and dependency while insisting that no new paradigm will be proposed. The objections to these paradigms are familiar enough and there's no need to restate them here. Still this is not just a time of 'waiting for a text'. Several new departures in development thinking parallel general tendencies in social theory such as the problematization of modernity, poststructuralism and postmodernism. Development discourse is examined in Foucauldian terms of power/knowledge (DuBois 1991, Escobar 1985, Marglin and Marglin 1990, Sachs 1992a), deconstructed (Johnston 1991), subjected to archaeological excavation (Sachs 1999), or juxtaposed with explorations of the postmodern (Schuurman 1993, Slater 1992) and the postcolonial (Kapoor 2008). These contributions expand on the critiques of Eurocentrism, Orientalism and occidental cultural homogenization in postcolonial and cultural studies. No doubt the debates on postmodernity and multiple modernities carry major implications for development theory for they are concerned with redefining 'development' writ large.

These contributions are often limited by their preoccupation with discourse. While deepening our critical insight they don't offer alternatives. Following postmodern interrogations of modernization, modernity as a theme is making a comeback, but now in the plural – as modernity 'reworked', neo-modernization theory, or new modernity. The latter involves the notion of 'risk society' and the idea that all societies, developed and developing, are exposed to ecological and other risks (Beck 1992).

Many discussions attribute greater coherence and consistency to development theory than it possesses. Thus in being criticized as the 'religion of the West' (Rist 1997) or as the 'myth of development' (Tucker 1999), developmentalism is homogenized and treated as if it were cut from a single cloth. The deconstruction of development texts is not the same as unpacking development theory, disaggregating its lineages, dimensions and projects. The very notion of *development* is increasingly being bracketed. The questioning comes from various directions: from deconstructions of development discourse but also from the momentum of globalization on account of which the special status of developing economies – the original rationale of the development argument – is gradually being eroded. In this context, structural adjustment represents a radical break with the development tradition, less because of its neoliberal thrust than because of the implicit argument that *all* societies must adjust to global economic imperatives. The implication is that either development is gradually fading out as an outdated perspective belonging to a bygone era of economic apartheid, or it is broadened to apply to all societies, as a global logic. If this were the case it would be logical to assume that the content and meaning of development would change too.

These various notions – deconstruction of development, structural adjustment, globalization, global risk – seem to point in a similar direction: the demise of 'development' and its gradually emerging reconstruction as *world development*. A related question is the relationship between endogenous and exogenous dynamics in development, which may also point towards a reconceptualization of development as a global problematic.

This chapter develops three arguments. First, it argues that development thinking has not been the single paradigm for which it has often been taken but that it has been a heterogeneous set of approaches all along, that has been not only variable over time but diverse at any given time. Second, it zeroes in on one particular unresolved dilemma in several forms of development thinking: the tension between *endogenous* and *exogenous* dynamics in development. Third, it explores the idea of rethinking development as a process that is not reserved to 'developing countries' but that *all* societies are developing, as part of a global process. Thus it juxtaposes development discourse and globalization. I argue that globalization should neither be blocked out or ignored, in the name of delinking, import substitution or neomercantilism, nor unconditionally embraced. The term I propose for this in-between position is *critical globalism*.

The first part of this chapter takes the form of development discourse analysis. The second part continues with meta-theoretical reflections. Discourse analysis makes subjectivities transparent, which may offer grounds to renegotiate subjectivities; but it is limited in that it does not *per se* engage objective dynamics. So in the third part the mode of argument changes as well. The closing argument on development and globalization seeks to gather the insights gained from analysing development discourse and to combine these with changes in objective circumstances so as to arrive at critical policy orientations.

Notions of change

There is a tendency among users as well as critics of development theory to attribute to it a certain coherence and consistency with the exception of one or other favourite cleavage. This easily produces a dichotomous view of development theory, as in Marxism versus neoclassical economics, mainstream versus counterpoint, etc. Development theories promote façades of consistency as part of their single-minded future-building project. Critics contribute to it by following the logic of binary opposition. It may be fruitful instead to view development theory *in the plural*, not as the unfolding of a grand paradigm neatly bifurcating in contesting models, but as a hybrid made up of uneven elements, of borrowings and incursions from alien sources and improvisations spurred on by crises. In a word, to consider the inconsistencies of what goes under the heading of development theory.

Robert Nisbet is widely regarded as an authoritative source on the history of western notions of change while he is also a spectacular representative of the tendency to 'homogenize' developmental thinking. In *Social Change and History* he maintains that 'for twenty-five hundred years a single metaphoric conception of change has dominated Western thought' (1969: 211). The theory of social development, in his view, derives from the ancient metaphor of *growth*. With the Greeks this took the form of *cycles* of change; in the Christian version formulated by Augustine it was modified to an *epic* form, still cyclical but without recurrence; and by the seventeenth century it was modified to produce the modern idea of linear progress. In the eighteenth century this set of assumptions engendered the idea of 'natural history' and in the nineteenth century, the theory of social evolution that was common to Hegel, Saint-Simon, Comte, Marx, Spencer, Morgan and Tylor. This theory, according to Nisbet, regarded change as natural, immanent, or proceeding from forces within the entity, continuous, directional, necessary, corresponding to differentiation in society, typically moving from the homogeneous to the heterogeneous, and finally, as proceeding from uniform causes.

Nisbet concedes that in twentieth-century social science there was a revolt against evolutionism, replacing unilinear evolutionism with multilinear evolution, but maintains that even the critics reproduced the underlying metaphor of growth: 'although they were denouncing the schemes of social evolution, they were accepting at full value the concepts of change that underlay the theory of social evolution' (1969: 225). That is, the belief in origins, immanence, continuity, uniform causes, etc., is reproduced in twentieth-century conceptions of social change. This bold thesis raises several questions: is this representation plausible, or does it in itself reflect a belief in origins and continuity?

A different way of reading the development of development theory may be genealogy in Nietzsche's sense. Nietzsche, as Foucault reminds us, was opposed to the search for 'origins': 'because it is an attempt to capture the exact essence of things, their purest possibilities, and their carefully protected identities; because this search assumes the existence of immobile forms that precede the external world of accident and succession'. However, Foucault continues, 'if the genealogist ... listens to history' he finds behind things 'not a timeless and essential secret, but the secret that they have no essence or that their essence was fabricated in a piecemeal fashion from alien forms' (1984: 78). An example of the preoccupation with origins is Hegel: 'The principle of development involves also the existence of a latent germ of being – a capacity or potentiality striving to realize itself. This formal conception finds actual existence in spirit; which has the history of the world for its theatre, its possession, and the sphere of its realization' (quoted in Nisbet 1969: 159).

For Nietzsche this would be an example of the 'Egyptianism' of philosophers, the obstinate 'placing of conclusions at the beginning' (in Foucault 1984: 90). History is replaced by metaphysics, by Neoplatonic essences beyond time. Let's contrast this with Nietzsche (1976: 470): 'By searching out origins, one becomes a crab. The historian looks backward; eventually he also *believes* backward'.

Nisbet's history of the idea of development as a continuous outgrowth of the Greek metaphor of growth exhibits not only the preoccupation with origins and continuity but also an essentialism of ideas. It lays claim to a grand cohesiveness of western thought, uniting the pagan and Christian, classical and modern notions in a single weave. It sets the west apart from the rest of the world while tacitly removing the main lines of cleavage within western thought, those separating ancients and moderns, religious and secular elites, elites and dissidents (such as Nietzsche's *esprits libres*). An exercise in high humanism, it produces an elite representation of western notions of change, with the classics duly towering above subsequent thinkers as the true ancestors of western thought.

What faithful conformism to begin with the Greeks, the proverbial 'cradle of western civilization'. Why not consider the divergencies *among* Greek notions of change? For example among the Peripatetics, Aristotle's followers who along with the Neoplatonists adhered to a cyclical notion of time, whereas the Stoics moved away from this and historians such as Herodotus and Thucydides broke altogether with the doctrine of recurrence.

In his essay on Chinese 'Attitudes toward time and change as compared with Europe', Joseph Needham groups non-Christian Greek thought together with Indian thought and the Hindu and Buddhist notion of the endless repetition of the wheel of existence. Needham refers to 'the intense history-consciousness of Christendom' and contrasts linear Judaeo-Christian time to cyclical Indo-Hellenic time. With regard to China he concludes: 'Strange as it may seem to those who still think in terms of the "timeless Orient", the culture of China was, on the whole, more of the Iranic, Judaeo-Christian than of the Indo-Hellenic types' (Needham 1981: 131). This gives us a rather different view of the distribution of civilizational perceptions of change and a totally different map of world history than Nisbet's. The grounds for the singularity of the west as a special case, a deviation from the 'general human pattern', are eliminated.

Why not highlight, rather than continuity and uniformity, the *discontinuities* and divergencies in western notions of change? Western views, of course, have been an amalgam, as we can see, for instance, in the *mélange* of Christian views in Augustine's time and later in the return to cyclical thinking in Nietzsche ('*ewige Wiederkehr*', eternal recurrence), Spengler and Toynbee (Needham 1981: 128). A re-examination of western notions of development reveals a far more heterogeneous and uneven history replete with moments of improvisation, dissonance, discontinuity. Leaving aside that Nisbet simplified the notions of change of Greeks and Christians – which he nuanced in later work (1980) – let's turn to the moderns.

Nisbet rightly mentions that the nineteenth-century theories of social development applied to different entities – to reason for Turgot and Condorcet, to knowledge and civilization for Comte, to freedom for Hegel, to democracy for Tocqueville, to the forces of production for Marx, to social institutions for Spencer, to kinship, property and civil government for Morgan, to legal institutions for Maine, to culture and religion for Tylor. Nisbet insists: 'it was the *entity* … for which natural development in time was claimed. It was *not* the sum total of geographical areas on earth' (1969: 167). But this is not the whole story of the theory of social evolution. Evolutionist stages theories, such as that of Victorian anthropology – primitivism, savagery, barbarism, civilization – were also taken to apply to human cultures which were identified with societies (Stocking 1987). Theorists of social evolution regularly applied their views to geographical areas – Hegel on Africa, Marx and Wittfogel on Asia are familiar examples.

Nisbet's focus is on development conceived as natural and endogenous to the entity or society, but another dimension to nineteenth-century developmental thought which he glosses over is development arising from *exogenous* influences and conditions – from diffusion, international influences, or what we would now call globalization. Marx's theory is both: 'the new grows in the womb of the old' refers to endogenous, organic growth; whereas his statements on capitalism as a 'permanently revolutionizing force', on its progressive effects on the 'rural idiocy' of the countryside and of colonialism on 'stagnant' societies refer to external dynamics.

Nisbet is sensitive to western ethnocentrism: 'No one can miss the fact that in every instance – there is no exception – the direction of change found by the evolutionist was toward the specific set of qualities possessed by Western Europe alone' (1969: 169–70). But, just as geography is missing, the imperial setting is absent from his account. It has been argued that imperialism is marked by 'the primacy of the geographical', for it is after all 'an act of geographical violence' (Said 1993: 225). Though this is a particularly narrow reading of imperialism that overlooks political economy (which may well transcend geographical, territorial boundaries), geography should not be ignored.

Nisbet's argument of continuity overlooks the shifts in western developmental thinking and papers over the dynamics over time of European views. In brief, seventeenth- and eighteenth-century views were ambivalent about Europe's status in the world and looked up to models such as China, Turkey, Persia and the noble savages of America, the Pacific and Africa. Only in nineteenth-century theories of social evolution did the European will to power prevail; they took a single-focused form which provided greater consistency, particularly during the second half of the century, than before or after.[1]

If Nisbet's representation is fundamentally flawed, how can we account for the fact that his kind of view has found such wide acceptance? A related question is to what extent we can recognize the same implicit model of endogenous, organic growth in contemporary development theory.

Development theories in the plural

If we consider twentieth-century development thinking and its theoretical lineages, does Nisbet's metaphor of growth hold? Is the tenor one of continuity and consistency or one of disparity and improvisation? The term 'development theory' suggests a coherence that in fact is hard to find. What we do find is a plethora of competing and successive currents, schools, paradigms, models and approaches, several of which claim to exclude one another. For a start, development theory refers to two terrains which have converged only at certain junctures: development sociology and development economics. Further distinctions run between theory and ideology, policy and practice.

Development sociology has been by and large the critical successor to the nineteenth-century theories of social development. Development economics, on the other hand, owes its origin to a deviation from late nineteenth-century economic orthodoxy. Kurt Martin (1991) has made the interesting argument that development economics resuscitates and revisits the classical political economy of Smith, Ricardo and Marx, who were development economists in that their basic problematic was the transition from an agrarian to an industrial society. Neoclassical economics came into being only after 1870 as a theory of fully industrialized economies (FitzGerald 1991).

'Development' if understood as the problematic of the transition from agriculture to industry has been revisited and reinvented several times over; it has been a question facing several generations of late developers. It was the question facing central, eastern and southern European economies during the early twentieth century: hence the involvement of central Europeans in the early stages of modern development theory. Hence Alex Nove's claim that development theory was 'born in Russia in the twenties' (Martin 1991: 28). Thus several modern development theories replicate earlier findings.

The formative period of 'modern' development economic theory was the 1940s and 1950s. The colonial economies were the *terrain* of development theory but the problematic was that of *transition* or, in a word, industrialization. Thus as 'colonial economics' transmuted into 'development economics' it borrowed from existing theories of transition, from classical political economy or from other 'late developers'.

For instance, the theory of unequal exchange was originally advanced in 1929 as an argument for protecting industry in agrarian countries (Martin 1991: 38). At the time unequal exchange was viewed as a feature of centre–periphery trade. In his 1928 analysis of European capitalism Werner Sombart applied it to Britain as the dominant centre, and central, eastern and southern Europe as exploited and dominated peripheries. The terminology of centre and periphery derives from a late nineteenth-century discourse of German political geography in which the term *Randlage* was used for periphery. For geographers such as Friedrich Ratzel this discourse carried definite political, nationalist overtones, as part of the rivalry between Germany and Britain.

Via Dietrich Haushofer it entered the discourse of geopolitics of national socialism and informed the urge for *Lebensraum* (Nederveen Pieterse 1989: ch. 1). Accordingly, the centre–periphery argument served nationalism in both offensive (national expansionism) and defensive (protectionism) modes. In the 1960s it was reutilized as a cornerstone of dependency theory. In Arghiri Emanuel's contribution to dependency theory, unequal trade came to describe the dualism of the world economy between north and south.

The premise of modern (that is, postwar) development economics was that it was a separate branch of economics, different from economics in the industrialized countries and from neoclassical equilibrium theory. State intervention and planning, along with accumulation and growth, were part of its 'founding discourse', which showed general affinities with Keynesianism. Foreign assistance, accompanied by the idea of mutual benefit, was another feature of the original discourse. In this respect it diverged from both neoclassical economics and Marxism.

In relation to international trade, again radically different theoretical outlooks prevailed. On the one hand were liberalism and the tradition of the Manchester School, following the Smithean premise that free trade and the international division of labour based on comparative advantage would eventually benefit all countries; on the other was neomercantilism, arguing, in the footsteps of Alexander Hamilton and Friedrich List, that infant industries require tariff protection. Mainstream economic theory from the 1870s onward promoted the free trade argument, while the neomercantilist policies which sheltered the late developers (the American Republic, later followed by Germany, France, Russia) were relegated to the margins, as deviations from the norm, to be reclaimed later as part of dependency theory and as an argument for tariff protection in less developed countries.

From the outset development thinking has been marked by an uneven and contradictory patchwork with divergent paradigms operating in different terrains and sectors: in industrialized economies, neoclassical economics coexisted with industrial policy; in trade, liberalism in theory coexisted with neomercantilism in practice; in finance, versions of monetarism prevailed. Each of these divergent perspectives and policy orientations made its imprint on developing economies, simultaneously in different sectors, although usually articulated under the umbrella of an overarching development rhetoric. Which development posture prevailed reflected the historical bloc of class alignments that held the upper hand.

As a concept, 'development' papers over the different interests involved in economic, social and political change. 'Development' suggests the possibility of a package formula in which all these interests come to some form of crystallization and convergence. As such it displays an intrinsically positivist bias. Obviously, social and economic change is always a field of contestation among different stakeholders. Each of these constructs a story – of the past, present and future – to validate its claims. A political economy of development theory (as a subset of the general sociology of knowledge) might not have too much difficulty in identifying the shifting 'historical blocs' that have set the agenda of development ideology at different points in time,[2] except, of course, that at no time has it been a single or uncontested agenda.

New trades and manufactures (Manchester School) contested the political economy of monopoly enterprise (mercantilism and the old colonial system). The political economy of competition capital and manufacturing was contested by finance capital (monetarism). All along, the political economies of capital in their different articulations have been contested by the political economies of labour (trade unionism, syndicalism, Marxism, socialism). The claims of national firms and agricultural interests (protection) have been contested by internationally oriented enterprise (free trade), etcetera. These various sets of contradictions have been played out through contestations between alignments of interests favouring either state intervention or market forces. Like masks in a puppet show, both 'state' and 'market' have themselves signified complex fields of forces and interests. 'State' and 'market' have been on either side of these contesting forces. The state has been the meeting place where a political and social contract between the diverging interests was fashioned.

Accordingly, development thinking implicitly carries two layers of meanings: an actual diversity of interests and perspectives, and a hegemony, that is, an inherently unstable settlement of these differences resulting in a development posture. The hegemonic effect occurs at both national and international levels. In a sense there are as many ideologies of development as there are players in the field, but some players are more equal than others.

In the 1960s what consensus existed in development economics was destroyed, 'so that it is no longer possible to talk of a mainstream of development economics' (Martin 1991: 55). In the 1970s the Chicago version of monetarism became dominant. Monetarism is not to be equated with neoclassical equilibrium theory: it is 'little more than a revival of nineteenth-century bankers' principles of "sound money" – currency convertibility, stable parity, fiscal thrift, low wages and minimal government influence in business' (FitzGerald 1991: 15).

The ensuing wave of neoliberalism rejects the 'limitations of the special case' and argues that poor countries are poor mainly because of mismanagement. Put in another way: the compartments which hitherto separated development economics from the mainstream economics which prevailed in industrialized economies, international trade and finance, fell away, so development economics is being integrated into general economics. Whether there is a ground for a separate theory of development is one of the key debates (Hettne 1995, Lal 1995; Martin 1991: 55). Structural adjustment programmes follow from the demise of separate development economics.

These shifts of alignment make for a second rupture in the history of 'development'. The postwar career of development has typically been one of state intervention. The period 1980–2000 in many parts of the world witnessed the marginalization of the state and the ascendancy of market forces. The renewed predominance of finance capital since the 1970s and the cycle of debt expansion and debt crisis turned the IMF and World Bank into arbiters of development policy, with the bankers' orthodoxy of sound money, or monetarism, being recycled as the newest beacon on the development horizon. Robert Kuttner notes that under these circumstances what public sovereignty remains 'has been entrusted to perhaps the most conservative and market-oriented of all public institutions – central banks ... the triad of central bankers, IMF, and World Bank has been so thoroughly creditor-oriented that it might as well have been the House of Rothschild or the House of Morgan' (1991: 260–61). In the alignment of the late twentieth century, as in the late nineteenth century, finance capital predominates as the cement of the historic bloc that frames 'development'.

Along with the discourse the models shifted – no more United States and American Dream, no more China, Cuba, Tanzania, Nicaragua either, but the accumulation models of the NICs of East Asia. It spelled the 'end of the Third World' (Harris 1986) and of Third Worldism. In the process another contradiction emerges, another instance of development double-speak for the East Asian experience is not unfettered market-led development but, on the contrary, the model of the developmental state (Chang and Grabel 2004, Johnson 1982, White 1988). In other words, contemporary development ideologies are again highly diverse and deeply divided discourses.

These divergencies can be observed on the level of development *theory*, which has been increasingly diversifying (Booth 1994b); development *ideology*, where neoliberalism is well past its peak; and development *policy*, which is inspired as much by ad hocism and pragmatism as by ideological posturing. Here from time to time I will use development *thinking* as a middling term, indicating the mixed character of development speak – an uneven *mélange* of theoretical precepts, ideological subscriptions and political preferences.

One line of thinking holds that the dividing line between development successes and failures in terms of growth doesn't run between models or theories, but that what matters more than the 'model' is how it is implemented. Thus, what matters is not whether or not a state intervenes but what *kind* of state intervenes and in what political culture. Several Asian countries have implemented NIC strategies with strong doses of state intervention, which has generated high growth rates in many countries, but not in the Philippines and Sri Lanka. To explain this variation, factors such as economic and political history, political institutions (Litonjua 1994) and ethnic politics and crony capitalism have been brought in.

It is difficult to oppose privatization in general if privatization can also serve as a barrier against corrupt politicians. This however does not settle the problem of accountability; on the contrary, market forces are still less accountable than state bureaucracies. The question, then, is not one of state versus market but rather points towards democratization and reforms that make both the state and corporations more accountable.

A sobering awareness is that matters are not simply decided on the basis of models. Policy implementation is affected by factors such as political culture, historical itineraries, and location in the regional and international environment. Thus the World Bank too, in the actual implementation of its policies, is more concerned with negotiation than with simply imposing its economic model (Mosley et al. 1991). In the process we are referred back to what development economists call 'noneconomic factors'.

Modernization revisited

In development sociology the leading paradigm has been modernization. Modernization theory took shape in the 1950s in the US and bears an American stamp – if we recall that Dahrendorf called the US the country of *angewandte Aufklärung*, the applied Enlightenment. When the US entered its era of globalism, a 'can do' attitude characterized its approach, as in the functionalist modernization advanced by Hoselitz: 'You subtract the ideal typical features or indices of underdevelopment from those of development, and the remainder is your development program' (Andre Gunder Frank in Worsley 1984: 18).

Most forms of evolutionism conceived of development as being natural and endogenous, whereas modernization theory makes room for exogenous influences. Modernization theory is usually referred to as a paradigm, but upon closer consideration turns out to host a wide variety of projects, some along the lines of *endogenous change*, viz. social differentiation, rationalization, the spread of universalism, achievement and specificity; and others involving projects of *exogenous change*: the spread of market relations or capitalism, technological diffusion and industrialization, westernization, nation-building (nationalism as a derivative discourse) and state formation (as in postcolonial inheritor states). If this diversity *within* modernization is occasionally recognized, still the importance of exogenous influences is considered minor and secondary.

> I do not view 'modernization' as a single, unified, integrated theory in any strict sense of 'theory'. It was an overarching perspective concerned with comparative issues of national development, which treated development as multidimensional and multicausal along various axes (economic, political, cultural), and which gave primacy to endogenous rather than exogenous factors. (Tiryakian 1992: 78)

This may be the steepest contradiction within modernization theory: between modernization as an endogenous and an exogenous dynamic. It may also be a profound contradiction in development thinking generally: the hiatus between development as an endogenous process and as externally induced change, under the aegis of imperialism, capitalism, globalism.

The theory of *dualism*, developed in the 1940s and 1950s by Boeke, Lewis and Kuznets, accommodates this contradiction with the idea of a traditional and modern sector. In effect the traditional sector represents endogenous growth and the modern sector the interaction with outside forces, in infrastructure, production techniques, trade, values and aid. The diffusion approach was institutionalized in the 'geography of modernization', focusing on transportation and on core urban areas as the vehicles for the 'mobilization of the periphery' (Brookfield 1975: 110–16). Phrased in another way, there is a hiatus between development theory as a national project and as an international or global dynamic. From the outset the main development theories, both economic and sociological, have been a national, or more accurately, a state project. Neomercantilism, 'socialism in one country', Keynesianism, self-reliance, all represent state projects. By contrast, the market-oriented approaches of neoclassical economics and neoliberalism have been equally comfortable in national *and* international domains.

This may give us a clue as to the impasses of development theories. The major turns in development have been shaped by supranational dynamics entirely or mostly outside the scope of standard development theory: the breakdown of the Bretton Woods system, the emergence of OPEC, the gradual shift from the Atlantic to the Pacific era, the shift to flexible production, financial crises in emerging economies. Time and again *crisis* has been a more formidable teacher than theory: the energy crisis, debt crisis, ecological crises, financial crisis, food crisis – and each crisis concerns supranational dynamics.

Neo-Marxism, dependency theory, world-system theory follow the external model: capitalism flows in, travels from the centre to the periphery, 'external areas' are incorporated into the world system. Their positive programmes, however, at any rate in the case of dependency theory, defend development as a national logic. F.H. Cardoso's notion of 'associated dependent development' did take into account external influences. The difference between Bill Warren and most dependency thinkers was that Warren followed a transnational and diffusionist approach to accumulation and development whereas the dependentistas operated within nationalitarian logic. Likewise, the key concepts of critical and alternative development thinking implicitly echo and revisit endogenous development as the norm: the self-reliance, autocentric development and delinking advocated in some forms of dependency theory, historicist views on modernization, polycentrism, indigenization, and 'another development'.

The *unit* of development, however, is not a given or a constant. The *boundaries* between what is internal and external are by no means fixed. Development discourse and its implicit assumption of the 'country', 'society', 'economy' as the developing unit paper over this issue and assume much greater national cohesiveness and state control than is realistic. This relates to the familiar question of the reach and strength of the state (Migdal 1988). The assumption has been questioned on several grounds. The classic argument of world-system theory maintains that it is not the society that is the developing unit but the 'world system' (that is, the unit integrated by an international division of labour of goods necessary for social reproduction). Michael Mann (1986) contends that the very term 'society' is misleading and proposes instead 'social networks' that sprawl across borders. Crossborder economies such as the Pearl River delta in China and the Riau triangle between

Indonesia and Singapore have inspired ideas of regional economies (Chen 2005, Ohmae 1995) and crossborder enterprises such as the Maquiladores at the Mexican–US border have also drawn attention. The unit of development is shifting further in light of the concern with regions and localities as sites of development, which finds expression in the regionalist turn (Amin and Thrift 1993) and 'new localism' (Goetz and Clarke 1993).

The nation state is caught in a dialectic of subnationalism and supranationalism. Still, the weakening of the state is by no means a straightforward process. 'One of the paradoxes of the late twentieth century is that the tendency of the state to intervene in economic affairs has increased – political rhetoric notwithstanding – at a time when the effectiveness of its interventions has declined' (Griffin and Khan 1992: 64). There is no question as to the central and enduring importance of the state. In Robert Kuttner's words, 'until world government arrives the nation state is the necessary locus of social contracts between market and society' (1991: 9). Unfettered markets increase inequality, and in the age of information economies, which puts a premium on human resource development, inequality is an economic liability. These arguments go far beyond the ideological dispute of state versus market; the real issue is the *kind* of role that the state is to play. Martin Carnoy (1993: 91) contends, 'the role of the nation-state in creating an innovation society is thus absolutely crucial to the well-being of its citizens in the information age'.

The policy options in most countries remain narrow: internationalization or globalization meaning liberalization; state-led internationalization with restrictions and regional cooperation; and alternative or 'another' development.[3]

Theorizing world development: critical globalism

The argument of this chapter is that an essentialist notion of development, of good, natural, endogenous development, bedevils development thinking. What else is the notion of 'stunted development' (Marx on Ireland), 'stagnation' (Marx on India), underdevelopment (dependency theory), 'maldevelopment' (Amin 1990c) but the deviation from a norm of good, that is, natural development? This may explain the appeal of Nisbet's approach for it asserts an organic model of development as the norm. Even modernization thinking, which is highly diffusionist in policy, remains endogenist in theory. As such it can be assimilated into the general strain of 'organic development'.

In addition to the trend toward discursive consonance there are political reasons why endogenism is appealing. The politics of development, from the earliest 'late developer' to the latest, has in the main been state politics. Endogenous development, which is intrinsic to the developing entity, is by definition controllable by the state. The career of modern development theory is synchronic with the career of decolonization and to a considerable extent it has served as a state doctrine of new nations. If endogenism is a powerful political tool, it is also a prism through which exogenous influences can be negotiated, a screen behind which contradictions can, in the name of the 'national interest', be concealed. In the age of globalization, however, endogenism backfires and a new settlement is required.

The weakness of the endogenous outlook on development is its single and narrow focus. In turning one's back on and seeking shelter from international turbulence one in fact makes development more vulnerable to it. Accordingly what is needed is to rethink development as a regional, transnational, global project so the international domain is not left to the strong players and their 'might is right' alone; in a word, to theorize world development. Hettne (1990: 34) contends 'that the crisis in development theory is a reflection of the disparity between the growing irrelevance of a "nation-state" approach and the prematurity of a "world" approach'.

Part of the problem of development thinking is the hiatus between development economics and development sociology. Or, phrased otherwise, its lack of comprehensiveness: *market*-oriented approaches marginalize the state; *state*-oriented approaches marginalize market forces; both marginalize society; *civil society*-oriented approaches marginalize the state and often the market as well, and transnational forces remain largely untheorized. Market-oriented globalism (neoliberalism, monetarism, structural adjustment, transnational capitalist class, export-led growth) clashes with state-oriented endogenism or indigenization (delinking, import substitution), leaving social forces (grassroots, NGOs, informal sector) in no man's land.

Critical globalism means theorizing the entire field of forces in a way that takes into account not just market forces but also interstate relations, international agencies and civil society in its domestic and transnational manifestations. This is an argument for interdisciplinarity in development studies and for a critical engagement with globalization, avoiding the clichés of globo-speak as well as of anti-globalism.

This brings us to the question of the relationship between globalization and development. If delinking is no longer a viable option (Chapter 4 below), neither is globalization *tout court* an attractive avenue. It might be argued that globalization is the successor paradigm to dependency, except that it is not a paradigm but a shorthand description of a set of processes. What is relevant is an underlying shift in attitude: if from the point of view of dependency theory, exogenous influences have been viewed with suspicion, from the point of view of globalism, they are celebrated.

There is a wide spectrum of positions. Extreme globalization thinkers (such as Friedman 2000, Ohmae 1992) celebrate globalization and present it as global destiny; a destiny that resembles a worldwide duty-free store. In denouncing the 'tyranny of globalism', Neo-Marxists in effect reassert the primacy of endogenous dynamics (Petras and Brill 1985). But, even if corporate globalization is the issue, is the alternative to retreat to statism or endogenism?[4]

The problems with this position are several. First, globalization is narrowed down to globalism, which in turn is identified with market internationalism. Globalization is then no more than a trendy term for advanced capitalism or neoliberalism masquerading as global momentum. But this only captures one face of current globalizations. The second limitation is historical shallowness. Globalization is not a new dynamic; it would be so only and typically from the point of view of the endogenist reading of history. Arguably, though, globalization has been a long-term process and what distinguishes contemporary globalization is that it is accelerated. The third aspect that is overlooked in this position is that globalization does not come alone but as a package. Speed is not all that distinguishes contemporary globalization. Globalization presently is much more than merely intensified economic internationalization because it comes together and is interwoven with the growth of the information economy and the onset of flexible production systems (e.g. Castells 1993).

Cardoso (1993) brings various elements, old and new, together. There is frustration that has not changed: 'the South is in double jeopardy – seemingly able neither to integrate itself, pursuing its own best interests, nor to avoid "being integrated" as servants of the rich economies' (1993: 156). And there is a recognition of change, for globalization, according to Cardoso, necessitates the 'redefinition of dependency'. Cardoso notes that the south has lost its great comparative advantage, the abundance of land, mineral resources and cheap labour, for these are no longer of vital importance to the globalized economy, and the second major change is that economic development now affects all of society, for the democratization of society and state are now necessary conditions for organizational and technological innovation. The bottom line is that only one choice remains: 'either the South (or a portion of it) enters the democratic-technological-scientific race, invests heavily in R&D, and endures the "information economy" metamorphosis, or it becomes unimportant, unexploited, and unexploitable' (1993: 156).

Obviously not all developing countries are able to connect with the new global economic dynamics. Castells observes the emergence (or consolidation) of a Fourth World: 'within the framework of the new informational economy, a significant part of the world population is shifting from a structural position of exploitation to a structural position of irrelevance' (1993: 37). Cardoso concurs: 'they will not even be considered worth the trouble of exploitation, they will become inconsequential, of no interest to the developing globalized economy' (1993: 156). This is hardly a new theme. Decades ago a similar point was made about the lack of interest of multinational corporations in investing in peripheral countries; but because of structural changes in the world economy it has taken on a new gravity and a new, rough edge.

'Globalism' means either fostering or managing globalization. Critical globalism refers to the critical engagement with globalization processes, neither blocking nor celebrating them. As a policy framework for developing countries it refers to an engagement with globalization processes that is both cautious and forward looking, weighing different types of capital flow, financial transactions and technological transformations. If Samir Amin proposes selective delinking, critical globalism may be summed up as selective globalization. The keynote of globalization is that the nation state can no longer be taken for granted as the unit of development; crossborder transactions and micro- or macro-regionalization have become major avenues of development. As a global agenda, critical globalism means posing the central question of global inequality in its new manifestations. As a research agenda, it entails identifying the social forces that carry different transnational processes and examining varying conceptualizations of the global environment and the globalizing momentum; an analysis of global babble and whose interests it serves.

What, under the circumstances, is the meaning of world development? Because of the combined changes of globalization, informatization and flexibilization there is a new relevance to the notion that 'all societies are developing'. This is not just an agreeable sounding cliché but a reality confirmed by transformations taking place everywhere, on macro as well micro levels. The whole world is 'in transition'.

One way to read the current dispensation is that the gap between the most advanced semi-peripheral countries and core countries is narrowing, whereas the gap between these and peripheral countries is widening. Paul Collier (2007) refers to 'the bottom billion'. There is a new meaning to Trotsky's law of combined and uneven development. The scope of economic innovation combined with the operation of the 'law of the retarding lead' (or the dialectics of progress) places new investors in technology, infrastructure and human resource development in several respects in a similar position as the conventionally industrialized countries. If we compare the profiles of economic renewal and industrialization strategies in the United States (e.g. Kuttner 1991, Reich 1983) with those of South Korea, or for that matter Brazil, there is considerable overlap. Thus, the 1986 industrial technology White Paper of the Korea Industrial Technology Association mentions as development targets for the 1990s the realization of advanced industrial society and the establishment of knowledge-intensive industries; as regards technology strategies, the continuous supply of high-quality brainpower and R&D for future-oriented projects and advanced high technology development; and as regards leading industrial sectors, information industry, advanced materials, bio-engineering and systems engineering (Lim 1995: 2). This is the convergence thesis of industrial societies revisited, but on different grounds and combined with new patterns of disjuncture.

Yet the unit of development is no longer what it used to be. The conceptualization of the unit of development that was relevant politically and economically under the previous dispensation changes under the sign of globalization. The unit is no longer simply national (to the extent that this endogenist political fiction was relevant at all) but increasingly regional, local. Thus, the Frostbelt of traditional industries in the United States has been decaying while Silicon Valleys are prospering. Within countries there are growing regional disparities. In the twenty-first century the stilted schema of core–semi-periphery–periphery, all along geopolitics translated into economic geography, are still less adequate than they used to be.

In these circumstances the notion of world development takes on different meanings. One window is the growing awareness of global risk, involving ecological hazards but also phenomena such as currency instability. Accelerated globalization heightens the need for global governance. The fact that world development takes place at different speeds and makes for a world of 'variable geometry' (to borrow a term used for the European Union) itself calls for global engagement and management. For marginalized countries and regions do find niches in the interstices of the maelstrom of globalization – through labour migration, crime networks, drug trafficking, political and cultural defiance. Religious and ethnonationalist resurgence in a globalized world of instant communication, portable technological capabilities and two-way migration flows has become a neighbourhood affair.

Another window is the role of the state in relation to economic development in the context of globalization: this may well be a greater role but especially a different role, considering that the state is no longer the same: it has been internationalized. A further window is that, because of new disjunctures, there is a new relevance to the project of global reform. Represented at various junctures by the New International Economic Order project, the Brandt, Brundtland and South Commission Reports, supported by the 'middle powers', the Non-Aligned Movement and G77, and now spearheaded by the World Social Forum and several regional alternatives, this remains one of the key dimensions of reorienting development. Global reformism is host to many projects, such as the formation of an international public sector or the project 'towards an international social welfare state' and global social policy (Deacon et al. 1998, Pronk 1990, 2000). Global democratization is a vital part of this agenda, including the democratization of international institutions, the reform of the United Nations and the Bretton Woods institutions. Griffin and Khan (1992) see three possible scenarios in which global governance may develop. One is the gradual withdrawal of the United States from international governance. An alternative is de facto international governance by entities such as the G7, bypassing established institutions and constituting a global plutocracy. The third script is a consensus in favour of the reform of existing institutions or the creation of new ones, strengthening the multilateral approach to international governance. They favour the latter option and advocate better structures of global governance, including the reform and strengthening of the UN system, bringing the Bretton Woods institutions under UN supervision and introducing international taxation. Even though political conjunctures have not been favourable to fashioning a global reform coalition, this remains a crucial agenda for development reconceived as world development. There are subjective dimensions to these concerns as well.

In international relations the concern with cooperation, rather than conflict, has been termed an 'institutionalist' approach. In this context, institutions are understood as 'recognized patterns of practice around which expectations converge' (Oran Young in Keohane 1984: 8).

It is not obvious how this relates to the grassroots, small-scale, small-is-beautiful approach of alternative development. The weakness of the alternative development approach as it stands is that it neglects the role of the state and the local/global nexus. A question looming in the background is whether social movements and NGOs should serve as buffers against globalization, providing shelter from the storm, shielding local culture, local identity, or whether their role should be to connect regions and communities to world society and the global economy. It bears pointing out that NGOs, especially international NGOs, are *part* of globalization, when viewed multidimensionally. If this is the premise, then for NGOs to block globalization *tout court* is one hand doing what the other doesn't know. As NGOs are part of a globalizing ethos, what they do and can do is to negotiate the *kind* of globalization they seek to promote and be part of. They can use their influence to make and shape the case for social development, not just as a matter of tinkering at the margins but as representing the cutting edge of contemporary development (cf. Chapter 8). What NGOs have stood for, that 'development is for people', now ranks higher on the agenda than ever. A case can be made (developed in Chapter 8) that the lessons of East Asia and the combined package of globalization/informatization/flexibilization converge on some of the points that NGOs have been pleading for all along: human resource development, social infrastructure, social institution building. In East Asia this has generally been done by developmental states while NGOs flourish in a democratic climate. NGOs can play key roles in the development of social institution building, which, according to the new institutional economics, is part of the crux of development success or failure.

The question of whether NGOs should connect with or disconnect from globalization is a non-issue. The position of specific NGOs in globalization processes depends on their place in the spectrum of types of NGOs. Transnational advocacy NGOs can contribute to shaping national and international opinion climates in favour of democratic global governance. Part of this horizon is collective action operating across national and zone boundaries, as part of transnational civil society. Global democratization requires several intermediate steps conceptually and strategically, but that is not the subject here (cf. Nederveen Pieterse 2000a).

The outpouring of books in western sociology concerned with problematizing modernity (e.g. Beck 1992, Toulmin 1990) inspired by post-structuralism and globalization (Bauman 1992) carries a potential for the renewal of development thinking and a new critique of modernization theory, especially if taken in combination with non-western studies interrogating modernity.[5] Development thinking needs to leave totalizing paradigms behind and choose diversified approaches, recognizing the heterogeneous, multivocal character of development theories. Doing so ties in with the premise in development research of no longer homogenizing the 'Third World' and seeking general theories and explanations, but focusing instead on the diversity of development circumstances.[6] When globalization and diversity are combined, as in 'glocalization', globalization can be conceptualized as changing patterns of diversification.

Notes

1 This is discussed at greater length in Nederveen Pieterse 1989 (ch. 15) and 1994.

2 This relationship between interests and development discourse is suggested for development ideology and not for development theory, which has greater autonomy.

3 On alternative development see Chapter 6 and on 'alternatives to development' see Chapter 7 below.

4 Cf. Hettne (1990: 244): 'there have been two kinds of bias in development theory: endogenism and exogenism. Both approaches are, if carried to their extremes, equally misleading. The obvious remedy is to transcend the dichotomy and find a synthesis'.

5 The historicist approach to modernization and the notion of multiple paths of modernization are well established in China, Japan and India (Singh 1989). In a broad way this parallels the theme of polycentrism, as against Eurocentrism (Amin 1990a). Of some relevance also is the older tradition of comparative political studies (e.g. Macridis and Brown 1964). Cf. Chapter 2 above.

6 One option is to work with typologies. The regulation school offers neostructuralist typologies based on regimes of accumulation and modes of regulation; Mann (1986) focuses on different forms of organizational power; Mouzelis (1988) is concerned with modes of domination. These typologies differ from the bloc approach (north–south), from the continental or regional approach (Europe, Asia, etc.), from the civilizational approach (Huntington) and from the determinist, base–superstructure categories used in Neo-Marxist (mode of production), dependency and world-system theories (core, semi-periphery, periphery), for they are neither geographical nor economistic.

4

Delinking or Globalization?

To those who are familiar with his earlier work, Samir Amin's new books are not really new; they mostly provide elaborations and further arguments in support of his theses rather than breaking new ground. But they do offer an opportunity to reconsider the arguments of an outspoken dependency thinker and a way to measure what has changed since the time that Samir Amin, with Andre Gunder Frank, Giovanni Arrighi and Immanuel Wallerstein, represented some of the most exciting work in global political economy. Revisiting these positions is an opportunity to gauge how this familiar family of perspectives of development Marxism is withstanding the time test of plausibility.

The focus of this chapter is Amin's argument of delinking – a keynote of his thinking and one of his distinctive contributions to alternative development thinking. Delinking or autocentric development, as the positive part of his dependency argument, remains a significant policy orientation – at minimum as the counterpoint to and polar opposite of what we now call globalization and globalism. The proposition of delinking, advanced in earlier works, is taken up in relation to cultural politics in *Eurocentrism* (EC: Amin 1989), frontally in *Delinking* (DL: Amin 1990a), updated in *Maldevelopment* (MD: 1990c) and figures with less emphasis and under different headings in subsequent work (1997, 1999, 2004, 2006).

Amin cannot be accused of optimism. He objects to forward development approaches such as the 'global Keynesianism' of the New International Economic Order proposals and the Brandt and Brundtland Reports, because the assumption that autocentric development would not be in conflict with worldwide interdependence is 'based on a naive illusion as to the laws governing existing world capitalism' (MD: 60). Nor does the share the optimism about NICs and he rejects the category 'semi-periphery' proposed by adherents of world-system theory: 'the NICs are not semi-peripheries on the way to catching up but in every sense the real peripheries of tomorrow' (DL: xi). He notes that NICs are the most indebted of all developing countries and predicts: 'The real periphery of tomorrow will be the NICs of Asia and America ... while the African "fourth world" will no longer represent the "typical periphery", but the last remnants of the periphery of yesterday en route for destruction' (MD: 65). Well into the twenty-first century, this is completely belied by developments that make some emerging societies – particularly those of East Asia, China and India – central to the world economy and drivers of global growth, rather than its dependent coat-tails.

Structural adjustment, in his view, is just another instalment of the liberal utopia, which is doomed to fail because it ignores the fundamental factor of unequal development as the reality of capitalism. This reality is 'recolonization, sweetened by charity' (DL: xi). The choice facing third world countries therefore is 'adjustment or delinking' (MD: 70). In brief,

> delinking is the refusal to submit to the demands of the worldwide law of value, or the supposed 'rationality' of the system of world prices that embody the demands of reproduction of world capital. It, therefore, presupposes the society's capacity to define an alternative range of criteria of rationality of internal economic options, in short a 'law of value of national application'. (MD: 70–71)

The social forces that are to carry this programme are a 'popular alliance' forged by 'the revolutionary intelligentsia' made up of organic intellectuals. In political terms, delinking is a national and popular project. Amin envisages 'national popular states' along the lines of people's democracies on the model of Maoist China (MD: 189). This project belongs to the 'second wave of national liberation': while 'the first wave of national liberation is spent', 'the forces entrusted with the second wave – with its national and popular content – have not yet been assembled around an adequate alternative plan. We are passing through a trough in the wave, shown by this disarray and intellectual and political surrender' (MD: 73).

Several obstacles on the way fall under the heading of 'the cultural aspect', which is taken up in all three works. The closing chapter of *Delinking* asks, 'is there a political economy of fundamentalism?' and contrasts fundamentalism and rationalism as irreconcilable approaches. In *Maldevelopment*, 'the cultural dimension of development' comprises ethnicity (essentially, according to Amin, a matter of ruling class competition) and the Nahda (the movement for 'reawakening' in the Arab world from the late nineteenth century). In *Eurocentrism*, Amin engages the 'cultural constraints' on the path towards delinking at a fundamental level as part of a wide-ranging historical exposition. *Eurocentrism* may be the most interesting of these books because it seems to be a novel departure in Amin's work: a political economist venturing into culture, the traditional stepchild of Marxism.

Amin seeks to steer clear of culturalism ('a tendency to treat cultural characteristics as transhistorical constants', EC: 6) as well as 'vulgar Marxism'. He takes issue both with westernization ('superficial', leads to 'compradorization') and cultural nationalisms ('feed fundamentalism', MD: 72). Amin makes a number of interesting, at times penetrating, observations on cultural history. The opposition Orient/Occident in his view is not tenable:

> The opposition Greece = the West/Egypt, Mesopotamia, Persia = the East is itself a later artificial construct of Eurocentrism ... the geographic unities constituting Europe, Africa, and Asia have no importance on the level of the history of civilization, even if Eurocentrism in its reading of the past has projected onto the past the modern North–South line of demarcation passing through the Mediterranean. (EC: 24)

Amin draws attention to the legacy of Hellenism that permeates both Christianity and Islam and that has been inappropriately annexed to Europe. This approach parallels Martin Bernal's *Black Athena*. In an interesting aside Amin observes that Hellenism 'was inspired by Buddhist thought, encountered in Afghanistan' (EC: 65), a reference to Ghandara civilization.

Amin questions two erroneous axioms in western thought: 'The first is that internal factors peculiar to each society are decisive for their comparative evolution. The second is that the western model of developed capitalism can be generalized to the entire planet' (EC: 109). Besides, of course, there is a fundamental tension between these assumptions. Interesting, furthermore, are Amin's discussions of early Islamic metaphysics and later the Nahda.

It follows on from his critique of culturalism that Amin acknowledges the plasticity of culture. He rejects, therefore, 'the sharp, cutting judgements that have been made about Christianity, Islam, Hinduism, Buddhism, Confucianism, Taoism, and animism, claims that certain religious conceptions were "openings" to progress and others obstacles' (EC: 84). Instead he recognizes the flexibility and *'plasticity of religions'*: 'religions are transhistorical, for they can readily outlast the social conditions of their birth' (EC: 84). Thus Islam 'has proven itself as flexible as its rival twin, Christianity; an Islamic "bourgeois revolution" is both necessary and possible, even though the concrete circumstances of the region's contemporary history have not allowed it so far' (EC: 65). In line with this general view, Amin rejects Weber's Protestant ethic argument: 'My thesis is not Weber's, but the thesis of a Weber "stood on his feet" ... Weber considers capitalism to be the product of Protestantism. I am suggesting quite the opposite: that society, transformed by the nascent capitalist relationships of production, was forced to call the tributary ideological construct, the construct of medieval scholasticism, into question' (EC: 86). In other words, capitalism generated Protestantism. These critiques of culturalism are pertinent at a time that encompasses revival of culturalist arguments, such as the Confucian ethic, the enemy image of 'Islamic fundamentalism' and Samuel Huntington's 'clash of civilizations'. But several questions arise. Does Amin manage to stay clear of 'vulgar Marxism'? How does Amin's rejection of Islamic fundamentalism differ from the mainstream western position?

Amin's analysis is based on a schema in which modes of production correlate with cultural and ideological patterns, in brief, as follows (Figure 4.1):

Mode of production	Culture
Communal	Ideology of nature
Tributary	Religion, metaphysics
Capitalism	Economism

Figure 4.1   *Mode of production and culture*

The notion of a tribute-paying mode of production, ranging from the empires of antiquity to feudalism, was first advanced in *Unequal Development* (Amin 1976). Each mode includes central and peripheral variations, in line with Amin's insistence on the fundamental nature of centre–periphery relations. Thus Confucianism in China was the ideology of a fully developed tributary mode of production, whereas Japan was a peripheral society in relation to China and Shintoism an underdeveloped version of a tributary ideology.

Even though Amin warns against the aspiration to formulate 'general laws' and thence the slippery slope of a cosmogony *à la* Engels (EC: 30), it is difficult to see how his own schema escapes this fate because likewise it relies on general laws. Although Amin is circumspect in some of his formulations, his analysis nevertheless consistently follows the base–superstructure schema, squarely within historical materialism. In his words, 'The religious revolution takes place on its own terms' (EC: 87), that is, Protestantism develops on its own – in the trail of and conditioned by capitalist development. The problem with the reflection theory of culture (culture reflecting material conditions) is that it becomes impossible to conceptualize 'cultural contradictions', for instance those observed by Daniel Bell (1978). This kind of base–superstructure logic we no longer find in current global political economy, at any rate not in Harvey, Jameson or Cox. But then, they do not take on grandiose historical analyses on the basis of scant sources.

Eurocentrism, then, is not a novel departure theoretically; in fact, Amin restates and elaborates on what he wrote on the relation between modes of production and culture in works dating back to the 1970s.[1] Amin's approach, as a circumspect reformulation of historical materialism, is generally steeped in nineteenth-century epistemology, and accordingly his reading of history is itself deeply Eurocentric. The categories of barbarism for the communal mode and civilization for the tributary mode (EC: 15–16) come straight out of the textbook of Eurocentrism. Amin's repeated recourse to the 'Socialism or Barbarism' rhetoric again reinvokes the evolutionist framework. Correlations between production systems and culture were first formulated in the French and Scottish Enlightenment and later entered Victorian anthropology and the analytics of Marx and Engels. Here they are recycled as instruments of historical analysis, without a sense of the historical character of the categories themselves.

A Eurocentric bias also comes across in some of the fine print of his history. Amin's reading of the Renaissance as the birth of Eurocentrism recycles another Eurocentric cliché: 'Things begin to change with the Renaissance because a new consciousness forms in the European mind' (EC: 75). According to Amin, we now say that this was due to the emergence of capitalism, but 'at the time, Europeans attributed their superiority to other things: to their "Europeanness", their Christian faith, or their rediscovered Greek ancestry ... Eurocentrism in its entirety had already developed' (ibid.).

This is an odd argument. First, it is an endogenist perspective on changes taking place in Europe, as if these were not conditioned by developments outside Europe. Secondly, why focus on the Renaissance – why not on the Crusades, as the first episode of Christendom trying to break out of its encirclement by the worlds of Islam and Byzantium? Thirdly, *which* Renaissance? The fourteenth and fifteenth centuries, the standard favourite from the Enlightenment to the present, or the twelfth-century Renaissance – that stood on the shoulders of the Islamic eleventh-century cultural awakening?[2]

That 'Eurocentrism in its entirety had already developed' by the fifteenth century is an unhistorical claim. Eurocentrism, in Amin's view, 'implies a theory of world history and, departing from it, a global political project' (EC: 75). For one thing, 'Europeanness' (rather than *christianitas*) does not come into the picture until the eighteenth century; the emergence of a 'European' consciousness dates from *circa* 1700 (e.g. Lively 1981). Why make such odd and unnecessary claims? This matches his criticism of Edward Said, according to whom Orientalism had its beginnings in the Middle Ages – and hence does not correlate with the epoch of capitalism. Since Amin rebukes Said for not acknowledging the differences between medieval Orientalism and the nineteenth-century version, he opens himself up to the same criticism by not acknowledging the differences between Renaissance Eurocentrism and the nineteenth-century version. As a consequence he constructs Eurocentrism as a static and monolithic concept.

Amin takes on 'Islamic fundamentalism' as one of the culturalist constraints on the path towards delinking and because in the Islamic world it is itself an alternative project of delinking. Amin rightly criticizes the general clamour about Islamism in the west: 'There is an element of hypocrisy on the part of the West in lamenting current Islamic fundamentalism when it has fought in every way possible against the progressive alternative' (MD: 109). Yet the foundation of his own critique is the cliché dichotomic view of fundamentalism versus rationalism: 'Rationalism and fundamentalism constitute two states of mind irreducible to one another, incapable of integration' (DL: 184). This dichomotizing view is an instance of a Marxist allegiance to Enlightenment thinking at a time when this was left behind as too simplistic in most other quarters. The tension between science and religion, rationality and the irrational, is now perceived as far more problematic than in the age of Voltaire and Diderot. A more complex frame of analysis would enable us to see the modern and rational features (in a context of limited political options and vocabularies) of the Islamist turn, an approach which is now common to all but the most parochial western accounts (e.g. Esposito 1992).

Amin's predictions are consistent with his analysis: in a book first published in 1985 he predicts that the socialist countries (the USSR, China and others) will seek 'to retain control of their external relations' rather than submit to the exigencies of capitalist expansion, and predicts catastrophe as a result of these developments in ten years' time (DL: xi).

All these features – evolutionism, Renaissance worship, dichotomy rationalism and irrationality, predictions of catastrophe – belong to a familiar profile: it may not be enough to be a Neo-Marxist to be free from the rendezvous with nineteenth-century epistemology. Neo-Marxism does not mean reconstructed Marxism. Amin devotes an unremarkable chapter to the Eurocentric lineage of Marxism in which he observes that 'Marxism was formed both out of and against the Enlightenment' (EC: 119). Marx shared the excessive optimism prevalent in the nineteenth century, but actually existing capitalism has not homogenized but polarized the planet, and hence Amin's analytic medicine is, predictably, unequal development and centre–periphery contradictions. This step from Marxism to Neo-Marxism leaves all the other questions about the Eurocentric lineages of Marxism unsettled – thus, how can one repudiate Eurocentrism and yet continue to talk of barbarism and civilization as if we were still in the nineteenth century? Why, for all its powerful analytics, does Marxism keep being delivered in units of pig iron?

Unequal development becomes the answer to all questions. It is Amin's talisman against liberalism as well as classical Marxism, the backbone and central tenet of his perspective. As a general view this is problematic in several respects. First, Amin presents unequal development not only as the basic law of capitalist development but in his view also the tributary mode is marked by centre–periphery relations (the Islamic world and Europe, China and Japan). In fact, the relationship between feudal China and Japan is presented as proof of the general validity of the centre–periphery principle, for this 'has produced the same "miracle" witnessed in the Mediterranean region: the rapid maturation of capitalist development in the periphery of the system' (EC: 64). Thus peripheries in the tributary mode have a head start in capitalist development. This sounds like Trotsky's law of combined and uneven development, fine-tuned by means of his argument of the advantage of backwardness. If this were valid as a general law we would expect the Mongol empire to have had a head start in capitalist development. Second, if in Amin's view there is a dialectical relationship *between* the tributary and capitalist modes, then it follows that a dialectics *within* the capitalist mode would be equally plausible. There is no acknowledgement, however, in Amin's work of such dynamics in capitalist relations. Quite the contrary. Hammering on centre–periphery contradictions and rejecting the notion of semi-periphery, Amin does not show any awareness of historical movements of rise and decline within capitalism: centres declining to peripheries, peripheries ascending to core status – even though this is a well-developed line of analysis (e.g. Friedman 1982). In line with the principle of perpetual polarization, peripheries ever remain peripheries: 'all the regions that were integrated in the world capitalist system with peripheral status have remained like that to the present ... New England, Canada, Australia and New Zealand were never peripheral formations; by contrast, Latin America, the Caribbean, Africa and Asia – with the exception of Japan – were and have remained so' (MD: 169).

Third, 'centre' and 'periphery' are adopted as unproblematic categories across history, as transhistorical coordinates – as if these nodal points themselves are not historical constructs, which cannot simply be extrapolated backward or forward in time. Thus, in the context of post-Fordism and flexible accumulation, centre and periphery carry quite different meanings than in the context of Fordism and, in turn, during the accumulation regimes of competitive and monopoly capitalism. These notions need to be rethought and reworked, as part of a historical economic geography, or what Foucault called a 'history of space'. Moreover, there have been episodes of peripheries playing a central role (e.g. OPEC provoking the 1973 energy crisis). In fact, it may be necessary to cut and paste these polarities, as in the 'pericentric' theory of imperialism.[3] Furthermore, in the context of the coexistence and articulation of modes of accumulation within the same space, spaces are layered in fulfilling multiple configurations – central in some relations, peripheral in others.

Amin rejects culturalism because of the tendency to treat cultural forms as transhistorical constants, but historical materialism is not exposed to the same scrutiny: its coordinates are unreflexively presented as transhistorical constants. Unequal development, centre and periphery are used as analytical tools as if they are constants from feudal times through the stages of capitalist development. Apparently Amin views unequal development as a transhistorical law of evolution. Thus stretched over time, the argument becomes proportionally thin and it becomes imperative to take into account counter-tendencies, which are absent in Amin's account, except for the instances mentioned. The result is a one-dimensional and one-sided representation of history. With respect to capitalist development, the overall result is a monolithic view in which polarization is recognized as the only dynamic. Amin's ignoring the dialectics within capitalist development is the corollary of and rationale for posing an alternative external to 'the system'. This is precisely the point of delinking.

The original form of delinking (decoupling, dissociation) was *mercantilism*, a strategy of states in the early stages of industrialization: close the borders to foreign products to protect infant industries. This was an option mainly for larger countries, such as China and India, which had the potential to effect an industrial transition on their own. At present levels of technology, industrialization without foreign investment has become unrealistic: the cost and quality differential between domestic and imported end products has become too great. Besides, this was a matter of delinking for relinking, '*reculer pour mieux sauter*', re-entering the world market once a certain level of competitive ability had been achieved. Presently, on the basis of backward technology, relinking would hardly be possible. The second form of delinking was disengagement from capitalism as part of the *transition to socialism*. This strategy of neomercantilist closure and 'socialism in one country' was not voluntary but imposed from without. A subsidiary plot in this scenario was a strategy of weakening world capitalism from without: 'in time, if enough peripheral societies are closed, the capitalist world system will shrink, and ... this shrinkage will reduce prosperity in the core' (Chirot 1977: 169). If this might still have been believable in the 1970s (in combination with capitalist crisis), it is no longer now. Rather, capitalism is expanding with new variations of capitalism. The third form of delinking has been part of *national liberation* and anti-imperialist in content. With the wave of decolonization past and non-alignment at its lowest ebb, this is no longer on the cards. All along delinking has also been a statist project, premised on a strong and hard state capable of imposing tight controls and political repression. Now with higher levels of communication and mobility, even if this kind of state-controlled closure were considered desirable, the scope for this option has considerably narrowed, if not vanished.

The politics of delinking is the litmus test of Amin's perspective. But this case is not as obvious as it appears because his views have been changing over the years. In the early 1980s Amin defined delinking as semi-autarky (Amin 1982: 225). Now Amin repeatedly points out: 'De-linking is neither commercial autarky, nor chauvinist culturalist nationalism' (MD: 231). In every definition and discussion, Amin presents delinking as a national project that is to be based on a national and popular alliance. One wonders how this is to materialize in an age of postnationalism. In yet another formulation, delinking parallels *polycentrism*. Polycentrism (originally inspired by Togliatti) has been an ambiguous turn in Amin's thought. Does it supersede unequal development and centre–periphery relations? Doesn't it reproduce 'centrism' and centre–periphery relations on other, regional or internal, levels? Earlier, in 1982, Amin cautioned against 'regional subimperialisms' and 'mini-hegemonisms' in Latin America, the Middle East, Africa and Southeast Asia. Now a section heading puts it in these terms: 'the genuine long-term option: transnationalization or a polycentric world and broad autocentric regions' (MD: 228). If delinking is now in effect redefined as an autonomous form of regionalization, how then is this to be carried off by a national and popular alliance? How does this mesh with delinking as a 'law of value of national application'? Are nationalism/populism not superseded by regionalization?

Amin's current formulations of delinking are so broad and opaque that delinking can mean almost everything to everyone, to the point that his prescriptions become self-contradictory. Delinking can mean, presumably, a popular anti-western, anti-capitalist posture – yet Amin precisely wants to save 'the universalism begun by capitalism' 'at the level of a popular, cultural and ideological universalism' (MD: 231). Delinking can mean self-reliant development: as such it is meaningless because self-reliance has long been a universally endorsed development cliché. Or delinking can mean regionalization – which is also an increasingly widely endorsed policy orientation. The problem is that the centrepiece of delinking, autocentric accumulation, is a loose screw because the *unit* that is to be autocentric, the nation or the region, is not defined, or rather its definition can shift according to circumstances. With respect to southern Africa, Amin speaks of delinking as a regional scenario (Amin et al. 1987) but in subsequent statements on the future of South Africa he continues to view delinking as a national agenda (Amin 1992). It is not possible on the basis of Amin's formulations to distinguish delinking as a strategy of national or regional self-reliance.

On an empirical level, too, Amin's general arguments have been belied by ongoing developments, more clearly in the twenty-first century than during the eighties and nineties: the deepening of globalization; the ongoing development of new industrializing countries; strengthening south–south trade and cooperation; and the development of regional associations and trade agreements across centre–periphery boundaries (NAFTA, ASEAN, APEC, SAARC, EU, EFTA).

In a world in which countries in the south vie for preferential trade access to markets in the north and for foreign investment, technology and finance, delinking is not the most obvious policy option. Actual delinking has been the shortest way to the Albania effect: isolation from foreign trade, technology, finance, communications, and the obverse of the universalism that Amin advocates. A number of African countries have been virtually cut off from global connections – Amin calls this 'passive delinking' (MD: 65; DL: xi). The record of voluntary delinking includes, besides Albania, Sekou Touré's Guinea, Pol Pot's Cambodia, Yemen, North Korea and Burma, while Saddam Hussein's Iraq was rather an instance of involuntary delinking. Delinking has also meant linking up with socialist bloc countries, an option that since 1989 has no longer been open. Due to the deepening of globalization, including technological and cultural changes, the balance has long shifted to the disadvantage of the strategy of closure.[4] More than ever, delinking has become a cul de sac.

It is not surprising that at present the only ideologies of delinking that remain are neither industrialization strategies nor part of a transition to socialism. Radical Islamism is civilizational in emphasis – its economic foundation is oil revenues and as such it is a distributionist mode of rentier development; a posture rather than a strategy. Green projects, also endorsed by some indigenous peoples, envisage delinking along the lines of localist 'small is beautiful', 'no growth' scenarios (discussed by Amin in MD: 165–73). Small Maoist currents in the Philippines, and Sendero Luminoso in Peru, have upheld delinking with an emphasis on anti-imperialism that is low on economic strategy.

Instead of delinking, regional cooperation has increasingly become a major (alternative) development strategy – as a way to negotiate and navigate globalization (Gray 1993, Oman 1993) rather than as a buffer against globalization. Now that national delinking is no longer a viable option Amin is reformulating delinking in such a way that it is a form of regionalization. None of the current forms of regional cooperation in the south (e.g. the Maghrib Union, Mercosur, Central American cooperation), however, subscribes to regional delinking or 'collective self-reliance'. Rather the objective is, through pooling resources and sovereignty, to achieve economies of scale and scope, to attract more foreign investment by increasing market size and to arrive at a stronger bargaining position vis-à-vis external forces. Regional integration, then, is a function and subsidiary mode of globalization and not a counter to globalization.

The problem with Amin's position is that delinking offers a rhetoric of autonomy in combination with a multipurpose politics. It is a posture rather than an analytic or a distinct policy. The most troubling problem of the delinking posture is that it is a posture of retreat, of turning one's back on the big bad world – in a world in which strength is generated through an engagement with realities, no matter how unpleasant, and dialogue with opponents. 'In this world, the only thing worse than being part of the evolving economic hierarchy is being excluded from it' (Henwood 1993: 8).

Amin's perspective on development is narrower even than world-system theory. World-system theory at least acknowledges dynamics and dialectics within capitalist development; the notion of semi-periphery is part of that. Frank, Arrighi and Wallerstein never agreed with Amin's delinking strategy. In their view delinking had been neither successful nor voluntary. At the same time, world-system theory also theorizes capitalism as a closed system and shows the same tendency of seeking an alternative external to it, as in the simplistic thesis of 'antisystemic movements'. Conversely, Amin views social movements as *part* of the system (MD: 111). In other words, among the rejectionists of capitalism there are marked differences as to where to find the exit from capitalism.

Amin's politics is statist. For Amin the state is 'the means to national protection and assertion, the instrument of what we have called "de-linking"' (MD: 181). This places Amin squarely within the original tradition of national liberation. That he opposes neoliberalism is clear enough, but he does not seem to follow the subsequent developments – the development of an argument encompassing a state regulatory role along with other public agencies and NGOs. The greatest weakness of this body of work, ultimately, is that it is theoretically unreflexive, reproducing an unreconstructed Neo-Marxism without adequately reflecting on its own principles of analysis.

There are underlying problems with this outlook, which are not confined to Samir Amin. One is the tendency towards stereotyped thinking about capitalism in terms of general laws of motion of capital written on stone tablets. While the greatest contribution of Marxism has been its powerful analytics in showing the varieties of capitalism, the greatest weakness of Marxism has been to underestimate the varieties of capitalist development.[5]

Notes

1 In particular Amin 1980, chs 2–4.
2 Episodes discussed in Nederveen Pieterse 1989, ch. 5.
3 The pericentric theory of imperialism is discussed in Nederveen Pieterse 1989, ch. 1.
4 Compare the balance sheet Chirot draws up on 'the issue of closure' (1977: 203–8).
5 The varieties of capitalism and their interactions are taken up in Chapter 11 below. This discussion does not address Samir Amin's later works, but over time there is little change in the structure of his arguments.

5

The Cultural Turn in Development: Questions of Power

After the cultural turn has upset most social sciences, it finally comes to economics and to the bundle of practices called development. Why is culture being introduced into development discourse? Western ethnocentrism as the implicit culture of developmentalism is no longer adequate in the age of accelerated globalization (or 'polycentrism in a context of high interaction'). In relation to global concerns such as ecological questions the west is no privileged interlocutor. The old paradigm of modernization/westernization is no longer valid, not just on account of polycentrism but also in view of the questioning of modernity. Questioning western itineraries is no longer an anti-imperialist preoccupation but a matter of soul-searching in the west. The waning of Cold War ideologies has shifted the goalposts and ethnic and religious movements emerge in their stead. Hence 'culture' has taken on a novel prominence.

How is culture 'put into' development discourse? The current reproblematizations don't start from a blank slate but rework established discourses. The articulation of culture and development is both a renegade notion at odds with established practices and a new brick in the wall of clichés. Culture comes into development studies at a time of retreat from structural and macro approaches in favour of micro and actor-oriented approaches (e.g. Long and Villarreal 1993). If agency is prioritized over structure (such as the state, the national economy), the cultural worlds and maps of meaning of actors become vital variables. The move from structures to actors may be described, in part, as an informalization of development and, in that context, culture tends to be viewed as, so to speak, the structure of the informal. The crucial weakness of culture and development discourse, at any rate policy-oriented discourse, is that it misses the point that culture is an *arena of struggle*. Culture is treated as if it is or conforms to a structure, on the analogy of the state or nation – existing out there, as an ambience one can step in and out of, a resource to be tapped, as national culture or, given the fragmentation of nations, as local culture. This chapter first discusses national culture, then local culture. National culture is worth considering also for the sake of raising the question as to whether the present preoccupation with local culture risks repeating the same mistakes as were made by the talk of national culture earlier on. The key questions are questions of power: how are culture and power conceptualized in these discourses?

The penultimate section returns to culture and development discourse, under the heading 'add culture and stir'.

National culture

The discourse of national culture carries instrumentalist overtones: culture as a device in nation building. Following the tracks of decolonization and Third World nationalism, anti-colonialism involved a cultural argument all along. Thus Amilcar Cabral argued in 'National liberation and culture':

> A nation which frees itself from foreign rule will be only culturally free if … it recaptures the commanding heights of its own culture, which receives sustenance from the living reality of its environment and equally rejects the harmful influences which any kind of subjection to foreign cultures involves. Thus one sees that if imperialist domination necessarily practices cultural oppression, national liberation is necessarily an act of culture. (Cited in Miller 1990: 46)

The liberation movement, according to Cabral, must bring about 'a convergence' toward 'a single national culture', which itself is a step toward 'a universal culture' (ibid.). Nationalism, then, is a step towards cosmopolitanism (cf. Cheah 1998). Fanon, likewise, devoted a chapter to 'national culture' in *The Wretched of the Earth* (1967). This outlines three phases in the cultural development of colonized peoples: (1) assimilation of the culture of the colonizer; (2) recollection of original cultural resources, but removed from the masses; and (3) combat, revolution and the formation of a national culture in which the artist 'rejoins the people'. Cultural struggles in South Africa, Palestine and Northern Ireland show similar politicized discourses. In South Africa it prompted the slogan of 'cultural weapons' as Inkatha's response to the ANC's 'culture as a weapon'.

In postcolonial countries calls for 'cultural protectionism' are not uncommon. Thus, in an African context, 'the New African Cultural Order would consist of researching and safeguarding the African personality and culture. This is a task for every one of us, but it must be stimulated and coordinated by conscientious, capable and responsible African politicians' (Gbotokuma 1992: 28). In the Philippines, Renato Constantino criticizes the 'new cultured Filipinos' as 'a breed apart from the mass of Filipinos', 'a class without roots – adopted children of a foreign culture'. 'In the end, it is the people and their culture that will endure. National culture will be developed by and will emerge from the real people' (1985: 48–9).

There are several strands in this discourse: identifying cultural identity with the nation; subsuming culture under a political agenda; nominating politicians as custodians of culture; a culture talk derived from other discourses – from politics of struggle, or from economics Soviet style, in the 'commanding heights'. Culture is denied autonomy and encapsulated in the political discourse of 'anti-colonialism equals nationalism'. The same options that pertain to the postcolonial nation are extended to culture. Dependency theory – which serves as the political economy of third world nationalism – is stretched to apply to culture: protectionism, dissociation, endogenous development are prescribed for national culture as they have been for the national economy. What ensues is cultural dependency theory.

The national culture argument also structures the wider terrain. As John Tomlinson notes: 'a majority of the discourses of cultural imperialism, and certainly those with the most prominence – the UNESCO discourse, that thematized by the term "Americanisation", much of the talk of media imperialism – treat the issue as one of domination of national culture by international culture' (1991: 73). UNESCO's institutional discourse follows the same nationalitarian tracks: '*National culture* is the mould into which, by the very nature of UNESCO as an inter-national body, cultural identity tends to be squeezed' (ibid.: 72). Another current in UNESCO discourse is pluralism and in this context cultural identity is discussed in terms of 'people' rather than 'nations'. However:

> The UNESCO discourse cannot negotiate this complexity with any coherence. In its recommendations on the issue of cultural domination it urges member states to: 'strengthen national languages with a view to affirming cultural identity and helping it to recover its natural role which is that of expressing the different aspects of activity and life and thereby furthering national development'. (ibid.)

References to 'cultural democracy' (Makagiansar 1979) are not sufficiently clear to settle these issues. When virtually all societies are multicultural in composition, equating cultural identity with national identity is a fallacy, as is obvious, for instance, in the case of language as a centrepiece of cultural identity.

With respect to cultural imperialism the 'national' formulation breaks down, as Tomlinson points out, in two ways: 'not only may there be difficulty in identifying a unified national cultural identity in the "invaded" country, but the same might be said of the putative "invader". What, then, is the "American way" that threatens global hegemony?' (1991: 74).

'National culture' discourse displays a particular logic. In postcolonial countries, at least in the new nations among them, there has been a replication of the process of nation building in the west. In France, as the saying goes, it took two hundred years to create 'Frenchmen'. In late nineteenth-century Europe, nation building was in its most intense phase – by means of public education, the mass production of monuments and the large-scale invention of traditions (Hobsbawm and Ranger 1983). It concerns, in effect, a process of state building through nation building. In postcolonial countries the erection of prestige architecture has the function of creating markers for national consciousness and identity, in the process inviting genuflection before the nation's leadership (Schudson 1994). This has also been a profoundly gendered process: the state (masculine) protects (nurtures, guides) national culture (feminine); nationalism has been a profoundly masculinist discourse. The relationship between feminism and nationalism, west and south, has been fraught with ambivalence (e.g. Enloe 1990, Kandiyoti 1991).

In western countries the project of nation building involved intense strife because it intervened in the existing cultural division of labour along lines of region, religion, language, class, gender. The *Kulturkampf* in Germany is a case in point. What ensued was not cultural homogeneity but rather state-managed settlements. Dutch pillarization, in force from 1917 to the 1960s, is an example. The construction of national identity, then, is a matter of cultural struggle, which is usually conducted along lines of language, religion or region. The contemporary terminology for this kind of conflict is ethnicity.

National culture can serve as a first-rate excuse domestically and internationally. Thus culture has been working overtime in Japan:

> When 'culture' is used to explain Japan, statements such as 'we do this because it is our culture' (i.e. 'we do this because we do this') are not perceived as tautology but are believed to give a valid reason for accepting all manner of practices whose political nature has been lost sight of. Culture thus becomes an excuse for systematic exploitation, for legal abuses, for racketeering and for other forms of uncontrolled exercise of power. In the international realm, culture is made an excuse for not living up to agreements and responsibilities, and for not taking action in the face of pressure from trading partners. (Wolferen 1990: 322)

When, several years ago, the Dutch minister of foreign affairs protested against the execution of political prisoners in Indonesia after they had been imprisoned for many years, his Indonesian counterpart pointed out that this was in character with Indonesian culture.

Accordingly, subsuming cultural identity under national identity is not an innocent move. Endorsing the myth of national culture and cultural unity, it glosses over the dark side of nationalism. The politics of nation building involves the marginalization of aliens, the suppression of minorities and of indigenous peoples – a process captured under the heading of internal colonialism. While national monuments are being erected, outside the glare of the spotlights aliens are expropriated, minorities constructed and refugees created. The harvest of these policies is ethnic mobilization for, in virtually all cases of ethnopolitics and movements for regional autonomy or secession, the main catalyst is the state imposing monocultural control (Nederveen Pieterse 2007). National culture serves as a code for state culture.

Local culture

National culture as the corollary of nation building has been part of modernization discourse. Culture and development discourse is primarily concerned with local culture. 'The first cultural dimension of development is the local level' (Kottak 1985: 46); national culture is next in the line of priorities, followed by the culture of the planners.

Privileging local culture is interpellated with several arguments. In the strong version of this perspective the local is mentioned in one breath with the grassroots, indigenous, informal. In some culture and development arguments (e.g. Verhelst 1990) these are viewed as the last frontier of cultural authenticity. The tendency is to view local culture in terms of prelapsarian purity and unity, homogenizing the local community as the last stand of *Gemeinschaft*, in a manner reminiscent of the way ethnographers used to speak about 'their' villages, or their cultures, as cultural wholes or configurations. The local as a privileged site may imply an argument about how culture develops: organically, from below and within, by way of 'roots', according to a horticultural anthropology.

Since this is the terrain of the return of anthropology, it is worth taking into account that 'anthropological "culture" is not what it used to be' (Clifford 1992: 101). Clifford elucidates: 'Anthropologists, as Geertz has written, don't study villages, they study *in* villages. And increasingly, I might add, they don't study in villages either, but rather in hospitals, labs, urban neighborhoods, tourist hotels, the Getty Center' (1992: 98).

In many postcolonial countries, the state and nation have been to a significant extent a terrain constructed by colonial administrations – the irony of Cabral, Fanon and others is that the trophy gained in the victory over colonialism was colonialism's legacy. Secondly, it is the terrain of the postcolonial state – and as such the arena of multicultural strife. Local culture, likewise, is not an uncontaminated space but a field criss-crossed by traces of migrants, travellers, traders, missionaries, colonizers, anthropologists. This awareness is part of the ongoing reorientation in ethnography: 'In much traditional ethnography ... the ethnographer has localized what is actually a regional/national/global nexus, relegating to the margins a "culture's" external relations and displacements' (Clifford 1992: 100). Or, in the words of Gupta and Ferguson (1992), conventional anthropology allowed 'the power of topography to conceal successfully the topography of power'. According to James Boon: 'What has come to be called Balinese culture is a multiply authored invention, a historical formation, an enactment, a political construct, a shifting paradox, an ongoing translation, an emblem, a trademark, a nonconsensual negotiation of contrastive identity, and more' (1990: ix, cited in Clifford 1992: 100).

Thus to situate the local is to view it in its multiple external connections and, next, to regard its performative, dramatic character – the local as a *project* enacted in relation to the regional, national, global; or, the local as strategy, device, ruse. Its 'truth', then, is as much without as within: in the negotiation of external boundaries. In a comparable fashion, the dynamics of ethnicity may be best approached not from within, by stepping into the intricacies of ethnic identification, but from without – in terms of competition with other groups, postnationalism, the retreat of the state, the dialectics of globalization and localization (Nederveen Pieterse 2007). One option is to take stock of the traces of travellers and the role of strangers (e.g. Shack and Skinner 1979). Conventional wisdom has it that underneath a veneer of modernity lurks perennial African 'tribalism' – in line with an essentialist view of tribe as primordial group attachment; until it is found that the tribes have been in large measure colonial and missionary constructs (e.g. Vail 1989). Then, there is the anecdote

> about a prominent member of an East African tribe, a professional philosopher, who had an interest in reviving traditional practices. As it turned out, the old ways and customs had been discarded and forgotten even by the elders of his tribe. The main repository of knowledge about the past was located in ethnographies published in Europe and the United States. He realized he needed an anthropologist as a consultant. He had no difficulty finding someone to take the job. (Shweder 1993: 284)

This is by no means without precedent. *Négritude, Africanité* and Afrocentrism borrowed extensively from European or American ethnography: Marcus Garvey and Aimé Césaire derived their images of Africa from the German ethnographer Leo Frobenius; Senghor borrowed from Lévy Brühl; Melville Herskovitz's work shaped African-American 'roots' thinking. Azania, the authentic African name for South Africa, was plucked from a novel by Evelyn Waugh. Ethnographers have generously fed this current, for instance Maquet's book on *Africanity* (1972) or Placide Tempels' work on *Bantu Philosophy* (see Hountondji 1991). The return of anthropology then may also bring the return of anthropological myth. In Roger Keesing's words (1987: 168), 'We anthropologists have a disciplinary vested interest in portraying other people's culturally constructed worlds as radically different from our own. We are dealers in exotica'.

Of course, recourse to 'tradition' is also tenuous for other reasons. Thus, according to Kaarsholm, in an African context what is at issue is 'a variety of often conflicting frameworks and discourses – African political, cultural and ethnic traditions, colonial and anti-colonial traditions, traditions of government, the traditions of nationalism and of modern political and cultural institutions. They are all full of contradictions within themselves and do not represent unambiguous positions *vis-à-vis* development' (1991: 4).

Like national culture, local culture is a terrain of power with its own patterns of stratification, an uneven distribution of cultural knowledge and boundaries separating insiders and outsiders – hierarchical or exclusionary politics in fine print. The dark side of local culture is local ethnocentrism or, in other words, ethnic fundamentalism. Certainly, local maps of meaning are of vital importance, but so is the awareness that 'Cultures are webs of mystification as well as signification' (Keesing 1987: 161). Gender is part of local constructions.

> Consider a New Guinea culture that consigns women to lifelong jural minority under male control, defines their essential nature as polluting and polluted, extracts their labor in lifelong drudgery for the service of men, excludes them from ritual and political life, all as ordained in the eternal nature of the cosmos and the rules of the ancestors … it is a smallish group of 'experts' in any generation

who – at least for myth, ritual, and other realms of religion – play the major part in creating and changing the culture. The rules of the ancestors and gods seem in such cases to be quite literally man-made. (Keesing 1987: 166)

No wonder that amidst the upsurge of ethnic mobilization women find themselves in a position of 'double jeopardy': under pressure from majority racism and minority sexism at the same time (e.g. Wallace 1992).

As Van Nieuwenhuijze remarked, westerners did not just venture out on a civilizing mission but also in search of the Golden Fleece (1983: 26). In the epoch of third worldism, of Che Guevara and 'one, two, three Vietnams', third world nationalism represented this golden fleece – national culture as the frontier of honour against imperialism, multinational capitalism and Coca-Colonization. In the age of globalization, local culture represents the treasure trove of the Golden Fleece – perhaps the world's last. The world's indigenous peoples are the last custodians of paradises lost to late capitalism, ecological devastation, McDonaldization, Disneyfication and Barbiefication. With ecological pressures mounting worldwide, this ethos is gaining ground as if queuing up for the last exit.

In each case, the national and the local serve as a frontier – against imperialism, capitalism, consumerism, developmentalism. The border of national culture, guarded by the postcolonial state and by dependency theory, did not hold. Culture and development discourse in its strong form pleads for an alternative development based on local culture. It attempts to erect boundaries in a time of boundary crossing. It welcomes crossing disciplinary boundaries in order to strengthen the case for erecting cultural boundaries. As such it reflects a politics of nostalgia.

Culture/power

How is power theorized in these discourses? Two very distinct theories of power are at work. The national culture perspective tends to follow a deductive approach in which culture is viewed as derived from macrosocial powers. Thus, according to Ernesto García Canclini, 'To analyse culture was equivalent to describing the manoeuvres of dominant forces', an approach that has been guilty of 'over-estimating the impact of the dominant on popular consciousness' (1992: 21).

In contrast, the local culture perspective follows an inductive approach: 'the inductivists are those who confront the study of the popular by beginning with certain properties which they suppose to be intrinsic to the subordinate classes, or with their genius, or with a creativity that other sectors of the population have lost, or with oppositional power as the basis of their resistance' (Canclini 1992: 20).

The inductive approach has been influenced by anthropological culturalism and populism. Its weaknesses are that it explains cultural difference but not inequality, decontextualizes the local, and tends to equate 'popular culture' with 'tradition'. As different strands in this perspective

Canclini identifies the biologico-telluric approach, which relies on 'innate forces' in people/nature relationships (as in *Blut und Boden*, blood and soil); and a statist version which holds that the state gives expression to popular values, a view that leads back to the national culture perspective (1992: 27–30).

Most relevant to culture and development discourse is yet another strand. In Latin America, 'Given the crisis in the political apparatuses and the ideological models, a belief in the "natural purity" of the people as the sole recourse is re-emerging amongst "movements of the base", "alternatives" and groups emanating from the populist parties' (ibid.: 31). This kind of perspective informs the strong version of the local culture view along with the grassroots-oriented alternative development approach, at times homogenizing the subaltern, at other times ascribing a romantic role to grassroots intellectuals (e.g. Escobar 1992b).

Anthropological holism as an ethnographic rhetoric and hermeneutic strategy – one of the sources of inspiration of culture and development – is under attack for underestimating the unevenness of power and the role of elites within indigenous communities (Keesing 1987, Thornton 1988).

Too often power is viewed only as state power, or power exercised with sovereignty, whereas it is more appropriate to view power as a social relation diffused throughout all spaces. However, it is true that differences in scope matter and that the power of a household head differs from that of the head of a multinational corporation. Another limitation is the tendency to think of power in terms of simple schemas, reducing the field of hegemony to a polarized contest between dominant and subaltern forces. Hegemony may be better thought of as an ongoing jostle, ever in motion and requiring continuous effort. Though the situation of polarization between dominators and the dominated is extraordinary, it rules political discourse as if it were routine and everyday. What *is* everyday are the little tactics of survival and quiet encroachment and subtle acts of subversion (Bayat 1998; Scott 1985, 1991). But even in polarized situations – such as the condition of *indigenes* in parts of Latin America – it is important to monitor the actual transactions taking place and to probe into the nodal points of interaction. Patterns of exchange between classes and politics of patronage, collective and personal, may be a more valid perspective than the schema of resistance and politics of struggle. One way to engage this perspective is to examine consumption patterns in popular strata (Canclini 1992: 41–4). Commodity chains and exchange relations reveal interclass relations and situate the local in wider networks (Appadurai 1986).

Add culture and stir

Culture has been part of development thinking all along, though not explicitly so. In the 1960s instilling 'achievement orientation' was a strategy geared to building entrepreneurial spirit, deriving from the American culture of entrepreneurialism and the idea that attitudes matter. Economic growth strategies have been based on the culture of economism. Structural adjustment programmes reflect a culture of economic globalism. These positions reflect different inflections of the ethnocentrism of western developmentalism (Chapter 2 above).

Culture and development (C&D) discourse is a significant improvement on the pattern of implicit cultural bias. Recognizing development practices as culturally biased and specific introduces cultural reflexivity, which of course forms part of a broader tide of awareness of cultural difference. An implication is to reconnect development with anthropology – reconnect in that colonial administrations relied on anthropological research. Presently this takes the form of development anthropology (Huizer 1993, Rew 1993) and *Entwicklungsethnologie* or development ethnology (as in the journal of that name) in Germany, as a supplement to development sociology. *Entwicklungsethnologie* is concerned not only with analysing local settings but also with 'the comprehension of the project itself as a problem of intercultural exchange and an arena of competing interests' (Antweiler 1993: 40).

C&D incorporates conventional anthropological methods such as participant observation, tailored to the development culture of projects, along with participatory or action components: Participatory Action Research, Rapid Rural Appraisal, Goal Oriented Project Planning and beneficiary assessment of projects (Salmen 1987), which may or may not be combined with a critical attitude to development and a general context of 'emancipatory knowledge'.

Though the cultural turn in development is a welcome turn, C&D raises questions. C&D policy discourse leans towards simplifications and 'add culture and stir', or the failure to reproblematize development. Other problems are the reification of culture and the reification of modernity and turning to applied anthropology at a time when anthropology is in crisis.

Development *policy* discourse is where the cultural turn in development makes its greatest impact. Here it is a follow-up to the notion that development in order to be effective must be participatory (itself a successor to the top-down 'mobilization' for development discourse). Sometimes this C&D policy talk is so superficial, however, that it is not only bogus and absurd but also meaningless. Thus the Dutch development cooperation policy document *A World of Difference* (Ministry of Foreign Affairs 1991) asserts that 'Culture must be the basis of sustainable development' and development must be 'embedded in culture'. Obviously *any* development strategy is 'based on culture', if only because it is not possible to operate outside culture, as long as we adopt the anthropological understanding of culture as all learned and shared behaviour and ideas. Culture with a big C is another option – as in using popular theatre to popularize family planning or AIDS containment; but this is clearly too narrow a view. The normative statement that development must be 'embedded in culture' glosses over the character of development as a cultural performance in itself: implicitly the reference is to the culture of 'others', of the 'developing' entity, and in an opaque sort of way it is a statement about development as an engagement with cultural difference.

In development, culture is discussed primarily in relation to economic rather than political or social development, which reflects the order of priorities in development culture. Other discussions focus on culture in relation to development projects (Crehan 1991). Discussions focused on politics often take the form of arguments in favour of decentralization and local government (e.g. Mhlaba 1991). Generally, however, C&D policy discourse tends to be a depoliticizing vision because by inserting culture it takes the politics out of development, while taking the politics out of culture by assuming established cultural boundaries. C&D runs the risk of adding culture to the development repertoire like an additional coating or local Vaseline, without necessarily changing the development agenda itself.

Add culture and stir, or the failure to reproblematize development, is a prominent feature of C&D policy. The case for C&D is generally made in instrumental terms, as a means to explain project failures and improve on the success rate of projects. *The Economist* publishes a steady stream of advertisements for anthropologists to join regional development banks and the World Bank. This is practical from the point of view of the development machinery, questionable from the point of view of the ethics of anthropology, and business as usual for the recipients of development politics on the ground. It parallels 'business anthropology' or using anthropological insights and methods to facilitate doing business across cultures.

The point of C&D is to rethink development and the intercultural relations that are implicitly negotiated in development from the point of view of anthropology and cultural critique. For this to work out, what is required is a further development of C&D theory; it may be argued that the failure to reproblematize development is a function of the reification of modernity. The beginnings of culture and development discourse include Talcott Parsons' pattern variables, for affective neutrality, universalism, etc., are themselves cultural traits. Reifying modernity and underestimating the complexity of modernity follows on from the habit of dichotomic thinking, which is as deeply entrenched among the critics of developmentalism as among its adherents. Simplistic schemas – tradition/modernity, premodern/modern, south/north – implicitly cloud over theory. Modernity may be better conceived in the plural, as modernities (Eisenstadt 2002).

A manifestation of the cul-de-sac of C&D theory is anti-development thinking (Chapter 7). Obviously the rejectionist position is not the best platform for redefining development. Foucauldian discourse analysis is long on history and short on future, strong on critique and weak on construction. It has room only for a reactive position of resistance rather than a proactive perspective of imagining and developing alternatives. This is a limitation of the Foucauldian approach in relation to development discourse as it is in relation to other terrains.

In many ways the agenda of C&D parallels that of alternative development (Friedmann 1992; see also Chapter 6 below). A singular difference is the priority given to culture, so the key issue is how culture is conceptualized. The tendency toward the reification of culture is part of a tradition that is deeply entrenched within and outside anthropology of identifying culture with territorial units. National culture and local culture are obvious examples of this outlook. In C&D, practices are considered to be 'embedded' in a matrix of meaning and the tendency is to view this matrix as belonging to a social group and, next, to localize this group.

A ramification of the local culture argument is *ethnodevelopment*, for which Stavenhagen (1986) made a case. Although this notion is understandable in its original context of internal colonialism, it potentially parallels apartheid and 'separate development'. Taking *ethnos* (people) as a starting point for development does not settle matters because it ignores the fundamental character of development as an intercultural transaction: ethnodevelopment means narrowing development to its endogenous dimension. In addition, ethnic culture is no more homogeneous than national culture, for ethnic groups are crosscut by multiple differences along lines of gender, class, place, religion, ideology.

The Dutch development policy document *A World of Difference* avoids the national culture fallacy by identifying communities as the bearers of culture, with a general orientation of pluralism and fostering cultural difference, which is a welcome qualification in view of the limitations of the concept of community (e.g. Young 1991).

The counter-argument to the territorial reification of culture is that culture cannot be localized because it is not in itself a spatially bounded category. If culture is territorialized, as in national culture or local culture, the boundaries are, ultimately, political frontiers that require political analysis. Culture is intrinsically *translocal* because human learning is. At minimum, then, what is required is to differentiate between open and closed concepts of culture, between translocal and territorial notions of culture (Nederveen Pieterse 2003).

One can also think in terms of historical layers of culture and intersecting circles of cultural influence. For instance, in Pakistan traces of a deep historical layer of the Indus Valley Mohenjodaro culture mix with the intersecting spheres of influence of Central Asian, Arab and South Asian cultures, all leaving their imprint on language, technology and identity (Junejo and Bughio 1988). In addition, the distinct regional cultures of Baluchistan, Sind, the Punjab and others are overlaid by Islamic culture as well as by rural/urban and gender differences across the regions. Within urban culture we can further distinguish various occupational circles such as the cultures of the military, the bureaucracy, traders, and so on. Somehow perched on top of this is 'national culture' (Jalibi 1984). What then is the statement that 'development must be based on culture' supposed to mean?

An interesting way of thinking about this is to examine how cultural diversity and exchange have influenced 'development' (see Griffin 1996, UNDP 2004, World Commission 1996). Another way of thinking about this is in terms of cultural mixing and hybridity. From the point of view of any given place, cultures are hybrid: their wholeness consists in their being situationally relevant, strategic sets of borrowed improvisations (Nederveen Pieterse 2003). The localization of culture can be questioned from the point of view not only of history but also of geography and the 'place'. What comes to mind is Deleuze and Guattari's argument of deterritorialization and David Harvey's (1993) work on space and place: 'from space to place and back again'. Doreen Massey argues for a 'global sense of place': 'a sense of place which is extra-verted, which includes a consciousness of its links with the wider world, which integrates in a positive way the global and the local' (Massey 1993: 66). Rethinking boundaries in the age of cultural translation is a keynote of Bhabha's (1994) work.

The issue is not simply bringing anthropology back into development, but what kind of anthropology – conventional anthropology or reflexive anthropology? C&D connects development and anthropology at a time when anthropology is in crisis, including the crisis of representation in anthropology and of the authority of the ethnographic text. In response, Marcus and Fischer (1986) propose 'the repatriation of anthropology as cultural critique', which means in effect the merger of anthropology and cultural studies. In leaning on applied anthropology C&D tends to ignore poststructuralist anthropology and its critical innovations, and looking south to postcolonial countries it ignores cultural studies in post-imperial countries as well as in the south.

Cultural studies involve different outlooks. For instance, *popular culture* is a more fruitful notion than local culture (or than national culture) because its hybrid character – mixing high and low culture, local and global cultural flows – is implied from the outset (e.g. Rowe and Schelling 1991). By using such concepts several unnecessary dichotomies that burden C&D can be overcome on a more subtle and more productive level of analysis and, ultimately, policy.

An element that tends to be relegated to the background in C&D literature is engaging with capitalism – as if the shift toward a cultural outlook is a shift away from political economy. This is short-sighted because it glosses over 'development' as a stand-in for and attempt to manage and steer the spread of capitalist relations and ignores a wide body of literature on the cultural dynamics of global capitalism and uneven development (e.g. Comaroff and Comaroff 2001, Pred and Watts 1992, Taussig 1980).

Table 5.1 gives an overview of the place of 'culture' in development thinking. This concerns the overt, explicit relation to culture; implicitly development itself, of course, is a cultural angle, though not self-reflexively so. Modernization and neoliberalism are, likewise, cultural outlooks.

Table 5.2 gives an overview of dimensions of and perspectives on culture and development. When UNESCO declared the World Decade for Culture and Development in 1988–97, its key point, that development must resonate with culture, was widely accepted. UNESCO's report *Our Creative Diversity* discussed several dimensions of culture and development, matching especially points 2, 3 and 4 in the table below. Occasionally the discussion refers to deeper levels, such as points 5 and 7.

Table 5.1 *Development theories and culture*

Theories	Relation to culture	Keynotes
Classical	Culture neutral (but implicitly Protestant ethic)	Industrialization, example Britain
Modernization	As obstacle ('tradition' as resistance to change)	Westernization, example US. Instill achievement orientation
Dependency	As political resource: 'national culture'	Anti-imperialism. Cultural dependency theory: indigenization, dissociation
Alternative development	As a resource: local and national	Indigenous knowledge; decentralization of knowledge
Neoliberalism	Instrumental; culture as a resource in marketing and innovation	Market culture (individualism, competitiveness, consumerism)
Human development	As an economic resource (human capital, cultural capital)	Example East Asia
Post-development	As a resource: local culture	Cosmovision and resistance, example Zapatistas

Table 5.2 *Development and culture*

Development and culture	Questions
1. Development is culturally neutral.	But 'development' is a cultural construction.
2. Development must be based on culture.	On whose culture, which culture?
3. Development must be based on local culture.	What is local? Reification of 'community'?
4. Development must take into account cultural diversity.	Diversity according to rural/urban, class, gender, age, region, religion, language.
5. Culture is a development resource.	E.g. cultural capital, social capital.
6. Development is an *intercultural* process.	Across transnational, regional, national and local culture, so *both* globalism and endogenism are inadequate.
7. Development *as* culture.	If development is improvement, what is 'better'?

The cultural turn in development is not without its ironies. The tables are being turned, as is altogether appropriate in the throes of globalization.

> Over the last few years, at various meetings of men and women and representatives of majority and minority groups from First and Third World countries, I have found that the indigenous 'voice' of the Third World is most likely to be voiced by a Westerner, while the voice of Western theory often comes straight out of Africa or Japan. The effect of all that intellectual place switching is to induce a sense of metaphysical jet lag across genders, cultures, and continents and to open up a conversation about the full range of interpretive possibilities for thinking about the significance of 'difference'. (Shweder 1993: 282)

Development is a cultural practice and in this respect development as a category is no different from culture in that both are elusive concepts. Defining them is as difficult as, to use a Spanish proverb, putting pants on an octopus. Development thinking if considered carefully is a series of improvisations and borrowings, zigzagging over time, a hybrid project intellectually and politically, and not nearly the consistent edifice that both its adherents and opponents tend to consider it. The transformations denoted as 'development' change along with the tides and currents of conventional wisdom (Chapter 3).

Development is intrinsically an intercultural transaction. At the cusp of the millennium, culture is the major marker of *difference*. It assumes the role that religion performed in the Middle Ages, biology ('race') in the eighteenth and nineteenth centuries, along with time (evolution), and ideology during the first part of the twentieth century (Robertson 1992: 98–9). As such, culture has come to mean 'otherness'. Taken in this sense the statement that culture must be the basis of development, reads: the other (others, otherness) must be the basis of development. Development politics, then, is a politics of difference, navigating and negotiating multicultural cohabitation locally and globally. The differences at stake are multiple and diverse, not just between developed and developing zones and countries, but also within them and crosscutting the difference between developing/developed.

Conventional developmentalism can be viewed as a form of 'symbolic violence': 'the violence which is exercised upon a social agent with his or her complicity' (Bourdieu and Wacquant 1992: 167). Understanding development as a politics of difference is a step towards making development practice self-conscious with regard to its political and cultural bias, a step towards a practice of reflexive development.

C&D may offer relief from development steeped in Eurocentrism, occidental narcissism or trilateralist arrogance, but the remedy against the chauvinism of 'great traditions' is not to adopt the inverse missionary position and the chauvinism of 'little traditions'. C&D is not simply a matter of including culture but also of interrogating culture as a terrain of power, culture as ideology. Anti-ethnocentrism, as David Crocker (1991) points out, may ultimately be based on another partial, particularist perspective. This is a question that is not settled in C&D. The alternative advocated by Richard Rorty (1991) is 'anti anti-ethnocentrism', or returning towards the historical tradition of one's own group as the basis for moral judgement. This is the position of what he terms postmodernist bourgeois liberalism. This tradition, however, can be interpreted in many ways; in the case of the United States it is read differently by Allan Bloom and Noam Chomsky, and on the basis of the tradition there is no way of deciding among these readings, precisely because the tradition is heterogeneous and mixed. What is needed is to find a sense of balance that does not yield to futures mapped from above or to nostalgia for the rear exit, a new sense of balance between universalism and localism.

Development and cultural liberty

In view of the political spillover of ethnic and religious movements – as in the former Yugoslavia, Iraq, Afghanistan and several Muslim countries – the policy relevance of the cultural dimensions of development is increasingly prominent. So it plays large in a Human Development Report devoted to culture (UNDP 2004). As its title indicates, *Cultural Liberty in Today's Diverse World*, the report deals not merely with cultural diversity but also with cultural liberty, which, it argues, is its novel contribution to the debate. Liberty or freedom is the report's leitmotiv: 'If what is ultimately important is cultural liberty, then the valuing of cultural diversity must take a contingent and conditional form. Much will depend on how that diversity is brought about and sustained' (16). In often paraphrased wording it adopts 'a freedom-based defence of cultural diversity' (23). From this premise follows on a critique of cultural conservatism:

> Being born in a particular cultural milieu is not an exercise of freedom – quite the contrary. It becomes aligned to cultural liberty only if the person chooses to continue to live within the terms of that culture, and does so having had the opportunity of considering other alternatives. The central issue in cultural liberty is the capability of people to live as they would choose, with adequate opportunity to consider other options. (16–17)

The report reiterates that 'tradition should not be confused with freedom of choice' and cautions that 'defending tradition can hold back human development' (88). On the same premise the report criticizes identity politics and quotes Anthony Appiah on the 'imperialism of identity': 'it is crucial always to remember that we are not simply black or white or yellow or brown, gay or straight or bisexual ... but we are also brothers and sisters; parents and children... let us not let our racial identities subject us to new tyrannies' (18). The report, rightly in my view, draws attention instead to multiple identities, but it carries this too far:

> People must be free to choose how to define themselves and must be afforded the same rights and opportunities that their neighbours enjoy. This Report asserts that a main hope for harmony lies in promoting our multiple identities ... [T]he recognition of multiple and complementary identities – with individuals identifying themselves as citizens of a state as well as members of ethnic, religious and other cultural groups – is the cornerstone of cultural liberty. (42, 73)

The report becomes unreal when it argues that identity is a matter of individual choice and it is up to individuals to decide which of their identities matters most, which may be theoretically true but ignores the fact that most people live their lives as part of communities. Besides, dominant discourses and structures of power often reinforce and perpetuate particular identities.

A chapter on 'Confronting movements for cultural domination' discusses coercive movements that oppose cultural liberty in the name of cultural superiority on an ethnic or religious basis. It also discusses restrictive measures against them (such as institutional barriers against coercive political parties, legislation and judicial intervention) but rightly argues that the most effective way to marginalize extremism is to strengthen democratic processes, which includes concerns such as paying attention to school curricula. The closing chapter focuses on three policy challenges: indigenous peoples and extractive industries; the trade in cultural goods; and migration. Its contributions are generally what one would expect in a brief 20-page treatment and further reiterate the cultural liberty approach: 'globalization can expand cultural freedoms only if all people develop multiple and complementary identities as citizens of the world as well as citizens of a state and members of a cultural group' (89).

The report follows the World Commission on Culture and Development Report, *Our Creative Diversity* (1996), but it bears little relation to the culture and development literature. Earlier work examined the cultural assumptions of development thinking and cooperation, from Eurocentrism to racial bias. This literature is reflexive and self-critical and its major concern is to make development efforts more effective and participatory by taking into account social diversity and local culture (Schech and Haggis 2000). Gone in this report is the reflexive and self-critical character, gone is the critique of Orientalism; instead criticism squarely targets cultural conservatism and extremism – the opponents of cultural liberty.

About development the report is brief: 'there is no clear relationship between culture and development'. 'Work ethic, thrift, honesty and openness to strangers can play a role in economic growth ... But there is no grand cultural theory of development here', as econometric evidence shows (38, 39). The report rejects cultural determinism to explain economic development – from Weber's Protestant ethic (at times Catholic countries were growing faster than Protestant countries) to claims made in Harrison and Huntington's (2000) work *Culture Matters*. It rightly rejects the cliché of western liberty and Oriental despotism: 'The history of the world does not suggest anything like a division between a long-run history of Western toleration and that of non-Western despotism ... the very idea of democracy, in the form of participatory public reasoning, has appeared in different civilizations at different periods in world history' (21).

The report notes the difficulties of measuring cultural liberty and developing a cultural liberty index because of limited data and conceptual and methodological problems. It attempts to operationalize cultural liberty by measuring its opposites in two forms of exclusion: living mode exclusion ('when the state or social custom denigrates or suppresses a group's culture, including its language, religion or traditional customs or lifestyles') and participation exclusion ('social, economic and political exclusion along ethnic, linguistic or religious lines').

The report rejects as myths that cultural diversity inevitably leads to clashes over values and that cultural diversity is an obstacle to development.[1] Fair enough; but would it not be appropriate in a Human Development Report on cultural diversity to take a further step and at least explore that cultural diversity may be *conducive* to development? Yet the *economics* of cultural diversity barely come up. The strongest claim is: 'As this Report argues from beginning to end, attempts to suppress and assimilate diverse cultural groups are not only morally wrong – they are often ineffective, heightening tensions' (44). Two pillars that remain are moral considerations and preventing or managing conflict. Precisely where one would have expected a reflection on correlations between multiculturalism and development this is entirely absent, bar a passing mention of the economic benefits of migration.

There would be several routes towards a political economy of multiculturalism and development. Keith Griffin, a member of the World Commission on Culture and Development, makes a strong case that cultural diversity, past and present, is conducive to development, particularly with a view to the innovative contributions of migrants (Griffin 2000a). Another option is to link up with the learning approach in development economics, including 'learning what one is good at producing' as well as 'learning to learn' (Rodrik and Hausman 2003) and under which conditions combining diverse cultural databases and institutional practices enhances investment decisions and economic performance. This also involves taking up questions of intercultural social capital (Nederveen Pieterse 2007). Cultural economy approaches hold that economics is not merely a social and political but also a cultural phenomenon (Amin and Thrift 2004), which points to a political economy of multiculturalism. This human development report, however, is long on norms and policy prescriptions and short on economics.

According to the report, 'human development aims at expanding an individual's choices' (93), which is odd because one would think that development is above all a social, not an individual project; though it is consistent with the analytical roots of the human development approach in liberalism (Chapter 8 below). Like most development studies the report is short both on history and on theory. The report makes selective references to the massive literature on ethnicity, ethnic conflict, religion and multiculturalism. The argument for cultural liberty is an odd duck in the massive literature on religion, ethnicity and ethnic conflict and novel in this debate. It does fit with Amartya Sen's argument of *Development as Freedom* (1999) and its functionalist application of a rights-based liberalism. To this report Sen contributed a background paper on 'Cultural freedom and human development'. As a broadsheet against exclusion the report doesn't discuss the exclusions and shortcomings of liberalism itself, which are firmly on the record, for instance in the history of colonialism (Mehta 1997, Metcalf 1998) and in relation to multiculturalism (see Parekh 2000).

The core problem of liberal multiculturalism is that it provides a solution for which there is no problem and a remedy for which there is no ailment; a world of optional multiple identities in which individuals can choose their identity is a world that doesn't need multicultural policies (Nederveen Pieterse 2007). The central paradox of this report is that it wants all-round cultural inclusion – but not cultural conservatism; it wants multicultural democracy – but not cultural conservatism. But who can define and decree what is conservative? In effect, this takes the politics out of culture and identity. Campaigns against extremism usually target the extremism of 'others' and are oblivious to one's own extremism.

The report reads as a compendium of liberal multiculturalism policies – straightforward, plain speaking, but mostly obvious and difficult to implement. The report acknowledges the problems that arise from integrating multicultural policies into human development strategies and from its liberal policy recommendations. Thus while education in one's mother tongue is no doubt a value, it notes that there are practical and economic impediments to doing so. Yet these reservations don't feed back to the recommendations: 'In the big picture the arguments for these policies are clear. But for policy-makers the contradictions, trade-offs and clashes with other aspects of human development can monopolize their attention' (45). These fundamental problems are discussed in throwaway lines on 'a history of power relations' that leave matters open and to which there is no follow-up. Thus, for all its plain-speaking clarity this is actually a confused and confusing document. At times its pronouncements seem to address a parallel universe: 'The central issue in cultural liberty is the capability of people to live as they would choose, with adequate opportunity to consider other options. The normative weight of freedom can hardly be invoked when no choice – real or potential – is actually considered' (17).

In sum, this report presents problems. First, when it claims that 'defending tradition can hold back human development' it restates the old-fashioned modernization vs. tradition approach. Second, when it poses cultural liberty as the framework for culture and development, it views developing countries' cultures through the lens of western values. Third, by offering freedom as the answer to every problem it places the cart before the horse. Policies informed by norms rather than by the difficult trade-offs of actual development policy belong to the world of ideology.

The report brings us into an arena of freedom and its opponents. In approach and language it reads like an American take on culture and matches an American policy agenda. If one would want to align development cooperation with, say, the war on terrorism, this would be the way to go. One would first declare the aim of development to be freedom; second, one would aim to defend and spread a 'culture of freedom' and oppose any form of cultural conservatism. To demonstrate even-handedness one would also roundly criticize extremism in the west such as extreme right wing parties and Christian fundamentalism. Third, one would weave this into development cooperation and conditionality. Thus the promotion of cultural liberty and the struggle against extremism would become strands of good governance.

Turning to culture and development generally, a key point made in this chapter is the significance of cultural difference within developing countries. A trend in many culture and development discussions is to focus on north–south relations and northern cultural bias, as in classic discussions of Eurocentrism and Orientalism. But, of course, ethnic stratification and cultural 'divisions of labour' within developing societies are at least as important, if not more, for they may involve institutionalized racism on the part of elites and bureaucracies (Jonsson 1999; Nederveen Pieterse 2007). Culture is charged with power at every turn.

Note

1 This is a common negative finding, though it runs against conventional wisdom. Thus an earlier study finds that 'ethnic, linguistic and religious differences are not significantly related to the growth rate in GDP per capita. States with minorities seeking greater autonomy need not press the minorities to conform to the cultural norms of the majority community to enhance economic performance' (Lian and Oneal 1997: 61).

6

My Paradigm or Yours? Variations on Alternative Development

> Human nature being what it is, while everyone likes to be a social engineer,
> few like to be the objects of social engineering. (Ashis Nandy 1989: 271)

This chapter is an inquiry into critical currents in development thinking. The objective is to go beyond the fraternity of rhetorical consensus in criticizing mainstream development and to hold the claims and aspirations of these critical positions themselves against the light. The focus is not only on the critical but also on the affirmative part of these positions. This exercise is not meant as a critique for critique's sake; the question is what these positions tell us analytically and where they lead us in terms of policy and action.

My views on alternative development have been changing over the years. Initially my impression was that alternative development presents a loose profile of critical sensibilities and alternative practices that leaves so many areas open that its claim to present an alternative model or paradigm to mainstream development thinking is exaggerated and misplaced. Further delving and reading enthusiastic accounts (such as Carmen 1996, Korten 1990, Max-Neef 1991, Rahman 1993) persuades me that there is a profound and principled challenge to mainstream developmentalism. Possibly this can take the form of an alternative development paradigm, but closer reflection on this position and its ramifications causes me to question this. I wonder not only how such an alternative development paradigm should be conceived, in terms of analytics and politics, but also whether thinking in terms of paradigms is appropriate at all.

Rather than pursue a single line of argument I have decided to keep these changing positions and moments of reflection in this chapter. Doing so enables me to look at alternative development from more angles and probe further than if I were just presenting a single line of argument. Others may have experienced a similar process of questioning. The structure of the chapter, then, roughly follows the logic of these three positions: (1) alternative development as a loose profile; (2) alternative development as a paradigm; (3) a post-paradigmatic way of thinking about alternative development. Each of these is a different way of constructing alternative development and the relationship to mainstream development. Each of these has its chemistry, reasoning and limitations. During this stroll past alternative development positions my own views shift from critical to supportive to revisionist. Advancing three arguments allows me to say more than if I would just present one; nevertheless the third position is the one I arrive at by travelling through the others.

The argument runs as follows. Alternative development has been concerned with introducing alternative practices and redefining the goals of development. This has been successful in the sense that key elements of both have been adopted in mainstream development. Even if not consistently practised it is now generally accepted that development efforts are more successful if the community participates. NGOs now play key roles on the ground and in development cooperation. This success reflects not simply the strength of NGOs and grassroots politics but also the 1980s roll-back of the state, the advance of market forces and the breakdown of regulation. All the same, the goals of development have been generally redefined. It is now widely accepted that development is not simply a matter of GDP growth, and human development is a more appropriate goal and measure of development. This also means that alternative development approaches have become less distinct from conventional development discourse and practice since alternatives have been absorbed in mainstream development. In the context of alternative development several pertinent positions and methodologies have been developed – views on the agency, methods and objectives of development. However, alternative development approaches have failed to develop a clear perspective on micro–macro relations, an alternative macro approach, and a coherent theoretical position, although it is often claimed that there is an alternative development paradigm. But is the concept of paradigm appropriate to contemporary social science? Besides, is formulating the relationship between alternative development and mainstream development as a paradigm break substantively tenable and politically sensible?

These reflections on alternative development are followed by queries on mainstream development, which is increasingly caught on the horns of a dilemma between the aims of human and social development and the constraints of structural adjustment and global monetarism represented by the international financial institutions. Presently, unlike the 1970s, the big hiatus no longer runs between mainstream and alternative development, but between human and alternative development on the one hand and the 'Washington consensus' of structural reform on the other (see Chapters 8 and 11 below).

Alternative development

To start with there are different ways of conceiving what alternative development is about and what its role is. Alternative development can be viewed as a roving critique of mainstream development, shifting in position as mainstream development shifts, as a series of alternative proposals and methodologies that are loosely interconnected; or it can be viewed as an alternative development paradigm, implying a definite theoretical break with mainstream development. It can be viewed as concerned with local development, with alternative practices on the ground, or as an overall challenge to the mainstream, and part of a global alternative. In many discussions this question of the status and scope of alternative development remains unsettled.

An elementary distinction, following Sheth (1987), runs between structuralist and normative approaches to development alternatives. This involves two basic differences. Structuralist approaches, such as dependency theory and the Keynesian reformism of the new international economic order, emphasize structural macroeconomic change – just as mainstream modernization thinking does – whereas alternative development emphasizes agency, in the sense of people's capacity to effect social change. The second difference is that dependency critiques of mainstream development do not usually question development *per se* but only *dependent* development (or underdevelopment).

A basic question is whether alternative development is an alternative way of achieving development, sharing the same goals as mainstream development but using different means, participatory and people-centred. It would seem this way if we consider the enormous increase in development funds being channelled through NGOs during the past decades (which well exceed the total annual disbursements through the IMF and World Bank). This suggests a peaceful coexistence between mainstream and alternative development. Yet the usual claim is that alternative development refers to an alternative *model* of development. Let us consider how this claim runs.

In the 1970s dissatisfaction with mainstream development crystallized into an alternative, people-centred approach to development. According to the 1975 report of the Dag Hammarskjöld Foundation 'What now? Another development', development should be 'geared to the satisfaction of needs', 'endogenous and self-reliant' and 'in harmony with the environment'. Whether this was meant to be an alternative practice of development apart from the mainstream or whether it was also to change mainstream development was not quite settled. This approach has been carried further under the heading of alternative development. Over the years alternative development has been reinforced by and associated with virtually any form of criticism of mainstream developmentalism, such as anti-capitalism, Green thinking, feminism, ecofeminism, democratization, new social movements, Buddhist economics, cultural critiques, and poststructuralist analysis of development discourse.

'Alternative' generally refers to three spheres – agents, methods and objectives or values of development. According to Nerfin (1977), alternative development is the terrain of 'Third System' or citizen politics, the importance of which is apparent in view of the failed development efforts of government (the prince or first system) and market forces (the merchant or second system). Often this seems to be the key point: alternative development is development *from below* and 'below' refers both to community and to NGOs. In several respects alternative development revisits Community Development of the 1950s and 60s. Community Development goes back to American social work, which entered colonial development via British colonialism and supplemented modernization efforts in the 1950s (Carmen 1996: 46–7). This genealogy accounts for the ambiguity of some of the key terms in alternative development such as 'participation'.

Alternative development is often identified with development-by-NGOs (e.g. Drabek 1987). But given the wide variety of NGOs and NGO practices, the equation 'alternative development is what NGOs do' is obviously inadequate. NGO ideology is organization-led and too limited to account for alternative development. Alternative development involves further distinguishing elements with respect to development methodology (participatory, endogenous, self-reliant) and objectives (geared to locally defined needs). But is saying that development must be undertaken from within and geared to local needs an adequate way of redefining development, or is it only a polemical position? The alternative referred to is alternative in relation to state and market, but not necessarily in relation to the general discourse of developmentalism. It would be difficult to maintain that alternative development has evolved a theory, although Hettne (1990, 2008b) among others tries to make such a case, arguing that it represents a counterpoint to mainstream development.[1]

Thus Friberg and Hettne (1985: 207) argue that 'opposed and dialectically related to the predominant paradigm, there has been a Green Counterpoint'. They relate this historically to the 'populist tradition' including narodnism (that is, populism in Russia), criticisms of the division of labour, the 'return to Gemeinschaft', as well as 'Third World populism', Gandhi, Maoism and Buddhist economics. Their premise is a radical questioning of development:

> it is the development process itself which engenders most of our problems ... If we have been floating along the stream of evolution, we are now starting to doubt whether it will carry us to the promised land. Instead we hear the roaring from the approaching waterfall. Almost all the traditional indicators of development have changed their emotional loading from plus to minus. (ibid.: 215)

A critique of capitalism is part of this perspective: 'The capitalist economy is in fact a parasite upon the non-capitalist economy', capitalism is a form of 'shifting cultivation' (233–4). They anticipate the 'possibility of a slow decline over the coming 500 years without any particular dramatic events as the turning point' (234) and envision a post-capitalist world, to which there are two different roads: the Red road of continued modernization toward a socialist world order, and the Green road of demodernization, cultural identity, self-reliance, social justice and ecological balance (234–5). The 'global Green movement', in their view, derives strength from three different sources: traditionalists in the peripheries, marginalized people at the middle level, and postmaterialists in affluent societies at the centres. Nations founded upon ancient nations or civilizations, such as China, Iran, Egypt, Vietnam, and also Mexico, Turkey, Japan and India, can be 'seen as the main sources, actual or potential, of alternatives to the Western model of development' (238), which is an interesting thesis in the days of China booming and 'India everywhere'.

This shows how quickly sensibilities date, or at any rate their articulation, and brightly illustrates features that run through various forms of alternative development thinking.

- The tendency to represent alternative development as a counterpoint that unites all dissident social forces critical of development, which in turn reflects a desire to forge a grand coalition of opposition forces.
- The tendency to equate development with modernization and alternative development with demodernization, premised on the 'incompatibility between modernization and human development' (ibid.: 235).
- The tendency to view alternative development as an alternative *external* to the mainstream, a counter-utopia carried by social actors in the interstices of the mainstream and in countries supposedly outside the thrust of western developmentalism; in other words, an oasis, enclave or 'liberated zone' approach to alternative development.
- The alignment of all forms of criticism of mainstream development together as if they form a cohesive alternative, but all good things together do not necessarily make a great thing. Friberg and Hettne mention 'possible priority conflicts between the subgoals of development' (220), but maintain that they form a coherent whole.

This particular formulation of alternative development is clearly dated and marked by the 1980s upsurge of Green movements. It is a prelude to the post-development perspective that took shape in the 1990s (Chapter 7 below). In later work, Hettne (1990, 1992, 2008a) abandoned the demodernization/anti-development perspective. Weaknesses of this position (anticipating the discussion of post-development in the next chapter) include the following:

- 'Mainstream development' is simplified as a single, homogeneous thrust toward modernization, and its diversity, complexity and adaptability are underestimated.
- While the theoretical claim is for a dialectical relationship between the mainstream and alternatives, the actual argument takes the form of a simple dualistic opposition and the dialectics, the ways in which mainstream and alternatives shape and influence one another, slip out of view.
- In order to maximize the opposition between the mainstream and alternatives, the appeal of the mainstream to various constituencies is underestimated.

Several of these features replay the narrative of anti-capitalist opposition. The tendency to transpose forms of struggle opposing early industrial capitalism to late capitalism indicates a failure of oppositional imagination. It recycles a struggle scenario under different circumstances and envisions no path but that of rejectionism. This is one of the problems of alternative development: post-conventional ideas straitjacketed in conventional political imaginaries. In the process alternative development is loaded with aspirations beyond its scope. Subsequent claims for alternative development by Hettne and others have been more modest and this kind of grandstanding now takes the form of post-development. Broadly speaking, then, the development terrain seems to be marked out into three overall positions: mainstream development (which is by no means a coherent position), alternative development (which involves a range of perspectives) and post-development.

A hostile criticism would be that this approach, inflated to 'alternative development', is pretentious because it suggests more than it can deliver, unclear because the difference between what is alternative and what is not is not clarified, and fuzzy to the point of hypocrisy because it sustains the overall rhetoric of development while suggesting the ability to generate something really different within its general aura. Alternative development has been fashionable because it coincided with a crisis in development thinking and because it matched general doubts about the role of the state, both among neoliberals and from the viewpoint of human rights. 'Alternative' discourse was a way of being progressive without being overly radical and without endorsing a clear ideology; it could be embraced by progressives and conservatives, who both had axes to grind with the role of states. It was a safe, low-risk way of being progressive and its structural obscurity ensured broad endorsement. It was a postmodern way of being post-ideological. It was everyone's way out except that of the last bureaucrat.

Hettne (1990) presents 'Another development' as a combination of basic needs, self-reliance, sustainable and endogenous development. Attractive as this *mélange* looks it also presents a problem. All good things put together do not necessarily add up to a paradigm. Part of this is the problem of articulation (cf. Laclau and Mouffe 1985). To the extent that each of these discourses has its own logic and autonomy, there is no guarantee that they will blend well together. Their actual course depends on their articulation with other discourses, which may turn out to be progressive or conservative. There is no preordained outcome to the politics of hegemony. At best this gives us an unstable articulation, which is too weak a basis to constitute an 'alternative model'. Ethnodevelopment may clash with eco-development or may take an ethnonationalist turn. Self-reliance may require economies of scale, which clash with ethnodevelopment. Feminism may clash with indigenous patriarchy, and so forth. Risking flippancy, one might say that the kind of world in which alternative development works is a world that doesn't need it. Thus, though pertinent as an orientation, it is too unstable and narrow to serve as a 'model'.

Hettne seeks to establish a sharp boundary between mainstream development and alternative development but fails to do so. Hettne's schematic representation of mainstream development theory versus counterpoint theory overrates the coherence and consistency of 'development'. Besides, if alternative development is defined as a counterpoint to mainstream development, it is reduced to a reactive position: if mainstream development shifts, so would alternative development. Furthermore, the alternative components mentioned by Hettne are no longer distinctive: participation and sustainability have long been adopted in mainstream development and basic needs have been abandoned.[2]

The problem is that there is no clear line of demarcation between mainstream and alternative: alternatives are coopted and yesterday's alternatives are today's institutions. The difference between mainstream and alternative, then, is a conjunctural difference, not a difference in principle, though it tends to be presented as if it is. In itself 'alternative' has no more meaning than 'new' in advertising. With Nandy (1989) we might term this the problem of the 'standardization of dissent'. In this sense alternative development replicates 'the value of the new', which is a pathos intrinsic to modernity (Vattimo 1988). As such alternative development partakes of the momentum of modernity and the evergreen hope that the future will redeem the present.

So far, then, it would be difficult to claim that alternative development represents a paradigm break in development, for it lacks sufficient theoretical cohesion. Alternative development reflects certain normative orientations, follows disparate theoretical strands, is in flux, not fully developed, and its status remains unclear. Part of the polemics of development, and situated on its cutting edge, it's made up as one goes along and remains intrinsically controversial and unsettled. Understandings of alternative development vary widely: whichever aspect of mainstream development the spotlight is on, alternative development is held up as its counterpoint. If mainstream development is viewed, as it has been through most of the career of modern developmentalism, as state-led, then alternative development is associated with the informal sector, social movements and NGOs. If mainstream development is viewed under the sign of liberalization, as has been the case since the 1980s, then the alternative becomes ... the state. Thus, under the heading of *Alternative Development Strategies in sub-Saharan Africa*, Stewart, Lall and Wangwe (1993) argue for import-substitution industrialization and state protection for industry, a strategy which, in other contexts, was part of mainstream repertoires.

This variability is intrinsic to alternative development to the extent that alternative development is by definition reactive, contrapuntal. At a time when there is widespread admission that several development decades have brought many failures, while the development industry continues unabated, there is continuous and heightened self-criticism in development circles, a constant search for alternatives, a tendency towards self-correction and a pattern of cooptation of whatever attractive, fashionable alternatives present themselves. Accordingly, the turnover of alternatives becoming mainstream has speeded up; the dialectics of alternative development and mainstream development have accelerated.

Green thinking about sustainability, a radical position twenty years ago, has long been institutionalized as 'sustainable development'. The informal sector, a twilight zone unnoticed by mainstream developers mesmerized by the state, has been put in the limelight by Hernan de Soto (1989) and embraced by establishment development agencies. The accompanying message of deregulation and government rollback of course beautifully matches the prevailing neoliberal outlook. NGOs, after decades of marginality, have become major channels of development cooperation. Governments go non-governmental by setting up government organized Non Government Organizations. In countries such as Mozambique and Bangladesh the resources of NGOs, domestic and international, exceed those at the disposal of government. Women's concerns, once an outsider criticism, have been institutionalized by making women and gender preferential parts of the development package. Criticism of foreign aid as development assistance has led to its being renamed 'development cooperation'. Capacity-building, which used to be missing in conventional development support, is now a major objective. Mega-summits by UN organizations in Rio, Cairo, Copenhagen, Beijing or Bali, by Habitat International and the WTO, have been forums for aligning official and unofficial discourses. Thus, forms of alternative development have become institutionalized as part of mainstream development and at times have overtaken mainstream development, to the point that MAD, or mainstream alternative development, may be a fitting notion. This turn of affairs is not incidental but a logical function of the way the overall development process is moving.

We can regard alternative development as either an open-ended poser or a set of ideas and practices that in time have been institutionalized, and while critically scrutinizing the latter we can keep open the former. The advantage of alternative development as an open-ended poser is that it provides a flexible position of critique. Of course, this principle can be adopted without reference to 'alternative development'; indeed, development itself can be defined as a 'constant consideration of alternatives' (Coetzee 1989: 11). A disadvantage is that without a theory, alternative development is like a ship without a rudder.

Alternative development paradigm

While much alternative development thinking makes a diffuse impression, this has gradually been giving way to a sharper and more assertive positioning on account of several trends.

1. The enormous growth of NGOs in numbers and influence generates a growing demand for strategy and therefore theory.
2. The importance of environmental concerns and sustainability has weakened the economic growth paradigm and given a boost to alternative and ecological economics.
3. The glaring failure of several development decades further unsettles the mainstream paradigm of growth.
4. The growing challenges to the Bretton Woods institutions lead to the question of whether these criticisms are merely procedural and institutional (for more participation and democratization) or whether they involve fundamentally different principles.

These diverse trends generate various lines of tension. One line of friction runs between the general alternative development preoccupation with local and endogenous development and the growing demand for *global* alternatives. Globalization under the sign of the unfettered market is denounced because it clashes with endogenous development, while the mushrooming of NGOs itself demonstrates the growing momentum of global civil society, in other words representing another arm of globalization. Another line of friction runs between diffuse alternative development and an alternative development paradigm, the former implying a soft and the latter a hard boundary with mainstream development, and theoretical openness or closure. These tensions find expression in more or less subtle differences among alternative development positions.

In view of the holistic aspirations of alternative development it would be desirable for disparate alternative development knowledge pools to be grouped together; yet in view of the different functions that alternative development fulfils – animating local development, guiding international NGO strategy, informing global alternatives – this will not necessarily happen. Alternative development serves dispersed discourse communities. International NGOs tend to look both ways, at local grassroots development *and* global alternatives. These different functions overlap and intersperse and are not necessarily incompatible, but rhyming them requires making them explicit, which is not often done, and an effort at synthesis, which requires more reflection on local/global and micro/mega interconnections than is common in most alternative development thinking.

Oddly, in view of the claim to an alternative development paradigm and its growing appeal, attempts to theoretically develop alternative development have been relatively few.[3] There may be several reasons for this. Alternative development tends to be practice-oriented rather than theoretically inclined. The world of alternative development is not a library world. Part of alternative development logic is that as development is people-centred, genuine development knowledge is people's knowledge and what counts is local rather than abstract expert knowledge. With the local orientation comes a certain regional dispersal in the literature, which looks like a scattered archipelago of primary local knowledges, with scant overarching reflection. Alternative development travels under many aliases – appropriate development, participatory development, people-centred development, human-scale development, people's self-development, autonomous development, holistic development; and many elements relevant to alternative development are developed under headings such as participation, participatory action research, grassroots movements, NGOs, empowerment, conscientization, liberation theology, democratization, citizenship, human rights, development ethics, ecofeminism, diversity, critical pedagogy, etc., which does not facilitate generating a coherent body of theory. Many alternative development sources do not refer to one another but keep on generating alternatives from the ground up, reinventing the wheel without outlining fundamentals or generating 'expert ' debate. In part this reflects the 'alternative' character of alternative development, in the sense of a habitus of subversion, an intuitive aversion to method, to systematization and codification, which implies a distrust of 'experts' and even of theory. Yet this weakens the claim to deliver a different paradigm.

Alternative development is not necessarily anti-theoretical but it is intellectually segmented. The work of several alternative development authors can be contextualized in terms of their social location. David Korten is an NGO strategist who contributes both to local development and global alternatives. John Friedmann is primarily concerned with local and regional planning. Anisur Rahman mainly addresses local and grassroots development. Manfred Max-Neef and Hazel Henderson are alternative economists, the former engaged with local development and the latter with global alternatives. Training, teaching and research are other contexts in which alternative development is being articulated, across a wide spectrum from small local institutes to university programmes.[4]

Critics of the Bretton Woods institutions increasingly claim to present a paradigm shift in development. The same elements keep coming back: 'equitable, participatory and sustainable human development' (e.g. Arruda 1994: 139); 'the values of equity, participation and environmental sustainability, as well as improving physical well-being' (Griesgraber and Gunter 1996a: xiv). Is this sufficient as the basis of a new paradigm? It concerns the 'how to' of development rather than the nature of development as such. It identifies aspirations rather than attributes of development. Hence it can easily be 'added on' to mainstream development discourse and indeed often is. Since mainstream development nowadays embraces and advertises the same values, the outcome is a rhetorical consensus rather than a paradigm break.

Rahman (1993) contrasts a consumerist view of development, in which people are the passive recipients of growth, with a creative view, in which people are the creative forces, means and end of development, for development is people's self-development. This refers to a set of normative orientations rather than to a different explanatory framework. Such elements add up to a distinctive alternative development profile, but not to a paradigm. The distinctive element of alternative development should be found in the *redefinition* of development and not merely in its agency, modalities, procedures or aspirations.

Dissatisfaction with development-as-growth is an increasingly common position, not just since the Club of Rome's report *The Limits to Growth* (Meadows et al. 1972). Yet if development is not about growth, what is it about? One option is to redefine development as social transformation (e.g. Addo et al. 1985). This is like saying that development is change – change from what to what, what kind of change? 'Good change', according to Robert Chambers (1983). Institutional transformation adds concreteness, but remains vague. Korten (1990) defines development as a transformation towards justice, inclusiveness and sustainability. Again these are normative clauses, but an ethics of development (Gasper 2004, Goulet 1992) does not add up to redefining development. Alternatively, might the character of alternative development be found in a distinctive *development style*? Max-Neef mentions 'avoiding bureaucratization' and for Korten the surest way to kill a social movement is to throw money at it. The downside of this position is the romanticization of social movements (as in post-development).

It may be argued that theory is a central concern of alternative development, for it is about the redefinition of development. Korten (1990: 113) notes that 'it is impossible to be a true development agency without a theory that directs action to the underlying causes of underdevelopment. In the absence of a theory, the aspiring development agency almost inevitably becomes instead merely an *assistance* agency engaged in relieving the more visible symptoms of underdevelopment through relief and welfare measures.' Indeed, 'an organization cannot have a meaningful development *strategy* without a development theory' (114). Korten proposes a redefinition of development as follows: 'Development is a process by which the members of a society increase their personal and institutional capacities to mobilize and manage resources to produce sustainable and justly distributed improvements in their quality of life consistent with their own aspirations (67). The same point in different wording: 'The heart of development is institutions and politics, not money and technology, though the latter are undeniably important' (144). 'The most fundamental issues of development are, at their core, issues of power' (214). The issues that Gunnar Myrdal raised in *An Asian Drama* (1968), issues of land ownership and the distribution of power, issues that have been papered over by community development and other fads, which made little or no difference in relation to poverty – these fundamentals are now placed centre-stage.

This position may be distinctive enough to establish a break with conventional development. For Korten it constitutes a break with the various approaches that coopt alternative values by 'adding them on' to the growth model. 'The basic needs strategies that gained prominence during the 1970s, and are still advocated by organizations such as UNICEF, are a variant of, usually an add-on to, a classical growth-centered development strategy' (44). The same applies to the approaches that have been concerned with giving structural adjustment a 'human face'. 'The basic services for which they pleaded were best characterized as a facade, putting a more palatable face on actions that are based on flawed analysis and theory, rather than coming forward in support of more basic, but politically controversial reforms' (45). The report of the World Commission on Environment and Development on *Our Common Future* (1987), known as the Brundtland Report, is also criticized for merging sustainability and growth in the notion of 'sustainable growth' (166).

A further question is whether, beyond an alternative definition of development, alternative development has a distinctive methodology, epistemology and policy agenda. A review of alternative development positions on questions of agency, endogenous development, indigenous knowledge and development cooperation, may serve to fill in and give substance to an alternative development paradigm or profile and also to detect whether there are contradictory elements among them. Since the literature is extensive, uneven and dispersed this is only a provisional review.

Agency

With regard to agency there have been marked changes over time in alternative development thinking. Generally alternative development combines the aims of development and emancipation. As development 'from below' it is part of the general concern with civil society. In 1970s alternative development manifestos the forces that were to carry and implement 'another development' were the community and informal sector, or the 'third system'. Of the big three – state, market, society – the emphasis was entirely on society as the foundation for another development. Clearly, at the time, alternative development was a protest position against state-led development. The strength of NGO discourse is also a weakness: neglecting the role of the state. Thus the rise of NGOs may be viewed as de facto part of the neoliberal 'counter-revolution' in development. When in the 1980s the private sector came to be viewed as the leading sector of development, the scope of alternative development widened to include the state. Thus Friedmann (1992) and others argue that a strong civil society and a strong state go together. A strong, activist state in this view does not necessarily mean a dominant state. In alternative development the role of the state is to act as an enabler, a facilitator of people's self-development. For the state to perform such a role democratization is implied.

What about the third of the big three – market forces? Gradually this is being roped in, moving beyond not only anti-state but also anti-market understandings of people-centred development. 'Step-by-step we have moved to a recognition that government, business and voluntary organizations all have essential roles in development' (Korten 1990: 95). Not only practices but also prescriptions increasingly involve synergies between government, NGOs and firms, and elements such as fair trade, corporate codes, socially responsible business, and banking. Thailand's Five Star Partnership Programme integrates the efforts of government, NGOs, the private sector, religious communities and academic institutions to facilitate community and provincial development. Sato and Smith (1996) present this as a practice exemplar which is part of an alternative development paradigm. A trend at the other extreme is for the market logic to take over to the point that private aid, as part of the development industry, becomes a business undertaking (Sogge 1996).

NGOs

The struggle of alternative development, according to Smitu Kothari (1994: 50), is 'nothing short of reversing the conquest of society by the economy'. This calls to mind Sukhamoy Chakravarty's saying that the market is a good servant but a bad master (quoted in Hettne 1992). Where the state has little autonomy in relation to business interests, foreign or domestic, social forces can act as countervailing power. In a situation where forces such as strategic business groups, multinational corporations or multilateral agencies seek to influence or capture the state, organized civil society can operate as a check on the 'privatization' of the public sphere.

The political economy of *dependencia* involved Third World intellectuals relying on the state and on the emergence of a national bourgeoisie. As intellectuals of Third World nationalism and anti-imperialism, at times they played the part of alternative mandarins. What is the political economy of alternative development? Which political and social forces sustain the world of everyday and really existing alternative development? Whom does alternative development discourse serve? Who are funding NGOs and alternative development consultants (Sogge 1996)?

NGOs have become part of the development industry, another component in the package. The rise of NGOs during the 1970s and 1980s was both a by-product of and compensation for the wave of neoliberalism (Duffield 1996). Civil society, social movements and NGOs are a mixed bag, all the more because, mushrooming amidst the breakdown of regulation (or informalization), they are unregulated. Some NGOs such as church organizations were active long before the development era. There are steep differences between NGOs as public service contractors and people-oriented NGOs (Edwards and Hulme 1992). NGOs suffer similar problems (bureaucratization, hierarchy, scale, corruption, dependence) as with any organization. If they are sites of power outside the reach of the state, they are within the reach of donors, who in turn move in the orbit of their funders, state or private, and their cultural and discursive agendas (see Black 1992, on the career of Oxfam). NGOs can function as parastatals, subcontractors of the state or governmental NGOs (GONGOs), but outside the channels of accountability and control. NGOs can just as easily be conservative agencies, such as evangelical movements broadcasting the theology of quiescence or the prosperity gospel of individual achievement, charismatic movements propagating new forms of ritualism, not to mention agencies such as the Summer Institute of Linguistics which is on record as having served as a CIA conduit.

Development NGOs have been denounced as 'new missionaries' engaged in recolonization, as 'unguided missiles' (Hanlon 1991) or as 'the new East India Company' (Burne 1995). They have been accused of neutralizing popular resistance and facilitating popular acceptance of structural adjustment (Arrelano-Lopez and Petras 1994). NGOs can contribute to democratizing development (Clark 1991), serve as vehicles of transnational networking building global civil society (Henderson 1993), as liaisons in 'innovation networking' (Mytelka 1993), or as channels of outside interference beyond the control of normalized politics and international relations (e.g. African Rights 1994). In the United States fake grassroots movements-for-hire or rent-an-NGO will promote corporate causes (Greider 1992). NGOs are now viewed with less naivety and more discrimination concerning the institutional, discursive, economic and political constraints under which they operate.

New politics

Alternative development literature is sprinkled with pleas for unity. In India, Smitu Kothari notes, 'The pervasive fragmentation of the entire democratic spectrum has to be replaced by coalescing our dispersed efforts' (1994: 51). In part this reflects a nostalgia for the 'old politics' characterized by clearly divided camps and neat ideological boundaries. Laclau and Mouffe (1985) contrast this with hegemonic politics which is characterized by unfixed identities and fragmented space, in which nodal points nonetheless matter. In hegemonic politics coalitions are not stable as in the old-time coalitions because the subjectivities are not as stable. Alternative development may involve novel coalition politics of new and old social movements, with a view to a new convergence of concerns and interests, in relation both to local and to global politics. The case for a 'convergence of radicalisms' fails to persuade because in these kinds of pleas the interests, identities and subjectivities involved tend to be taken as static and given, rather than as constructed in the process of articulation.

In alternative development, agency can be defined narrowly or broadly; it can be defined loosely, in diffuse alternative development, or sharply, in the alternative development paradigm. At any rate, what is more appropriate than a static coalition politics or a new kind of political 'unity' is the idea of *synergies* among pluralistic actors, synergies that are flexible and mobile and do not require ideological consensus. Thus, the World Bank's NGO desk is making tripartite negotiations between government, NGOs and international institutions a feature of its approach. Defining development policy as public action is an approach that involves synergies among diverse actors and across sectors.[5]

Endogenous development

The notion of the 'endogenous' refers to a social, cultural and symbolic space. Endogenous development implies a refutation of the view of development = modernization = westernization. Self-reliance, then, does not simply concern the means but the end of development: the goals and values of development are to be generated from within. 'Development is endogenous – there are no front runners to be followed' (Rahman 1993: 217). An implication is that modernity is viewed as generated *from within*. Modernization then is not a matter of just importing foreign models but also the 'modernization of tradition'. Imported modernization means the destruction of existing social and cultural capital – as in the clichéd modernization view of tradition as 'resistance to change', modernization as the development of enclaves (rooted in colonialism) and the resulting dualistic structure.[6] By contrast, modernization-from-within means the revalorization and adaptation of existing social and cultural capital. Rahman relates how traditional self-help groups in West Africa, the Naam, have taken on other functions. A broad stream of literature discusses many instances of grafting development onto 'traditional' organizations (Burne 1992, Carmen 1996, Pradervand 1989, Verhelst 1990). These instances open up our understanding of development as well as modernity. The 'modernization of tradition' releases local and popular energies in a way that the modernization approach of top-down mobilization and outside-in imposition could never achieve.

An endogenous outlook is fundamental to alternative development. Yet endogenism is difficult to turn into a 'hard' principle. Generally the boundary between inside and outside is one of the fundamental problems of development thinking (e.g. Gordon 1991). For what is the *unit* of development? The conventional framework used to be the 'society' (read nation, read state), a position that was challenged by Wallerstein (1979) who argued that the actual unit of development is the world-system (that is, the zone integrated by a division of labour in the production of goods necessary for reproduction). Alternative development introduces a diffuse range of alternative sites of endogeneity: people, community, local, grassroots.[7] Who are the *people* in 'people power'? Is it 'people' or 'the people' – in which case we are back with 'society'? Or does it involve a class element, as in 'popular sectors'? If endogenous means within the community, it leads to the question of ethnodevelopment (see below). If endogenous means within society, it leads to the question of globalization and the blurring of borders. External change agents or *animateurs* often play an important role in stimulating local processes or acting as brokers: this is another limit to endogeneity as a horizon (a point made by Friedmann 1992).

How far to take endogenism? For instance, are Islamic development approaches part of alternative development? They are endogenous, geared to basic needs, participatory and sustainable. Does this also apply to Islamist grassroots organizing, for instance in Egypt, Turkey, and for that matter Algeria (cf. Ibrahim 2008)? The community activities of Shiv Sena in Mumbai, an extreme right wing Hindutva organization, have been praised for their alternative development efforts (Esman and Upton 1984: 8). Organizations such as the Tamil Tigers (LTTE) are also known as effective community organizers. After endogenism the next stop may be ethno-chauvinism.

Ethnodevelopment

Endogenous development implies that each society should find its own strategy. But what is a society? An idea originally advocated by Rodolfo Stavenhagen (1986), with reference to the indigenous peoples in Latin America, and taken up by Hettne (1990), is ethnodevelopment. According to Friberg and Hettne (1985: 221), states are 'artificial territorial constructions' and 'small communities of human beings are the ultimate actors'. 'The concept of nation-state implies that the territorial boundaries of the state coincide with the boundaries of a culturally homogeneous nation. This is the exception rather than the rule in a world with about 1500 peoples or nations but only 150 states.' Therefore, 'The tribes and nations of the world are much more basic units of development, because they allow for the forging of a genuine consensus between their members. Normative convergence can only be obtained where people share a framework of social reasoning' (ibid.).

Under the guise of alternative radicalism, this is not merely nostalgic and conservative but also reactionary. It evokes false notions of 'consensus' and group boundaries based on a reification of *ethnos* = community. Friberg and Hettne note that 'Modernization always implies the decline and disintegration of natural communities' (1985: 233). First, this narrows modernization to exogenous modernization, eliminates the idea of modernization-from-within and thus denies the very idea of endogenous development. Second, should one accept these criteria as part of alternative development, it would mean alternative development upholding the same arguments as right wing opponents of multiculturalism in the west (and not only in the west): in the name of 'natural communities', immigrants can be banned; in the name of 'cultural homogeneity' as a condition for sharing 'a framework of social reasoning', multiculturalism can be declared inoperable. 'Natural communities' is the terminology of blood and soil politics. It is the kind of terminology that the followers of Hindutva in India would embrace. Endogenous development hardened to ethnodevelopment is a programme for separate development, for neo-apartheid and Bantustan politics, a programme for inward-looking deglobalization in the age of accelerated globalization.

This is alternative development at its worst. It evokes the spectre of ethnofundamentalism. The reasoning is insinuating: 1,500 peoples, therefore 1,500 nations-in-waiting? Once 'genuine consensus' among group members is the working criterion, an infinitesimal process of fissure is on the cards. In the contemporary world of 'ethnic cleansing' this sounds unbelievably naive. There may be constructive ways of valorizing ethnicity, for example in conjunction with local culture and the policies of decentralization. But a prerequisite for reconstructing ethnicity is deconstructing it, in the sense of recognizing its constructed character (Nederveen Pieterse 2007), and not recycling static notions such as 'natural communities' and blood and soil politics.

'Green authors tend to visualize the future as a world of cooperating and federated natural communities without strong centre–periphery gradients between them' (Friberg and Hettne 1985: 223). A further perennial problem of visualizing a future of autonomous communities, as in Green notions of bioregionalism, is that the relationship *among* communities or regions, which are inevitably differentially endowed in terms of resources, is not settled (cf. Young 1991). Friberg and Hettne are aware of the dark side of populism and the possibility of eco-fascism; they mention the resemblance of the Green movement to 1930s fascist movements and their emphasis on nature and folk culture (226).

Methodology

The hallmark of alternative development methodology is participation. Participatory Action Research, Rapid Rural Appraisal, as well as conscientization, critical pedagogy and empowerment are further elements in the alternative development repertoire. These elements are not specific or exclusive to alternative development. They have been developed in education, liberation theology and general development studies. Arguably what is specific to alternative development is the local and popular context in which they are applied. Participation is a deeply problematic notion; it is an improvement on top-down mobilization, but it remains paternalistic, unless the idea of participation is radically turned around, so that governments, international institutions or NGOs would be considered as participating in people's local development.[8]

Epistemology

Korten (1990) mentions the phenomenon of 'believing is seeing', or paradigms controlling perception. We tend to select and suppress information according to our beliefs. Alternative development in this sense claims a 'Copernican revolution' in understanding development. The key resource becomes not the country's aggregate GNP but people's creativity. This would also imply, for instance, that 'poverty' as such disappears as a clear-cut development indicator. Poverty as an indicator follows on from the development-as-growth paradigm: 'the poor' are the target of development because they lack economic resources. But if development is not about growth but about institutional transformation, then the concern is not merely with economic capital but as much with social, cultural, symbolic and moral capital and in these respects poor people can be rich. This introduces different distinctions such as the 'rooted' and the 'uprooted' poor (Carmen 1996). Stereotypes of poverty as wholesale deprivation, the 'culture of poverty', etc., are disabling elements of development discourse. They evoke the notion of development as external intervention. The keynote of alternative development epistemology is local knowledge.

Indigenous knowledge

Another keynote in alternative development and post-development thinking is critique of science. In India, the work of Ashis Nandy, Shiv Vishvanathan, Claude Alvares and Vandana Shiva is part of a wider critique-of-science movement. Vandana Shiva (1991) criticizes the Enlightenment model and seeks to formulate 'an alternative development paradigm'. Critique of science is also well developed in Latin America. According to Escobar (1992b), western science through development exercises a form of 'cultural violence on the Third World' and what is needed are 'alternative conceptions of knowledge'.

Critique-of-science movements involve dissident intellectuals, popular organizations and NGOs who oppose mainstream development expertise and policy, and network with movements in the west and Japan. Beck (1992) regards critique of science and technology as the main form of struggle in the 'new modernity' of 'risk society'. In view of the globalization of risk – such as global ecological hazards, the export of polluting industries and waste materials, the risks of biogenetic engineering, the spread of reproduction technologies – this is rapidly becoming a global contestation. In the south, 'indigenous knowledge' is a countervailing position to western science.

Tariq Banuri formulates a cultural critique of modernity focusing on what he calls the 'impersonality postulate of modernity: That impersonal relations are inherently superior to personal relations' (1990: 79). This yields a continuum of contrasting positions: with respect to ontology – from individualism to holism; with respect to cosmology – from instrumentalism to relational context; and epistemology – from positivism to hermeneutics. These contrasts parallel Carol Gilligan's (1982) distinction between masculine/feminine and impersonal/relational perspectives.[9] Banuri links a Foucauldian agenda of 'resurrection of subjugated knowledges' to a vision of the future in the south and argues in favour not only of a 'decentralized polity, economy, and society' but also of epistemological decentralization.

The problem, however, with the poststructuralist turn in development thinking is the same with poststructuralism in general: the critique of the Enlightenment easily slips into an adoption of the 'other Enlightenment' – romanticism and an unreflective reverence for tradition and community; or a postmodern conservatism, which in the end is barely distinguishable from anti-modern conservatism. Critique of science is inherent in late modernity and thus also in development thinking in its late phase; but it can take an unreflective or a reflexive form. If unreflective, it verges on anti-intellectualism, or possibly, intellectual anti-intellectualism.

The notion of indigenous knowledge has developed out of the regard for local knowledge (Brokensha et al. 1980; Chambers 1983; Hobart 1993). 'To ignore people's knowledge is almost to ensure failure in development' (Agrawal 1995b: 3). Indigenous knowledge, or the practical knowledge of people in other cultures, gives substance and depth to otherwise rhetorical categories such as endogenous development.[10] Yet it is difficult, as with other alternative development orientations, to turn indigenous knowledge into a clear-cut principle in view of the absence of a hard boundary between indigenous and other forms of knowledge. After all, what is 'indigenous'? This too is a construction and one that is not devoid of romantic overtones. Agrawal (1995a) makes a persuasive case that there are no principled grounds on the basis of which indigenous knowledge can be distinguished from scientific knowledge. Rather than pursuing indigenous knowledge per se, Agrawal advocates combining and blending knowledge systems. This caution is not meant to neutralize criticisms from an 'indigenous' point of view but is a necessary qualification if we want to take these concerns seriously, for instance in relation to questions such as indigenous intellectual property rights or traditional resource rights (Posey 1994).

Development cooperation

With redefining development comes a different assessment of international development cooperation. The general trend is away from development assistance to cooperation and partnership. As Korten notes, the consequences of development assistance or international aid have all too often been anti-developmental: 'it *reduces* capacities for sustained self-reliant development' (1990: 139). Conventional development assistance is a matter of 'moving money' rather than 'building capacity'. This involves the familiar distinction between relief (welfare) and development: 'Where the needs are chronic, rather than temporary, increasing the amount of humanitarian assistance, especially food aid, is likely to exacerbate the problem' (ibid.).

The principle of people's sovereignty or popular legitimacy as the basis of sovereignty involves a redefinition of development cooperation as principally a matter of people-to-people relations in which governments play a mediating and enabling role. Development cooperation then needs to be redefined as a process of 'mutual empowerment' (Korten 1990: 146–7; see also Duffield 1996).

If we would group the elements discussed above as an alternative development model in contrast to a conventional development model centred on growth, the result might be as shown in Table 6.1. The question still remains as to whether this would constitute an alternative development paradigm or just a profile; for now, the slightly more neutral terminology of models is adopted. Since profiles in each model differ over time, several boxes indicate multiple options.

Accepting these as the contours of an alternative development paradigm has several attractions. Alternative development ceases to be *any* alternative in relation to mainstream development. Alternative development as a diffuse

Table 6.1   *Contrasting development models*

Models	Growth	Social transformation
Objectives	Accumulation	Capacitation, human development
Resources	Capital, technology, trade, foreign investment, external expertise	Human resources, social capital, local knowledge
Features	Growth-led	Equity-led
Agency	State-led or market-led	People, community. Synergies between society, government, market
Epistemology	Science	Critique of science, indigenous knowledge
Modalities	Exogenous examples, demonstration effect, modernity vs. tradition, technology transfer	Endogenous development, modernization from within, modernization of tradition
Methods	Import substitution industrialization, export-led growth, growth poles, innovation, structural adjustment	Participation, sustainability, democratization
Social policy	Trickle-down. Safety net	Trickle-up. Social capacitation through redistribution
Development cooperation	Aid, assistance	Partnership, mutual obligation
Indicators	GDP	Green GDP, Human Development Index, institutional densities

position might be effective for alternative development as critique but not as a programme to be implemented. An alternative development paradigm might help the chances for alternative development to gain recognition and institutional support, which is necessary if it is no longer about marginal local initiatives supported by NGOs, but if it aims to be a large-scale over-haul of development as such. If alternative development is about wide-ranging synergies between communities, government agencies, international institutions and business, then its profile must be both distinct enough and acceptable enough to generate support in institutional circles and diverse interest communities. Yet this raises different questions. A serious discussion of alternative development as a paradigm would involve its negotiation and fine-tuning in wide circles. This treatment cannot prejudge such a broad discussion; but what it does raise is a more fundamental question: whether the notion of paradigm is applicable at all.

Paradigm politics

The world is tired of grand solutions. (Manfred Max-Neef 1991: 110)

To match Kuhn's concept, a paradigm shift in development would have to meet three conditions: it must provide a metatheory, be accepted by a community of practitioners, and have a body of successful practice, including exemplars that can be held up as paradigms in practice. Sato and Smith (1996: 90) mention these requirements, but their brief chapter fails to deliver a metatheory. In my view more fundamental questions need to be asked. What is the status of a paradigm and is this concept and that of paradigm shift relevant to social science? A paradigm in the sense of Thomas Kuhn (1962) refers to the explanatory power of a theoretical model and its institutional ramifications for the structure and organization of science. The point of Kuhn's analysis is a critique of positivism, particularly in the natural sciences. Kuhn's position was that social science is 'pre-paradigmatic' because a scholarly consensus such as exists in physics or biology is not available in social science.

If we consider this more closely, in the social sciences positivism is largely a past station, except in some forms of economics. The interpretative character of social science has become widely accepted since phenomenology, hermeneutics and the linguistic turn. Also if one does not accept discourse analysis and deconstruction as analytic instruments, the time of blind faith in models and grand theories is past. It is generally understood that social sciences are of an extraordinary complexity because they involve political processes that are reflexive in nature, in the sense that social actors will act upon any theory, which is thus modified in action. Constructivism is widely accepted as a theoretical framework in relation to social phenomena as well as in relation to social science theories, which of course are also social phenomena. In constructivism, notions of paradigm and paradigm shift are built in. Pierre Bourdieu's (1988) analyses of social science in action are an example and so is his notion of reflexive sociology. It follows that in relation to reflexive social science the concept of paradigm does not hold and that social science is basically 'post-paradigmatic' or, at least, non-paradigmatic. In social science 'paradigm' may be used in a loose sense but it does not serve the same function of a critique of positivism as in the natural sciences, nor does it adequately describe the organization of science.

Recent years have witnessed an outburst of claims for new paradigms in social science, development studies included – a kind of new paradigm epidemic. Paradigm shift is a central theme of postmodernism (Bauman 1992, McHale 1992, Santos 1996) and also figures in claims for 'new science' (Capra 1988). Lipietz (1995) presents political ecology as a new paradigm. Hazel Henderson's work centres on paradigm shifts (1991, 1996a, 1996b). Mahbub ul Haq (1995) proposes a human development paradigm. Norman Long's (1994) 'actor-oriented paradigm' refers to a critique of structuralist approaches in development and a return to anthropological sensibilities.

What is the point of these exercises in a general context of reflexive, constructivist social science? It does signal a watershed, at minimum a more reflexive mentality in social science. But is borrowing from the natural sciences an appropriate move? One impression is that the claims to paradigm shifts primarily serve a political purpose. What is at issue is a claim for political unity and convergence: by emphasizing the intellectual convergence of diverse elements, the chances for a political cohesion of diverse constituencies may be enhanced. Part of the appeal of Kuhn's paradigm shift is the element of revolution or a drastic break in intellectual and therefore political practice. But in fact in current usages paradigm is used in a broad and loose sense of an 'intellectual framework', similar to discourse and *episteme*, and not in Kuhn's more specific sense of an explanatory framework that defines the practice of 'normal science'. More often it concerns normative values rather than explanatory and metatheoretical frameworks.

Development, even though it hinges on theory as the beacon of policy, is more concerned with policy than explanatory frameworks. In development, the claim of a paradigm shift means that a policy framework has changed. Thus, ul Haq's human development paradigm refers to a set of normative orientations – equity, sustainability, productivity, empowerment – and not merely to a different explanatory framework. There are still further reasons why the notion of a paradigm shift may not apply to development or alternative development.

The first consideration is diversity in the south. If conventional developmentalism (growth, modernization, neoclassical economics) is no longer acceptable because of its linear logic and universalist pretension, why should an alternative development paradigm hold? There are now 'five Souths' (Group of Lisbon 1995) and a wide range of local variations within each of these: how could a single paradigm encompass such a diversity of development paths, needs and circumstances? Besides, would a new orthodoxy really be desirable? Is what is needed not rather a post-paradigmatic perspective? The diffuseness of alternative development may also be an analytical advantage. Alternative development as a loosely interconnected ensemble of sensibilities and practices is more flexible in resonating with diverse situations than an alternative development paradigm. While a paradigm shift implies a revolution in relation to past work, it means routinization in relation to future work. It would fix a practice of 'normal development'. In view of the diversity and flux of the development field such routinization may precisely not be what is desirable. In other words, the urge toward paradigm renewal may itself be inappropriate.

Further considerations in relation to an alternative development paradigm are the following.

- The various elements of the alternative development package are each meaningful but none of them can be turned into a firm, hard principle: it follows that alternative development as a paradigm cannot stand up either. The strength of alternative development positions is critical, rather than programmatic.
- The elements of the alternative development paradigm are contradictory. In effect endogenism as a principle annuls any general formulation of alternative development. 'If the people are the principal actors in the alternative development paradigm, *the relevant reality must be the people's own, constructed by them only*' (Rahman 1993: 220, emphasis in original). By this logic, how can there be a general alternative development theory, let alone a paradigm? There can only be a sprawling archipelago of local alternative perspectives.
- The valorization of indigenous knowledge has similar implications. Giving the alternative development paradigm the status of a metatheory – the usual way out of 'Zeno's paradox' ('the Cretan says that all Cretans are liars') – does not work in this case because it establishes outsiders as experts over insiders.

There is also an institutional dimension to this question. There may be political advantages as well as disadvantages to a sharp break with mainstream development. Sanyal (1994) argues that alternative development has withered because it has not found institutional support since agencies, bureaucracies and ministries cannot handle sharp discontinuities in principles and practices (discussed further under 'Mainstream development' below).

The above considerations apply to the *broad* alternative development paradigm (*à la* Hettne, Rahman, Carmen and others), while the Bretton Woods challengers propose a much narrower alternative development paradigm of equitable, sustainable and participatory development. Here a different problem applies: the distinction between the *narrow* alternative development paradigm and mainstream development exists as a rhetorical claim only, for the sole distinctive feature is the insistence that development be equitable. This implies a critique of the trickle-down principle of neoclassical economics; but that too, even in the mainstream, is nowadays hardly a controversial point. This, then, is a clear instance of 'paradigm politics'.

Mainstream development

Mainstream development here refers to everyday development talk in developing countries, international institutions and international development cooperation. It now seems a long time since development was defined as growth and simply measured by means of per capita GNP. Gradually, starting with basic needs and other heterodox approaches in the 1970s, development has been redefined as enlargement of people's choices and human capacitation (Sen 1985) and as if people, basic needs, health, literacy, education and housing matter. The Human Development Index has become an influential standard. People-centred development has become a mainstream position.

Hence there is now considerable overlap between mainstream and alternative development, which share much the same rhetoric, ideals and definition of development: participation, work with the poor and vulnerable groups, local action. This overlap is not always apparent from alternative development discourses, which often tend to stereotype mainstream approaches. This may be a matter of institutional lag or ignorance about changes in the mainstream; or antagonistic posturing in terms of 'us' and 'them', building up the alternative appeal by emphasizing the backwardness of the mainstream. Adherents of alternative development hold different views on the nature of the relationship between alternative and mainstream development. Two extreme positions are that alternative development is to be as distinct and separate from mainstream development as possible (e.g. most Bretton Woods challengers, Kothari, in some respects Korten), or that continuity between mainstream and alternative development both exists and is desirable (e.g. Wignaraja 1992). Most proponents of an alternative development paradigm posit a contradiction between growth and structural reform on the one hand and alternative development on the other. Ul Haq, as a proponent of human development, does not see a contradiction between human development and structural reform. His human development paradigm is identical to the alternative development paradigm except that, characteristically, it includes *production* as a core value.

This also implies a tension between alternative and human development. The limitation of human development, according to some, is that critical concerns are being instrumentalized short of the overhaul of the development-as-growth model, so that in effect development business-as-usual can carry on under a different umbrella. What we see is still a 'fetishism of numbers' (Max-Neef 1991). Friedmann (1992) mentions, besides human and citizen rights, 'human flourishing' as the value orientation of alternative development, precisely to counteract its operationalization in indices such as the Human Development Index. This affirms that alternative development is about something beyond merely another set of measuring standards, which is a point worth making – but only if we *also* consider the importance of indices such as HDI in influencing policy frameworks (Henderson 1996b; ul Haq 1995). Implementation is desirable, practicalities are prosaic, and institutions need measurements. Human flourishing exceeds but also requires human development. In analogy with Moser's (1991) argument on gender needs, one could say that alternative development is not only about practical but also about strategic needs, that is, a profound redistribution of resources within societies and on a world scale. Except that the alternative development paradigm stakes an even larger claim: the total overhaul of development.

According to Rajni Kothari (1993b), alternatives have been coopted, resulting in 'a world without alternatives'. Kothari complains of 'deep cooptation': not only organizations but also mentalities have changed, a critical edge has been lost. He observes 'the consumerism and commercialisation of diverse human enterprise, the basic crisis of vision – in a sense, an end of "alternatives" in the real and comprehensive sense of the term' (1993b: 136). This kind of pessimism, while understandable, seems somehow illogical: what reason is there to assume, short of a fundamental shift in human nature, that the creativity that has given rise to alternatives in one context will not find different avenues of expression, whatever the circumstances and indeed prompted by them? That emancipation can be successful should not be held against it – although it often is, as if a Sisyphean task were a seal of purity. Of course, Kothari views cooptation not as success but as capitulation; but isn't the record much more varied? Cooptation, besides being logical in view of how the development field is structured, may be desirable if it means a greater chance that once-marginal views are implemented. There is cause to regret cooptation mainly if one regards alternative development as a position external to the system; but this kind of island mentality is as sterile, as delinking, as a national development strategy. Governments and NGOs are factually interdependent in terms of agenda setting and funding. The entire field is changing, including government organizations.

An intermediate option is the 'growth plus' approach: growth *plus* redistribution, participation, human development, or 'sustainable growth'. 'Redistribution with growth' was a prominent position in the 1970s (Chenery et al. 1974). Structural adjustment with a human face has been an in-between position (Jolly 1986). Korten views 'adding on' as a weakness of alternatives and therefore seeks to establish as sharp as possible a break with conventional positions. However, from the point of view of institutional acceptance and policy implementation, 'adding on' may rather be a source of strength, because for bureaucracies in welfare ministries and international agencies total breaks are much more difficult to handle than additional policy options (Sanyal 1994). In view of such ramifications, is it necessary or wise to formulate alternative development as anti-growth? Ul Haq argues for continuity rather than a plain contradiction, between growth and human development. In his view the key issue is the *quality* of growth. Ul Haq builds on the redistribution with a growth position; the difference is that, while arguing for theoretical continuity and policy refinement, he also claims the status of a new paradigm and a 'revolutionary' role for human development. A different consideration is that substantively the nature of economic growth itself is undergoing rethinking, also in the north. An increasingly prominent line of research concerns the links between growth and social development and the idea that social capital is crucial to economic development (see Chapter 8).

Conclusion

Development is not what it used to be. It might be argued that the big hiatus in development now no longer runs between mainstream and alternative development but within mainstream development. Mainstream development now incorporates many alternative development elements and practices. It is the vast stretch of contemporary mainstream development, from the Bretton Woods institutions all the way to grassroots empowerment, which makes for its cacophonic character. Broadly speaking, the divide now runs between human and alternative development, on the one hand, and the number-crunching approach to development, the positivism of growth, on the other. Institutionally this rift runs between the UN agencies and the IMF, with the World Bank straddled precariously somewhere in the middle.

The differences between alternative and human development are significant enough but not as wide as those between them and the 'Washington consensus', or what remains of it. Human development is better positioned institutionally than alternative development, from the UN system to economics and social welfare ministries in the south; on the other hand, it tends to be bureaucratic in outlook. The bottom-line agency of the human development approach is the state, whereas the agency of alternative development is local and social movement activism. To alternative development there is a protest element against development-business-as-usual, which represents a grassroots take on development that is probably irreplaceable; witness contributions such as participatory action research. Alternative development brings anthropology into development. Yet, alternative development cannot walk away from the role of the state. Education, health care and infrastructure cannot be left to local alternative development. Economic development requires state action. More recent alternative approaches argue that a strong civil society needs a strong state (Brohman 1996, Friedmann 1992). This also follows on from the need to combine micro and macro development approaches. Human development provides an enabling perspective on the developmental role of the state. Thus, together, alternative and human development represent a combination of local, grassroots and state perspectives. Both approaches involve different perspectives on global reform. Neither is complete; alternative development cannot do without the state; human development cannot function or flourish without an active civil society, nationally and internationally. What matters, after all, is the direction and character of overall development. In this context the differences between alternative and human development are relatively minor.

The key issue is the relationship between social and human development and the policies followed by international institutions.

Notes

1   The idea of counterpoint is inspired by Wertheim's theory of emancipation in which counterpoint plays a key role (Wertheim 1974; cf. Nederveen Pieterse 1989, ch. 3, 'Counterpoint and emancipation').

2   In the 1995 edition of his book, Hettne fine-tunes his position on alternative development in terms of three principles: 'The principle of territorialism as a counterpoint to functionalism. The principle of cultural pluralism as a counterpoint to standardized modernization. The principle of ecological sustainability as a counterpoint to "growth" and consumerism' (1995: 199). These reformulations are hardly improvements. Territorialism is a spatial demarcation of development that is as problematic as ethnodevelopment. Cultural pluralism is now widely accepted and thematized in the culture and development approach (Chapter 5 above). Contrasting sustainability and growth is crude; ul Haq's point that what matters is not growth but the quality of growth is more to the point.

3   Sources include the Dag Hammarskjöld Foundation (1975), Nerfin (1977), Wolfe (1981), Klauss and Korten (1984), Drabek (1987), Korten (1990), Hettne (1990), Max-Neef (1991), Friedmann (1992), Rahman (1993), Carmen (1996) and a wide array of articles in books and journals (such as *International Foundation for Development Alternatives*, which dissolved in the early 1990s, and *Alternatives*). Critiques of alternative development are Latouche (1993), Sanyal (1994) and Cowen and Shenton (1996: 457–72).

4   This is the context of Carmen (1996), Coetzee (1989), Guha and Vivekenanda (1985) and also of my work. I used to teach in an MA programme on Politics of Alternative Development Strategies at an international graduate school in development studies. As an anthropologist by training and after years spent living in countries in the south, my interests range from local development to global alternatives.

5   See Wuyts et al. 1992. Brown and Ashman 1996, 1999, discuss factors that make intersectoral cooperation fail or succeed.

6   New modernization theory, as So (1990) notes, takes into account traditions as sources of innovation and not just as 'resistance to change'.

7   Sundaram (1994) draws a distinction between 'development from below', which he views as the domain of local, district or regional government, and 'development from within' as the terrain of the village or grassroots. This distinction between endogenous (local government) and within (village) is unusual. I owe this reference to Aurora Galindo.

8   See critiques of participation by Estava 1985b, Nederveen Pieterse 1992b, Stiefel and Wolfe 1994, Cooke and Kothari 2001.

9   Western social theories, according to Banuri (1990), view everything – exchange, production, jurisprudence, education, political science, etc. – through the prism of impersonality. Banuri cites Ashis Nandy's definition of progress as 'an expansion of the awareness of oppression' (1990: 91). Gilles Deleuze said about Foucault, 'You have taught something absolutely fundamental: The indignity of speaking on someone else's behalf' (quoted in

Banuri: 96). From this follows a critique of the role of the expert: 'It is not for the outside expert to insist that the goals which he or she thinks worth pursuing are the ones which should be pursued by all societies ... the crisis if any stems precisely from the centralized intervention itself' (97). He concludes that 'the main task of the theorist ... is to help strengthen resistance against oppressive institutions'. See Cowen and Shenton (1996: 453–61) on the ironies of this position.

10 A relevant journal is *Indigenous Knowledge and Development Monitor*. In 1993 a Foundation for the Promotion of Indigenous Knowledge Based Development was set up in Mysore, India, along with a Centre for Advanced Research of Indigenous Knowledge Systems. See Goonatilake 1999.

7

After Post-development

> The idea of development stands like a ruin in the intellectual landscape. Delusion and disappointment, failures and crime have been the steady companions of development and they tell a common story: it did not work. Moreover, the historical conditions which catapulted the idea into prominence have vanished: development has become outdated. (Wolfgang Sachs 1992b: 1)

Along with 'anti-development' and 'beyond development', post-development is a radical reaction to the dilemmas of development. Perplexity and extreme dissatisfaction with business-as-usual and standard development rhetoric and practice, and a disillusion with alternative development, are keynotes of this perspective. Development is rejected because it is the 'new religion of the West' (Rist 1990a), it is the imposition of science as power (Nandy 1988), it does not work (Kothari 1988), it means cultural westernization and homogenization (Constantino 1985) and brings environmental destruction. It is rejected not merely on account of its results but because of its intentions, its worldview and mindset. The mindset of economism implies a reductionist take on existence. Thus, according to Sachs, 'it is not the failure of development which has to be feared, but its success' (1992b: 3).

Post-development starts out from a basic realization: that attaining a middle-class life style for the majority of the world's population is impossible (Dasgupta 1985). In time this has led to a position of the total rejection of development. In the words of Gustavo Esteva,

> If you live in Mexico City today, you are either rich or numb if you fail to notice that development stinks ... The time has come to recognize development itself as the malignant myth whose pursuit threatens these among whom I live in Mexico ... [T]he 'three development decades' were a huge, irresponsible experiment that, in the experience of a world-majority, failed miserably. (1985: 78)

Post-development overlaps with western critiques of modernity and techno-scientific progress, such as critical theory, poststructuralism and ecological movements. It parallels alternative development and cultural critiques of development. It stands to development as 'deep ecology' does to environmental management. There are different strands to this way of looking at development. *Anti-development* is rejectionism inspired by anger with development business-as-usual. *Beyond development* ('*au delà de développement*') combines this aversion with looking over the fence. In *post-development*, these are combined with a Foucauldian methodology and theoretical framework of discourse analysis and a politics inspired by poststructuralism. These positions are not all consistent and besides, as a recent approach, post-development thinking is not theoretically developed. The overlap among these sensibilities is sufficient to group them together here under the heading of post-development.

Development is the management of a promise – and what if the promise does not deliver? Living in Chiapas or other oppressed and poor areas, chances are that development is a bad joke. The question is what is to be done with this assessment. Post-development is not alone in looking at the shadow of development; all critical approaches to development deal with its dark side. Dependency theory raises the question of global inequality. Alternative development focuses on the lack of popular participation. Human development addresses the need to invest in people. Post-development focuses on the underlying premises and motives of development, and what sets it apart from other critical approaches is its rejection of development. The question is whether this is a tenable and fruitful position.

In the 1980s these views crystallized around the journal *Development: Seeds for Change*. They have been taken up by intellectuals in Latin America (Esteva, Escobar), India (see Dallmayr 1996 on the 'Delhi school'), Pakistan (Rahnema and Bawtree 1997), Malaysia (Just World Trust 1995), France (Latouche 1993), Switzerland (Rist 1997), Germany (Sachs 1992a), Belgium (Verhelst 1990), England (Seabrook 1994), Ireland (Tucker 1999), and Japan (Lummis 1991). They have become prominent since they coalesce with ecological critiques and ecofeminism (Mies 1986, Shiva 1988b) and through bestsellers such as Sachs's *Development Dictionary*.

First we will consider some of the overt positions of post-development – the problematization of poverty, the portrayal of development as westernization, and the critique of modernism and science. The argument then turns to the methodological dimension of discourse analysis of development. We will then look at the difference between alternative development and 'alternatives to development'. The reasons why this difference is made out to be so large are, in my interpretation, anti-managerialism and dichotomic thinking. This exposition closes with a discussion of the politics of post-development and a critical assessment.

Problematizing poverty

An insight that runs through post-development is that poverty is not to be taken for granted. In the words of Vandana Shiva:

> Culturally perceived poverty need not be real material poverty: subsistence economies which serve basic needs through self-provisioning are not poor in the sense of being deprived. Yet the ideology of development declares them so because they don't participate overwhelmingly in the market economy, and do not consume commodities provided for and distributed through the market. (1988b: 10)

Poverty is in the eye of the beholder. Sachs (1989) distinguishes between *frugality*, as in subsistence economies; *destitution*, which can arise when subsistence economies are weakened through the interference of growth strategies; and *scarcity*, which arises when the logic of growth and accumulation has taken over and commodity-based need becomes the overriding logic. In this early work, Sachs's policy recommendation is to implement growth strategies with caution, building on frugal lifestyles. This matches the recommendations made by 'ecological developers' all along, such as the agronomist René Dumont (1965, 1974), to follow growth strategies in tandem with appropriate technology and the maximum use of local resources. But the rejection of either growth or development does not follow.

'Poverty' is not simply a deficit, for that is simply to adopt the commodity-based perspective of the north; 'poverty' can also be a resource. Attributing agency to the poor is a common principle in alternative approaches such as conscientization *à la* Paulo Freire, human-scale development (Chambers 1983, Max-Neef 1982, 1991), participatory action research and the actor-oriented approach. According to Rahnema, poverty is real enough, but is also a culturally and historically variable notion. 'The way planners, development actomaniacs and politicians living off global poverty alleviation campaigns are presenting their case, gives the uninformed public a distorted impression of how the world's impoverished are living their deprivations. Not only are these people presented as incapable of doing anything intelligent by themselves, but also as preventing the modern do-gooders from helping them' (1992: 169). This is a different issue: it concerns the representation of poverty. By way of a counterpoint, Rahnema draws attention to 'vernacular universes' that provide hope and strength; to the spiritual dimension ('Most contemporary grassroots movements have a strong spiritual dimension'; 171); and to 'convivial poverty', 'that is, voluntary or moral poverty' (171). This suggests an affinity with the lineage of the Franciscans, liberation theology and Gandhian politics.

In this view, it is the economism of development that is truly pauperizing. While these considerations may be valid up to a point, a consequence is that poverty alleviation and elimination, for what these efforts are worth, slip off the map. Another problem is that less market participation does not necessarily imply more social participation, lest we homogenize and romanticize poverty, and equate poverty with purity (and the indigenous and local with the original and authentic). The step from a statistical universe to a moral universe is worth taking, but surely a moral universe also involves action, and which action will follow?

Development = westernization

> The debate over the word 'development' is not merely a question of words. Whether one likes it or not, one can't make development different from what it has been. Development has been and still is the *Westernisation of the world*. (Serge Latouche 1993: 160; emphasis in original)

According to Escobar, the problem with 'Development' is that it is external, based on the model of the industrialized world, and what is needed instead are 'more endogenous discourses'. The assertion of 'endogenous development' calls to mind dependency theory and the 'foreign bad, local good' position (Kiely 1999). According to Rajni Kothari, 'where colonialism left off, development took over' (1988: 143). This view is as old as the critique of modernization theory. It calls to mind the momentum and pathos of decolonization, the arguments against cultural imperialism, Coca-Colonization, McDonaldization, Disneyfication, Barbiefication and the cultural homogenization thesis according to which western media, advertising and consumerism induce cultural uniformity.

All this may be satisfying, like the sound of a familiar tune, but it is also one-sided and old-fashioned. In effect, it denies the agency of the south. It also denies the extent to which the south owns development. It entirely overlooks – as do development studies generally – the deep lineage of development thinking in the reformers in the south, from Muhammad Ali in Egypt, the Tanzimat reforms during Ottoman rule, Japan's missions to the west followed by the Meiji Restoration, and the *científicos* in Latin America. A common strand in these projects is an awareness of a technology and development gap with the west and attempts at catching up. In the early twentieth century, this drives the Young Turks and Young Persians, Kemalism in Turkey, and inspires catch-up ideologies such as *seonjinguk* in South Korea. All this reflects Eurocentrism but also transformation drives which are at times inspired by non-western examples. Thus, *seonjinguk* in South Korea at some point may also reflect Japan's rise and its victory in the war with Russia.[1]

Several recent development perspectives originate to a considerable extent in the south, such as dependency theory, alternative development and human development. Furthermore, what about 'easternization' as in the East Asian model, touted by the World Bank as a development miracle? What about Japanization, as in the 'Japanese challenge', the influence of Japanese management techniques and Toyotism (Kaplinsky 1994)? At any rate, 'westernization' is a lumping concept that ignores diverse historical currents. Latouche and others use the bulky category 'the West', which in view of steep historical differences between Europe and North America is not really meaningful. This argument also overlooks more complex assessments of globalization. A more appropriate analytic is polycentrism. Then, the rejoinder to Eurocentrism is not third worldism but a recognition that multiple centres, also in the south, now shape development discourse (Amin 1989; see also Chapter 2 above). In the twenty-first century this is more appropriate than ever (see Chapter 12 below).

Critique of modernism

Part of the anti-western sentiment is anti-modernism. No doubt development suffers from a condition of 'psychological modernism', has erected monuments to modernism, a vast infrastructure and big dams – placing technological progress over human development. States in the south have used science as instruments of power, creating 'laboratory states' (Scott 1998, Visvanathan 1988), as in Rajiv Gandhi's high-tech modernization drive in India and Indonesia's experiment in aircraft technology. In Latin America, the work of the *cientificos* is not yet complete. Brazil's commitment to high modernism is on display in Brasilia (Berman 1988). Islamabad in Pakistan is another grid-planned capital city without heart or character. The 1998 nuclear tests in South Asia were another rendezvous of science and *raison d'état* (Subrahmanyam 1998). For Gilbert Rist development thinking represents the 'new religion of the West' (1990a), but indeed the worship of progress is not reserved for the west.

Aversion to modernism also exists in the west; rationalism is one face of the Enlightenment and romanticism is another. There are many affinities and overlaps between critical theory and the counterculture in the west (Berman 1988, Roszak 1973, Toulmin 1990) and anti-modernism in the south. Schumacher ('small is beautiful') found inspiration in Buddhist economics (Wood 1984) and Fritjof Capra in eastern mysticism, while Ashis Nandy's outlook has been shaped by Freud, the Frankfurt School and Californian psychology.

Part of the critique of modernism is the critique of science. A leitmotif, also in ecological thinking, is to view science as power. 'Science' here means Cartesianism, Enlightenment thinking and positivism, an instrument in achieving mastery over nature. Critique of Enlightenment science runs through the work of Vandana Shiva (1991). But this is not a simple argument. For one thing, science has been renewing itself, for example in quantum physics and chaos theory, and undergoing paradigm shifts leading to 'new science'. In addition there are countertrends within science, such as the methodological anarchism of Feyerabend and the work of Latour (1993). In social science, positivism is no longer the dominant temperament; increasingly the common sense in social science is constructivism. In economics positivism prevails, but is also under attack. Thus, for Hazel Henderson economics is not science but politics in disguise (1996b). A clear distinction should be made between *critique of science* and *anti-science*. Acknowledging the limitations of science, the role of power/knowledge and the uses made of scientific knowledge does not necessarily mean being anti-science. Critique of science is now a defining feature of new social movements north and south (Beck 1992). Ecological movements use scientific methods of monitoring energy use, pollution and climate changes. 'Green accounting' and 'greening the GDP' use scientific standards, but for different ends than previously. Anti-development at times sounds like Luddism, with more rhetoric than analysis and not altogether consistent (e.g. Alvares 1992).[2] From a third world viewpoint, too, there are other options besides anti-science (e.g. Goonatilake 1999).

It is more appropriate to view modernism as a complex historical trend, which is in part at odds with simple modernization. Thus, the dialectics of modernity are *part* of modernity and have given rise to critical theory, reflexive modernity and so forth. Ironically, aversion to modernism as style is also an expression of high modernism, late modernity and postmodernism (cf. Chapters 9 and 11 below).

Development as discourse

According to Escobar, the 'discourse of Development', like the Orientalism analysed by Edward Said, has been a 'mechanism for the production and management of the Third World ... organizing the production of truth about the Third World' (1992b: 413–14). A standard Escobar text is: 'Development can best be described as an apparatus that links forms of knowledge about the Third World with the deployment of forms of power and intervention, resulting in the mapping and production of Third World societies' (1996: 213).

Discourse analysis forms part of the 'linguistic turn' in social science. It involves the careful scrutiny of language and text as a framework of presuppositions and structures of thought, penetrating further than ideology critique. Prominent in literature criticism, discourse analysis has been applied extensively in cultural studies, feminism, black studies, and now in social science generally. Discourse analysis contributes to understanding colonialism as an epistemological regime (Mitchell 1988), it can serve to analyse the 'development machine' (Ferguson 1990) and development project talk (Apthorpe and Gasper 1996, Rew 1997) and has become a critical genre in development studies (Crush 1996a, Grillo and Stirrat 1997). Discourse analysis applied to development is the methodological basis of post-development, which in itself it is not specific to post-development; what is distinctive for post-development is that from a methodology, discourse analysis has been turned into an ideological platform.

Escobar (1992b: 419) concurs with Gustavo Esteva that development is a 'Frankenstein-type dream', an 'alien model of exploitation' and besides reflects urban bias. 'The dream of Development is over' and what is needed is 'Not more Development but a different regime of truth and perception' (ibid. 412–14). Escobar refers to a 'group of scholars engaging in the most radical critique of Development' viewed as the 'ideological expression of postwar capital expansion'. In this view, World Bank studies and documents 'all repeat the same story'. 'Development colonized reality, it became reality'. It 'may be now a past era'. 'The dream of Development is over' (419). To 'establish a discontinuity, a new discursive practice' it is appropriate to 'undertake an archaeology of Development' (414–15). To effect change means to effect a 'change in the order of discourse', to open up the 'possibility to think reality differently'. The grassroots orientation disrupts the link between development, capital and science and thus destabilizes the 'grid of the Development apparatus' (424).

Escobar's perspective provides a broad and uneven *mélange*, with exaggerated claims sustained by weak examples. Broad in combining vocabularies: poststructuralism, social movement theory and development. Uneven in that the argument centres on anti-development but makes no clear distinction between anti-development and alternative development. Exaggerated in that his position hinges on a discursive trick, a rhetorical ploy of equating development with 'Development'. This in itself militates against discourse analysis, caricatures and homogenizes development, and conceals divergencies within development. His perspective on actual development is flimsy and based on confused examples, with more rhetoric than logic. For instance, the claim that the World Bank stories are 'all the same' ignores the tremendous discontinuities in the Bank's discourse over time (e.g. the redistribution with growth in the 1970s, structural adjustment in the 1980s, poverty alleviation and the knowledge bank in the 1990s). And while Escobar and Esteva associate 'Development' with urban bias, the World Bank and structural adjustment in the 1980s have been precisely aimed at correcting 'urban parasitism', which had long been a standard criticism of nationalist development policies (a classic source here is Lipton 1977).

Alternatives *to* development

Many of the concerns of post-development are not new and are shared by other critical approaches to development. Post-development parallels dependency theory in seeking autonomy from external dependency, but is now taken further to development as a power/knowledge regime. Post-development faith in the endogenous resembles dependency theory and alternative development, as in the emphasis on self-reliance. Whereas dependency thinking privileges the nation state, post-development, like alternative development, privileges a local and grassroots autonomy. Alternative development occupies an in-between position: with post-development it shares the radical critiques of mainstream development, but it retains a belief in and accordingly redefines development. The record of development is mixed and includes achievements, so what is the point of rejecting it *in toto*? In many ways the line between alternative and post-development is quite fine, again except for the rejection of development.

Scanning 'the present landscape of Development alternatives' looking for 'a new reality', Escobar is 'not interested in Development alternatives, but rather in alternatives to Development'. Alternative development is rejected because 'most of the efforts are also products of the same worldview which has produced the mainstream concept of science, liberation and development' (Nandy 1989: 270). Latouche (1993: 161) goes further:

> The most dangerous solicitations, the sirens with the most insidious song, are not those of the 'true blue' and 'hard' development, but rather those of what is called 'alternative' development. This term can in effect encompass any hope or ideal that one might wish to project into the harsh realities of existence. The fact that it presents a friendly exterior makes 'alternative' development all the more dangerous.

This echoes Esteva's fulmination against those who 'want to cover the stench of "Development" with "Alternative Development" as a deodorant' (1985: 78).

Latouche examines 'three principal planks of alternative development: food self-sufficiency; basic needs; and appropriate technologies' and finds each of them wanting (1993: 161). In fact these were part of 'another development' in the 1970s and are no longer specific to alternative development in the 1990s, if only because they have entered mainstream development discourse. Latouche maintains that:

> The opposition between 'alternative development' and *alternative to* development is radical, irreconcilable and one of essence, both in the abstract and in theoretical analysis ... Under the heading of 'alternative development', a wide range of 'anti-productivist' and anti-capitalist platforms are put forward, all of which aim at eliminating the sore spots of underdevelopment and the excesses of maldevelopment. (159)

At this point other arguments come into the picture: anti-managerialism and dichotomic thinking. These are not necessarily part of the explicitly stated post-development view, but they might explain the size of the gap between alternative development and post-development.

Anti-managerialism

Development thinking is steeped in social engineering and the ambition to shape economies and societies, which makes it an interventionist and managerialist discipline. It involves telling other people what to do – in the name of modernization, nation building, progress, mobilization, sustainable development, human rights, poverty alleviation, and even empowerment and participation (participatory management). Through post-development runs an anti-authoritarian sensibility, an aversion to control and perhaps an anarchist streak. Poststructuralism too involves an 'anti-political' sensibility, as a late-modern scepticism. If the public sphere is constructed through discourse and if any discourse is another claim to truth and therefore a claim to power, what would follow is political agnosticism. This also arises from the preoccupation with autonomy, the problem of representation and the indignity of representing 'others'.[3]

Douglas Lummis declares an end to development because it is inherently anti-democratic (1991, 1994). Viewing development through the lens of democratization is pertinent enough, not least in relation to the Asian authoritarian developmental states. Nowadays development managerialism not only involves states but also international financial institutions and the 'new managerialism' of NGOs. All of these share a lack of humility, a keynote of the development power/knowledge complex. In post-development there is suspicion of alternative development as an 'alternative managerialism' – which may make sense in view of the record of many NGOs (e.g. Sogge 1996). So what to do? Emery Roe's response, in a discussion of sustainable development as a form of alternative managerialism, is 'Nothing' (1995: 160).

However, as Corbridge argues, 'an unwillingness to speak for others is every bit as foundational a claim as the suggestion that we can speak for others in an unproblematic manner' (1994: 103; cf. Corbridge 1998). Doing 'nothing' comes down to an endorsement of the status quo (a question that returns under the politics of post-development below). Gilbert Rist in Geneva would argue: I have no business telling people in Senegal what to do, but people in Switzerland, yes.[4] This kind of thinking implies a compartmentalized world, presumably split along the lines of the Westphalian state system. This is a deeply conventional view, ignores transnational collective action, the crossover between social movements and international relations, the trend of post-nationalism and the ramifications of globalization. It completely goes against the idea of global citizenship and a 'global civil society'. Had this been a general view, the apartheid regime in South Africa would have lasted longer. Under the heading of 'post' thinking, this is actually profoundly conservative.

Dichotomic thinking

Post-development thinking is fundamentally uneven. For all the concern with discourse analysis, the actual use of language is sloppy and indulgent. Escobar plays games of rhetoric: in referring to development as 'Development' and thus suggesting its homogeneity and consistency, he essentializes 'development'. The same applies to Sachs and his call to do away with development: 'in the very call for banishment, Sachs implicitly suggests that it is possible to arrive at an unequivocal definition' (Crush 1996b: 3). Apparently this kind of essentializing of 'development' is necessary in order to arrive at the radical repudiation of development, and without this anti-development pathos, the post-development perspective loses its foundation.

At times one has the impression that post-development turns on a language game rather than an analytic. Attending a conference titled 'Towards a post-development age', Anisur Rahman reacted:

> I was struck by the intensity with which the very notion of 'development' was attacked... I submitted that I found the word 'development' to be a very powerful means of expressing the conception of societal progress as the flowering of people's creativity. Must we abandon valuable words because they are abused? What to do then with words like democracy, cooperation, socialism, all of which are abused? (1993: 213–14)

There are several problems with this line of thinking. First, some of the claims of post-development are simply misleading and misrepresent the history of development. Thus Esteva and others in the *Development Dictionary* (Sachs 1992a) refer to Truman in the 1940s as the beginning of the development era. But this is only one of the beginnings of the application of development to the south, which started with colonial economics; besides, development has an older history – with the latecomers to industrialization in central and eastern Europe, and in Soviet economic planning. Second, dichotomic thinking, pro- and anti-development, underrates the dialectics and the complexity of motives and motions in modernity and development. Even though at given points particular constellations of thinking and policy seem to present a solid whole and façade, there are inconsistencies underneath and the actual course of development theory and policy shows constant changes of direction and numerous improvisations. Thus, some speak of 'the chaotic history of development theory' (Trainer 1989: 177) and 'the fashion-conscious institutional language of development' (Porter 1996). Third, post-development's take on real existing development is quite narrow. The instances cited in post-development literature concern mainly Africa, Latin America and India; or reflections are general and no cases are discussed (as with Nandy). The experience of NICs in East Asia is typically also not discussed: 'the assertion that "development does not work" ignores the rise of East Asia and the near doubling of life expectancy in much of the Third World' (Kiely 1999: 17).

The politics of post-development

Strip away the exaggerated claims, the anti-positioning, and what remains is an uneven landscape. Eventually the question to ask is: what about the politics of post-development; fine points of theory aside, what is to be done? Post-development does make positive claims and is associated with affirmative counterpoints such as indigenous knowledge and cultural diversity. It opts for Gandhian frugality, not consumerism; for conviviality, à la Ivan Illich, for grassroots movements and local struggles. But none of these is specific to post-development and they do not necessarily add up to the conclusion of rejecting development.

Forming a position in relation to post-development might proceed as follows. Let's not quibble about details and let's take your points on board and work with them. What do you have to offer? This varies considerably. Sachs (1992a) is a reasonable refresher course in critiques of development. Latouche's arguments are often perceptive and useful, though they can also be found in alternative development sources (such as Pradervand 1989, Rahman 1993) and are mostly limited to sub-Saharan Africa. A commonsense reaction may be: your points are well taken, now what do we do? The response of Gilbert Rist is that alternatives are not his affair.[5] The general trend in several sources is to stop at critique. What this means is an endorsement of the status quo and, in effect, more of the same, and this is the core weakness of post-development (cf. Cowen and Shenton 1996).

If we read critiques of development dirigisme, such as Deepak Lal's critique of state-centred development economics – which helped set the stage for the neoconservative turn in development – side by side with post-development critiques of development power, such as Escobar's critique of planning, the parallels are striking.[6] Both agree on state failure, though for entirely different reasons. According to Lal, states fail because of rent seeking; Escobar's criticisms arise from a radical democratic and anti-authoritarian questioning of social engineering and the faith in progress. But arguably, the net political effect turns out to be much the same. In other words, there is an elective affinity between neoliberalism and the development agnosticism of post-development.

Escobar offers an outspoken post-development position but is also contradictory. On the one hand he caricatures 'Development' and argues for 'alternatives to Development', but on the other, he pleads for redefining development. Other positions, such as that of Sachs, are both more limited and more consistent – all past and no future. *The Development Dictionary* features critiques of the market, state, production, needs, etc., which are historically informed but overstate their case and offer no alternatives, and ultimately fall flat. Recognizing the power/knowledge nexus in discourse, Escobar proposes 'the formation of nuclei around which new forms of power and knowledge can converge' (Escobar 1992b: 424). Basic to his approach is the 'nexus with grassroots movements'. He evokes a 'we' that comprises 'peasants, urban marginals, deprofessionalized intellectuals' (following Esteva 1985). What they share is an 'interest in culture, local knowledge', a 'critique of science' and the 'promotion of localized, pluralistic grassroots movements'. In another passage, grassroots movements include: women, ecological movements, peasants, urban marginals, civic movements, ethnic minorities, indigenous peoples, popular culture, youth movements, squatter movements, and Christian base communities. Their common features, according to Escobar, are that they are 'essentially local', pluralistic, and distrust organized politics and the development establishment.

As nodal points Escobar mentions three major discourses – democratization, difference and anti-Development – which can serve as the 'basis for radical anti-capitalist struggles'. What is 'needed is the expansion and *articulation* of anti-imperialist, anti-capitalist, anti-productivist, anti-market struggles' (1992b: 431). Again, as in 1980s alternative development discourse, this is the aspiration to construct a grand coalition of opposition forces, now combined with a Foucauldian search 'toward new power-knowledge regimes' (432). The desire for a grand oppositional coalition involves the evocation of a 'we' that, in the desire for discontinuity, claims to capture all social movements in the 'Third World', now under the heading of anti-Development. 'Many of today's social movements in the Third World are in one way or another mediated by anti-Development discourses ... although this often takes place in an implicit manner' (431). In the west, social movements militate against commodification, bureaucratization and cultural massification; in the Third World, according to Escobar, they militate 'against bureaucratization achieved by Development institutions (e.g. peasants against rural development packages, squatters against public housing programmes), commodification, capitalist rationality brought by Development technologies' (431).

This is clearly a biased representation: social movements in the south are much too diverse to be captured under a single heading. Many popular organizations are concerned with *access* to development programmes, with inclusion and participation, while others are concerned with alternative development and renegotiating development, with decentralization, or alternative political action. 'Anti-development' is much too simple and rhetorical a description for the views of the 'victims of development'. Indeed 'victims of development' is too simple and biased a label (Woost 1997). This view suffers from the same problems as early alternative development arguments: it underestimates the desire for and appeal of development and engages in 'island politics' or politics of marginality. Besides, it is contradictory. In its reliance on deprofessionalized intellectuals and a distrust of experts, post-development rubs shoulders with anti-intellectualism, while it also relies on and calls for 'complex discursive operations'. Post-development no longer focuses on class interests and is post-Marxist in outlook, yet Escobar also reinvokes radical anti-capitalist struggles. Like some forms of alternative development, post-development involves populism, now seasoned by an awareness of the articulation effect; yet its striving for a new articulation of anti-imperialist, anti-capitalist and other movements is populist.

At the same time, the political horizon of post-development is one of resistance rather than emancipation. Made up of resistance *à la* Scott, it participates in the 'romance of resistance' (Abu-Lughod 1990). Its other component is local struggles *à la* Foucault. Earlier I argued that, in post-development, discourse analysis is used not merely as an analytical instrument but as an ideological tool (Chapter 1); this becomes apparent when it comes to politics. As many have argued (Hoy 1986, Said 1986), Foucault's imagination of power is an imagination without exit. Foucault engages in a 'monologue of power' (Giri 1998). In the footsteps of this logic, post-development takes the critique of development to the point of retreat. Retreat from business-as-usual can be a creative position from which an alternative practice may grow. Thus critical theory and its negation of the negation, though pessimistic in outlook, has served as a point of reference and inspiration, for instance to the social movements of the 1960s. But the imaginary of power that inspires post-development leaves little room for forward politics.

The quasi-revolutionary posturing in post-development reflects both a hunger for a new era and a nostalgia politics of romanticism, a glorification of the local, grassroots, community with conservative overtones. Different adherents of post-development advocate different politics. Escobar opts for a 'romance of resistance'. Gilbert Rist's politics are those of a conventionally compartmentalized world. Rahnema opts for a Confucian version of Taoist politics (cf. Chapter 9 below). Ray Kiely adds another note:

When Rahnema argues that the end of development 'represents a call to the "good people" everywhere to think and work together', we are left with the vacuous politics of USA for Africa's 'We are the World'. Instead of a politics which critically engages with material inequalities, we have a post-development era where 'people should be nicer to each other'. (1999: 24)

In the *Power of Development*, Jonathan Crush offers this definition: 'This is the power of development: the power to transform old worlds, the power to imagine new ones'. The context is a comment on a colonial text: 'Africans become objects for the application of power rather than subjects experiencing and responding to the exercise of that power' (1996b: 2). Crush comes back once more to the power of development: 'The power of development is the power to generalize, homogenize, objectify' (22). There is a disjuncture between these statements. While the first is, or seems to be, affirmative, the other two are negative. Clearly something is lost in the process. It is what Marx called, and Schumpeter after him, a process of 'creative destruction'. What happens in post-development is that of 'creative destruction' only destruction remains. What remains of the power of development is only the destructive power of social engineering. Gone is the recognition of the creativity of developmental change (cf. Goulet 1992). Instead, what post-development offers, besides critique, is another series of fashionable interpretations. Above all it is a cultural critique of development and a cultural politics (Fagan 1999). This reflects on more than just development; 'development' here is a stand-in for modernity and the real issue is the question of modernity.

Coda

Post-development is caught in a rhetorical gridlock. Using discourse analysis as an ideological platform invites political impasse and quietism. In the end post-development offers no politics besides the self-organizing capacity of the poor, which lets the development responsibility of states and international institutions off the hook. Post-development arrives at development agnosticism by a different route but shares the abdication of development with neoliberalism. Since most insights in post-development sources are not specific to post-development (and are often confused with alternative development), what is distinctive is the rejection of development. Yet the rejection of development does not arise from post-development insights as a *necessary* conclusion, that is, one can share its observations without arriving at this conclusion: in other words, there is no compelling logic to post-development arguments. From the critique of development imposed from above as a one-size-fits-all regime does not follow development agnosticism but rather development pluralism.

Commonly distinguished reactions to modernity are neo-traditionalism, modernization and postmodernism (e.g. McEvilley 1995). Post-development belongs to the era of the 'post'– poststructuralism, postmodernism, postcolonialism, post-Marxism (post-capitalism?) and at times seems 'lost in the post'. It is premised on an awareness of endings, on 'the end of modernity' and, in Vattimo's words, the 'crisis of the future' (1988). Post-development parallels postmodernism both in its acute intuitions and in being directionless in the end, as a consequence of the refusal to translate, or a lack of interest in translating, critique into construction. It also fits the profile of the neo-traditionalist reaction to modernity. There are romantic and nostalgic strands to post-development and its reverence for community, *Gemeinschaft*, the traditional, and there is an element of neo-Luddism in the attitude toward science and technology. The overall programme is one of resistance rather than transformation or emancipation.

Post-development is based on a paradox. Though it is clearly part of the broad critical stream in development, it shows no regard for the progressive potential and dialectics of modernity – for democratization, soft power technologies, reflexivity. Thus it is not difficult to see that the three nodal discourses identified by Escobar – democratization, difference and anti-development – *themselves* arise out of modernization. Democratization continues the democratic impetus of the Enlightenment; difference is a function of the transport and communication revolutions, the world becoming 'smaller' and societies multicultural; and anti-development elaborates the dialectics of the Enlightenment set forth by the Frankfurt School. Generally, the rise of social movements and civil society activism, north and south, is also an expression of the richness of overall development, and cannot be simply captured under the label 'anti'. Post-development's source of strength is a hermeneutics of suspicion, an anti-authoritarian sensibility, and hence a suspicion of alternative development as an 'alternative managerialism'. But since it fails to translate this sensibility into a constructive position, what remains is whistling in the dark. What is the point of declaring development a 'hoax' (Norberg-Hodge 1995) without proposing an alternative?[7]

Alternative development thinking looks primarily at development from the point of view of the disempowered, from bottom-up, along a vertical axis. It combines this with a perspective on the role of the state; in plain terms: a strong civil society needs a strong state (Friedmann 1992). Post-development adopts a wider angle in looking at development through the lens of the problematic of modernity. Yet, though its angle is wide, its optics are not sophisticated and its focus is blurred. Its take on modernity is one-dimensional and ignores different options for problematizing modernity, such as 'reworking modernity' (Pred and Watts 1992), or exploring modernities in the plural (Eisenstadt 2002, Nederveen Pieterse 1998b). More enabling as a position is reflexive modernity and a corollary in relation to development is reflexive development (Chapter 11 below).

In my view post-development and 'alternatives to development' are flawed premises – flawed not as sensibilities but as positions. The problem is not the critiques, which one can easily enough sympathize with and which are not specific to post-development, but the companion rhetoric and posturing, which intimate a politically correct position. 'Alternatives to development' is a misnomer because no alternatives to development are offered. There is no positive programme; there is critique but no construction. 'Post-development' is misconceived because it attributes to 'development' a single and narrow meaning, a consistency which does not match either theory or policy, and thus replicates the rhetoric of developmentalism, rather than penetrating and exposing its polysemic realities. It echoes the 'myth of development' rather than leaving it behind. Post-development makes engaging contributions to collective conversation and reflexivity about development and as such contributes to philosophies of change, but its contribution to politics of change is meagre. While the shift toward cultural sensibilities that accompanies this perspective is a welcome move, the plea for 'people's culture' (Constantino 1985) or indigenous culture can lead, if not to ethnochauvinism and 'reverse Orientalism' (Kiely 1999: 25), then to a reification of both culture and locality or people. It presents a conventional and narrow view of globalization, equated with homogenization. On a philosophical level we may wonder whether there are alternatives to development for *homo sapiens* as the 'unfinished animal', that is, to development writ large, including in the wide sense of evolution.

Notes

1 cf. research by Jongtae Kim, University of Illinois, Urbana-Champaign.
2 Alvares (1979) proposes appropriate technology as an alternative approach.
3 In some ways this matches the weary anti-politics sensibility of intellectuals in eastern Europe (Konrád 1984). On representations of others, according to Crush, 'The current obsession with Western representations of "the Other" is a field of rapidly diminishing return' (1996b: 22).
4 In correspondence with the author.
5 At a seminar at the Institute of Social Studies, The Hague.
6 Both papers are reproduced side by side in Corbridge 1995.
7 For a similar critique of post-development see Robins 2003.

8

Equity and Growth Revisited: From Human Development to Social Development

Redistribution with growth was prominent in the 1970s but was sidelined during the neoliberal era and is currently being revisited. East Asian experiences are noted for high growth rates but they can also be considered with a view to equity. The human development approach makes a strong case for combining equity and growth along the lines of human capital; this can be extended with a stronger perspective on the social dimension – as social development. Studies of welfare states add depth to equity-growth arguments. Economic sociology addresses questions of embeddedness, social capital, networks and trust. By combining a variety of arguments on equity and growth, this chapter seeks to arrive at a new overall perspective on social development.

On the occasion of the World Summit for Social Development in Copenhagen in 1995, benevolent statements were issued on the relationship between growth and equity such as 'Economic growth and social development impinge on each other, i.e. broadly effective social progress is not possible without a socially oriented economic and finance policy' (Development & Cooperation, 1, 1995: 12). Here I probe such rhetorical statements to find a core of policy-relevant thinking.

In the framework of Copenhagen followed by the Millennium Development Goals the dominant tendency has been to relegate questions of social development to poverty alleviation. It may be necessary, however, to challenge the Washington consensus not merely in policy terms, to produce an adjustment of structural adjustment, but also in fundamental terms. Revisiting Keynesian strategies (Singer 1996, Townsend 2004) is important, but one wonders whether they are viable in the context of accelerated globalization. Here I explore the equity-growth argument.

First let me briefly discuss two alternative positions: *rejecting growth* or, alternatively, pursuing *equity without growth*. A prominent set of positions rejects growth for various reasons, such as ecological views, according to which more is not better, and alternative development, according to which what matters is not growth but development that is equitable, sustainable and participatory, views that are often accompanied by rejecting growth *per se*. In view of the ecological and resource limits to life on the planet these are serious and pressing considerations (Sachs 2008). Post-development rejects not only growth but also development as such. A general problem with these positions (discussed in Chapters 6 and 7 above) is that the target is too wide: what should be at issue is not growth but the quality of growth. Exploring this is the point of juxtaposing growth and social development. Clearly 'growth' is a deeply problematic category. The mere question of how growth is defined and measured raises numerous problems. Simply rejecting growth, however, leaves us with too narrow a position and too narrow a coalition to implement whatever policies seem desirable.

At a general level it may be argued that what many people desire is not growth but change, transformation. Marshall Berman refers to 'the desire for development' (1988: 47). The point is not to go against this desire, or complex of desires, not to adopt a confrontational approach, a politics of purity or abstinence, which invokes resistance, but to transform and channel desire, or, at the risk of sounding patronizing, an education rather than a suppression of desire. The marketplace represents powerful and dynamic forces that resonate with deep-seated drives – not merely to 'accumulate, accumulate' but also to 'change, change' and 'improve, improve'. Market forces or excess market forces alienate and marginalize many, but is the appropriate response to ignore or marginalize market forces in return? A wiser course is to explore what common ground exists between the market and social development, or the scope for a social market approach, considering that the problem is not the market but the unregulated market.

A different option is to pursue *equity without growth*. This kind of approach has been referred to as 'support-mediated security'.[1] This may give us the 'Kerala model' with advanced social policies and comparatively high levels of education, health and female emancipation. From the mid-1970s, as Kerala was acquiring international model status, it was slipping into crisis, including 'severe stagnation in the spheres of material production, soaring unemployment, acute fiscal crisis and erosion of sustainability of the social welfare expenditures' (Isaac and Tharakan 1995: 1995).[2] Growing unemployment because investors shun a state where unions, with the backing of the state government, are strong; at least that is the position of the local right wing backlash, which matches international press comments. This refers us to the familiar tales of western welfare states in the era of post-Fordism, globalization and 'social dumping'. Aside from the deeply politicized question of how to account for the Kerala crisis, one conclusion is that 'in the absence of economic growth it is difficult to sustain, much less expand, welfare gains' (Isaac and Tharakan 1995: 1993), an equation that also applies to other developing countries that have followed the social welfare approach such as Costa Rica, Sri Lanka, Mauritius and Jamaica (Townsend 2004: 54).

So we turn to equity with growth, regrouped under the banner of social development. The point here is not to make a case for social development in *moral* terms, in the name of solidarity, compassion or decency. Thus, according to Galbraith, 'in the good society there must not be a deprived and excluded underclass' (1996). It is not that such moral considerations are irrelevant but that they are of limited purchase. Moral economies and discourses are unevenly distributed, so achieving a political consensus purely on moral grounds is unlikely. Moral arguments invite trade-offs – the importance of economic growth may outweigh the appeal of moral policy. Since in conventional views growth is supposed to trickle down, morality would be merely a matter of time: in time growth policies will generate moral outcomes. Hence moral considerations tend to be practically out-flanked and too easily neutralized by growth policies.

Neither is the point to make a *political* case for social development. Social and welfare policies enhance political stability and legitimacy, but in doing so they also invite trade-offs – between political legitimacy and political efficacy. A classic position is that collective demands are to be restrained, so collective interests do not crowd out state autonomy and undermine the state's capacity to undertake reforms. The absence of social development may prompt uncontrolled informalization, such as a growing underground economy and ethnic and religious mobilization.

These are all important considerations but they are not the main line of argument followed here. Rather, the point is to consider the case for social development on *economic* grounds, in relation to growth itself. Or, to examine whether, how, to what extent and under which circumstances social development is good for economic growth and beneficial to business; the point is to explore the scope for market-friendly social development. This line of thinking involves classic debates – on the welfare state, on the 'big trade-off' between equality and efficiency (Okun 1975), on modernization and equality. Here I revisit this question by considering several lines of research to see what the present scope is of social development arguments and whether their combination yields new insight. This is worth doing, considering that 'there is no very strong tradition of doing macroeconomics as if poor people and social processes mattered' (Taylor and Pieper 1996: 93).

Relevant lines of research include the following.

1. Redistribution with growth. Prominent in the 1970s, these views are currently being revisited along with Keynesian perspectives.
2. Lessons from East Asia. Often discussed with a view to the role of state intervention, they can also be considered with a view to equality.
3. Human development. This approach makes a strong case for combining equity and growth along the lines of human capital but leaves the social dimension underexplored.
4. Lessons from welfare states and the scope for combining social policy and development.
5. New institutional economics provides institutional analyses and economic sociology addresses questions of embeddedness, social capital and trust.

Other bodies of literature are relevant to social development – such as comparative studies of social security, the regulation school, post-Fordism, associational democracy – but fall outside this treatment. The point of this exercise is to find out what they add up to when various arguments on equity and growth are grouped together and, by adding novel elements that are not usually combined with social development, to arrive at a new overall perspective.

Social development

Let me first explain in what sense I use social development. A narrow meaning of social development is public welfare policies of health, education and housing. This approach, as Midgley (1995) points out, suffers from compartmentalization: the separation of social policies from development policies. The Copenhagen summit and the Millennium Development Goals reproduce this tendency: social development usually ends up in the basket of poverty alleviation (UNRISD 1995). For the same reason, the present argument does not concern the social economy, progressive market or socially responsible business, cooperatives or fair trade. Not because they are not important, but because they represent a compartmentalized or, at least, a partial approach. The focus is on the overall economy rather than on particular segments. Secondly, social development can be used in contrast to economic development.[3] The third option, which is followed here, is to view social development in a substantive and comprehensive manner with equal emphasis both on the 'social' and 'development': in other words, an integrated approach to social concerns and growth strategies.

A fundamental reason for taking this course is that the distinction between the economic and the social is only recent and tenuous. Karl Polanyi (1957) made the point all along that the market and the economy are embedded in the social. Timothy Mitchell notes that 'the idea of the economy in its contemporary sense did not emerge until the middle decades of the twentieth century' (2002: 4). Its emergence, according to Mitchell, is not just another social construction or a different mode of representation, but also a reorganization and transformation of the political process and relations of exchange. On similar grounds Ha-Joon Chang argues, 'in the final instance there can be no meaningful distinction between economic policy and social policy'.

> The separation of economic policy and social policy implicitly assumes that it is possible to objectively define an economic sphere that should (and does) operate according to some 'scientific' economic logic and a social sphere where we may want to (but are normally advised, by those 'hard-nosed' economists, not to) override the economic logic with 'ethical' considerations (such as better income distribution, employment creation, protection of human rights, and so on) despite the 'inefficiencies' that such action is going to create. (2004: 248)

Thus the very distinctions between the economic and the social that frame the field and the debate are contested. Both the economic and the social are, from a broader point of view, 'political' categories and representations and the very terminology 'social policy' flags a relative position in the first place. As Ha-Joon Chang notes:

We seem to use the term 'economic policy' as a shorthand for a policy whose underlying structure of rights and obligations is relatively uncontested (or, more likely, should not be contested according to the point of view of the person making the particular distinction) and 'social policy' as a shorthand for a policy whose underlying structure of rights and obligations is more contested. (2004: 250; cf. Elson 2004)

How then to define social development? Midgley defines social development as 'a process of planned social change designed to promote the well-being of the population as a whole in conjunction with a dynamic process of economic development' (1995: 25). 'Planned social change' carries dirigiste overtones, though actually Midgley argues for 'managed pluralism'.

The discourse of social development used by governments, international institutions and many NGOs is social policy, which usually means a social engineering, managerial approach. This is apparent if we leaf through the reports submitted to the World Summit for Social Development.[4] Several bodies of literature reviewed here reflect this tendency, except for economic sociology, which looks at the social from the ground up. We might term this a society-centred approach to social development, or social development from below. Actual social security concerns much more than government social policy such as family and local networks (e.g. DSE 1994, Hirtz 1995). As Ann Davis remarks, 'Of course, social work agencies are only one way of replenishing family and friendship networks' (1991: 84). When social security falls outside conventional social policy, how could a conventional approach to social development be adequate? Accordingly, implicit in 'social development' are multiple layers of meaning: whether social development is compartmentalized as social policy or whether it is viewed as an overall approach; and with regard to the agency of social development, whether it is managerial, from above, or society-centred, from below.

Redistribution with growth

In the 1970s' growth and redistribution literature several currents of thought came together. Adelman and Morris (1967) developed an approach to social development influenced by modernization theory; their social development index may be read as a modernization index.[5] At a time when Keynesian demand management played a prominent part, Gunnar Myrdal adopted a productivist or supply-side approach. According to Myrdal, 'welfare reforms, rather than being costly for society, actually lay the basis for more steady and rapid economic growth' (quoted in Esping-Andersen 1994: 723; see also Myrdal 1968). In presenting redistribution as a *precondition* to growth, Myrdal followed a Swedish tradition. 'The unique contribution of Swedish socialism was its idea of "productivist" social policy. Its leading theoreticians stood liberalism on its head, arguing that social policy and equality were necessary preconditions for economic efficiency, which, in turn, was a prerequisite for the democratic socialist society' (Esping-Andersen 1994: 713).

The Swedish concept of a 'productivist social justice' in which 'the welfare state invests in optimizing people's capacity to be productive citizens' contrasts with 'the strong Catholic influence in Continental European welfare states [which] has resulted in a policy regime that encourages women to remain within the family' (1994: 722). The productivist approach to social justice addresses the standard criticism of Keynesian policies that they focus on demand and ignore supply factors.

We find echoes of productivist arguments in the human development approach and the regulation school. Arguably Swedish productivism and human development share a common root in Joseph Schumpeter's emphasis on supply factors in economic development which influenced both lineages. Schumpeter's approach differs fundamentally both from Keynes's preoccupation with demand and demand management and from von Hayek and Mises' approach, his contemporaries in Vienna, and their radical rejection of the state, which in Schumpeter's view is a necessary handmaiden of capitalism. Keynes inspired the post-Depression career of European social democracy; it is more concerned with avoiding crises and downturns than with promoting upturns. Hayek and Mises inspired (or more precisely, matched) the Anglo-American approach to capitalism and their views became policy with the Reagan and Thatcher administrations. Schumpeter's approach was a seminal influence both on Japan's industrial policy (the Schumpeters made many visits to Japan in the 1930s) and on Sweden's welfare state, in the Rehn-Meidner model that combined an emphasis on industrial innovation and full employment with generous social provision. Large corporations were allowed to accumulate tax-free reserves as long as they spent them on research and development (McCraw 2007). Thus we can find the contours of Schumpeter's supply-side approach in East Asian economies from Japan to Korea and Singapore. Osvaldo Sunkel's account of Latin American neostructuralism offers a similar profile.

> It is not demand and markets that are critical. The heart of development lies in the supply side: quality, flexibility, the efficient combination and utilization of productive resources, the adoption of technological developments, an innovative spirit, creativity, the capacity for organization and social discipline, private and public austerity, an emphasis on savings and the development of skills to compete internationally; in short, independent efforts *from within* to achieve self-sustained development. (Ramos and Sunkel 1993, quoted in Sunkel 2008: 65–6)

The postwar development approach is often referred to as the Keynesian consensus, which makes sense because it was premised on the state as central actor in the economy. Yet key ideas and policies of this period – such as Big Push and Rostow's stages of growth – were supply-side policies, and in this sense to characterize this era as Keynesianism is a misnomer.

In a well known World Bank-sponsored study, Hollis Chenery and associates (1974) argued that egalitarian and developmental objectives are complementary, a position that favoured a redistribution of income and assets to the poorest groups. *Redistribution with Growth* and sequel studies (such as Adelman and Robinson 1978) were inspired by a dissatisfaction with the course followed during the first development decade. In the 1980s, this egalitarian approach was outflanked and clipped by the rise of monetarism, supply-side economics and neoconservatism. It makes sense to revisit these arguments, taking into account subsequent trends and addressing the misgivings about dirigisme, rents and rent seeking, welfarism and dependency.

In the 1990s, the idea of redistribution with (or for) growth regained some ground in mainstream development policy, with some new inflections: a general concern with social indicators in measuring development, to the point of redefining development itself; an emphasis on human capital; and a growing critique of trickle-down. *Advancing Social Development*, the World Bank's report to the Copenhagen summit, notes: 'How growth affects poverty depends greatly on the initial distribution of income. The more equal the distribution of income to start with, the more likely it is that poverty will be reduced for a given increase in average income' (1995: 4–5). Hence the World Bank's recognition of the importance of safety nets for the poor when implementing deficit reduction (23). This World Bank package includes 'promoting labor-demanding growth, investing in people, providing safety nets, and improving governance' (48). In this fashion, social development is assimilated as part of structural reform – as a supplementary safety net, as structural adjustment with a human face, or as 'stage two' of structural reform and the political stabilization of reform policies.

In view of the importance of the initial distribution of income and its effect on poverty alleviation, would merely installing safety nets be logical or adequate? It would seem that to achieve these effects more far-reaching measures are called for. In addition, what is at issue are structural reform policies and their economic rationale. The actual challenge is to examine the nexus not merely between income distribution and poverty alleviation but also between equity and growth. Redistribution with growth, in a mix of productivist and demand management elements, also informs South Africa's Reconstruction and Development Programme (cf. Moll et al. 1991).

Lessons of East Asia

Equitable development policies are widely recognized as a crucial factor in East Asian development. Thus 'there is substantial evidence to suggest that equity in income distribution and decent welfare systems are friends not enemies of growth, a pattern strikingly clear for Japan, Taiwan, Hong Kong, Korea and Singapore where equity and growth have gone hand in hand' (Weiss 1996: 195). World Bank studies acknowledge that one of the initial conditions for rapid growth in East Asia

> was the relative *equality of income* in the first generation NIEs [Newly Industrializing Economies]. This factor was more of a change brought about by policy than an inheritance. Most other low- and middle-income countries were not able to achieve similar equality of income or assets. Large land reform schemes in both

Korea and Taiwan, China, did away with the landholding classes and made wage income the main source of advancement. Public housing investments in Singapore and Hong Kong were early priorities of governments bent on maintaining a national consensus on development policies. (Leipziger and Thomas 1995: 7)

This point is often noted: 'some of the advantages of the rapidly growing East Asian countries were their unusually low initial income inequality in 1960 and their labor-demanding pattern of growth, which tended to reduce income inequality over time' (World Bank 1995: 5).

Education policies are part of this equation. The World Bank study on *The East Asian Miracle* 'shows that the single most important factor in launching the miracle countries on a path of rapid, sustained economic growth was universal or near-universal primary school enrolment ... In 1960 Pakistan and Korea had similar levels of income, but by 1985 Korea's GDP per capita was nearly three times Pakistan's ... In 1960 fewer than a third of the children of primary school age were enrolled in Pakistan while nearly all were enrolled in Korea' (ibid.: 34).

Such evidence is less conclusive in Southeast Asia. In Malaysia between 1970 and 1990 the New Economic Policy established an inter-ethnic trade-off between Bumiputras and Chinese (economic gains for the Malays and political citizenship rights for the Chinese, without an infringement on their economic position) that was made possible by rapid growth rates and foreign investment and resulted in equity between Malays and Chinese (but excluded the inhabitants of Sabah and Sarawak, the indigenous Orang Asli, and Indians) (Gomez 1994, Jomo 1995). Policies pursuing equity and growth have been less in evidence in Thailand, play a minor part in Indonesia and have been absent in the Philippines.

While the elements of equity in the growth path of East Asian NIEs are noted in World Bank and other studies, they are not often highlighted. In Leipziger and Thomas's *Lessons of East Asia* they figure in the text but not in their 'Development Checklist', which features items such as selective industrial policies and directed credit (1995: 2). Debates on the East Asian NICs have concentrated on the question of the efficacy of government interventions – as the primary challenge to neoclassical economics and its emphasis on trade liberalization as the clue to Asian economic success. The question of the 'governed market' (Wade 1990) or 'governed interdependence' (Weiss 1996) and the everlasting debate on state or market (Wade 1996) has tended to overshadow other issues such as equity and growth. In an Asian perspective on the 'East Asian Miracle' study, equity and growth, or 'shared growth', is mentioned in passing while the emphasis is on the institutional capacities of government (Iwasaki et al. 1992, Ohno 1996: 20).

The emphasis on the authoritarian character of Asian regimes (which is itself a variation on the well-worn theme of 'Oriental despotism') biases the discussion. References to Confucianism and 'Asian values' are not particularly helpful either. The first distinctive feature of East Asian authoritarian government is that it has been *developmental* – unlike, say, Somoza's authoritarianism or that of predatory states; the second is that in significant respects it has been *cooperative* in relation to the market and society – unlike Pinochet's regime in Chile. The third is that it has not only disciplined labour but also capital. What has been overlooked or downplayed is the coordinating character of government intervention in East Asia and the ingenious political and social arrangements which have been devised in order to effect social policies in a market-friendly fashion, or, vice versa, to effect market support strategies in a society-friendly fashion (Ohno 1996, Weiss 1996). Specific examples include state support for small and medium-sized businesses in Taiwan (Hamilton and Woolsey Biggart 1992), Singapore's housing policy (Hill and Kwen Fee 1995, Rodan 1989) and Malaysia's new economic policy. China's experiences in combining the market economy and social development are also worth examining (Gao 1995, Griffin 2000b).

Human development

> Empowerment is not only democratic, it is efficient. (Griffin and McKinley 1994)

The human development (HD) perspective takes the further step of making a general case for the nexus between equity and growth. According to Keith Griffin (1996: 15–17), 'under some circumstances, the greater is the degree of equality, the faster is likely to be the rate of growth'. His considerations include the cost of the perpetuation of inequality and that inequality undermines political legitimacy while 'modern technology has destroyed the monopoly of the state over the means of violence'. Furthermore, 'measures to reduce inequality can simultaneously contribute to faster growth'.

> There is much evidence that small farms are more efficient than either large collective farms of the Soviet type or the capitalist latifundia one finds in Latin America and elsewhere. A redistributive land reform and the creation of a small peasant farming system can produce performances as good, if not better than those of other agricultural systems. The experience of such places as China and Korea is instructive ... what is true of small farms is equally true of small and medium industrial and commercial enterprises. An egalitarian industrial structure, as Taiwan vividly demonstrates, can conquer world markets. (Griffin 1996: 17; cf. Fei et al. 1979)

Further elements mentioned by Griffin are investments in education – 'There is probably no easier way to combine equality and rapid growth. The whole of East Asia is testimony to the veracity of this proposition' – and the liberation of women. 'A final example of the falsity of the great trade-off is the liberation of women. Equal treatment of women would release the talent, energy, creativity and imagination of half the population' (ibid.: 17; cf. Buvini et al. 1996).

A broadly similar case is made by ul Haq, who mentions 'four ways to create desirable links between economic growth and human development'

(1995: 21–2): investment in education, health and skills; more equitable distribution of income; government social spending; and empowerment of people, especially women. Ul Haq proposes an HD paradigm of equity, sustainability, productivity, and empowerment (1995: 16). It is the element of productivity that sets this paradigm apart from the alternative development paradigm. This refers to the supply-side factor as the nexus between equity and growth.

This position is not necessarily controversial from the point of view of neoclassical economics. HD owes its definition to the emphasis on the investment in human resources, human capital, which is prominent in the East Asian model and Japanese perspectives on development and is now a mainstream development position. The growing knowledge intensity of economic growth, as in innovation-driven growth and the emphasis on research and development and technopoles, reinforces the argument that an investment in human capital fosters growth. Ul Haq rejects the idea that adjustment and HD would be antithetical, either conceptually or in policy: 'Far from being antithetical, adjustment and growth with human development offer an intellectual and policy challenge in designing suitable programmes and policies ... The challenge of combining these two concerns is like that of combining the conflicting viewpoints of the growth school and the distribution school in the 1970s' (1995: 7–8). The same reasoning informed 'structural adjustment with a human face' (Jolly 1986).

> It is not difficult to find confirmation for human capital arguments in neoclassical economics: welfare economics and human capital theory provide important market-conforming justifications for a range of social policies, most notably for public health and education ... neoclassical economics is inherently theoretically elastic. The theory of market failure may, in fact, justify a 'residual' welfare state, while information failure theory can be applied to argue for a fully fledged, comprehensive welfare state. (Esping-Andersen 1994: 712)

Nevertheless, the author continues, neoclassical economics emphasizes the efficiency trade-offs associated with welfare policies, specifically negative effects on savings (and hence investments), work incentives, and institutional rigidities (as with respect to labour mobility). In other words, neoclassical economics can both acknowledge and deflect welfare arguments by treating them as subsidiary to growth as the primary objective, so that in the end welfare policies end up on the backburner. The key aim should be, rather, to zero in on those elements in the equity–growth debate which are controversial or which open up the framework of neoclassical economics.

The HD approach skirts rather than confronts this issue. This follows on from the fact that HD follows the human capital argument, which is part of rather than outside the paradigm of neoclassical economics. In addition, in assuming the *individual* as the unit of human development HD shows that its intellectual roots are in liberalism.[6] HD may also be interpreted as the lessons of East Asia translated into general policy. As such, one way of reading it is as a meeting point between the authoritarian state and the neoliberal market with the state acting as the supplier of human skills to the market through human resource development programmes, packaged to achieve effective global competition. Merging social concerns and market concerns is excellent, but the question is, on which terms? According to ul Haq there is no contradiction in principle between structural reform and HD, it is only a matter of designing the right policy mix. This means that HD may be institutionally and ideologically acceptable to all sides. Since HD does not challenge but goes along with market logic, it does not in a principled way address the problem of the unregulated market.

HD has been inspired by Amartya Sen's (1985) capabilities approach to development. An obvious question is, if capacitation is the objective and measure of development, then who defines capacity, ability or human resources? What about the disabled, unwed mothers, the aged? What about human traits that *cannot* be translated into economic inputs, resources?[7] Besides, if capacitation and the enlargement of people's choices are the yardstick of development, as HD would have it, should we also consider, say, the Medéllin Cartel as a form of capacitation and enlargement of people's choices? As Des Gasper (2004) argues, to Sen's capabilities approach there is no moral dimension. To the extent, then, that HD does not challenge neoliberalism and the principle of competitiveness but endorses it, HD may enable development business-as-usual to carry on more competitively under a general 'humane' aura. Then, social development, sharpened and redefined in a wider framework, is a more inclusive and enabling perspective than human development.

Lessons of welfare states

Looking at social development side by side with the welfare state serves two purposes. It bridges the increasingly artificial divide between developed and developing countries and it helps to clear the path from economic generalizations to institutional and political questions. It might also, on the other hand, confuse issues: equity–growth policies do not necessarily have to take the form of the welfare state, which is a specific institutional arrangement.

It is not difficult to find econometric confirmation for the general positive correlation between equity or equality and growth: 'virtually every single statistical study concludes growth is positively related to equality' (Esping-Andersen 1994: 723); 'most econometric studies conclude that inequality is harmful to growth' (725). However, aside from methodological limitations, a fundamental theoretical fallacy is implicit in this approach. Ironically, this echoes the fallacy inherent in neoclassical economics, namely the tendency to abstract economic factors from institutional and political dynamics. According to Esping-Andersen, 'the narrowly economic framework of the neoclassical model' is the reason for 'the curious gap between theoretical claims and empirical findings'. 'The model is consistent only when it leaves out political and social variables; studies that incorporate them invariably produce contradictory results' (724).

The welfare state may also be thought of as a particular way in which the economy is embedded in society. 'The welfare state is not something opposed to or in some way related to the economy; it is an integral element in the organic linkage of production, reproduction and consumption ... what we think of as the postwar welfare state is but one crucial regulatory element in the Fordist system of mass production' (Esping-Andersen 1994: 716–17). The failure of welfare states lies not so much in fiscal strain but can rather be seen as a 'manifestation of a mounting incompatibility between a fossilized welfare state, on one hand, and a rapidly changing organization of production and reproduction, on the other hand' (717). This refers to a series of shifts – toward service production, of industrial production to NICs, from standardization to flexibility, and from the Fordist family to women's economic independence, dual-earner households and non-linear life patterns. In welfare arrangements, this may involve shifts toward the Schumpeterian workfare state (Jessop 1994) and toward welfare pluralism (Mishra 1996).

The reorganization of production is a function of new technologies and changing consumer demand (flexible accumulation) as well as globalization and the rise of the NICs. The crisis of welfare states, then, is also, in part, the other side of the coin of East Asian economic success. For instance, 'the redistributive Keynesian demand-stimulus policy, which served very well to assure adequate demand for domestically produced mass-consumption goods ... became increasingly counterproductive when such goods originated in Taiwan and Korea' (Esping-Andersen 1994: 717). This suggests that the framework in which equity and growth are conventionally considered – the society or nation state – needs to be opened up, eventually to a global scope.

Studies of welfare states highlight their diversity. This includes distinguishing between residual welfare states (USA), lean welfare states (Switzerland, Japan), productivist welfare states (Scandinavia), and the Rhineland welfare states, which tend to uphold status differences rather than being egalitarian. These distinctions may be merged with dynamic arguments on the relationship between equity and growth.

Arguments on the relationship between equity and growth coined in general terms are superseded by 'more complex, interactive models that posit curvilinear relationships between welfare states and economic performance' (Esping-Andersen 1994: 723). Such arguments suggest that up to a certain point the welfare state will have a positive influence on economic growth but that this then turns increasingly negative. Another curvilinear model suggests that 'full employment is best secured in countries where collective institutions (and the Left) are either very weak or very strong ... In the former case, labor market clearing is largely left to naked market forces; in the latter, to political management' (724). Accordingly,

the effect of a welfare state cannot be understood in isolation from the political-institutional framework in which it is embedded ... there may exist a trade-off between equality and efficiency in countries where the welfare state is large and very redistributive but in which the collective bargaining system is incapable of assuring wage moderation and stable, nonconflictual industrial relations.

Thus, in concrete terms, a Swedish, Norwegian, or Austrian welfare state will not harm growth, while a British one will (even if it is smaller) ... if we turn to a dynamic interpretation, the evidence suggests that as long as a large and redistributive welfare state is matched by neocorporatist-style political exchange mechanisms, equality and efficiency are compatible; when the capacity for harmonious political bargains ceases to function, the same welfare state may threaten economic performance. (725–6)

One line of argument is that once a certain level has been reached, growth yields diminishing returns in terms of welfare and wellbeing (Daly and Cobb 1994), which calls to mind an earlier argument of Keynes on the diminishing returns of the pursuit of surplus (Singer 1989).

Similar dynamic and curvilinear arguments have been made in relation to 'social capability': 'a country's potential for rapid growth is strong not when it is backward without qualification, but rather when it is technologically backward but socially advanced' (Temple and Johnson 1996: 2). How to define and measure 'social capability'? Putnam (1993) looks at associational membership and survey measures; Myrdal (1968) considers levels of mobility, communication and education. Temple and Johnson focus on 'social factors that play a role in the speed of catching up' and define social capacity narrowly as 'the capacity of social institutions to assist in the adoption of foreign technology' (1996: 1, 3). They follow the Adelman and Morris index of social development and conclude from their findings that the 'relative importance of investments in physical capital and schooling appears to vary with the extent of social development' (41).

Social capital

This brings us to the wider question of the institutional embeddedness of social policies. At the end of the day arguments about equity and growth cannot be made in generic terms. They are political questions or, more precisely, for their economic rationale to be operative they depend on institutional arrangements and political settlements. New institutional economics focuses on the institutional requirements for economic growth such as legal frameworks and structures of rights, while the growing body of work on the sociology of economics examines the embeddedness of economic behaviour.

The standard literature on social development is, as mentioned before, dominated by questions of social policy. Literature on economic performance increasingly turns towards social issues (e.g. Granovetter 1992, Stewart 1995), but on an entirely different wavelength. Since the two fields hardly meet it is an interesting exercise to consider their possible intersections. They concern two dimensions of social development: social policy and the economic significance of social networks and relations of trust, which is often summed up under the heading of social capital. Social capital refers to a widely ramifying range of arguments, with various possible intersections with social development, depending on which angle on social capital one adopts.[8]

For Bourdieu (1976) a key concern is that of the relations among economic, social, cultural and symbolic capital, which he regards as cumulative and interchangeable. Current interest is more concerned with social capital as a clue to economic capital, an asset in the process of accumulation. Social capital in this sense may be appropriated in a right wing perspective, in which civil society serves as a counter (rather than as a complement) to the state. According to Fukuyama, 'The character of civil society and its intermediate associations, rooted as it is in nonrational factors like culture, religion, tradition, and other premodern sources, will be key to the success of modern societies in a global economy'(1995: 103). Building intermediate associations may be an alternative to the role of government and to 'social engineering', which are held to be a dead end. Left wing takes on social capital make a similar case, but this time aiming to address not state failure but market failure. With a view to the success of corporatist strategies in East Asia and continental Europe, various forms of 'concertation' may be recommended as a redress for market failure. Communitarianism emphasizes building community and civic virtue. In Britain, rethinking social democracy combines ideas about rebuilding community, the social market or social economy (Sheffield Group 1989) and 'stakeholder capitalism' (Hutton 1995) with the renewal of democracy, as in associative democracy (Amin 1997, Hirst 1993).

These concerns overlap with an extensive literature on industrial districts and local economic development, which goes beyond agglomeration economies and transaction cost arguments to incorporate relations of trust (Harrison 1992, Ottati 1994) and institutional densities (Amin and Thrift 1993) as elements that go into the making of regional economic performance. Politics of place may also involve local culture as a dimension of economic performance (Hanloe et al. 1990; Lash and Urry 1994). Analyses of the 'Third Italy' from the point of view of associative economics also refer to local democracy as an economic asset. This may take the form of New Left productivism, centred on 'the popular construction of cooperation through citizenship and authentic participation, in politics and the workplace' (Amin 1997: 316). In this context the informal economy may be viewed as a permanent arrangement, which may be further developed, for instance in the form of labour exchange networks (e.g. exchanging child care for gardening), in combination with an active and capacious state.

These right wing and left wing takes on social capital are both upbeat, optimistic, in viewing social capital as an avenue either to outflank the state or to combine a strong civil society, strong state, strong economy. Social capital has thus become a new terrain of rhetorical positioning and ideological contestation, which calls for greater analytic clarity.

Quite influential in putting social capital on the map has been Putnam's (1993) study of the course of administrative decentralization in Italy since the 1970s. According to Putnam, those regions in Italy, in the north, which have a historical legacy of civic associations and participatory local government have reacted well to administrative decentralization in terms of regional government and economic performance; while the Mezzogiorno, which has been governed historically along centralized and vertical lines, shows high rates of failure both in administration and economic achievement. His conclusions come down on the side of 'history as destiny' and carry a conservative bias. Putnam's work has been criticized for misconstruing 'path dependency', misreading Italian history and stereotyping the south (Levi 1996, Sabetti 1996). Besides, this approach leaves no room for the possibility of nurturing or generating social capital. The record of several countries shows that the vicious circle can be broken. In East Asia policy interventions have been able to create economically enabling political and institutional conditions within reasonably short time spans, even in countries that had been used to vertical and centralized government. In other words, levels of trust are not simply historical givens but can be fostered through an appropriate policy mix. Policy performance can be a source of trust, not just a result.

Notions such as social capital and the social market carry a double meaning: they refer to the socialization of the market and at the same time to the instrumentalization or commodification of social relations. The notion of 'trust as a commodity' exemplifies this double move (Dasgupta 1988). Likewise, there are different dimensions to embeddedness. At a general level, the point is that the economy is embedded in society; down the ladder of abstraction, any market relationship is embedded in a specific social configuration. A few considerations may clarify the range of applicability of social capital. (1) Social capital is particularistic. To networks there are boundaries, and boundaries are exclusionary. 'Neighborhoods ... are a source of trust and neighborhoods are a source of distrust. They promote trust of those you know and distrust of those you do not, those not in the neighborhood or outside the networks' (Levi 1996: 51). The other side of embeddedness is exclusion; the other side of trust is risk. Social capital then may be a strategy of risk management. (2) Social exclusion and closure facilitate trust and cooperation by ensuring the predictability of relations and preventing the leakage of resources. (3) Concentrating social capital has long been a fundamental strategy of power: witness the circles of privilege of aristocracies, 'old boy' networks, clubs, inner circles, secret societies, lodges, sects and crime networks. It has also been a strategy of subversion, insurgence, revolution, or the conquest of state power: witness the Jacobins, Carbonari and the cells in international communism. Women's networks have cultivated sisterhood and autonomy. Features in common include boundary-establishing rituals of initiation that serve to concentrate social capital, create bonds of obligation, establish a circle of trust and a common frame of understanding. (4) Cooperation can also be a competition strategy. Examples range from alliances, non-aggression pacts or peace treaties to firm mergers, all of which seek to reduce risk.

As Coleman notes, 'most forms of social capital are created or destroyed as by-products of other activities' (1988: 118). The question is what difference policy can make, in other words, can social capital or civic participatory culture in some fashion be nurtured, fostered, or harnessed as part of social development policies? In addition, to look for enabling features of social capital one must look not merely at internal relations within groups but also at relations *among* groups. Under what conditions do we get widening circles of social capital?

On the premise that embeddedness involves inclusionary and exclusionary elements, the work on ethnic economies may serve as an example (Light and Karageorgis 1994, Waldinger et al. 1990); the informal economy may also be a field of inquiry (e.g. Portes 1994). An interesting line of research is not merely ethnic economies but *inter-ethnic economies*, in other words the development or generation of trust across ethnic boundaries (Nederveen Pieterse 2007). For instance, the Chinese diaspora in the Pacific Rim countries involves not merely ethnic enclave economies but also a wide range of collaboration with locals, such as joint ventures (Seagrave 1996). What attitude governments take in relation to these forms of cooperation can make a huge difference. The New Order government of Suharto utilized the Chinese business community as a classic 'trading minority', 'the Jews of the East' – keeping them politically dependent, with limited political rights, while nurturing relations with a small coterie of tycoons (Irwan 1996); whereas the Malaysian new economic policy (1970–90) was able to strike an inter-ethnic deal.

It would follow that a policy of *democratization*, rather than polarization, of inter-ethnic relations can contribute to economic achievement. This may be an instance with wider implications. Social development in this sense refers to policies promoting social trust among and across diverse communities – classes, status groups, minorities, etc. It may also refer to the creation of social infrastructure such as housing, schools, clinics, water supply; or asset development among low-income groups to encourage savings among the poor, which will foster social investments (Midgley 1995: 160). Government can play a facilitative role, in the form of managed pluralism. Synergies between regional, urban and local economic development are another relevant approach. The principle of cooperation also applies to relations among firms and between firms and subcontractors (see e.g. Dore 1992 on goodwill in Japan).

An extensive literature documents intersectoral cooperation and synergies in the context of community or local economic development (CED, LED). This approach may also have international, macro-regional and global implications (cf. Gerschenkron 1992, , Kuttner 1991, Thrift and Amin 1997). The emerging theme of transnational social policy is worth considering (Deacon et al. 1998). A further proposition is that of a World Social Development Organization to effect economic and social policy jointly on a world scale (Petrella 1995: 22). Examining transnational social capital in the informal (Portes 1996) and the formal sector (Strange 1996) may enrich these propositions.

Conclusion

> Economic growth does not cause an increase in the quality of life, but an increase in quality of life does lead to economic growth. (Mizanur Rahman Shelley, Center for the Study of the Global South 1994: 62)

Structural adjustment programmes and social safety nets make up a convenient combination, and so do the 'Washington consensus' and the Copenhagen summit. In this configuration, social development is a matter of tidying up after the market: a polarizing mode of economic growth, followed by social impact studies to assess its pauperizing impact and poverty alleviation measures to compensate for the immiserization effect. This is the repair or damage control mode of social development. Upon closer consideration it is not so much social development as social fixing and political risk management. Along the way, however, social inequality entails not merely a moral cost and political consequences: 'there is a point at which social injustice undermines economic efficiency' (Center for the Study of the Global South 1994: 15).

In development theory a distinction runs between development as planned change or engineering, and development as immanent change, a process from within (Cowen and Shenton 1996). Modernization theory followed a logic of development from above and outside. Structural adjustment follows in the same footsteps. Modernization policies in the past, and at present the application of liberal productivism to developing countries, first *destroy* existing social capital for the sake of achieving economic growth, and then by means of social policy seek to *rebuild* social tissue. Obviously along the way there is a lot of slippage, displacement, and realignment of power relations. Pursuing Darwinist economics and then sending Florence Nightingale after to tidy up the damage is a cumbersome and economically counterproductive approach to development.

The point of this chapter is to take social development beyond poverty alleviation toward a substantive and proactive approach. The second objective is to go beyond the human capital approach of human development. A productivist approach to social development involves not merely investing in education, health, housing – the standard fare of human capital approaches – but also accommodating and investing in networking across communities and groups and designing enabling institutional environments – in other words, a social capital or participatory civic society approach. As a supply-side approach, that is, enhancing productivity and output rather than promoting consumption, this addresses the criticism of Keynesian demand stimulus policies on the part of the supply-siders of the 1980s. To address the problem of technological change and jobless growth requires a wider approach of investment-led growth (cf. Griffin 2000a).

On several grounds and in multiple fashions – human capital, social capital, democratization – social development can contribute to overall economic achievement. In the words of Amin and Thrift (1997: 160), 'the argument within socioeconomics that there can be a close connection between democracy and economic success is to be welcomed in our market-driven age'. If the market dominates it might as well serve socially useful purposes.

The neoclassical trickle-down argument cannot be made in generic terms because outcomes will vary according to the political and social circumstances;

for the same reason, equity-growth or *trickle-up* arguments cannot be made in general terms either: as such they would have very limited purchase. A social productivist approach might require an interventionist, developmental state,[9] but this may be too heavy-handed. A more modest approach is managed pluralism (Midgley 1995). Intersectoral synergies between local government, NGOs and people's organizations and firms are another field of cooperation (Brown and Ashman 1999, Wignaraja 1992).

Managed pluralism involves political regulation. Merging social and market concerns also involves the development of collective bargaining systems. This may be difficult to achieve in segmented societies. Ethnic segmentation is a case in point; caste and class antagonism is another obstacle. A civic culture that strongly privileges individualism, as in North American free enterprise culture, may be more conducive to a casino mentality than to socially inclusive political settlements. Even so, one application of this kind of approach would be to review affirmative action policies in the United States and reservations policies in India. For these, legacies need not to be taken as destinies. The point of the social development approach is not to provide a menu but to suggest a direction of analysis and policy. Social development, redefined in a wide sense, can serve as an orientation for a new social contract and as such become a new assembly point for development.

Notes

1 In considering infant mortality rates, Drèze and Sen (1989) distinguish two patterns: growth-mediated security, in which the crucial factor in lowering infant mortality rates has been growth and employment (e.g. in Hong Kong, Singapore, and South Korea), and support-led security in which infant mortality rates have come down although growth rates have been low (in Chile, Costa Rica, Jamaica, and Cuba during the 1970s). The latter countries have since changed course or been overtaken by events: Chile embarked on a different course under the Pinochet regime; Costa Rica and Jamaica have implemented macroeconomic reforms since the 1980s; Cuba's economy is stagnant.

2 On the Kerala model see Robin 1992. 'The open unemployment rate is around three times the national average ... Kerala has earned the dubious distinction of being the only state in India whose real social expenditure has decreased during 1985–86/1991–92 period, compared to the decade 1974–75/1984–85' (Isaac and Tharakan 1995: 1996). Cf. Tharamangalam 1998 and 'The Kerala model of development: a debate'.

3 This is a British usage, parallel to, for example, social anthropology; e.g. Booth 1994a.

4 For instance, Indonesia's report to the Copenhagen summit is entirely framed by the 'Presidential Instruction No. 5/1993 regarding the Intensification of Efforts to Alleviate Poverty', the so-called IDT Program (IDT Program Implementation Guide, Jakarta, National Development Planning Agency and Ministry of Home Affairs, 1994). A report such as *Social Dimensions in the Agenda of the IDB* (Inter-American Development Bank 1995) is also confined to social policy. By contrast,

the parallel meeting organized by NGOs followed a different track. An example is the Philippine Rural Reconstruction Movement's *The Way of Power: Development in the Hands of the People* (Quezon City 1994), which develops a civil society and grassroots-centred Sustainable Rural District Programme, in other words, a social action and participatory policy approach. Several submissions combine social action and policy approaches, from below and above, such as Møller and Rasmussen (1995). UNRISD (1995) reviews various approaches, from poverty alleviation to participatory social policy and notions such as promoting global citizenship; cf. Mkandawire 2001, 2004.

5 The components of the Adelman-Morris index of social development are size of the traditional agricultural sector; extent of dualism; extent of urbanization; character of basic social organization; importance of indigenous middle class; extent of social mobility; extent of literacy; extent of mass communication; crude fertility rate; degree of modernization of outlook (in Temple and Johnson 1996: 10).

6 Cultural bias may be another limitation to HD. Griffin and McKinley (1994) seek to accommodate this by making HD responsive to cultural difference and disaggregating HDI according to ethnic groups within society. Griffin (2000b) considers cultural difference as an engine of economic growth.

7 Paul Streeten (in ul Haq 1995: xi) mentions the conflict between human resource developers (who emphasize HD as a means to growth) and humanitarians (who view it as an end and are also concerned with the unproductive and unemployable).

8 This context only allows a brief engagement. There is now a broad stream of publications on social capital particularly in economics and political science.

9 Or, an 'intelligent' or educator state that is ahead of civil society, such as France and Singapore; a principle that is not part of the Anglo-American tradition, which leans towards the minimal state.

9

Critical Holism and the Tao of Development

For Vincent Tucker

Life is poetic and harsh, momentary and evolutionary, personal and abstract, physical, emotional, mental and intuitive. Human experience is layered and multifaceted, but social science, circumscribed by a Cartesian and Newtonian matrix of knowledge, captures only a narrow slice of experience. Disciplinary boundaries further narrow and theories bend the range. Development processes likewise take place across dimensions – on a physical level, in an eco-logical framework, as shifts in social relations, changes in emotional landscapes, on a mental plane, in a political field, a historical context, on a moral plane and in a universe of meaning. Given the partial nature of development theories – which reflect disciplinary territories (and policy interventions) which, in addi-tion, reflect political and institutional interests – the development field is carved up in many ways. How then do we arrive at a comprehensive approach? If we opt for a holistic approach it may produce syntheses that are too quick and whose centre of gravity is located outside social science, for instance in ethics, so they yield commentaries with outsider status. One can identify the world of development as 'a totality of fragments' and the world of capitalisms as one of 'difference within a structured totality' (Pred and Watts 1992: 11), yet that does not tell us very much. In fact the notion of 'fragments' implies some kind of pre-existing wholeness. Responding to this dilemma is the context of this chapter. This is a reflexive chapter that is concerned with questions of general methodology and the philosophy of development.

Remedying remedies

This treatment is inspired by Vincent Tucker's work on critical holism, which he developed in relation to the sociology of health. He combines the sociology of health with critical development studies. In criticizing the role of transnational pharmaceutical industries and their commercialization of health he arrives at a new combination of concerns – holism and critical thinking, or holism with a bite, holism with an attitude. Part of this is an anthropological sensitivity to cultural dimensions of development (Tucker 1996b), a personal engagement with healing, which include fol-lowing a holistic health course and taking a degree in holistic massage, and interests ranging from music to psychotherapy.

Tucker's starting point is modern medicine, or the biomedical approach: the 'clinical gaze', 'a pill for every ill' (1997: 37), 'a magical fix for all ailments' (30), and the idea that 'health = doctors + drugs' (1996a: 17); a hegemonic system sustained and propagated by medical professionals and pharmaceutical industries. All along his interest has been not only in the politics of dependence in the south and Ireland but also in the possibilities for dependency reversal (Tucker 1996c) and, likewise, in alternatives to conventional medicine. In this respect his approach differs from treatments of modern medicine which are primarily critical (e.g. Kothari and Mehta 1988; Nandy 1995). He contrasts modern medicine with an emerging 'new holistic health paradigm' (1997: 32), which is considered at several levels. 'The emergence of the holistic paradigm will require not only a change in the practice of medicine and health care, but also in the knowledge system and the model of science on which it is based. It will also require changes in the institutional fabric of health care' (ibid.). His approach is concerned with extending holism itself: 'it also addresses weaknesses in holistic thinking and practice by incorporating into the model perspectives from more critical traditions of public health' (1996a: 1). For instance, Fritjof Capra's work 'like most approaches to holism, is less well developed when it comes to incorporating social, economic and cultural systems into the model' (1997: 42). Hence, Tucker distinguishes between

> two versions or tendencies in holistic thinking. One focuses primarily on the individual organism. Most holistic health practice belongs to this tendency. It differs from biomedicine in that in its diagnostic techniques and therapies it takes into account a broader range of systems, which include the biological, the energetic, the psychic, the interpersonal and the spiritual. While it is more cognisant of the social and environmental factors which impact on the health of the individual, and takes these into account in its diagnosis, it does not provide ways of analysing or intervening in these macro systems. The second version of holism derives from the more sociological approach of Engels and Virchow... It also derives from the public health tradition. It encompasses economic and political systems as well as biological and environmental systems and is based on the notion that health and illness are not simply biological phenomena but are socially produced. This more sociologically informed holism has been further developed by Marxist political economy and radical development theory... (1997: 42)

Tucker then initiates a further move. While the sociological tradition 'adds a critical edge often missing in holistic health practice ... it has little to contribute to our understanding of the personal and interpersonal dimensions of illness and wellbeing' (1997: 43). Finally: 'The critical combination of these two perspectives, which forms the basis of an expanded and more critical notion of holism, can provide a comprehensive alternative to the biomedical model' (ibid.).

Vincent Tucker's synthesis involves multiple movements: from biomedical reductionism to holism, from individual holism to sociological holism, from sociology and political economy to holism in personal, interpersonal and spiritual dimensions. The components of critical holism are spelled out in several places: 'a critical synthesis of holistic medicine, political economy, development theory, environmentalism and feminism ... a theoretical synthesis of holistic theory, Marxist political economy and culture critique' (1996a: 3); 'critical holism encompasses social, economic, political and environmental systems including world systems' (ibid.: 41). In health practice this yields the following combination:

> A holistic perspective on health promotion, while not excluding biomedical interventions, may include public health practices, environmental campaigns, political action, educational activities and complementary forms of medicine. It will include not only changes in personal life style, but also collective action to challenge organisations and institutions ... which act in ways detrimental to public health. (1997: 45)

This is a high-wire synthesis. While it is developed in relation to health it addresses gaps in our knowledge that are of general relevance. Its triple movement – providing remedies and remedying not only the original deficiencies but also the shortcomings of the remedies as well – is welcome medicine in relation to development studies and social science generally. It involves a developed sense of balance. Thus, we all know, not only intellectually but viscerally, the limitations of modern medicine. We may acknowledge the merits of holism, though its weaknesses are also evident – no critical edge, no political economy. The reverse applies to political economy – materialist savvy and sociological finesse, but no emotional or spiritual depth. If in a combined movement we bring all these together, balancing the limitations of each with the strengths of others, we have a bridge of uncommon strength and sophistication. This has been Vincent Tucker's contribution. In passing, Tucker notes that his critical holism paradigm 'also provides a basis for elaborating a general theory of human development' (1996a: 1), so it is worth probing what would be the general ramifications of this synthesis. Generally, the limitations of a position or paradigm are often remedied by switching to another position while the limitations of *this* position are not addressed. People often move from one ideological fix to another. The result is the usual pendulum swing alternating between extremes – a common spectacle in everyday politics and theory, and an everlasting merry-go-round of limited options.

Critical holism is an uncommon synthesis. Criticism and holism refer to different modes of cognition. This makes it a welcome synthesis: without a critical edge, holism easily becomes totalizing, romantic, soggy; and without holism, criticism easily turns flat, sour.

If we re-code these sensibilities, perhaps the synthesis becomes easier. To 'criticism' there are several strands: it refers to the exercise of analytical faculties; it means a repudiation of 'faith' and dogmatism in the Enlightenment tradition; it entails a commitment to class struggle in Marxism; an emancipatory knowledge interest in critical theory; and equality and social justice in dependency theory. Key elements of criticism then are analysis, anti-dogmatism and social justice. How does this tally with holism as a concern for the whole, the totality? If we take criticism in its affirmative sense it means acknowledging dimensions which have been *left out*. Through criticism an inclusive knowledge is to be achieved, which represents those elements which are outside or not acknowledged in the status quo. Accordingly, criticism is also an attempt at healing in the sense of restoring wholeness – by acknowledging and rendering visible that which has been ignored, left out. In a broad sense both criticism and holism then refer to modes of healing: from the point of view of completeness in a societal sense by way of emancipation and justice, and from the point of view of wholeness in a multidimensional sense.

Conventional therapies implicitly refer to 'wholeness' through the notion of deficiencies. Through 'additives' or supplements, dietary or vitamin deficiencies can be remedied. Only here wholeness is confined to the physical sphere, which permits medicalization and 'fixing'. Modern medicine recognizes psychological dimensions of health, as in psychosomatic illness, but these are compartmentalized away in domains such as psychology, psychiatry, neurology. (Here the idea of multiple layers is well established – such as the id, ego and superego in psychoanalysis – but this hardly feeds back into conventional medicine.) The difference between holistic and conventional therapies is that the former acknowledge emotional, psychological, spiritual (and moral and social) levels of being as dimensions of health and well-being, and seek to integrate these into the healing process.

Wholeness, holism

> Once the whole is divided, the parts need new names.
> (Lao Tsu [sixth century BC], 1973: 29)

According to a dictionary of word origins, '*Whole* is at the centre of a tightly knit family of English words descended from prehistoric Germanic *khailaz* "undamaged"' (Ayto 1990: 573). Other members of this family include *hail* 'salute', *hale, hallow, heal, health* and *holy*. 'Etymologically, *health* is the "state of being whole"…. The verb *heal* [OE] comes from the same source' (277). '*Holy* originated as a derivative of the prehistoric Germanic adjective which produced modern English *whole*, and so its etymological meaning is perhaps "unimpaired, inviolate"' (285). In Germanic languages there is a connection between health, healing, holiness and wholeness which also exists in other language groups, as in Latin *salvus* 'healthy', *salus* 'bliss, health', in Irish *slan* 'healthy, whole', in Greek *holos* 'whole', and in old Indian *sarva* 'undamaged, whole' (de Vries 1963: 257). 'Saviour' (in Dutch *heiland*) means 'healer' and connects to the Greek *soter* (de Vries 96). The Dutch *genezen* (healing, healed) refers to the Gothic *ganisan* 'saved, healthy, holy', which may be connected to the Greek *neomai* 'I come back, come home'. According to an etymologist, this would give the meaning of 'coming home safely' (de Vries 82).

Health, then, refers to a state of wholeness, and healing is restoring a person to wholeness. Viewed in this light 'holistic healing' becomes a tautology, for apparently all along health basically means wholeness and healing 'making whole'. This tautology makes sense only in distinction to conventional medicine. Holism, in this context, appears to be a cerebral attempt at the *recovery* of interconnections that have been lost in the course of analysis, in the process establishing different connections.

Holism is defined as 'the theory that whole entities, as fundamental and determining components of reality, have an existence other than as the mere sum of their parts' (*Random House Dictionary of the English Language*, quoted in Craig 1992: 4).

> Jan Christiaan Smuts gave the word currency in his 1926 book *Holism and Evolution*, where he advocated the exploration of matter, life, and mind in relation to each other, rather than as isolable realms of existence. Since then, *holistic* has been applied to approaches and attitudes, in the humanities and the social sciences as well as the sciences, that privilege the study of a system over analysis of its parts. (ibid.: 4–5)

In Smuts' work wholeness and holism are used interchangeably. His book follows an essay of 1912, 'An inquiry into the whole'. *Holism and Evolution* is a high-minded work that was influenced by the Cambridge Platonists, Bergson's vitalism, and ideas of evolution from Darwin to de Vries (Meurs 1997). Holism in this work derives from the Greek *holos* and stands for 'the activity of the Whole'. 'Holism that is the ultimate activity which prompts and pulsates through all other activities in the universe' (Smuts, quoted in Meurs 1997: 115). The first chapter deals with 'The holisation of the whole', which refers to assimilation and homogenization processes (Meurs 1997: 118).

Apparently there is slippage between wholeness and holism. As a notion wholeness is evocative and descriptive, whereas to holism there is a programmatic element. Now *systems* thinking comes into the picture, as part of the analysis recovery syndrome. Once the analytical mode has generated distinctions and separations, systems thinking is an attempt to piece together again that which has been taken apart. The attributes of systems, however, are unlike the properties of wholeness. Holism may be a step forward in relation to the Enlightenment habit of taking everything apart but it's short of wholeness. Humpty-Dumpty put together again is not the same Humpty-Dumpty. *Esprit de système* is not the spirit of wholeness. More precisely, there are different notions of system. It derives from the Greek *synhistanai*, 'to place together', so to understand things systematically means to put them in a context and to establish the nature of their relationship. This relationship may be thought of as calculable and machine-like, as in mechanistic notions of system; or as approximate network relations, as in general systems theory (Capra 1996: 27f.). In social science the notion of system ranges from structural functionalism *à la* Parsons, and world-system theory, to the complex systems approach of Niklas Luhmann. In Luhmann's words, 'Sociology can only describe society in society … It is a science of the social system and a social system of science. To make matters even more complex, as a science and, as a social system, sociology is also an internal observer of whatever system it participates in' (quoted in Lee 1997: 15). One problem of systems approaches is that they imply a closure of the field; they achieve understanding (and manipulability) by framing the field, and even reflexivity may not remedy this.

It makes sense then to distinguish between wholeness and holism as perspectives with related but separate lineages: wholeness refers to a comprehensive field which may be divided up according to spiritual criteria (there are divisions also in mystical or magical universes); holism is the systemic or scientific recombination of fragments in a new totality. From a historical point of view, wholeness resonates with neolithic and older sensibilities, while holism brings to mind the technology and mindset of the industrial era. While there are continuities between wholeness and holism, 'this is not to say that the differences between modern holistic thinkers and earlier ones are easily reconcilable' (Dunn 1986: 3). Both are relevant angles, each with its range of applicability.

The slippage between wholeness and holism leaves room for a politics of holism. In combination with ideas on evolution, holism can apparently be taken in any political direction. Jan Smuts is a case in point. A Cambridge graduate, back in South Africa Jan Smuts became a general, Minister of Defence and Mining in the new republic and Prime Minister from 1919 to 1924 and during the Second World War. A pro-British Boer and an empire builder in the tradition of Cecil Rhodes, he was part of the Milner Group, and as a member of the British Imperial War Cabinet he was a party to the Balfour Declaration that partitioned Palestine and an active negotiator in the partition of Ireland (Nederveen Pieterse 1989, Quigley 1966, Sampson 1987). Smuts endorsed segregation and introduced pass laws. His views on the 'native question' in South Africa were much like those of Rhodes. Africans, 'if left to themselves and their own tribal routine ... do not respond very well to the stimulus of progress'. Therefore, in white areas 'the system should only allow the residence of males for limited periods, and for purposes of employment among the whites' (quoted in Minter 1986: 43).[1]

To wholeness there are obviously many dimensions. Wholeness is evoked in mysticism, myth, religion. Faces of wholeness in the theatre of the gods are Pan, who gives us the word for 'all', Okeanos or the world stream, and Varuna the encompasser. Wholeness carries intimations of the unity of being as in *unio mystica*, oceanic feeling, cosmic consciousness (Mehta 1989). Religion is replete with 'whole' metaphors, such as the tree of life, wheel of life, dharma, 'Thou art That', and other references to the inner interconnectedness of phenomena. Paradise is a state of wholeness and the fall means the loss of wholeness. Paradise regained is wholeness regained. In Christian theology 'the whole of creation' envelops the non-human world. A conventional difference between mysticism and religion is that, in the former, wholeness may be a matter of experience, while in religion it becomes a point of doctrine, so that religion relates to mysticism as abstraction does to experience. While some religions superimpose a 'monotheistic consciousness', 'our psyches are "polytheistic" by nature' and contain an inner pantheon (Ahmed 1997: 33, 36). Wholeness is woven into personal experience – in life's transitions, in love, in experiences of pain and healing, in peak experiences. The paradox of wholeness is the powerful materiality of life and the immaterial nature of the full realization of life. Wholeness includes 'life beyond', but there is no life beyond without life within. The materiality of life makes transcendence possible and constrains it, casting a spell of material life that is shattered only at life's edges – in peak experiences or in the face of death.

It is not difficult to read philosophy from Plato to Aquinas, Hegel to Heidegger as elaborations, systematizations of sensibilities originally set forth in vision, revelation, religion, although to say so is of course sacrilege in reverse. At least, this is the argument of the *philosophia perennis* (*à la* Huxley 1946). Neo-Platonism, one of the strands in idealistic philosophy, connects eastern religions with western philosophy (Nederveen Pieterse 1994). What comes to mind is Hegel's view of world history as a rendezvous with the unfolding *Geist*. Richard Rorty is reproached for his 'undifferentiated, monotonous holism' (Bhaskar 1991: 100), which involves yet a different meaning and facet of holism.

So as a theme, wholeness functions like a kaleidoscope of sensibilities. Among lineages of holism Vincent Tucker mentions ecological thinking in biology which spread to social science. Related currents are Gestalt psychology, psychotherapy and Buddhist thought (1997: 41). In social science wholeness is thematized in several ways. Marxism represents a commitment to 'the whole' within a materialist ontology. Harrod's plea for 'a re-search for a lost completeness' refers to a return to critical political economy (1997: 108). Gestalt psychology led Ruth Benedict (1935) to a view on cultures as wholes or 'configurations' organized around core meanings. Talcott Parsons' social systems approach is centred on structural differentiation and functional integration. Louis Althusser viewed societies as structured wholes.

In the social sphere wholeness is often associated with romanticism and nostalgia, as in the idealization of 'tradition', communitarianism and the idealization of 'community'. In politics it can involve homogenizing projects of 'totality', as in some types of utopian politics, or nostalgia for a lost political 'unity'. In this light, a dose of difference can be quite a relief. A different and concrete angle on wholeness is the social exclusion approach (Bhalla and Lapeyre 1997). In liberation theology's 'preferential option for the poor' this sensibility is stated affirmatively. For the architect Robert Venturi, part of postmodern sensibilities is 'the obligation toward the difficult whole' (McHale 1992: 3).

Contradictions of modernity

The question of modern medicine is a subset of a larger problem – the question of modernity and, in turn, the contradictions of modernity: in particular the contradiction between the 'two cultures', the scientific-technological and the humanistic cultures, the worlds of science and art. The core of scientific culture is often traced back to Descartes and his project of 'certain knowledge' on the basis of mathematics as a universal scientific method, or 'the world according to mathematics'. The mathematical mind abstracts, generalizes, dichotomizes and is given to formalism (Davis and Hersh 1986, cf. Passmore 1978).[2] Critiques of Cartesianism, in the company of Bacon and Newton, go back a long way, among others to the Neapolitan philosopher Giambattista Vico: 'Mathematics is created in the self-alienation of the human spirit. The spirit cannot discover itself in mathematics. The human spirit lives in human institutions' (quoted in Davis and

Hersh 1986: x; see also Pompa 1990). This general current of dissent is as old as 'the other West of William Blake and Paracelsus' (Nandy 1995: 60). A different twist to this kind of dispute is the argument between Habermas and Lyotard on the virtues of the Enlightenment and the debate on postmodernism.

There is something jarring about the way the tension within modernity is usually conceptualized and represented on either side of the argument. Viewing the relationship between scientific and humanistic cultures as a dichotomy itself follows a Cartesian paradigm. Representing this tension as a dualistic, polarized relationship gives either side the opportunity to profile its position and in the process exaggerate the issue. It is clearly a superficial representation from the outset. Viewing this relationship as a continuum of views that meet and diverge on multiple levels is much more adequate. In addition this involves a one-sided representation of the Enlightenment, which is a much more complex historical field than is granted in conventional views.[3] This is worth keeping in mind when considering the long-standing attempts to bridge these worlds and reintegrate the sciences and humanities. Siu's *Tao of Science* attempted such a reintegration long before Capra's *Tao of Physics*. Generally elements of this fusion include the following:

- *Ecology.* Ecological knowledge as part of a general systems approach and deep ecology (as in Arne Naess 1976).
- *History of science.* Joseph Needham's work on the history of Chinese science and technology and its influence on western science is part of a wider body of work documenting the historical connections between 'western knowledge and eastern wisdom'. The Enlightenment also includes figures such as Leibniz and Goethe who bridged western and eastern sensibilities. Later Werner Heisenberg was influenced by Indian philosophy through conversations with Tagore, and Niels Bohr was inspired by his visit to China (Weber 1982: 218). On a conceptual level, Kuhn's (1962) work on scientific revolutions debunked the self-representation of progress in science, and through the notion of paradigm shifts introduced a meta-level of analysis of scientific procedures and gatekeeping.
- *Physics.* Subatomic physics has generated findings that upset Descartes' certain knowledge, including Heisenberg's uncertainty principle, according to which the instrument of measurement affects the outcome, also known as the observer effect. In the 1920s Alfred North Whitehead developed an inclusive notion of reality beyond dualisms such as those of mind and matter: 'In a certain sense, everything is everywhere at all times. For every location involves an aspect of itself in every other location' (quoted in Siu 1957: 157). In quantum physics this has been taken further in David Bohm's (1980) work on the implicate order. Several of these reorientations have been grouped together under the heading of the holographic paradigm (Wilber 1982), building on Dennis Gabor's work on holography.
- *New science.* This includes developments such as catastrophe theory, chaos theory, complexity theory, fuzzy logic, the theory of emergence, self-organizing systems (Prigogine and Stengers 1984) and new trends in biology and mind-brain research.

Some of these reorientations turn on a fusion or complementarity of 'western knowledge and eastern wisdom'. What is the status of this fusion? To what extent is the new science a marginal concern? It is not quite so marginal if we think of developments such as chaos theory, which has found a wide application (Gleick 1988), including in business (Peters 1988) and social science (Anderla et al. 1997, Eve et al. 1997). The butterfly effect, or sensitive dependence on initial conditions, may be interpreted as an instance of the implicate order in action. Subatomic physics finds an application in nano technology and advanced materials research. What several accounts suggest is that on the other side of science we come out at findings that intimate an interconnectedness of being that is similar to what has been intuited in mysticism – arguably, a complementarity between 'moonshine physics' and ground-floor mysticism.[4] In this view, the splitting process carried all the way through, to subatomic quantums and quarks, arrives at the ultimate unity of all being, or the universe as a 'sea of quarks' (Adachi 1996). At these deeper strata, contradictions such as those between the sciences and the humanities unravel. They turn out to be 'regional contradictions' that make sense within a certain limited context, but do not hold in the larger field. It is true, of course, that the world of everyday action is not a world of quantums or quarks, yet on the level of the foundational claims of science and epistemology it does matter that the Cartesian and Newtonian premises apply within a narrow range only. This argument cuts two ways. While to all human faculties and expressions there may be a 'territorial drive' and an urge toward functional autonomy, by this wide-angled logic, all are part of the whole and cannot be denied their potential to contribute to wholeness. This also holds for mathematics – in Plato's words, God ever geometrizes; and for computers – without computers the intricate calculations that led to chaos theory could not have been generated. In other words, 'both reductionism and holism are necessary' (Capra in Weber 1982: 241). New science does not replace but supplements Newtonian science.

> Typically, the new paradigm demonstrates that knowledge gained under the old paradigm is true *under specific boundary conditions*. Thus, the rules of motion put forth by Newton are not demolished by Einsteinian physics, but are shown to be a special case of a larger, more inclusive physics ... Chaos and complexity do not 'overthrow' former conceptions and scientific knowledge, but merely supplement them. (Eve 1997: 275)

Development and high modernism

The contradictions of modernity are of profound relevance to development studies. Considering that development is applied modernity, all the contradictions of modernity are reproduced within development as dramatically unresolved tensions. Development theory is now being torn between paradigms – mainstream, alternative and post-development – or between internal and external critiques of development. What then is the relevance of these disputes over modernity for development studies and of attempts to reconceptualize or bridge these concerns? Arguably, the most fundamental question concerns the meaning of development, which in turn boils down to the question of what evolution is.

The social sciences have a long lineage, but as sciences they go back less than two hundred years. Development thinking goes back to nineteenth-century political economy, but modern development thinking is no more than fifty years old. In relation to the complexities of social life, at times development as applied social science gives the impression of navigating the ocean in a row-boat, or a Lego imitation of collective existence, in which mechanistic notions of social dynamics in tandem with political and hegemonic interests push and shove for the driver's seat. Really existing development has been an arena of ideological posturing or pragmatic reformism, either way involving brutal simplifications and crude interventions. At times in relation to the collective body, development interventions seem like performing surgery with a chainsaw. All the same, in some conditions surgery with heavy equipment beats no surgery at all, although even that depends on which side of the operation one is on.

Development knowledge is fragmented and characterized by discipline-centrism. 'The development process is compartmentalised by each discipline to suit its own areas of specialization, research methods, and theoretical frameworks' (Brohman 1995: 303). In this division of labour there has been a definite hierarchy.

> Development in its halcyon days was mainly economic development. Other disciplines entered the area apologetically or stealthily – as the supplementary knowledge of social structures facilitating or hindering economic growth, as insights into the psychological factors motivating or discouraging economic growth, as information about the political factors influencing economic decisions. (Nandy 1995: 146)

Meanwhile divergent theories have often been applied in different policy spheres and economic sectors at the same time, making real existing development a patchwork of zigzag premises and policies.

Development thinking is steeped in mathematics – a world of numbers, indicators and statistics. Neoclassical economics is a formidable instance of applied Cartesianism. Part of this is a rendezvous with intellectual and managerial power – the power to classify, administer and change the world. The theoretical and methodological characteristics of neoclassical economics – the assumptions of universal applicability, measurability, objectivity, formal modelling – make it a powerful instrument. Reductionism along with disciplinary fragmentation has made expert regimes and technocratic interventions possible, and has generously contributed to development policy failures. According to a former president of the American Economic Association, 'When you dig deep down, economists are scared to death of being sociologists. The one great thing [they] have going for [them] is the premise that individuals act rationally in trying to satisfy their preferences. This is an incredibly powerful tool because you can model it' (Charles Schultze in Brohman 1995: 302). Conventional development is a politics of measurement, a matter of 'fixing' within limited spheres, achieving desired change by manipulating indicators and modifying numerical relationships, such as the ratio of external debt to GDP, or debt to exports.

The gap between economic development and social and cultural development, or the hard and soft dimensions of development, is reproduced in the institutional division between the Bretton Woods institutions and UN agencies, in which the former hold the purse strings. Indeed, this mathematical universe is inhabited in many different ways. For the sake of macroeconomic and financial management – by the IMF and Bank of International Settlements; with a view to economic growth in combination with sustainable development and poverty alleviation – by the World Bank; with a view to human development and the indicators of schooling, health, housing, sustainability – by the UNDP. What they share is a commitment to social engineering.

The American psychotherapist Thomas Moore proposes to add another ailment to psychology's list of disorders:

> I would want to include the diagnosis 'psychological modernism', an uncritical acceptance of the values of the modern world. It includes blind faith in technology, inordinate attachment to the material gadgets and conveniences, uncritical acceptance of the march of scientific progress, devotion to the electronic media, and a life-style dictated by advertising. This orientation towards life also tends toward a mechanistic and rationalistic understanding of matters of the heart. (1992: 206)

Modern development has suffered from a severe case of psychological modernism, has erected monuments to modernism, placing technological progress over human development. In Latin America the work of the *científicos* is not yet complete. In Asia 'laboratory states' have used science as an instrument of power and reason of state (Visvanathan 1988). Modernization and development, including critical Marxist development thinking, have been 'scientist' in temperament. 'Science became the integrating myth of industrial society' (Berman 1984: 187), so it became the guiding light of development policy. Rationalization was the key to modernization, so it became the master key to development. This is the familiar Enlightenment headache syndrome. We now turn to the countermoves.

Shortcuts and other remedies

> Do you think you can take over the universe and improve it?
> (Lao Tsu [sixth century BC], 1973: 29)

Rather than another diagnosis, what the situation calls for is a scrutiny of remedies. Often what is presented as the way ahead is no more than a shortcut – the ailment may be diagnosed correctly but the remedy is not examined. Some medicine turns a headache into a migraine, induces medicinal toxification, or provides only temporary or local relief. So in considering remedies for the culture of high modernism we may apply Vincent Tucker's recipe of remedying remedies. Some of the antidotes to high modernism reproduce dichotomous thinking, skipping levels, and neolithic nostalgia, or framing contemporary dilemmas in anachronistic terms.

Positions and counterpositions in the development field often operate on the basis of simplistic dichotomies – such as modernity versus 'tradition', science versus indigenous knowledge, the impersonal versus the personal, the global versus the local. And critiques of development modernism often adopt dualisms that in effect replicate the dichotomous thinking of modernism. Does it make sense to subject modernity to the same simplistic treatment to which the project of modernity has subjected social life? We need to distinguish between the *project* of modernity and *really existing modernities* (and the sociology of modernity), which are far more complex than blueprint modernity. Opposition to modernization has been part of modern experience, and the dialectics of modernity include modernism as a cultural politics that at times runs contrary to modernity critical theory and reflexive modernity.

The world of post-development ranges from militant development agnosticism and rejectionism to the New Age thinking of the Schumacher College, which offers courses on 'Systems thinking and learning for change' and 'Buddhist economics'. There is a beatific island effect to this project. It describes itself as 'a truly Green oasis, a centre for deep green values expressed beautifully by people from all over the world' (1997).

At either end of the spectrum, adherents of post-development use statistics to make their case. 'For example, it has been estimated that a single edition of the *New York Times* eats up 150 acres of forest land' (Rahnema 1997: 379). According to Gustavo Esteva, 'if all countries "successfully" followed the industrial example, five or six planets would be needed to serve as mines and waste dumps' (1992: 2). Thus post-development too inhabits a mathematical universe. The opponents of abstraction, generalization, dichotomization and formalism often apply abstraction, generalization, dichotomization and formalism in order to make their case, also in the development field. While presenting itself as an external critique, post-development critique is external to (some of) the goals and not necessarily to the premises or the means of development. Some of the points of reference of post-development – the opposition to reductionist science and modernity (Alvares 1992, Nandy 1988) – are unreflective and dichotomous in their logic. They exhibit a similar polarized and dualistic thinking to that of modernization theory, which dichotomizes 'tradition' and 'modernity', and tend to fall into the trap of modernization in reverse. The question, however, is how to overcome dichotomies, not merely to change the direction of the current.

Majid Rahnema criticizes 'compulsory actomania' and the 'mask of love' in development aid. In his view what lies behind solidarity or 'charity' is 'the great fear we have of becoming fully aware of our powerlessness in situations when nothing can be done' (1997: 392, 393). Who are we to intervene in other people's lives? He recalls the Chinese notion *wu-wei*, which is variously translated as 'non-intervention' or 'action through non-action' (397). What is odd in Rahnema's treatment is that he proceeds to explain this Taoist notion by setting forth the Confucian 'arts of governance' and 'aesthetic order', as if he is oblivious to the tensions between Taoism and Confucianism, which run as deep as those between mysticism and official religion, and to

Confucianism's comeback as an ideological prop for authoritarian regimes. It may be argued that 'non-intervention' is a superficial translation of *wu-wei*. A relevant passage in the *Tao te Ching* is: 'Tao abides in non-action / Yet nothing is left undone' (Lao Tsu 1973: 37). 'Nothing is left undone' is not the same as doing nothing. Again, what is offered as the road ahead is a shortcut, a rapid and easy synthesis that does not do justice to the multiple dimensions of existence, each of which involves tensions which require engagement in their own right and appropriate to the level at which they are experienced. This is holism without a sufficient critical edge.

A polemical polarization that is similar in structure is taking shape in relation to globalization. Some who identify globalization with corporate, market-driven transnationalism opt, in reaction to globalization, for localization and, in a reaction to free trade, for 'new protectionism'. An example is the volume *The Case against the Global Economy and for a Turn toward the Local* (Mander and Goldsmith 1996). This position reduces globalization to economic globalization, confuses an opposition to neoliberalism with an opposition to globalization, and thus mixes up the current form of globalization with the underlying trend of globalization. This involves setting up a false dichotomy between the global and the local. The global and the local require and sustain one another in many ways. Examples of interpenetration are 'glocalization' and 'insiderism', or the thesis according to which transnational corporations can enter foreign markets effectively only if they become insiders; the argument according to which flexible specialization leads towards the relocalization of operations so as to be close to consumers, suppliers, competitors and high-skilled labour; the dialectics of globalization which show, for instance, that transnational corporations may well end up as active promoters of localism (Miller 1997); and a host of cultural studies which show that the global and the local are embedded in one another. A further argument is that the local itself is a construction, a performative stance that owes its meaning and dynamics to its relationship to wider units, including the global (Boon 1990). So on several counts the contrast between the global and the local does not work as a clear-cut distinction or as a dichotomy, because for either to function it requires the other.

'Identifying with the whole' is a formidable challenge and taking shortcuts is tempting. Part of the remedy for modernism is to recover lost sensibilities, a 'resurrection of subjugated knowledges'; or, 'rediscovering traditional knowledge' (Fals-Borda 1985). This may involve reconnecting with spiritual sources sidelined and bulldozed by the incursions of colonialism and modernization, for instance reinvoking the shaman (Nandy 1989). Max Weber had already pointed to charisma as a way out of the 'disenchantment of the world'. However, the problem with charisma is that it makes no distinction between Hitler and Gandhi. The shaman stands in contrast to the scientist and the priest, but that is only half the story; the other half includes the different types of shamans, for example distinguishing between the *brujo* or wizard and the *curandero* or healer. A recourse to cults is another option, with obvious limitations: 'cults can have either a tranquilizing or a liberating effect on people, depending, among others, on the leadership's inspiration and the social context' (Huizer and Lava 1989: 15). Morris Berman made a point about the 'flip side of Cartesianism' which, even if he overstates his case, is still valid:

> Why not abandon Cartesianism and embrace an outlook that is avowedly mystical and quasi-religious, that preserves the superior monistic insight that Cartesianism lacks? Why not deliberately return to alchemy, or animism, or number mysticism? ... The problem with these mystical or occult philosophies is that they share ... the key problem of all nondiscursive thought systems: they wind up dispensing with thought altogether. To say this is not, however, to deny their wisdom ... My point is that once the insight is obtained, then what? These systems are, like dreams, a royal road to the unconscious, and that is fine; but what of nature, and our relation to it? What of society, and our relationship to each other? ... In fact, it is but the flip side of Cartesianism; whereas the latter ignores value, the former dispenses with fact. (1984: 188)

'The commitment toward the difficult whole' is ill served by binarisms. What is needed is a combination of wholeness and difference, as in Vincent Tucker's synthesis. Shortcut holism may just produce neolithic nostalgia – revisiting Arcadia, which yields only temporary comfort, island paradises that provide merely local relief, a politics of ecstasy that produces a hangover. Recovering the wisdom of ages is needed, but not as a shortcut. What is needed, rather than simply flipping over to another extreme, is a new sense of balance, between science and art, fact and value, analysis and meaning. Nowadays this means bridging the development gap and crossing sensibilities ranging all the way from neolithic to post-industrial settings. It involves recognizing multiple dimensions of existence and, accordingly, multiple modes of cognition, which need to coexist rather than compete. The assumption that only a single mode of cognition should prevail implies skipping levels.

Towards the Tao of development

Vincent Tucker's critical holism cannot be readily translated into a general theory of development because, unlike in health, there is no holistic practice in development. Alternative development practices tend to be local and short of a holistic approach. While there is a mysticism of the human body, a theory and a practice (holistic medicine), there is no equivalent holism of the social field. This is the missing element. There are, so to speak, 'a thousand points of light', but they are scattered about, like 'ten thousand things' – local alternatives, cultural and spiritual alternatives, rival theories, counterpoints and countercurrents,[5] but there is no unifying, overarching paradigm as there is, up to a point, in relation to health. The appeal of critical holism is that it places holistic theorizing and practice in relation to collective existence on the agenda and thus renders it imaginable: at least steps can be taken in its general direction.

Since in its epistemology social science has been a follower of natural science, would it not be logical for it also to follow new developments in science, including new science? It would be, except that the extent of specialization has narrowed the nexus between the two. The present situation in social sciences and development studies is an uneven combination of trends – towards polemical antagonisms, partial recombinations and occasional syntheses.

Criticisms of Cartesian science also have deep roots in the south. Both science and a critique of science movements have played a role in development activism and popular movements (Zachariah and Sooryamoorthy 1994). One trend is to view science as a religion,[6] and as power. Suspicion of Enlightenment science is also a leitmotif in radical ecological thinking (e.g. Shiva 1988a). Science here stands for Cartesianism, Newtonian mechanism, positivism, an instrument to achieve mastery over nature. At times this presents a caricature of science that ignores ongoing developments in science and new science. Why should critique of science and of science-as-power mean being anti-science? This would be a Luddite view and at times 'anti-development' comes across as twentieth-century Luddism. Meanwhile science, of course, is a major instrument of ecological monitoring. The 'Limits to Growth' take the form of a mathematical argument. 'Green accounting' uses scientific measures to arrive at realistic costing and pricing. The critique of science is part of reflexive modernity. What this means is the integration of multiple knowledges within a larger framework.[7]

Positivism is no longer the dominant temperament in social science except in economics and number-crunching sociology. Increasingly the lead paradigm in social science is constructivism. In development studies, one-sided disciplinary perspectives are gradually in retreat and being relegated to the status of partial knowledge. A development economist can no longer afford to ignore politics, sociology, gender, ecology, culture; nor can a political scientist or sociologist afford to ignore economics. Most problems now faced in development require a combined approach, such as structural adjustment, currency instability, corruption, the environment, gender, poverty, conflict prevention, complex emergencies, post-conflict reconstruction. Many policies that are now initiated involve partnerships of different parties, joint efforts of government agencies, social organizations and firms. Clearly the 'partnership' gospel itself prompts new forms of critical engagement; but even so the field is changing profoundly. To make synergies possible in policy they must become part of development thinking. Also, now that participation and empowerment have become part of the mainstream, even if primarily in rhetoric, the bottom-up, ground-up sensibilities and local culture that were the domain of grassroots, activist and anthropological approaches need to be integrated into mainstream discourse. Many new concepts that are current in development talk imply a combination of disciplines: good governance, accountability, human development, institutional development. New theoretical perspectives are likewise interdisciplinary, such as new institutional economics and public action. We witness both a return to and a renewal of political economy and new combinations such as ecological economics (which is more than simply resource economics) and the sociology of economics. Economic sociology shows, for instance, that markets are socially embedded and politically constituted and vary culturally, and yields novel notions such as social systems of production

(Hollingsworth and Boyer 1997). At the same time these reorientations tend to be ad hoc and only dimly reflected in general theoretical reorientations or in everyday research, which remain empiricist. Disciplinary knowledge still ranks as foundational knowledge. Interdisciplinary research is more widely applauded than it is practised. A multidisciplinary approach refers to a combination and an interdisciplinary approach to an interaction of disciplines; a holistic approach is a step further. Holistic means integrated from the outset, which implies a revisioning of each discipline (a new view of economics, etc.[8]) and not just an adding up.

An example of holistic science is Gregory Bateson's synthesis, which Berman refers to as 'a non-Cartesian mode of *scientific* reasoning ... a methodology that merges fact with value and erodes the barrier between science and art' (1984: 232). For Berman this represents a general point of reference: 'I see our immediate future in a post-Cartesian paradigm, not in a premodern one' (271). The difference between Bateson's holism and the archaic tradition, according to Berman, is its 'self-conscious character' (272). Berman's *Reechantment of the World* is likewise a self-conscious re-enchantment.[9]

Considering that one of the problems of conventional development thinking is linearity, a relevant option is the application of chaos theory to development. In social science, chaos theory can be used as the basis of a non-modern social theory (Lee 1997) and with a view to public policy (Anderla et al. 1997; Elliott and Kiel 1997). A preliminary point is that there is no ready translation of chaos theory from natural to social systems (Elliott and Kiel 1997: 72). Chaos does not mean randomness or the absence of order; it refers to the unpredictability of the outcome of processes because of small differences in initial conditions. The butterfly effect, or a sensitive dependence on initial conditions, has its place in folklore:

> For want of a nail, the shoe was lost;
> For want of a shoe, the horse was lost;
> For want of a horse, the rider was lost;
> For want of a rider, the battle was lost;
> For want of a battle, the kingdom was lost!
> (Traditional, quoted in Gleick 1988: 23)

Chaos theory suggests distinguishing between different spheres of collective existence: those in which Newtonian dynamics prevail, and where robust policy interventions may be effective; and those in which non-linear dynamics predominate and where 'gentle action' is appropriate. In addition, chaos theory suggests an ecological perspective: 'If chaos theory is right, a myriad of interactions in the nonhuman world is required to support and sustain the human world. Perhaps the Gaia hypothesis is undergirded by the mathematics of chaos to a degree even its originator might be surprised to learn of' (Eve 1997: 279–80).

Thus, some spheres would lend themselves to intervention: 'In those cases where a stable and predictable response is known, related policy is eminently sensible. In areas such as tax expenditures where consumers and corporations do behave as Newtonian machines in response to interest rates or tax abatements, public policy is quite effective in altering behavior' (Elliott and Kiel 1997: 77). Whether this would apply in countries in the south with 'soft states' is an open question. Neoclassical economics with its assumption of atomistic individuals exercising rational choice proceeds as if *this* sphere is the only sphere. In reality the sphere in which this applies is quite circumscribed. Complexity is by far the more common condition, north and south. In the north this has led to an awareness of the limited effectiveness of social engineering and of the malleability of society as a fiction. 'As societies become more complex, even the most arduous efforts to change social dynamics provide only minimal benefit' (ibid.: 76). This insight has barely penetrated development thinking. Modernization efforts remain surgery with a chainsaw. Poverty alleviation remains a matter of advanced arithmetic. Now chaos theory confirms what anthropologists have known all along: that 'Complex adaptive systems often exist on the edge of chaos' (Eve 1997: 280; an example given is the irrigation system in Bali). Many so-called traditional ways of life involve a sophisticated, time-tested social and ecological balance. That outside interventions can do more damage than good is confirmed by the harvest of several development decades.

Where non-linear dynamics prevail, the counsel for policy is 'gentle action' (Elliott and Kiel 1997:73). This may be a more faithful approximation of *wu-wei* than 'non-intervention'. Thus, chaos theory yields a complex range of action orientations. Consideration for the ramifications of small differences can be translated in several ways – as a sensitivity to local conditions and cultural differences, and as an antidote to abstract models that gloss over local conditions and the actual implementation of development interventions. This is the point of the cultural turn in development, the return of anthropology to development. It also suggests a regard for the organizational and managerial dimensions of development on the ground and points to institutional analysis. A related consideration concerns the reflexivity of development as a form of applied cybernetics. Reflexivity here has two meanings – the self-referential character of development thinking, which in effect represents layer upon layer of reflexive moves, each a reaction to and a negotiation of previous development interventions, as an ongoing trial-and-error motion. And also the importance of subjectivities in the development process, the reactions of people on the ground to development plans, projects, outcomes, or people's reflexivity, which should be built into the development process. Steps in this direction include popular development (Brohman 1996) and public action theory.

The contributions of chaos theory to social science are preliminary and schematic. The distinction between linear and non-linear dynamics is of some use but too sketchy to be of much use. Already at times development processes are regarded as curvilinear, rather than linear.[10] Development refers both to a *process* (as in, a society develops) and an *intervention* (as in, developing a society). For Cowen and Shenton, this produces an intrinsic tension: 'Development defies definition ... because of the difficulty of making the intent to develop consistent with immanent development' (1996: 438).

Considering this kind of difficulty, would it make sense to think of the Tao of development? While the Tao of physics refers to a combination of physics and mysticism, the Tao of development is a more difficult combination because development is not merely a science or analytics (development theory) but also a politics. Taoism evokes an association of inaction, quietism. It is not clear whether this really applies to Tao, but there is no historical example of existing Taoism that disputes this, and historically there is a dialectic between Taoism and Confucianism.[11] Still this does not simply close the issue. For instance, by analogy, although existing socialism has not met expectations, Marxism continues to be relevant as a method.

One of the core problems of development is its pretentiousness, the insurmountable arrogance of intervening in other people's lives. This may be balanced by an equally pretentious notion, but an entirely different kind of pretension – the Tao of development. Setting a high goal for development may be better than setting no goal at all, or declaring development over and done with – as in post-development approaches – while, in the meantime, development business-as-usual goes on. Setting an elusive goal for development may be better than carrying on with development as a positivist politics of measurement; although when it comes to, for instance, poverty alleviation there will obviously be different opinions on this. The Tao of development means acknowledging paradox as part of development realities: such as the antinomies between measurement and meaning, between intervention and autonomy, or the tension between the local and the global. These antinomies are part of the perplexities of the human condition. Development participates in these perplexities and is not in some fashion outside or beyond them. Some will regard this acknowledgement of complexity as a gain, and others – who are fighting a different kind of battle – as a loss. The Tao of development is asymptotic – never entirely approachable, like an ever-receding horizon. What it involves is a subtle and sophisticated sense of balance across different dimensions of collective existence.

Balanced development in a conventional sense refers to a balance between economic growth and redistribution, and between growth across different sectors. Critical holism as a balancing act involves balance in a wider and more fundamental sense, across dimensions of collective existence, from the epistemological to the practical, which may take several forms.

- A *multidimensional* approach, or a balance between the horizontal and vertical dimensions of collective existence. The horizontal refers to the worldly and social spheres; the vertical refers to the inner dimension of subjectivities and meanings, to the depth of the social field, its layered character, which Anouar Abdel-Malek referred to as the 'depth of the historical field'.
- A *multifaceted* approach or a diamond social science, which reflects or shines light upon relations and dynamics across sectors (economy, politics, social, cultural) and levels (local, microregional, national, macroregional, global) and achieves a balance between them.[12] This might be termed Gestalt sociology.

- A *chiaroscuro* social science which abandons the assumption of full transparency of society. The assumption of transparency is what lent the Enlightenment its totalitarian bend, as in Bentham's panopticism and in socialist state ideology (Laclau 1990). This is a matter of modesty, a sense of the contingency of knowledge, or self-limiting rationality (Kaviraj 1992).[13] *Clair-obscur*, originally a term to describe the play of light and shadow in oil paintings, here refers to a sense of balance and interplay between that which is known and unknown, conscious and unconscious, the day and night sides of life.
- A distinction between and combination of objective and subjective dimensions of development. Development thinking is now increasingly anchored in people's subjectivities rather than merely in overarching institutions – the state or international institutions. While development thinking has become more participatory and insider-oriented, as in the actor-oriented approach (Long 1994), development practice has not been democratized, particularly when it comes to macroeconomic management, so there is a growing friction between development thinking and practice.
- A trend in local and increasingly also in large-scale development is towards partnerships across sectors, or synergies between different development actors – government, civic associations and firms. This is a marked departure from times when development was seen as either state-led, or market-led, or civil society-led (cf. Chapter 6). This might be considered a holistic approach;[14] but not a critical approach because talk of partnership in unequal relations of power is clearly apolitical (cf. Tvedt 1998: 224).
- Since development is concerned with the measurement of desirable change over time, it is chronocentric. For a more complex awareness, what is needed is combining multiple time frames and a balance between 'slow knowledge' and the 'fast knowledge' of instant problem solving. 'Slow knowledge is knowledge shaped and calibrated to fit a particular ecological context' (Orr 1996: 31). The conventional time horizon of development policy – the mid-term time span of a generation, or shorter, down to five years or so, in the case of planning, development projects and project-based lending – has changed with sustainable development and the implied notions of intergenerational equity and 'co-evolutionary development'. It is changing also as a consequence of the duration of the development era and the failures of 'development decades', which gradually bring to the fore the *longue durée* of development. Evolution, a long-time silent partner of development, is coming into the foreground.

On the whole, this sense of balance is better achieved in social science than in development studies; it is comparatively more developed in relation to situations that are geographically and socially nearer than those which are distant (as a function of insider knowledge); and more developed in relation to the past and in history (where hindsight makes it easier to acknowledge the complexity of motive, action and result) than in relation to the present or future. In forecasting and future projects, one-dimensional science and technology treatments, or the flat earth extended in time, are almost the norm, except in science fiction.

There is an affinity between spatially wide and temporally long approaches, or between globalization and evolution. Both are forms of holism, spatial and temporal. With evolution coming back to the foreground, ideas such as those of Teilhard de Chardin are making a comeback (e.g. Arruda 1996). Terhal has compared Teilhard de Chardin's ideas of 'evolutionary convergence', the noosphere and the dawn of collective reflection, with Kuznets and Wallerstein's perspectives on world development.[15] He finds that Teilhard underestimates social stratification and inequality in human evolution (1987: 228) and that there are elements of Eurocentrism to his work (266–7), which make it another instance of shortcut holism.

In Skolimowski's perspective too evolution is taking a reflexive turn: 'we are evolution conscious of itself' (1994: 92). For Skolimowski, 'the feast of life is participation' (157). For Stuart Todd, what follows from this perspective is that the clue for development is to 'align with life processes' (1997: 36). But this is too generic a recipe, like an all-purpose elixir, like Bergson's *élan vital*, for what are 'life processes'? Are not development and its contradictions themselves manifestations of 'life processes'? This introduces 'life processes' in a normative, discriminating sense, without providing the terms of distinction. Goonatilake (1991) introduces the notion of 'merged evolution' to characterize the situation in which through biogenetic engineering the strand of cultural evolution – which hitherto has run a separate course – merges with and impacts on biological evolution. This perspective distinguishes *and* combines: rather than positing a shortcut 'evolutionary convergence' it confronts the dilemmas of a real existing convergence.

As to globalization, critical holism calls for a perspective on world history and globalization beyond conventional disciplinary methodologies (e.g. Mazlish and Buultjens 1993). There is no doubt that the future lies with visions of cooperative globalization (as in Arruda 1996), in contrast to competitive globalization, although these cannot be neatly separated, because competition and cooperation are also two sides of the same coin. However, shortcut holism – which ignores or underrates inequality and difference – falls short as a remedy.

This sense of balance means treating development as a tightrope act. The source of critical holism is the field of health and healing, in which individual and collective concerns typically come together. Feminism is another approach in which personal and social concerns are combined by rethinking the boundaries between the private and the public, the personal and the political. These combinations, along with the idea of Gestalt sociology or social science, raise a further option: viewing social science not merely as explanation or as critique, the standard assignments of social science, but as healing, as socio-therapy. As there is therapy in relation to the individual body and psyche, can there be healing of the collective body? In popular culture the idea is not uncommon, as in Sinéad O'Connor's lyrics about Ireland: 'And if there ever is going to be healing, there must be remembering, and then grieving, so that then there can be forgiving' ('Famine', O'Connor 1994). In development work this is not such an uncommon idea either – after all, what else is post-conflict rehabilitation and conflict prevention? Both notions have emerged in relation to complex emergencies and ethnic conflict. Yet if the notion of development as healing sounds novel, it is presumably because it makes explicit that which has been implicit, and in doing so combines sensibilities which are usually kept neatly apart in separate boxes. These then are elements of the Tao of development: a holistic approach, a sense of balance across dimensions, a notion of collective healing. Critical holism in combining holism and difference merges these sensibilities in a balancing act.

Wholeness then should not be expected from a shortcut towards an undivided whole in a divided world but should be sought in a new balance. The counsel for development studies and social science is to distinguish between multiple spheres and levels, each of which requires engagement on its own terms, and not merely to contrast but to combine knowledges. As to implications for action and policy, this involves a case by case, contextual assessment of whether linear or non-linear dynamics prevail and whether robust or gentle action is appropriate. It also exceeds local alternatives. Critical holistic development includes macroeconomic management, global democratization and planetary ethics. Identifying with the whole means that development can no longer be simply geared to material aims and achievements but must include non-material dimensions, as in cultural development. It means that development can no longer be anthropocentric but must encompass the planetary ecology. Stretching the meaning of development to its fullest, it may be summed up as a collective learning process of human self-management according to the most comprehensive standards conceivable and practicable.

Notes

1 Note the reference to 'system' in this quotation. As Minter notes (1986: 42), several biographies try to whitewash Smuts's reputation as a humanitarian philosopher-statesman. Meurs (1997) presents him as an obstacle in the way of the architects of apartheid

2 'The computerization of the world represents an advanced stage of Cartesianism. Within that stage, programs become autonomous. We have even been given intimations of automated concept formulation and of action instigated as a consequence of such automation' (Davis and Hersh 1986: 303). Current developments in global currency trading are an example of automated action: triggers built into trading programmes set in motion a series of financial operations whose ripple effects can upset financial systems. For a more developed argument see Yurick 1985.

3 A standard omission in representations of the Enlightenment is that it was not only an epoch of rationalism, but also of romanticism, and that these occurred in combination. For instance, what is one to say of these statements of Diderot: 'what makes me angry is that the passions are never regarded from any but the critical angle. People think they do reason an injury if they say a word in favor of its rivals. Yet it is only the passions, and the great passions, that can raise the soul to great things ... The language of the heart is a thousand times more

varied than that of the mind, and it is impossible to lay down the rules of its dialectics' (quoted in Gay 1977: 188, 189).

4   The complementarity between new physics and mysticism is disputed by, among others, Wilber, who deems it a false complementarity and at most concedes that new physics *accords* with mysticism (1982: 166–79). While mysticism addresses all levels – physical, biological, mental, subtle, causal and ultimate – physics only pertains to a single level (159).

5   Besides alternative development literature, see e.g. Henderson 1996a, Whitmyer 1995, Roszak 1976.

6   'Positivism is just a crank religion' (Chris Mann in Dunn 1986: 2).

7   Capra gives another example of the integration of multiple knowledges: 'From the very beginning it was clear to me that there was no reason to abandon the biomedical model. It could still play a useful role for a limited range of health problems within a large, holistic framework, as Newtonian mechanics was never abandoned but remains useful for a limited range of phenomena within the larger framework of quantum-relativistic physics' (1988: 171; cf. Abraham et al. 1992).

8   According to Hazel Henderson (1996b), economics is not a science but politics in disguise.

9   This is not as clear with Toulmin, who advocates not the abandonment of modernity or a return to pre-modernity, but *humanizing modernity* and a return to the oral, the particular, the local, the timely (1990: 180f.).

10 E.g. Cowen and Shenton about Hegel's views on development: 'Unlike the linear image that the idea of progress evoked, the course of development was curvilinear or spiral-like, always impeded or arrested within its own logical structure' (1996: 130).

11 As to Taoism: 'It is inconceivable to a Taoist that Tao should be actualized in this world by human efforts because the core of Taoist doctrine is to teach its followers to transcend merely human affairs and psychologically dwell in "nothingness" (*wu*) so as to be in line with the "nonaction" (*wu-wei*) of the great *Tao*' (Wei-ming 1979: 10–11). Generally, while there have been episodes of a working balance between mysticism and official or state religion – between Buddhism and governance, Qabbala and Judaism, Christian mysticism and Christendom, Sufism and Islam, etc. – such episodes are not well known or readily accessible, so that they could act as sustainable examples.

12 Several significant books in social science achieve this in different ways. It applies to the oeuvre of Max Weber, Gramsci and Braudel and to books such as Wertheim's *Evolution and Revolution*, Stavrianos' *Global Rift*, Worsley's *The Three Worlds*, and David Harvey's *The Condition of Postmodernity*.

13 'I plead not for the suppression of reason, but an appreciation of its inherent limits' (Gandhi in Parekh 1997: 68).

14 This is the theme of a report in the *Irish Times* on social partnerships, particularly in disadvantaged areas. The partnerships include 'business, trade unions, farming organisations, schools, health boards, state agencies … and representatives from the local community' (Catherine Foley, 'The holistic way of solving problems', *Education & Living* supplement, 17 February 1998, pp. 2–3).

15 According to Teilhard de Chardin, 'Although mounting demographic pressure causes quite a number of evils at one level of human interaction', in principle it leads to 'social unification and a higher level of collective consciousness' (quoted in Terhal 1987: 176).

10

Digital Capitalism and Development: The Unbearable Lightness of ICT4D

The application of information and communication technologies (ICT) in development policies – in short, information-for-development or ICT4D – follows ideas of digital divide and cyber apartheid. This discussion situates ICT4D in critical development studies and global political economy and argues that information-for-development is primarily driven by market expansion and market deepening. As the latest accumulation wave, digital capitalism generates information technology boosterism and cyber utopianism with the digital divide as its refrain. The first part of this discussion criticizes the discourses and policies of bridging the digital divide; the second section views information-for-development as part of a package deal in which cyber utopianism is associated, not exclusively but primarily, with marketing digital capitalism. This is examined further in the third section on the relationship between digital capitalism and cyber utopianism of which ICT4D is a part.

The actual task of information-for-development is to disaggregate ICT4D and to reconsider ICT in development policy in this light. This is taken up in two sections that place ICT4D in the context of development studies and development policy. I argue that less emphasis on the internet and more on telephone, radio and television would normalize and ground the discussion. I conclude that the ICT4D discussion should move away from development aid, NGOs and externally funded digital projects and focus on the central question of disembedding technology from capital.

Bridging the digital divide

The digital divide, the theme of a dazzling outpouring of literature,[1] is typically portrayed in statistics, for instance 'the fact that half the world population has yet to make its first telephone call, or that the density of telephone lines in Tokyo exceeds that of the entire continent of Africa' (Campbell 2001: 119). Or, Manhattan has more internet providers than all of Africa (Fors and Moreno 2002). Eighty-eight per cent of internet hosts are in North America and Europe and 0.25 per cent in Africa (half of which are concentrated in South Africa). With 13 per cent of the world population, Africa has only 0.22 per cent of landline telephone connections and less than 2 per cent of global PC ownership (Ya'u 2004: 14).

The digital divide is a deeply misleading discourse: the divide is not digital but socioeconomic, but representing the divide in technical terms suggests technical solutions. It suggests digital solutions for digital problems (Cullen 2001; Warschauer 2003: 298). With the digital divide comes reasoning that correlates connectivity with development performance – 'Area A is rich, integrated into market relationships, and has a lot of telephones; area B is poorer, less integrated into market relationships, and has fewer telephones: therefore, a telephone rollout will make B richer and more integrated' (Wade 2002: 450). The next step is to equate connectivity and economic development and to view ICT as key to bridging the rich–poor gap and 'national "e-readiness" as a cornerstone of capacity building ... the discourse surrounding ICT has thus become part of developmental discourse itself' (Thompson 2004: 105).

Hence follows the policy of bridging the digital divide. Since digital capitalism doesn't go where profit margins are low such as rural areas and developing countries, the rationale of bridging the digital divide is that development intervention can make up for market imperfections and jumpstart connectivity on a nonprofit basis.

Bridging the digital divide has become a keynote of development policy, heavily promoted by major institutions. The World Bank and its Global Information and Communication Technologies Department launched the Development Gateway, InfoDev, the Global Knowledge Partnership, the Global Development Learning Network, World Links for Development, the African Virtual University and a host of other initiatives (Luyt 2004; Thompson 2004; Wade 2002). The G8 launched the Digital Opportunities Task or DOT Force which is endorsed by the UNDP (Shade 2003). The UNDP started the Sustainable Development Network Program and the Global Network Readiness and Resources Initiative, and has teamed up with Cisco Systems to offer ICT courses in developing countries (McLaughlin 2005). The UN is involved via the World Intellectual Property Organization (WIPO). Following the 1997 Basic Telecommunications Agreement the WTO looks further towards e-commerce (Shade 2003). The World Summit on the Information Society met in Tunis in 2005. Development cooperation in Australia, Canada, the Netherlands, Scandinavia and Switzerland, among others, sponsors digital projects in developing countries. NGO initiatives include Computer Aid International, World Computer Exchange and the International Development Research Centre (Ya'u 2004: 23).

In Thomas Friedman's book *The World Is Flat*, information technology is the key to bridging the development gap between the United States and India and to bridging the rich–poor gap. 'Three billion people–from India, China, and the former Soviet empire–walked onto a "flattened playing field." They can now "plug and play, connect and collaborate, more directly with your kids and mine than ever before in the history of the planet"' (Friedman 2005). The combination of rising educational levels in developing countries (at a time when the American educational system is showing weaknesses) and the business strategies of multinational companies, with ICT as an enabling factor, creates economic opportunities for developing countries. On the downside is a troubling message to Americans – over the next ten years up to 11 per cent of the American workforce may be outsourced (cf. Luyt 2004).

Call centres are opening from Argentina to Kenya and Russia. But are teleworking and teleservices beneficial to India and other information processing countries? They offer jobs to a new middle-class segment, but already after a few years the attrition rate in India is 30 to 35 per cent. 'Indian staff are required to keep odd hours, adopt American accents, and have few options for career advancement' (ibid.: 7). Call centres are a dependent economy geared to patrons and clients in the north to the point that Indians must adopt American names and fake identities. They are a pseudo transfer of technology which only transfers end-user capability.

> With the exception of some groups (like software programmers), it seems that most teleworkers who are predominantly women are receiving extremely low wages; and some of them work in the kind of modern-day sweatshop conditions that characterized export oriented manufacturing throughout the developing world. (De Alcantera, quoted in Ya'u 2004: 21)

At times information-for-development comes with an extra-terrestrial optimism (e.g. Alden 2003; Friedman 2000; Sims 2002) that is oblivious to the chequered history of international development efforts. Suddenly technology becomes a development shortcut, even though this flies in the face of obvious constraints. First, 'Relative to income, the divide today hardly exists' (Wade 2002: 444), so bridging the digital divide is actually about bridging income gaps, and here the evidence is that they are generally growing. Second, a major cause of growing inequality within and between societies since the 1980s is growing skill differentials and IT and digital literacy is a major part of this growing gap (Nederveen Pieterse 2004: ch. 5; Cornia 1999). Thus, bridging the digital divide as a means to narrow inequality in effect presents the problem as a solution. Third, 'the digital divide is increasing rather than decreasing' (Ya'u 2004: 24), which is plain given the rapid changes and competitive drives in the IT field. Fourth, research suggests that 'the digital divide will never be bridged': 'it would take Africa about 100 years to reach the 1995 level of Ireland' (ibid.). Bridging the digital divide is mopping up with the tap open. This presents us with the unbearable lightness of ICT4D and the illogical nature of bridging the digital divide.

Unpacking this approach, an obvious and often discussed problem is technological fetishism.[2] Some discussions argue that connectivity should be addressed not as a technological fix but as part of a capabilities approach and in terms of social capabilities. This is true, and by the same token it implies certain priorities: 'Once the illiteracy problem is solved (as in Kerala, India), cheap books are a great boon, but giving illiterate people cheap books does not solve illiteracy' (Wade 2002: 443).

ICT4D as a package deal

The wider issue is the package character of ICT4D and the interrelated nature of ICT components and the constellation it is part of. This suggests that the *means* of bridging the digital divide contradict the very idea of bridging: 'efforts to bridge the digital divide may have the effect of locking developing countries into a new form of dependency on the West. The technologies and "regimes" (international standards governing ICTs) are designed by developed country entities for developed country conditions' (Wade 2002: 443).

From the package character of ICT4D emerges the actual task of ICT4D, which is to unpack ICT4D so its development potential can be diagnosed and possibly harnessed.

Contemporary globalization is a package deal and ICT is deeply wired into this cluster. Information technologies and microelectronics-based telecommunications since the early 1980s created the possibility for the globalization of supply: the information and communication revolution cheapened long-distance communication and enabled plant relocation and outsourcing to low-wage areas. Information technology also enables providing global product information or the globalization of demand. While flexible production has come with growing research and development costs, it also comes with a shorter shelf-life for products and thus a pressure to expand market shares to amortize the cost of technology investments, thus generating incentives for global marketing and creating a global brand recognition. With advertising growing three times faster than trade and the global advertising boom comes the political economy of branding and the culture of logos. Information technology is also tied up with the globalization of competition; the changing dynamics of global inter-firm competition involve inter-corporate tie-ups, networking and mergers and acquisitions to manage the cost and risks of research and development and global marketing. Corporate mergers both downsize companies and seek to make brands stronger. ICT further provides the technical means for financial globalization, as in 24-hour electronic trading, which has come together with financial deregulation and 'securitization' or the dilution of the separation between banking and non-banking forms of corporate finance, which, in turn, enabled corporate globalization and the wave of corporate merger activity from the 1980s onward. One form this takes is the spread of new financial instruments such as options and derivatives.[3]

In a global political economy these trends are discussed under headings such as flexible accumulation and post-Fordism and as a mode of produc-tion. A mode of production or regime of accumulation combines systems of production (technologies and the organization of firms) and forms of regulation (the political and legal regulation of business and capital). This suggests that we cannot pick and choose elements from this configuration without in effect activating and transplanting much of or the entire con-stellation. This is already apparent at a technical level.

Complex ICT systems have 'layers' of components–including PCs, computer hardware, telecommunications, cables, software–and decisions made about standards for one layer in one part of a large organization can easily interfere with decisions about standards for another layer made in another part of the organization. Compatibility can take years to achieve at a huge cost, by which time new incompatibilities may have arisen. (Wade 2002: 448)

What is at stake in contemporary globalization is both different national capitalisms, each of which is dynamic and in flux, and the interaction of capitalisms, which is mediated through complex layers of technology, international finance, international trade, international institutions, macroeconomic policies, knowledge systems, legal standards and proprietary arrangements. Development policy is part of the interaction of capitalisms. The terms of this interaction are generally set by hegemonic powers and institutions.

Accordingly what matters too is with which perspective we approach these questions – from the inside (the advanced countries) looking out, or from the outside (from the point of view of developing countries) looking in. The development approach suggests the latter, whereas the realities of power and privilege imply the former. The trade-offs involved in investing in ICT tend to be viewed differently in developed countries than in developing countries: 'it does not make sense to have hospitals connected to the Internet when there are no drugs in the hospitals, or for schools that have no chairs to be connected to the Internet' (Ya'u 2004: 26). ICT4D reworks several familiar problems in development policy, some of which are sketched below.

Development policy is incoherent. Surely education is more important to development than digital access and is also a condition for digital literacy. Uneven education worries organizations such as UNESCO, which calls on states to devote as much as 26 per cent of their budgets to education (ibid.). Yet the structural reform policies advocated by the IMF and World Bank require cuts in public spending, including education. It does not make sense to cut education spending *and* argue for ICT4D, to erode basic capabilities and advocate fancy digital capabilities.

ICT4D implies the imposition of a development model. According to techno determinists the spread of technology equals development. This recycles conventional modernization thinking which ranges from Enlightenment positivism (and Lenin's formula of progress as 'Soviets + electricity') to postwar modernization theory. In this series ICT4D is Modernization 2.0 (Shade 2003: 14). Second, for neoliberal economists and entrepreneurs the spread of market forces equals development. Both these discourse communities make an instrumental use of information-for-development: what matters is technological transformation and market expansion. What these views share is at minimum development naivety, which may be both genuine and deliberate (involving not just the sociology of knowledge but also the sociology of ignorance). In defining poverty as the absence of technology and market forces they lack awareness of social development. In the process these views present the disease as the remedy and hegemony as freedom (cf. Shade: 117). More precisely, what is at issue is the imposition of a development model.

Time and again technological modernization has served as a means to effect political and economic reforms. Information technology also functioned this way in western countries – making reforms seem inevitable and thus selling the Reagan and Thatcher reforms in the US and UK ('There Is No Alternative') to trade unions and labour constituencies. ICT indeed is wired in many directions.

ICT promotion serves as a rationale for trade and investment liberalization in developing countries. As Ya'u notes, 'African countries that have undertaken the liberalisation of their telecommunication sector have ended one form of monopoly – state monopolies – and found themselves saddled with a new monopoly – that of foreign investors' (2004: 19).

ICT support also undergirds changes in development institutions. ICT promotion fits the World Bank's new career as Knowledge Bank. Joe Stiglitz's theory of information asymmetry as a cause of market imperfection provides the World Bank with a rationale to improve the functioning of markets by remedying information gaps; which sidesteps critiquing markets themselves (Thompson 2004).

ICT raises the question of appropriate technology. It may be true that in the information economy the cost of a copy is zero (Verzola 2004), but the cost of the delivery systems – infrastructure, electricity, hardware, software and human ware – is far from zero. Questions that are seldom asked are 'which technology is appropriate, are low-tech more appropriate than high-tech options, and for what are the technologies going to be used?' (Fors and Moreno 2002: 199). A further question is how do the returns on investments in ICT compare with returns on other investments?

ICT is designed according to the requirements of the prosperous markets. 'Developing countries are placed at a growing disadvantage by the software–hardware arms race in the global market for savvy computer users ... The effect of this technological arms race is to keep widening the digital divide between the prosperous democracies and the rest of the world' (Wade 2002: 452).

ICT privileges western content. While ICT places the emphasis on the channels of information, in the process it privileges western content. 'What does it mean that people have access to information or channels that they do not own? Citizens are provided access to channels over which they have no control. Increasingly, also, they are offered little or no real choice over content' (Ya'u 2004: 24).

Intellectual property rights presuppose western legal norms. Intellectual property rights and the harmonization of patent law are a major frontier of contemporary globalization (Drahos and Braithwaite 2002; Drahos 2003). As Ngenda points out, 'The international intellectual property model is a product of Western legal norms' (2005: 60). It carries the imprint of individualism and proprietary individualism such as the *droit d'auteur* (66).

The incentive for reward principle has become enshrined in the World Intellectual Property Organization (WIPO), along with the view that 'patent protection is an indispensable incentive to creative and inventive work' (67–8).

> Like too much of all good things, too much IP protection does not reward society. The intensification of intellectual property benefits the owners of the innovations, while society at large suffers welfare loss due to the rent-seeking or monopolistic behavior of knowledge economy firms that depend on patents, copyrights, and other IP rights regimes as their source of profit. (Parayil 2005: 48)[4]

ICT manufacturing does not necessarily add up to ICT diffusion. Latecomer nations lack the financial resources to invest in new technologies which also presuppose a business infrastructure in soft social capital such as appropriate institutions (Wong 2002: 168). While East Asian countries have been strong in electronics manufacturing they have been weak in services, especially financial services and knowledge-based services of the kind that use ICT. This was a factor in the 1997 Asian crisis. Disparities in ICT diffusion are significantly higher among Asian countries than among non-Asian countries; Japan and the four Asian NIEs rank above the norm in ICT diffusion, whereas the six Asian LDCs underperform, especially in the internet (Wong: 185). Thus there is a significant digital divide between the five more advanced countries of the region and the other developing Asian countries. Wong concludes that a high involvement in ICT production has little or no spillover effect in ICT diffusion.

Digital capitalism → cyber utopia

The digital divide theme is unusual because it is quite ordinary for new technology to spread unevenly, so why should digital technology be different? Now, however, cyber apartheid and information apartheid loom and, according to a flood of studies, we must get wired: schools, libraries, community centres, senior citizens in retirement homes, and the homeless, to meet their information needs (e.g. Stansbury 2003; Wicks 2003).

Media reports discuss, for instance, 'Ethiopia's digital dream' and the enthusiasm about applying IT in e-government, education and communications across the countryside, an aim that is pursued with great zeal despite poverty, and in the hope that digital solutions can make up for the lack of infrastructure (Cross 2005). Yet, looking at the fine print we find that to implement this the Ethiopian government and Telecommunications Corporation must team up with Cisco Systems and Business Connexion of South Africa; the reporter visited the country as a guest of Cisco Systems; which prompts the question, is this Ethiopia's digital dream or that of IT corporations? This illustrates a key dilemma of ITC4D. Part of this is what is known in economics as the expert service problem: the expert who is to diagnose the problem has a stake in its solution.

The boundary between ICT4D and ICT marketing is thin. ICT4D may be a terrain in its own right but it is also part of a general ICT boosterism in which ICT is the latest major wave of capital accumulation – think railroads, electricity and chemical industries in the nineteenth century and automobiles and telecommunications in the twentieth century. Each accumulation wave comes with its own boosterism: it is not sufficient for new products to be made – they must also be invested in, sold and used. They must be the talk of the town.

In the series of capital accumulation waves the ICT wave is a special case in that it is a highly capital-intensive sector that has not delivered on its promise; it has absorbed multibillion dollar investments in infrastructure (such as the Fiber Optic Link around the Globe and satellite systems) that are vastly under-used. ICT has been at the forefront of Transnational Corporation (TNC) operations; in the 1990s typically up to a third of American TNC investments in developing and emerging markets from Mexico to Russia went to the telecom industry (Schiller 1999). It is prime terrain for transnational mergers and acquisitions and mega corporations such as WorldCom, Vodaphone, Viacom, MCI and Mannesmann. ICT is both a dream space of multinational capital (according to former President Bill Clinton the internet should become a free trade zone) and the spearhead of market-led development in a world-to-come of minimal regulation, and typically faces preferences for the national regulation of telecoms.[5]

In Schumpeter's analysis of capitalism new technologies and inventions are the motor of capital accumulation. This also looms large in the long-wave approach to capitalism. But the cycle of emerging technologies from trigger to inflated expectations and overinvestment to maturity also involves cultural changes; it is also a hype cycle.

Accumulation boosterism is an exercise in the economy of appearances, which is about conjuring up economic opportunities as much as reflecting them, and in the process opens up frontiers (Tsing 2004). It is about the *aura* of innovation, the *creation* of markets, the effervescent *buzz* of entrepreneurial dynamism and expansion. The general propensity to drama in capital accumulation is enhanced in ICT because ICT *is* and is *about* the communications business. Just as broadcasters typically broadcast the gospel of broadcasting, ICT communicates the wonders of communication and preaches the ICT gospel. According to this accumulation script, ICT is essential to opening up new business opportunities, unprecedented translocal and global horizons and vast empowerment opportunities.

ICT4D is a strategic part of ICT expansion: ICT4D is digital capitalism looking south – to growing middle classes, rising educational levels, vast cheap labour pools, and yet difficult regulatory environments. It is about *market expansion* and converting unused capacity into business assets on the premise that new technology is the gateway to hope. And it is about the *deepening of the market* by pressing for liberalization, opening up spaces for competition and investment, bypassing regulations or devising new regulations that will shape the future.

One might view this as a marketing campaign for internet service providers (Gurstein 2003), but probably more is at stake. Brendan Luyt (2004) asks 'Who benefits from the digital divide?' and identifies several beneficiaries of cyber utopianism: information capital, elites and states in the global south, the development industry, and civil society groups and NGOs. Information capital stands to gain new markets and cheap labour. 'If the South increasingly assumes the role of information processor for the North and acts as a lucrative market for the new products of informational capitalism, this is not due to chance' (Luyt: 5). Measures against software piracy are a significant part of its interest: 'The Business Software Alliance, an organization initially established by several of the biggest names in the industry ... with the express purpose of fighting software copyright infringement, has been especially active in the developing world...'(ibid.: 4).

For elites and states in the global south where economic development is essential to state legitimacy, ICT4D serves as another development tool. For the development industry ICT is a strategic tool around which to fashion new public-private partnerships, matching the growing corporatization of development. Traditionally about 30 per cent of World Bank disbursements have gone to infrastructure projects in transport and communication which also aid transnational capital. Civil society groups and NGOs find in ICT a low-cost instrument to communicate with like-minded groups.

ICT4D is a prism in which profiles of neoliberal globalization are refracted. It stands at the crossroads of today's major forces in private, public and social spheres: telecoms, international institutions, states and civil society groups and cyber activists.

If we take a step back it is clear that a cyber utopia is an unlikely project. Digital capitalism has been in the forefront of the neoliberal globalization of the past decades. The telecom industry and the dotcom economy have been central to the economic expansion of the 1980s and 1990s (Schiller 1999). For Susan Strange (1996), telecoms were a key instance in the making of casino capitalism. Although the telecom industries don't rank among the Fortune 100 they include mega-conglomerates. Telecoms have been a major force in the worldwide neoliberal turn and several have also played a key part in the conservative turn.[6] As the saying goes, the media do not defend corporate capitalism, they *are* corporate capitalism. That the media are part of the problem is keenly understood in the United States.

From the early 1900s onwards, the United States has developed the world's most extensive communication infrastructure. Because of its large geography and thin population, radio, telephone and later television have played a large role in American society and, in addition, information technology is more developed than anywhere else. So, should ICT be able to bridge rich–poor gaps the United States would be the leading case. Digital divide arguments have led to providing local community internet access in schools and libraries (Menou 2001). But this has been to little or no effect, *n'en déplaise* techno determinism, public-private partnerships and silicon snake oil. Social inequality in the United States has *grown* significantly precisely since the 1980s and along with the ICT wave (Nederveen Pieterse 2008b). In the United States ICT has either been indifferent to or has contributed to increasing social inequality.

American telecoms have typically practised '"two-tier marketing" plans, polarizing products and sales pitches to reach "two different Americas" – rich and poor ... "Nobody puts as much effort into dual marketing as the telecommunications industry", stated *Business Week*' (Schiller 1999: 53). This has resulted in a sharply polarized provision of services, from telephone to internet access, privileging *power users*: 'Evidence mounted that the corporate-sponsored build-out of high capacity networks was systematically evading poor neighborhoods in order to concentrate on well-off suburban residences and business parks' (ibid.: 54). Internet access among blacks and minorities in the United States varies by income, so inequality is *social*, not digital. As Mark Warschauer notes, 'just as the ubiquitous presence of other media, such as television and radio, has done nothing to overcome information inequality in the United States, there is little reason to believe that the mere presence of the Internet will have a better result' (2003: 297; cf. Davis 2001; Schiller and Mosco 2001).

ICT4D and development studies

From the point of view of development studies we can situate ICT4D at various levels. First, technology represents knowledge and capability, and as such it forms part of a capabilities approach to development, notably the human development approach. Second, the new technologies are embedded in capital and as such they evoke development from above; most public-private partnerships around ICT are typically too technical and capital-intensive in nature to be participatory. Third, technology is a means of control; witness the surveillance capabilities of ICT (such as global positioning systems aligned with cell-phone signals) and the corporate campaigns against software piracy and open source software. Fourth, ICT revives the old debates on appropriate technology and dependent development (Hyder 2005).

The digital projects sponsored by foreign aid and implemented by NGOs display the usual dilemmas of alternative development; most projects are not locally owned and not sustainable and fold when the funding runs out (discussed below).

ICT is wired into contemporary accelerated globalization, which in development has meant structural adjustment and rolling back the developmental state in favour of market forces. Digital divide discourse is reminiscent of previous techno fixes that stressed the need for mechanization and tractors, infrastructure development or the construction of large dams, generally prioritizing capital needs over local needs. Software, the second digital divide, involves intellectual property rights, cognitive frameworks, cultural styles and vernaculars (such as English) that raise questions of

Table 10.1   *ICT4D and development policy*

ICT4D	Dimensions	Development
Technology	Capability	Human development
	Embedded in capital	Development from above
	As a means of control	Dependent development
Digital divide	Technological fetishism	Development as techno fix
Accumulation	Neoliberal globalization	Structural adjustment
Development aid	NGO projects	Alternative dependency
Software	Intellectual property rights	Monopoly rents
Human ware	Education	Human development

knowledge monopolies and cultural imperialism. 'Human ware', the third digital divide, returns us to the basic questions of education and human development, the familiar terrain of capability and inequality. Yes, education is a leveller *if* it is available and *if* it comes with other reforms – land reform, social provisions, etc. A précis of general development implications of ICT4D is in Table 10.1.

ICT4D and development policy

A contributor to a discussion on the implications of technological change noted:

> Poverty is a choice the world has made. It is a political choice. The information revolution will be another instrument to implement that choice. Only a governance revolution would represent a real change. And to link the information revolution with democratization is naïve in the extreme, parallel to the current leap of faith linking democratization and open markets. (quoted in Hedley 1999: 86)

Govindan Parayil offers a more benevolent view:

> What is most urgent is to find ways to integrate informational economy with traditional economy in a fair manner such that the asymmetric relationship between the two could be overcome ... While information and communications technologies, like any other general-purpose technology cluster, have the potential to benefit all, it is the unfair political economic context within which they are developed, deployed, and diffused that needs to be reformed or better reconfigured for equitable development... (2005: 49)

It's just that changing 'the unfair political economic context' is a tall order. The weary succession of development decades shows that it takes a lot more than technology and capital inputs to achieve development. Development policy is a terrain of hegemony and struggle, and policy compromises among hegemonic forces and institutions shape and obfuscate the terms and nature of this struggle (Chapter 1). Hegemonic compromises introduce development fads and shibboleths – such as good governance, transparency, democracy, civil society, participation, empowerment – which when all is said and done usually mean business as usual with fresh paint. ICT4D in most senses in which it is used is another development fad and part of the process of obfuscation. The problem is not just that many info development projects are under-funded and ill conceived or that ICT4D is driven by corporate interests; the deeper issue is that ICT4D is a Trojan horse that locks developing countries into an everlasting dependency.

The instrumental approach according to which information technology can be used and appropriated towards diverse ends and will serve either utopia or dystopia is contradicted by more complex assessments of the nature of information technology such as Bruno Latour's actor-network theory (Hand and Sandywell 2002).

First, from the point of view of development policy the emphasis on the internet is inappropriate, reflects class bias and is inspired by commercial interests. Of course, information technology is meaningful for social movements, as in the Zapatistas' use of the internet or the Filipinos' use of cell- phones in their people power interventions (Castells 1996; Léon et al. 2005), and enables 'organized networks' of many kinds (Lovink 2005). Yet the internet is principally a middle-class medium; as a medium, essentially an extension of the typewriter, it presupposes literacy and the ability to absorb or create content and digital literacy. It may be termed a Starbucks approach to ICT4D.

From the point of view of development policy it would be appropriate to place more emphasis instead on television, radio and the telephone. For instance, in Indonesia the internet is minuscule but radio and television are huge. Of 11 or so TV channels only one is a public channel, the others are commercial. Looking at the ordinary communication technologies grounds and normalizes our discussion: if some of the digital debates are over our heads because of novel technical and legal issues we are all quite familiar with the problems of ordinary mass media – problems of ownership, unequal services and access, commercial bias, and questions of content.[7] Obviously this is not a development shortcut; rather it can serve development ends only after several hurdles have been passed. Then media such as community radio can allow more local input and will have a greater outreach and development potential than the fancy digital media.

Another question is who is the agent of information-for-development? Here the role of development aid and NGOs may be overplayed. The digital NGO projects display the usual characteristics of alternative development: a reliance on project funding; uneven NGO unaccountability (to donors more than to communities); authoritarian or non-participatory management styles; non-replicable projects because they rely on specific capabilities and social capital, so most projects are not locally owned and not sustainable; and insufficient attention paid to the problems of 'scaling up' (Sorj 2003; Wade 2002). While the projects run they produce alternative dependency and when the funding dries up so do most projects.

Government-supported information projects with government providing the inputs of content (making access to government forms and licences available online) may be more viable than foreign aid projects, but usually fall short of their promise (Gupta 2005; Weerasinghe 2004) and turn citizens into customers (Wade 2002). India offers several good examples of developmental uses of the internet such as nonprofits that bring agricultural extension and other information to farmers in rural India,[8] for instance e-Choupal.[9] Several are supported by the government of India. Government-supported initiatives such as Drishtee use a kiosk-based revenue model to bring IT enabled services to the 'rural masses'.[10] Other projects focus on village level e-education.[11] However, as Sanjay Gupta (2005) notes, 'E-governance is limited to e-government or e-services. Little participation is granted to the beneficiaries in decision-making or the design of the initiatives. Few cater to the needs of the poorest of the poor; Drishtee, for example, does not even consider the lowest 25% income-wise as its clients'.

If we look to ICT4D as a new threshold in development policy rather than as another round of business as usual, then development aid on the part of bilateral or multilateral aid agencies or foundations, and also government-provided services, may not be the first place to look. Realistically, the first place to look is at IT services that are provided by the private sector.

In many developing countries village phone networks such as n-Logue in India and Grameenphone in several countries (www.grameenphone.com)[12] have made a considerable impact. Consider, for instance, the mobile phone coverage of Safaricom in Kenya (www.safaricom.co.ke). Many, often low-key, private sector enterprises and also entrepreneur networks (www.tie.org) use IT. There is no reason to overstate or exaggerate the significance of these initiatives; their purpose and reach are limited. But these private sector enterprises are not financially dependent upon external funding and, operating at low profit margins, they have a greater reach and are more sustainable than donor or public sector projects. India may have the edge among developing countries in digital literacy (high education levels, English language, development as a national priority, decentralized state, local developmental states), yet Sanjay Gupta notes:

> Only 10,000 of the over 600,000 villages have seen some Internet-based ICT for development initiatives, most of which have important ingredients missing: social focus, community-driven, need-based and local initiative ... Their business strategy has been primarily focusing on certain type of transactions: related to land and agriculture or the provision of government services. They are mostly undertaken by the private sector with the intention of making them financially sustainable and profitable. Few have the empowerment of the socially and economically underprivileged groups as an objective. ... Benefits for women in such initiatives are scarce, and little effort is made to encourage the use of services by women. Part of the problem is that most kiosks are operated by men, which discourages women from using them, given the social milieu in most parts of India. Also, content and services are more geared towards the needs of men rather than those of women. Most initiatives suffer from problems such as power cuts or lack of adequate power, and low-quality connectivity. (Gupta 2005)

But it is important to look beyond the attempts to bridge the digital divide by replicating and extending existing hardware and software technologies. Digital capitalism presents more pressing issues. Robert Wade notes that 'LDC governments should not take technological and international regimes as given … They need more representation in standard setting bodies and more support in the ICT domain for the principle that "simple is beautiful"' (2002: 444). What matters is to shift the discussion away from the assorted applications of information technology and onto the technologies themselves.

The core problem that ICT4D poses is *disembedding technology from capital*. This is the real challenge of info-for-development, which brings us back to old questions of technology transfer and to full technology transfer rather than pseudo or adaptive transfer.

During the Cold War years South Korea and Taiwan could disaggregate products and obtain their embedded technologies through reverse engineering and, by redesigning them, bypass property rights and acquire intellectual property. The WTO regime of intellectual property rights and the talks on the harmonization of patent laws seek to forestall and limit these options. China follows a different path and uses its market power and bargaining clout to disaggregate foreign direct investment packages to obtain not just end-user capability but also design technologies. But this route is not open to the smaller developing countries.

Digital capitalism poses the problem of technology dependency anew in both hardware and software. Efforts to develop appropriate IT hardware include simple computer (simputer), $100 laptop and one laptop per child (OLPC) projects. Entrepreneurs in China, India (Arifa 2002) and Brazil are developing low-cost designs that may provide 'Southern high-tech alternatives'. Whether they compete or cooperate in these efforts is now not the most important question. Countermoves in this situation are attempts to *re-embed technology in capital*, as in Microsoft teaming up with OLPC and providing its operating systems at cheap rates to avoid youngsters becoming computer literate without Windows; or Microsoft making software available to Indonesia with a steep discount.

The second major frontier is software and the free and open software systems (FOSS) movement. This is of special importance because intellectual property rights are a major site of north–south negotiation and contestation. With the advanced economies increasingly losing their edge in manufacturing, services and research and development to emerging economies due to offshoring and outsourcing, intellectual property rights are a major remaining advantage (leaving aside the ongoing international trade talks on agriculture and textiles). In software development many corporations large and small have a stake in outflanking Microsoft monopolies and instead developing and fine-tuning the Linux operating system and other open source systems because these allow for the reprogramming of core codes and may thus offer greater flexibility, stability and security (Weber 2004). Governments such as that of Brazil and other emerging information economies increasingly use Linux in government administration, with, additionally, a view to savings (Sugar 2005). Cyber activists and other 'organized networks' (Lovink 2005) also operate in this domain.

It would be a fantasy to think of a 'digital Bandung' or an 'IT Cancún' (similar to the walkout from the WTO talks in Cancún in November 2003 initiated by China, India, Brazil and South Africa and the Group of 21 developing countries). This assumes more policy cohesion than is now available. But there is room to strengthen this general approach and the convergence of interests of various stakeholders with a view, ultimately, to fashioning an alternative digital political economy.

We are on a major cusp in globalization. It may well be that in the next round of globalization the winners of the previous round – the United States, Europe and Japan – will be placed second. The growing imbalances in production, consumption, trade deficits and financial deficits, particularly in the United States, have become unsustainable. To a considerable extent courtesy of ICT, the old winners of globalization have been losing their production advantages to newcomers who combine low wages with a good infrastructure, capable workers and docile labour regimes, and now this also applies to information processing services. One advantage they can hold on to is intellectual property rights. As long as the advanced countries, more precisely, corporations in the advanced countries, can monopolize IPR and draw monopoly rents from IPR, they may be able to hold on to their advantage, which in other respects is slipping away. This means that ICT is not only important in its own right, but that it is also an arena in which at this stage the shape of globalization is being decided. The major tipping points here are FOSS, TRIPS and patent laws. Here we find major corporations, governments in the global north and international institutions on one side, and most developing countries on the other. This is the real frontier of ICT4D.

Notes

1 Google gave 6,260,000 entries for digital divide in August 2005 and over 4 million in June 2008.

2 'The digital divide is often portrayed in crassly reductive terms as a mere technological access problem that can be ostensibly addressed by providing cheap computing and communication technologies to the poor. However, the digital divide is not merely a technological problem due to the absence of connectivity or access to cyberspace. This instrumentally informed discourse on digital divide is a modernist tendency to unreflectingly categorize and compartmentalize complex sociotechnological changes into one-dimensional social problems in a bid to resolve them through simple technological fixes' (Parayil 2005: 41). Cf. Hand and Sandywell 2002.

3 Cf. Dicken 2007; also Nederveen Pieterse 2004: ch 1.

4 On wider criticisms of copyright see Smiers 2000.

5 'It was symbolic that, in many of the world's capital cities, postal or communications ministries were physically situated near the seat of power' (Schiller 1999: 48).

6 Media tycoons such as Rupert Murdoch and Conrad Black have backed conservative politics. Rupert Murdoch funds the *Weekly Standard*, the house magazine of American neoconservatives. Silvio Berlusconi in Italy, Thaksin Shinawatra in Thailand, and Hugo Slim in Mexico emerged as entrepreneurs through the telecom and info industry.

7 The 1970s discussion on the role of the media in north–south relations, under the heading of the New International Information and Communication Order, led to a stalemate, parallel to the New International Economic Order debate. The current World Summit on the Information Society (WSIS) discussions may be a replay of these power plays (cf. Hamelink 2004; Shade 2003).

8 See www.indiagriline.com, www.mahindrakisanmitra.com, www.agriwatch.com and http://www.mssrf.org. A website that gives comprehensive information on ICT initiatives in India is www.bytesforall.org. I owe these examples to Sanjay Gupta (2005); cf. Arifa 2002, Ashraf 2004, Chandra 2002, Prestowitz 2005, Singh 2002 and Wade 2002.

9 'e-Choupal is a web based initiative of ITC's International Business Division, offers the Farmers of India all the information, products and services they need to enhance farm productivity, improve farm-gate price realisation and cut transaction costs. Farmers can access latest local and global information on weather, scientific farming practices as well as market prices at the village itself through this web portal – all in Hindi. Choupal also facilitates supply of high quality farm inputs as well as purchase of commodities at their doorstep' (www.echoupal.com).

10 'The services it enables include access to government programs and benefits, market related information, and private information exchanges and transactions' (www.drishtee.com).

11 This involves projects such as 'Every Village a Knowledge Centre', http://www.mssrf.org/special_programmes/ivrp/ivrpmain.htm. 'Breaking the traditional confines of a school, Hole-in-the-Wall Education Limited takes the Learning Station to the playground, employs a unique collaborative learning approach and encourages children to explore, learn and just enjoy!' (www.niitholeinthewall.com). Cf. www.trai.gov.in

12 'With the assistance of n-Logue and the financial support from the State Bank of India, the LSPs recruit local entrepreneurs to set up and run village-based information kiosks. These kiosk owners are typically locally-based men or women who have at least a 12th Standard education, and demonstrate the ability and motivation to run their own business. Marketed under the brand name "Chiraag", which means enlightenment, these kiosks offer a variety of services aimed at providing benefit to rural areas while contributing the kiosk's sustainability' (www.n-logue.com).

11

Futures of Development

Whither development is an old question. Considering future trends in development by way of trend extrapolation, even if it is a limited exercise, provides an opportunity to uncover background questions. Clearly there is no single future trend. Secondly, complexity is a factor of growing importance. For some time the dominant mood in the development field has been scepticism bordering on pessimism – can't work, can't do. From a shortcut to utopia, development has become a dystopia.

This chapter probes futures of development. I take this up first by strolling through the current preoccupations of the major development theories and, by way of extrapolation, their likely future problematics. In bird's eye fashion this also recapitulates key themes of the book. The second section signals major changes in the development field and argues that these add up to a growing reflexivity concerning both modernity and development. In view of reflexive development and politics and forward options in philosophies and the politics of change, I redefine development, no longer as 'improvement', but as collective learning. The next section turns to reconstructions of development and argues that the era of neoliberalism is fading and in its stead a reform platform in development thinking is emerging. This is taken further in a new additional section on twenty-first century globalization and development policy.

Futures of development thinking

Let me start with a general note on development theory. 'Development theory' is a limited notion. The concepts of 'perspective' or 'analysis' are more adequate and make the point that theories matter as ways of seeing and analytics. Many 'development theories' are not development theories strictly speaking; they have been derived from other social sciences and are applied to development studies. The singular in 'development theory' is distracting because development problems typically require a combination of analytical perspectives. Development is multidimensional, so issues are not simply settled at one level. The terrain is complex from a theory viewpoint also, because there are multiple dimensions to development thinking – of explanation, methodology, epistemology, interest articulation, imagination and policy mobilization (Chapter 1).

The current array of perspectives in the development field represents a dispersal of stakeholders and interest positions (Chapter 1) which is likely to stay. This means that for each of the current development perspectives there is a set of options in facing changes and challenges. Accordingly, there are multiple analytical lenses through which to view futures of development and each shows different options. Several options are prefigured in current debates and others are hypothetical or can be inferred by logic. The starting point in this section is the existing set of development perspectives, each of which continues to renew itself. This is a sketch rather than an exhaustive treatment. Addressed are the major development perspectives: modernization theory, dependency, neoclassical economics, alternative development, human development and post-development.

Modernization theory

Current themes in relation to modernization theory include neo-modernization theory, which involves a revaluation of 'tradition', no longer as an obstacle but as a resource, and options such as the 'modernization of tradition' (So 1990, Tiryakian 1996). A practical application of this outlook is cooperation between development agencies such as NGOs and 'traditional' social organizations, which has been under way in many places.

Another trend is to view *modernities* in the plural. Developing countries no longer view themselves merely as consumers (Lee 1994) but also as producers of modernity, 'reworking modernity' and generating new and different modernities (Eisenstadt 2000). Voices in the majority world are now not merely critical of western modernity or argue for some kind of fusion, but also assert alternative modernities (e.g. Ibrahim 1996, Mahathir and Ishihara 1995, Wignaraja 2008). This may include engaging postmodernism, not merely as a condition (flexible specialization, post-Fordism, urban and social complexity) or a target of criticism but as a sensibility, a style and philosophical disposition (Giri 1998). Postcolonial studies and its destabilizing of modernist assumptions are part of this outlook (Kapoor 2007). Another complex assessment concerns neo-medieval modernity, notably in urban studies (AlSayyad and Roy 2006).

Dependency theory

Global political economy renews dependency thinking in a broad sense, with a focus on uneven global development (Amin 1997, Boyer and Drache 1996, Chossudovsky 1997, Hoogvelt 1997) and neoliberal globalization. A crucial distinction runs between globalization as *process* and as *project*, or between globalization as a historical trend and specific projects that seek to steer globalization, from the World Trade Organization to transnational women's organizations.[1] Rethinking dependency theory ranges from innovative historical revisions (such as Frank 1996, 1998; Hobson 2004), critiques of new industrialized countries (e.g. Bello 2002) and the renewal of structuralism (Kay 1998). According to Osvaldo Sunkel, in Latin America the response to neoliberalism is neostructuralism:

Neo-structuralism recognizes the insufficiencies of the structuralism of the 1950s regarding short-term macro-economic imbalances, overemphasis on import-substitution over interaction with the international economy, overburdened government intervention, etc., while defending the need for strong and deliberate long-term state policies to deal with the problem of overcoming structural heterogeneity and creating, complementing and regulating markets in the frequent cases of market absence, imperfections and failures, characteristic of the underdevelopment syndrome; ensuring, not necessarily by public enterprises, the provision of public goods such as transportation, energy, communications, and other long-term investments; promoting the diversification of production and exports to higher value added and technologically more advanced and competitive productive activities; actively supporting their penetration into foreign markets; widening the coverage and upgrading of the quality of education and social services in health, housing, and social protection, particularly for the poor and less well off; as well as implementing policies to ensure environmental sustainability and the achievement of a better regional balance. (Sunkel 2008: 65)

Neoclassical economics

In the 1980s Deepak Lal argued that 'the demise of development economics is likely to be conducive to the health of both the economics and the economies of developing countries' (1983: 109). How does the 'counter-revolution in development' shape up in the twenty-first century? Now structural adjustment no longer appears as the omega of development but as an intermezzo. Adjustments of structural adjustment policies have sought to give them a 'human face' with safety nets, poverty alleviation, or by making them more user-friendly and context- and country-specific. Bringing the state back in and good governance represent further adjustments (Kiely 1998, World Bank 1997). In the 1990s, the World Bank returned to its 1970s position in favour of equitable growth, producing a growing tension between the politics of the 'Wall Street–Treasury–IMF complex' and the World Bank's social or populist liberalism. The neo-conservative turn was another intermezzo. Bank directors (Wolfowitz, Zoellick) seeking to use the Bank as a strategic tool of American foreign policy did not enhance the Bank's standing in the development field. Obviously, the 'Washington consensus' is not what it used to be.

Alternative development

Mainstream approaches have coopted elements of alternative development such as participation. The strength of alternative development is a regard for local development and agency from grassroots groups and social movements to NGOs. With local development comes a concern with project failure, cultural diversity and endogenous development. The disaffection with the state in alternative development resonates with neoliberal misgivings about state failure and this conjuncture contributed to the great wave of 'NGO-ization' since the 1980s. NGO professionalization runs the risk of depoliticization and managerialism along with the erosion of state capabilities and an 'alternative dependency' on donor support and agendas. The policy of 'strengthening civil society' by supporting NGOs is deeply apolitical, ignores contradictions within civil society, overrates NGOs and weakens state capabilities (Tvedt 1998).

On the other hand, the blurring of the line separating alternative and human development approaches, or society and state-oriented perspectives, opens the way to synergies between civic organizations, local government and firms, which *may* contribute to supply-side social development (Chapter 8).

Alternative development thinking used to be strong on critique and weak on alternatives beyond local empowerment. Increasingly attention turns to global-scale alternatives 'beyond Bretton Woods', or 'alternative globalization' and the World Social Forum.

It may be argued that alternative development is no longer an appropriate heading and a more distinctive terminology would be welcome. Besides, alternative development is tainted by the discourse of strengthening 'civil society'. Alternative terminologies could be grassroots or 'popular development' (Brohman 1996); but such headings gloss over the trend of NGO professionalization, and alternatives beyond the local level (meso, macro, global alternatives) slip out of the picture. Another option is participatory development, but participation is too vague and too problematic to serve as a capstone (cf. Cooke and Kothari 2001). It may be possible to redefine core elements of alternative development (such as emancipation, transformation) more sharply and critically to distinguish participatory from mainstream approaches, but it is more realistic to concede that the era of 'alternative development' is over than to suggest a different heading. Reform *in* and *through* development is more important than defining a separate alternative development.

Human development

The human development approach extends to gender (as in the Gender Development Index), political rights (as in the Freedom Development Index) and environmental concerns (sustainable human development). Through regional human development reports such as the Arab Human Development Report, it extends to different regions and countries. In combination with participatory development, new fusions arise such as 'just development' (Banuri et al. 1997). Human security refers to a new combination at the conjunction of conflict and development (Naqvi 1996, UNDP 1994) and the problematic of 'linking relief and development' (Nederveen Pieterse 1998a).

A relevant theme for the human development approach is to examine the relationship between human capital, its starting point, and social and cultural capital. Bourdieu (1976, 1988) argued that the different forms of capital are related and interchangeable. For Bourdieu this served as an analysis of 'modes of domination'. These interrelations are significant from an analytical and policy view, as in new institutional economics (Harriss et al. 1995) and socioeconomics, the cultural turn in development and social capital (Fine 1999, Nederveen Pieterse 2007). Social capital figures in social and economic geography: clustering, 'institutional densities' and civic political culture may explain regional economic success or failure (Chapter 8). For instance, what underlies the success of micro-credit schemes may be that they build on people's social capital. Part of the cultural turn in development is a regard for local cultural capital, for instance indigenous knowledge. Cultural diversity and the mingling of different cultural flows (diasporas, migrants, travellers) have been potent ingredients in economic innovation and growth (Griffin 2000a, Nederveen Pieterse 2003, 2007).

The human development approach has all along pursued global reform, from the role of the UN system and the Bretton Woods institutions and the World Trade Organization (Singer and Jolly 1995) to macroeconomic regulation and global taxes (Cleveland et al. 1995). Global reform (discussed below) is likely to remain a major preoccupation.

Post-development

Anti-development has all along been concerned with local autonomy, at times advocating local delinking. A constructive turn is the nexus with ecological liberation movements (Peet and Watts 1996). Another concern is 'resistance to globalization' so anti-development and anti-globalization become synonymous: economic globalization is viewed as the main form of developmentalism at the turn of the millennium (Korten 1995, Mander and Goldsmith 1996). A local orientation risks overlooking wider dimensions. Thus, in this view, the Zapatista rebellion in Chiapas is concerned with local autonomy and land rights; but the Zapatistas also organize with a view to political reform in Mexico and global alliances of resistance (Castells 1997). The major limitation of the post-development approach is that it offers no significant future perspectives beyond local autonomy, so the most likely future of post-development is localism.

Table 11.1 is a précis using key words to characterize understandings of development according to the major development perspectives (column 1), ongoing revisions (2) and future options (3).

We stand on the shoulders of these perspectives, they make up our analytics and we perceive the development field through them, as if through a kaleidoscope, for they have been guiding lights through several development decades. Yet these optics are also coloured by old polemics, as strategic interventions and simplifications that made sense in contexts that, by and large, are no more. Each of these paradigms is swarmed around by a growing number of 'exceptions' that cannot be accommodated. Often they are no longer at the centre of our vision but at the periphery, so we can no longer see simply through but also past them. They are but one way of looking at development, only part of the toolbox.

Table 11.1   *Development perspectives and future options*

Theories and definitions of development	Recent themes	Future options

Modernization
Development is state-led growth
  Keynotes: industrialization,
  western model, foreign
  aid, linear progress,
  convergence
	Revaluation of
	  'tradition',
	  postmodernism, 'end
	  of history',
	  neomedievalism
		Modernities plural

Dependencía
Development is
  underdevelopment (or
  dependent development)
  by comprador bourgeoisie;
  or state-led autocentric
  development (associated
  dependent development)
  by national bourgeoisie
	Critique of NICs, new
	  international division of
	  labour, social exclusion.
	  Global political
	  economy: power and
	  economics, bring the
	  state back in. Uneven
	  global development
		Critique of uneven
		  globalization;
		  critique of BRIC

Neoclassical economics,
  neoliberalism
Development is market-led growth
  Keynotes: overcome
  state failure through
  structural reform
  (deregulation, privatization,
  liberalization) and get
  prices right
	Financial crises. Market
	  failure, safety net,
	  human capital, good
	  governance,
	  sustainability. Debt
	  reduction. New
	  institutional economics:
	  institutional analysis
		Regulation of
		  finance

Alternative development
Development is society-led,
  equitable and sustainable
	Coopted in mainstream
	  Decentralization
	  Professionalization.
	  Alternative globalization
		Social development
		  Global justice

Human development
Development is capacitation.
  Human resource
  development is the means
  and end of development,
  measured in Human
  Development Index
	Gender DI, Freedom DI,
	  human security, global
	  reform. Social and
	  cultural capital
		Social development
		  Global reform

Post-development
Development is destructive,
  immiserizing, authoritarian, past.
  Keynotes: discourse
  analysis, critique of science
  and modernity
	Local delinking,
	  ecological movements.
	  Deglobalization
		Localism

Development and complexity

This section takes up general analytical and methodological features of the development field and then considers changes that have taken place at an institutional level and general policy directions, recapitulating points made in previous chapters.

Table 11.2 *Another outline of the development field*

Agents	Perspectives	Policies	Conflict areas
IMF and World Bank	Neoliberalism, monetarism, social liberalism	Structural reform, structural adjustment (SA)	Adjust SA. World Bank vs. IMF. Poverty alleviation
WTO	Free trade	Trade-related intellectual property rights, Doha round to cut agricultural tariffs in north	With regions, states, trade unions, INGOs. Multilateral agreement on investment
UN system	Human development	Capacity building, human resource development, safety net, human security	Conflicts in UN system and between UN and international financial institutions, OECD. 20:20 compact
States	Medley of all approaches	Contending forces	Growth, social cohesion, poverty alleviation, environment, globalization, democratization
(I)NGOs	Human and participatory development	Empowerment, humanitarian assistance, lobbying, poverty eradication	Conflict with GOs, among and within NGOs. Tension between relief and development
Local actors	Alternative development and/or post-development	Autonomous development, democratization	Conflicts among locals about participation, autonomy, values

Development involves different stakeholders and actors who typically hold different perspectives and policy preferences. Yet these agents and their preferences should not be essentialized. Seen up close, each position itself is a cluster of positions and an arena of different views. Table 11.2 briefly sums up these internal differences, signalling salient bones of contention. Thus, in relation to structural adjustment there are conflicts between and within the Bretton Woods institutions, between and within the World Bank and the IMF, involving economic policy and the scope of poverty alleviation. Obviously all these characterizations are shorthand and meant only as illustrations of the present situation.

Development unfolds in diverse contexts of relations of power, cultural values, social practices, ecological conditions and historical itineraries. Development is intrinsically contextual. But these contexts are not sealed off from one another. Thus while cultural differences matter, they are not rigid boundaries; they are crossroads and traffic circles where different kinds of traffic meet. Development is an intercultural transaction (Chapter 5). This refers to the meanings of development as well as to implementation. Hence conventional modernization = westernization views, on the one hand,

and endogenous or indigenous development views, on the other, are both too simple. They are based on binary oppositions and privileging either end of the continuum of perspectives ignores the fact that actual development involves continuous traffic back and forth across the spectrum.

Profound changes take place in the development field, but assessing change is itself a complex operation, polycentric in meaning. So it's not easy to indicate a general direction in which changes in development thinking and policy point and still less to rank them in importance. With this proviso let's signal some of the most significant changes, focusing on the postwar period.

The first change concerns the understanding of the nature of development. Early efforts concentrated on the hardware of development, such as infrastructure, capital inputs and technology. The recent trend is to pay equal attention to the *software* of development, to institutions, processes and management, education and knowledge (e.g. World Bank 1997, 1998). Or to argue that development is essentially human software development, as in the human development approach and the World Bank's aspiration to become a 'knowledge bank'. The emphasis on knowledge parallels the general gravitation towards the knowledge economy. It implies a reorientation from a preoccupation with the exterior and façade of development (infrastructure, capital inputs) to its 'inner' conditions, and from a one-dimensional to a multidimensional understanding. This includes environmental management as a learning process. 'Sustainable development' is now part of any approach to development, which offers us the option of 'anthropocentrism with a human face' (Ariansen 1998).

Another major change is that the *unit of development* has become multi-scalar. This in turn affects the agency of development. If early on this was the state, now it includes international and regional institutions, market forces, urban and local government, civic associations (at multiple scales) and households. Development actors have become polycentric. Grassroots interests count more than previously. Hence development is no longer simply a geometry of power and a reshuffling of the status quo.

If previously the west dominated development thinking, perspectives from the south and Japan have become increasingly important.[2] While this happens at a policy level, it is paralleled in profound revisionings of history (e.g. Frank 1998). At the same time, development is no longer simply confined to the south. Since the former eastern bloc countries have become countries in transition toward market economies and democracies, development policies also apply here. Changes taking place in advanced economies – deindustrialization, flexibilization, migration, urban problems, regionalization – also lead to development policies, albeit at different economic and institutional levels. Accordingly, the line between 'developing' and 'developed' worlds has been blurring. The north faces questions on social exclusion (Gaventa 1998, Judt 1997, Young 1999), empowerment (as in urban empowerment zones and in management-speak), good governance (crony capitalism in the north requires transparency) and the renewal of democracy. Learning from the south takes place for instance in microfinance (Rogaly and Roche 1998).

There is a growing convergence of advanced countries and NICs. In light of technological change and globalization, NICs are developing much like advanced countries though starting from a lower base, with less stable institutions and less diversified economies. If we compare the forward policies of Germany with those of, for example, South Korea and Brazil, we will find broadly similar agendas, such as an emphasis on innovation-driven growth, human capital, technopoles, industrial districts, research and development and knowledge intensity (e.g. Connors 1997). This is 'betting on the strong', driven by the imperatives of global competitiveness and efficiency. The financial crises in Mexico, Asia and Latin America show the frailty of emerging markets. While the net figures in terms of productivity and exports may outstrip those of advanced countries, the institutional settings are more vulnerable. Meanwhile, as the gap between advanced countries and NICs is narrowing, the gap between both of these and the least developed countries is in some respects widening.

The sprawling delta of development actors and concerns raises the question of *policy coherence*: what understandings of purpose and process conceivably unite these diverse actors? In international cooperation, this is the issue of consistency – between bilateral and multilateral policies, between trade, finance and security policies and international development policies. This would imply a trend towards a broad collaborative understanding of development efforts. 'Participatory development' in this context signals an undercurrent of deep-seated change. Development action is dialogical, involving the concerted efforts of actors in different settings and at many levels. Social choice theory, public action and new institutional economics reflect this reorientation. At a policy level, it comes across in the concern with interactive decision-making, public–private partnership, empowerment, social inclusion, migration and managing urban problems.

However, the trend towards the democratization of development coincides with the simultaneous extension of transnational power structures and regimes. These twin trends are in contradiction. The democratization of development runs into the hurdle of power structures, from local landlords all the way to international financial institutions. This is not a simple opposition or contradiction that can be settled through conventional politics of resistance and contestation (e.g. Chin and Mittelman 2000), for democratization also requires institutionalization (deinstitutionalization and reinstitutionalization).

In a brief time span, there have been profound changes in the Gestalt of development. These changes do not all point in the same direction. There is a growing awareness of development as an asymptotic rendezvous, an undertaking that, like the horizon, recedes and changes as we approach. Development by this understanding is intrinsically uncertain and contested: coherence is a moving target; concertation is never fully achieved; dialogue is ever imperfect; software is never complete; learning never ends. In addition, development is not simply progress but the trial-and-error clarification, redefinition and management of progress. It concerns the translation of growing human capabilities into hardware and the translation of hardware into software, including collective reflection and institutions of collective management.

Complexity politics

These considerations affect the understanding and definition of development. It may be argued that in the absence of a simple yardstick, the conventional understanding of development as improvement is no longer tenable. Over time improvement has meant economic growth, modernization, nation building, industrialization, better life opportunities, enlarging people's choices, enhancement of capacities, rolling back the state, state effectiveness, good governance, sustainability, poverty eradication, poverty alleviation, social inclusion, and so forth. It follows from the different meanings of development over time (Chapter 1) that improvement is a historically contingent notion. It follows from the plurality of development actors that development is polycentric in its meaning, objectives, agency and methods of implementation and therefore what constitutes improvement in development is intrinsically contested. 'Development' is a moving target situated somewhere in between underdevelopment and post-development, to take two extremes on the continuum of perspectives (and we might add over-development). Actual development thinking and action are about finding a balance or accommodation between different actors, perspectives, interests and dimensions within specific historical, political and ecological settings, and thus requires a holistic approach (Chapter 9).

It remains attractive to understand development as improvement, but which improvement and how? Understanding development as improvement almost inevitably invites a one-dimensional perspective, privileging one or other dimension, and a managerial approach, whereas what actually constitutes improvement never is and never can really be settled. Consequently, development unfolds in a peculiar 'as if' mode: while everybody knows that development-as-improvement in any form is open to question, it seems necessary to proceed as if there is a consensus. Wouldn't it be more productive and appropriate then to make this contingency part of the understanding of development? This means redefining development as a *collective learning experience*. This includes learning about different understandings of improvement, as a collective inquiry into what constitutes the good life and sensible ways of getting there. Learning is open-ended. This also makes sense as a point about development methodology, in action and inquiry.

Learning is a theme of growing salience. Collective learning figures in organization studies and the 'learning organization' (Cooperrider and Dutton 1999, Senge 1990), local economic development and industrial districts (Lawson and Lorenz 1999), planning and sustainability (Meppem and Gill 1998) and risk analysis and disaster management (Comfort 1999). Collective learning is a way of looking at social action (Foley 1999); public action and social choice theories centre on collective learning and feedback processes. Thus local policy formulation and implementation is a 'social experiment requiring flexibility, experimentation and social learning with the people' (Olowu 1988: 17). Collective learning as the point of development places development policy discussions on a different footing: the focus shifts from the result to the process and to the role of complexity in development.

The diagnosis of complexity is often the endpoint of analysis or critique. An approach or policy is scrutinized and then criticized because it ignores certain elements and the conclusion is the diagnosis of complexity and the usual coda is a call for further research. Matters are complex and therefore ... This kind of weary note has been a standard conclusion in public administration. Matters are complex, therefore nothing or not much can be done, which celebrates the comforts of the status quo. This weariness informs the classic definition of public administration as the science of 'muddling through' (Lindblom 1959).[3] Thus complexity *per se* is easily a cul-de-sac. So if we have established the complexity of development, the next question is whether complexity is disabling or enabling.

Emery Roe in *Taking Complexity Seriously* argues for 'triangulation' or the 'use of multiple methods, procedures and/or theories to converge on what should or can be done for the complex issue in question' (1998: 5), including theories that defamiliarize the problem, considering that 'more conventional analytical frameworks, such as microeconomic analysis, are often part of the problem being analyzed' (23). One of the issues is management: 'the more managers (want to) manage, the more they (have to) confront the unmanageable. But it is equally true that the more unmanageable things are, the greater the pressure to manage them' (96). Following critical theory in the version of the journal *Telos*, Roe distinguishes between 'organic negativity', or resistance at a popular level, and 'artificial negativity', in the sense of disputes within the 'new class' of managers. A question that follows is whom triangulation serves. Is complexity analysis an instrument of managers or does it contribute to popular self-organization? This becomes a key issue in deciding whether complexity is disabling (leave it to experts) or enabling (creating an opportunity and necessity for democratization). A detour via the theme of reflexivity may yield further insight.

Modernity has resurfaced as a central theme in social science and has been reproblematized from various angles, as in notions such as high, late, advanced, neo, critical, reflexive, radical, post modernities. A strand that runs through these lines of questioning is that modernity has become its own problem. Ulrich Beck (1992) contrasts simple modernity concerned with 'mastering nature' with *reflexive modernity*, the condition in which the moderns are increasingly concerned with managing the problems created by modernity. Reflexivity figures in relation to the self, social theory, cultural studies, political economy, financial markets, organization studies and research methodology. New social movements are said to be reflexive in the sense of information-oriented, present-oriented and concerned with feedback (Melucci 1989).

Beck refers to the 'new modernity' as risk society, emerging in conditions in which scarcity is no longer the dominant theme because of the growth of productive capacities. Risk distribution society, which in Germany emerged in the early 1970s, is contrasted to scarcity society, which predominates in the south, where the primary concern is with modernization through techno-scientific development. All the same, scarcity societies and risk societies interact and overlap in various ways. First, they interact through the globalization of risk: through generalized effects such as the erosion of the ozone layer; through the commonality of anxiety; and boomerang effects of crisis in developing countries on developed countries and vice versa. Stagnation in advanced economies also affects the developing economies. Second, they interact through the export of risk to scarcity society. The relocation of traditional industries in the south is affected by different trade-offs between accumulation and risk in scarcity societies (witness the Bhopal disaster). Countries in the south may serve as an ecological waste dump also because of rural naivety in relation to industrial risk. Extreme poverty and extreme risk attract one another. Third, there is a north–south transfer of risk awareness, as mobilization arguments for social movements caution on technical grounds, government preparedness, etc. Critique of science and of corporate practices and PR, for instance oil companies and pharmaceuticals, is being transnationalized (as in campaigns critiquing Nestlé baby formula or Shell in Ogoniland in Nigeria). This is addressed in political ecology (Peet and Watts 1996). Environmental movements in the south also inspire collective action in the north (Martinez-Alier 2000).

These interactions are reflected in ongoing debates. Can we understand these debates better in light of the notion of reflexive development? Is there an emerging pattern of reflexive development? In the course of several development decades, development thinking and policy have become increasingly aware of failures and crises of development. Development also entails the 'production of errors'. Evaluation and impact studies have become a major industry alongside development programmes. New policies are increasingly concerned with managing the hazards, unintended consequences and side-effects brought about by development. In development theory this questioning is reflected in the rejection of developmentalism and linear progress. Critiques of the role of science and techno-scientific development lead to a revaluation of indigenous technical and local knowledge, which is a logical turn in view of the crisis of 'western' models.

This section develops four arguments: (1) Development thinking *is* reflexive. That is, almost invariably, development theory stems from a reaction to and thus also a reflection on the limitations of a preceding development policy or theory. (2) One way of looking at development thinking and policy over time is as a *layer* of reflexivities, that is, reflection upon reflection upon reflection. (3) Development thinking increasingly participates in the general trend towards reflexivity in and in relation to modernity. (4) Development thinking is not consistently and sufficiently reflexive; it should be more reflexive and its reflexivity should be thematized.

Arguably, there is both a historical and an emerging pattern of reflexive development. Critiques of development follow on from and lead to critiques of modernity and its consequences, and from the crisis of development policies. A feedback pattern is emerging in which development policy becomes increasingly concerned with the management of development itself. A similar process took place in modernity and, as an offspring of modernity, development participates in its dialectics.

Risk society, according to Beck, is a 'catastrophic society' replete with dystopias and subject to apocalyptic mood swings. In countries in the global south, extremes of pessimism are frequent – on account of negative growth, the failure of trickle-down and the consequences of development, populist swings in politics or the paralysis of politics, and double-dealing on the part of western institutions. The perplexities of progress are shared north and south. The modern crisis of techno-scientific progress translates into a crisis of development. 'Progress is a blank check to be honoured beyond consent and legitimation' (Beck 1992: 203) and now there is a breakdown of faith that technical progress equals social progress. It is no longer taken for granted either that the negative effects of technical progress can be treated separately, as the mere social consequences of technological change. A parallel questioning in development is whether growth equals development, and economic growth equals social development. Progress as a paradox is an established theme (e.g. Ashton and Laura 1999, Stent 1978). Ashis Nandy's (1989) definition of progress as 'the growing awareness of oppression' serves more as a warning signal than a guiding light. Probing the meaning of progress in the light of north–south differences goes back some time (e.g. Banuri et al. 1993) and 'redefining progress' has become a major preoccupation, both north (Halstead and Cobb 1996) and south.

Thus 'anti-development' thinking parallels critiques of progress, and post-development resembles the aprogrammatic, directionless, radical scepticism prevalent in postmodernism. The core problem posed in post-development is the question of modernity. However, to be 'for' or 'against' modernity is, either way, too simple a position. Post-development, as an uneven combination of postmodern methodologies and neo-traditionalist sensibilities, articulates profound sensibilities but is not policy-oriented and does not have a future programme. Reflexive development is more enabling as a perspective (Chapters 1 and 6). There are different stages and kinds of modernity and reflexive development critically negotiates modernity and development, short of rejection.

The deeper argument here is that *development has been reflexive all along*. According to the conventional interpretation, development thinking was an extension of 'progress', but Cowen and Shenton (1996) show that the origins of development thinking lie in the critique of progress. Classical political economy was a reaction to the social problems and dislocations brought about by industrialization, so the origins of development thinking lie in reflexivity in relation to industrialization and not simply in catching-up policies. In this light we can reread the seesaw history of economics and development policy as a series of reactions to and reflections on policy dilemmas caused by previous policies and conditions. Viewed in this way, the neomercantilism of the late industrializers (the American Republic, Germany, France, etc.) was a response to Britain's lead as the workshop of the world. Central planning and building 'socialism in one country' were variations along the same route. In Britain in the 1870s, neoclassical economists resumed the Manchester School legacy in order to capitalize on Britain's leading position. In the 1890s, bankers adopted monetarism and sought to control inflation in response to depression and the boom-and-bust cycle. During the 1930s Depression, Keynesian demand management sought to mitigate the business cycle and Fordism was founded on Keynesian principles. Neoliberalism in the 1980s was a response to the limitations of Keynesian demand management under conditions of 1970s stagflation in conjunction with technological and political changes. If the keynote of neoliberalism was state failure, the recent preoccupation has been market failure. The Third Way of New Democrats and New Labour was a flawed attempt at a new political balance.

In the development field, modern development theory, while rejecting the universal applicability of neoclassical economics, resumed the legacy of classical political economy and its responses to the social dislocation and instability brought about by industrialization. Its first orthodoxy was modernization and growth theory. Structuralism, dependency theory (resuming the legacies of Keynesianism and neomercantilism) and alternative development (resuming the legacy of populism) arose from the failure of modernization policies. The neoliberal counterrevolution (resuming the tradition of liberalism) was a rejection of orthodox development economics and state intervention. Post-development involves a rejection of conventional development and progress *in toto*. Human development builds on East Asian state-led development, resumes the growth and equity approach of the 1970s along with Rawlsian social liberalism, and rejects neoliberalism. Safety nets and structural adjustment 'with a human face', human security and poverty alleviation are responses to the limitations of neoliberal reform. This zigzag history is usually interpreted in terms of the pendulum swing of state–market predominance (with different emphases reflecting the changing status of various development actors). However, these historical processes also show a layering of reflexivities, represented in institutional changes and policy measures and accompanying shifting indices (Chapter 3).

A disadvantage of redefining development as collective learning is that it suggests an evolutionary linear process of accumulative knowledge. This can be remedied by considering learning as a nonlinear process. Another disadvantage is that it is apolitical, because where is the struggle in this framework? Do landlords, multinational corporations or governments yield their positions of privilege and power on account of learning and reflexivity? They do so only under pressure of collective action. Thus reflexivity must have a political edge and refer to social feedback loops that generate and inform a collective action that challenges and transforms power relations. It must refer to a reflexive politics that translates collective learning into a forward politics.

Reflexivity arises from a methodological and philosophical reflection on development, but it is not a purely intellectual process: it concerns ongoing political changes. Reflexivity is taken here not as an academic exercise but as *collective reflexivity*: a social awareness that unfolds as part of a historical process of changing norms, ideologies and institutions, which crumble and then regroup under different headings.[4] Collective reflexivity takes shape through changing institutions and policies, changing expectations and agendas. There is distortion along the way when reflexivity arising from particular circumstances is institutionalized, or abstracted as an ideology or theory, and applied out of context; these are problems of institutional lag, generalization and orthodoxy. Since theory implies generalization, this effect is inherent in economic and development theory. Specificity, diversity, contingency have only recently been adopted as principles of methodology and policy, and current development policies seek to strike a balance between specificity and generality.

Reconstructions

Like all social change, development unfolds in parallel universes. It unfolds as philosophies of change and politics of change, as structural and con-junctural changes, as local politics and as transnational regimes generated in faraway places.

The challenge facing development is to retrieve hope from the collapse of progress. The collapse of progress is not just an occasional episode of collective moodiness but also the onset of a different awareness. The Enlightenment has cast a long shadow. Through most of its career development has been steeped in authoritarian high modernism (Scott 1999), which is part of the failure of three development decades. But all along, as argued above, it has also been a series of responses to and negotiations of the crises of progress. The dilemmas of development parallel the dilemmas of modernity on one question at least: what of a politics of hope? In one view, the current situation is a retreat by intellectuals (Petras 1990), but is the recovery of old positions an option? Presently the development field is bifurcating into a managerial stream – managing development as part of development bureaucracies – and an interpretative stream whose major concern is to deconstruct development, to unpack its claims and discourses and, once that is done, to deconstruct the deconstruction, for deconstruction is a never-ending task. This is the interpretative turn in development studies. In the career of modernity, in the wake of the routinization and bureaucratization of modern institutions, intellectuals from legislators became administrators or interpreters (Bauman 1992), and for some time development intellectuals have been facing similar career options.

According to Rorty (1997), what good politics needs are not principles but 'stories', narratives. The reflexive turn is disabling if it leads to a cul-de-sac of pessimism. What matters is not just the method but the intention; what matters is not just deconstruction but why deconstruction. If the intention is to tell a story about the uselessness of stories, it will end up a thin story; if the intention is to tell a story about the significance of stories, it's a different story. Reflexivity is enabling if it is taken as the achievement of a new level of awareness, awareness of the meanings of trying as well as of failure.

Among the reconstructions discussed in the course of this work, the widest and most general forward reorientations are critical globalism (Chapter 3) and critical holism (Chapter 9). Critical globalism is taken further in concluding observations on global transformations below. Chapter 5 discusses development as intercultural transaction. Participatory development (Chapter 6) and supply-side social development (Chapter 8) are alternative politics and an alternative political economy of development and alternatives to neoliberalism. This poses the larger question of a coherent policy alternative to neoliberalism, after neoliberalism.

The development field is a field of hegemonic compromise that papers over the differences between the dominant stakeholders. These can be characterized as different modernities (sociology) or different capitalisms (political economy): Anglo-American free enterprise capitalism, Rhineland capitalism (west European social market capitalism), East Asian capitalism, the NICs, market socialism in China, transitional countries, the rentier capitalism of the oil-producing countries, etc. The differences among them reflect geographical locations, historical itineraries, the timing of development, levels of technology, cultural capital, institutional differences and resource endowments.[5] Typically, in line with their historical experiences, different capitalisms take diverse approaches to development; but development cooperation is also a transnational undertaking. The first synthesis in modern development was the Keynesian consensus, which reflected the experiences of European capitalisms (and east European socialism). The current successor to this approach is human development, which also reflects the experiences of east Asian state-led capitalism. The market-centred neoclassical approach as represented by the Washington consensus reflects the interests of Anglo-American capitalism. Both market- and state-led approaches vie for civil society endorsement and embrace 'participation' and seek to coopt the third major synthesis, society-centred participatory development.

The diverse approaches to development are being papered over in the hegemonic language of development. Who can reasonably object to 'good governance', 'democracy', 'civil society', 'transparency'? Of course, each of these needs to be unpacked. Thus, embedded in 'good governance' is the contentious idea that the free market and democracy go together. Viewed from this angle, development discourse appears as a large-scale spin-doctoring operation. During the 1980s the Washington consensus dressed up as a trilateral consensus and during the 1990s as a global consensus. The Washington consensus premise that 'economic growth is best furthered by more open trade, export-led growth, greater deregulation, and more liberalized financial markets' (Palley 1999: 49) was transmitted globally through the international financial institutions, the WTO and the G8.

Neoclassical economics and monetarism represent (a) good house-holding (don't spend more than you earn), (b) technical expertise, (c) a theoretical legacy, (d) an ideological mindset (deeply anchored in anti-communism), (e) an interest coalition and (f) policies biased towards the lead players. These dimensions cannot be neatly separated. The technical skills of economic and financial monitoring and planning are steeped in analytical and ideological assumptions, mental frameworks and institutional paths, such as competitiveness indexes, international credit ratings and banking policies. They assume Anglo-American capitalism, as the 'norm' of capitalism, and in the process represent the perspectives and interests of major financial institutions such as the Wall Street–Treasury–IMF complex. This approach faces mounting problems: growing inequality, financial instability and crisis management.

We inhabit a global theatre of the absurd, a winner-takes-all world in which the wealthiest billionaires own as much as approximately half the world population. The statistics are familiar.[6] If trickle-down does not apply in national economies it is even less valid at a global level. Global inequality, refracted in local inequality, goes together with environmental imbalances. In the world fashioned by Anglo-American capitalism, development and environment are the two central problems.

The Washington consensus is part of the problem. For decades, criticism of and protest against the Washington consensus has been plentiful,[7] but no coherent alternative has emerged. But over time several streams have been coming together. International civic organizations have long argued for an alternative to Bretton Woods (e.g. Griesgraber and Gunter 1996b, Niva 1999). Now there is a growing reform consensus in international development which includes reorientations in the World Bank and OECD (e.g. Edwards 1999). The Washington consensus itself has been cracking. Criticisms of the IMF's handling of financial crises show a rift within the Washington consensus: within the IMF (Camdessus 1998) and World Bank (Stiglitz 1998, 2006) and among free market advocates such as Jeffrey Sachs, who have come back on their endorsement. Dissident voices in Wall Street (Soros 1998) also plead for reform. These are signs of and responses to the growing difficulty of the neoliberal regime to reproduce itself. What used to be the Washington consensus has dwindled down to a Washington agenda. Financial instability poses risks even for the winners. Reform proposals converge on calls for financial re-regulation to control the flows of 'hot money' (Akyuz 2000). In the wake of the Mexican, Asian, Latin American and Russian crises, the IMF (and the US Treasury, which finances the bailouts) has been pondering the scope for re-regulation but has settled for transparency, in effect the worldwide alignment and standardization of accounting systems. If double book-keeping was essential to the rise of modern capitalism, the standardization of accounting systems is part of the globalization of capitalism.

Other approaches also have their problems, in part as a function of the Washington hegemony. Participatory development is an indication of a larger change that is imperceptibly taking place in political systems and cultures. It reflects a relative disempowerment of states and political systems in relation to development and technological change, which takes the form of depoliticization and technocracy, and repoliticization through the emergence of subpolitics, manifest in special interests, lobbying, social movements and localization, ethnic and religious mobilization. As both the cause and effect of democratization, civil actors seek empowerment, and the boundaries between political and non-political, public and private spheres have become increasingly fluid. Informalization and liberalization involve a transfer of responsibilities from government to NGOs and the emergence of parallel structures, for instance in welfare and public health. Thus in several sub-Saharan African countries, much of the health care and welfare sector has been subcontracted to foreign-funded NGOs. What are not being replaced, of course, are the procedures of accountability, inadequate as they were. Hence, the new democratic culture of which participatory development is part also has new democratic deficits. The problems of participatory development are in part a function of the Washington hegemony. While 'participation' has become the leading development talk since the 1990s, it is a highly elastic term.[8] The alternative platform matches the Washington consensus in the common theme of state failure, the trend toward privatization and informalization, that is, a greater role for firms and NGOs, and the discourse of civil society and democracy. The new policy agenda of civil society building and 'NGO-ization', community development and self-reliance, matches the new right agenda of government rollback and decentralization. Another problem is the alternative dependency through foreign-funded NGOs. According to Michael Woost, 'we are still riding in a top-down vehicle of development whose wheels are greased with a vocabulary of bottom-up discourse' (1997: 249).

In view of these problems, should we go back to the Keynesian consensus? Structural conditions are now different. If we look at the difficulties of welfare states in the north, could they survive in the south under much more difficult circumstances? The human development approach is state-centred at a time when government influence is being curtailed. The capabilities approach that underlies human development does not challenge power relations. There is no going back to governmentalism as it used to be; there is no going back to the daddy state because of changes in technology, organization, production, markets and consumption. The conjunction of the Washington consensus and the alternative platform is too significant to be simply a matter of ideological manipulation. The point then is to find a narrow path in which participatory approaches retain their meaning, the role of the state is reinvented through public sector reform, and the Washington agenda is reconsidered. This task is common to north and south. The general concern with public–private partnership and corporate citizenship is part of this change.

Participatory development (articulating social interests) and human development (articulating perspectives of states and international institutions) form a strategic combination for together they represent social, state and institutional perspectives. Until recently, the major rift in the development field ran between these approaches and the Washington agenda (discussed below).

Underlying this rift is the question of finding a way for the abstract indicators and narrow agendas of the world of finance to communicate meaningfully with the real world of social questions, work, poverty and human security. The core of the Washington agenda, free markets and sound money, is the ratio of the world of banking and finance as viewed through the lens of Anglo-American capitalism. Viewed from a global perspective, the Washington agenda is a minority concern, whereas social development is a majority concern. A major principle for reform in the development field is that the accommodation between different capitalisms should take place according to majority and not hegemonic interests.

Against this backdrop, the contours of a coherent alternative to neoliberalism may gradually be taking shape. This involves a new convergence in development thinking and a consensus that, though short of a global consensus, is broad and growing. The outlines of this reform platform include the following components:

- Investment-led growth and domestic demand-led growth. 'This is a strategy that lifts all boats, because demand growth in one country pulls in exports from others, so that all grow together' (Palley 1999: 50; see also Griffin 2000b).
- Human rights, core labour standards and independent unionism. Domestic demand-led growth requires rising wages and this entails evening the balance between capital and labour.
- Political reform and active democracy to counteract economic cronyism.
- Controls on short-term capital movements to require investors to commit for a minimum period.[9]
- Taxes on the buying and selling of currencies to curb financial speculation.
- Measures to prevent tax competition.
- Debt reduction for low-income countries (as in Jubilee 2000).
- Reform of the IMF and World Bank to make them more accountable.
- A review of global trade and investment institutions and policies.

These measures would contribute to evening the balance between capital and labour. A growing ensemble of social forces and political institutions shares this approach. In the south, this broadly matches the politics of reforming governments. It matches the *Alternativo Latinoamericana* (Conger 1999). It matches forward proposals in South Asia (e.g. Bhaduri and Nayyar 1996: ch 6). In the north, Third Way politics is a significant departure, not in terms of principles but in terms of establishing a centre-left political momentum. In terms of principles the Third Way is too vague (Giddens 1998); in practice, it has been driven by electoral opportunism and in delivery it has been too weak (Faux 1999, Ryan 1999). Labour, civic organizations, reform and Green parties might be able to carry the Third Way beyond electoral opportunism. In the United States, a coalition of leftist Democrats and labour adds up to a 'Main street Alternative' (Palley 1999).

In the UK, there are significant perspectives and political forces beyond New Labour (e.g. Hutton 1995) and similar conditions exist presently in most countries in the north.

Internationally the principles of a reform alternative to neoliberalism are broadly shared in the UN system and other international institutions. The World Bank's comprehensive development framework endorses pro-poor growth (e.g. Sen and Wolfensohn 1999). The IMF has begun to accommodate the social and human dimensions of development. In international the development cooperation, where criticism of policy incoherence has been rife (Smillie 1997), reform initiatives are now being widely shared, including by the OECD (Bernard et al. 1998). Labour internationalism and the ILO are significant forces. International NGOs and civic organizations have contributed significantly to changing public discourse and promoting public and private accountability.

Features of this reform platform are that it bridges concerns north and south, avoids old left orthodoxy and populism as well as right sloganeering and market worship, and combines national reform with global reform. It's not a matter of going back to conventional Marxism or Keynesianism. Several components of the Washington agenda – public sector reform to achieve effective government, good governance, accountability and transparency – are part of the reform agenda. A difference is that if accountability in the Washington formula refers primarily to international monitoring institutions and overseas investors through the standardization of accounting systems, in the reform agenda it refers primarily to accountability to the electorate.

Part of the reform platform is the awareness that no matter how ingeniously development is reinvented, it cannot be settled without global reform. Virtually all development approaches now engage the global level. In dependency thinking, this takes the form of criticizing uneven globalization. Neoliberalism involves the project of neoliberal globalization. Alternative development envisages alternative globalization and human development seeks global reform, while anti-development converges on anti-globalization. The global horizon is a compelling rendezvous, a prism in which all angles on development are refracted. This illustrates the dramatic salience of globalization as well as the diversity in development thinking. Since we have entered the era of global capitalism, while national settlements are important, global engagement is essential. Globalization requires political adjustments for all development actors, while development actors seek a political adjustment of globalization. The crossroads of globalization may be summed up as either neoliberal globalization or taking a developmental approach to globalization (Pronk 2000). A Keynesian approach to a global new deal could take the form of global neo-Keynesianism (e.g. Lipietz 1992). Straddling society-centred and state-centred approaches to global reform are proposals for global social contracts (Group of Lisbon 1995) and transnational social policy (Deacon et al. 1998). The challenge for a global development approach is to bring separate and opposing interests and constituencies together as part of a worldwide bargaining and process approach. Together with proposals for reform of the UN system and strengthening the international legal order, this adds up to a global reform platform.[10] At this point, development becomes world development, a horizon radically different from the original Gestalt of development.

Notes

1 Global neoliberal projects are discussed for example by McMichael 1996. Nederveen Pieterse 2000b discusses the distinction between globalization as process and as project.

2 A case in point is Japan's role in representing the 'East Asian Miracle', discussed in Wade 1996.

3 This has been the most quoted source in public administration for forty years.

4 Several perspectives focus on the reflexivity of the self (Giddens 1991, Habermas 1990, Taylor 1989) while others refer to reflexivity in a collective sense (Beck 1992, Foley 1999), including reflexive institutions (Fischer 1993) and reflexivity in financial markets (Soros 1998, 2008). Self-reflexivity and collective reflexivity combine in approaches that merge the personal and the political, such as feminism and new social movement research (Melucci 1989). An approach to NGOs combines a commitment to social justice with an attentiveness to interpersonal relations and psychological states (Edwards and Sen 1999). In discussing the work of Aurobindo, Pande and Habermas, Giri probes the relationship between individual and collective reflexivity (1998: ch. 11). A critical discussion of reflexivity is Lynch 2000.

5 Different capitalisms and different modernities are twin-track descriptions. Cf. Eisenstadt 2000, Nederveen Pieterse 2004 (Chapter 11).

6 Since the 1980s the gap between rich and poor countries has been widening dramatically. The poorest 20 per cent of the world population account for 1.3 per cent of total private consumption expenditure, while the highest 20 per cent, that is, those living in the highest-income countries, account for 86 per cent (UNDP 1998: 2). See Nederveen Pieterse 2004 (Global inequality, Chapter 5).

7 For example, Bienefeld 1994, Gills and Philip 1996, Cypher 1998. 'One country's exports are another country's imports, and this means that all cannot rely on export-led growth' (Palley 1999: 50). Export-led growth may lead to competitive devaluation and global deflation or a global shortage of demand (Greider 1997).

8 The World Bank publishes a *Participation Sourcebook* (1996). Arguably, it should not be 'community participation in development' but state and international agencies participating in community affairs.

9 Proposed by Soros 1998 and shared by Stiglitz 2006 and others (cf. Conger 1999: 383).

10 For example, Edwards 1999, Nederveen Pieterse 2000a, and Patomäki and Teivanen 2004 address global reform.

12

Twenty-first-century Globalization and Development

According to a recent headline, 'China says west's lack of market oversight led to subprime crisis'. A senior Chinese banking regulator points out: 'Western governments must strengthen their oversight of financial markets and improve cross-border regulatory cooperation if they are to avoid future global financial crises'.[1]

The tables are turning. The north used to lecture and discipline the south. In the twenty-first century not only has much of the south escaped this discipline – and repaid its debts to the IMF early – but some have started talking and acting back. These are not minor glitches. In the case of China it involves a $2 trillion question, which is approximately the size of its dollar holdings.

The first section of this chapter reviews major changes in twenty-first-century globalization. The second part turns to the significance of these changes and trends in development policies. With the unravelling of neoliberal capitalism, trends are towards a return of state-regulated capitalism. In relation to contemporary development strategies, I note three trends: newly industrializing countries in the global south have become important drivers of the world economy; the agency of development shifts from metropolitan centres to developing countries; and the pendulum swings from markets to states.

The development field is made up of diverse sets of relationships between societies and parts of societies at different levels of development. The fourth section addresses these relations under the heading of development pluralism. One of these relations, between industrialized and developing countries, between north and south, has been of pivotal importance, but the importance of international development cooperation is receding in the twenty-first-century and has been exaggerated all along.

In effect, at issue are two ruptures in the development field; first, the onset of the twenty-first-century brings much of the developing world outside the grasp of western institutions; second, the crisis of 2008 brings global slowdown and changes political economies and economic approaches in the west. The closing section reflects on the changes associated with the 2008 economic crisis (as shorthand for the crisis of 2007–2009).

Twenty-first-century globalization

The 1990s were marked by the dominance of neoliberal approaches. The problems were clear all along, certainly from development and social points of view, but as long as Anglo-American capitalism was thriving, many criticisms fell on deaf ears. Capital flowed to what seemed to be the most dynamic, innovative and profitable forms and centres of capitalism. Wall Street and London's City led the way and Tokyo and Frankfurt, Singapore, Hong Kong and Shanghai followed. Finance capital was crisis-prone, but the crises occurred, time and again, in the peripheries and semi-peripheries of world capitalism and served as tools to discipline emerging societies and to align their economies with dominant trends in the world economy.

In the twenty-first century the tide has turned. From the birth of the millennium, the landscape of capitalism, and hence the landscape of development, began to change. The United States experienced a series of crises: the dotcom collapse, the September 11 attacks, the Enron and Anderson series of corporate scandals, Hurricane Katrina, the subprime mortgage crisis and the financial crisis of 2008. The Federal Reserve's easy credit regime of low interest rates papered over economic problems by facilitating excessive borrowing by consumers, banks and hedge funds. Subprime mortgages were the latest extension of the pyramid scheme of Anglo-American capitalism. In August 2007 the credit levees broke and the housing bubble popped, producing a financial crisis larger and more serious than any seen since the Depression.

American capitalism has gone from crisis to crisis, with the management of each crisis precipitating the next. The crescendo of crises demonstrates the downside of neoliberalism, the flipside of deregulation. According to the new refrain, the market is *not* self-healing. Hence the massive government interventions in Wall Street and the new chorus: 'Goodbye capitalism American-style'.[2]

Financial crises used to take place in the emerging economies of the south. The crisis of 2007–2008, however, hit American and European banks while emerging markets were unscathed, at least initially. When the financial crisis brought about an economic slowdown not only in the US but also in Europe, its effects spread to emerging economies as well. For decades Wall Street financial powerhouses were the winners of globalization and the beneficiaries of financial turbulence; now sovereign wealth funds from the global south kept Wall Street banks afloat by buying into them. The funds came from two major sources: Asian countries' accumulated wealth from exports – with Singapore and China in the lead – and oil exporters – with the Gulf emirates and Norway in the lead. Who could miss the irony – the powerhouses of free enterprise rescued, for a while at least, courtesy of state capitalist institutions?

With the twenty-first century have come momentous changes.[3] Table 12.1 gives a schematic overview of the differences between twentieth- and twenty-first-century globalization and the emerging international division of labour; for discussion I would refer to the source (adapted from Nederveen Pieterse 2008a).

Table 12.1 *Trends in twenty-first-century globalization*

Pattern 1980–2000	Pattern 2000s
Trade	
North–south trade dominates	Growing south–south trade
US-led trade pacts dominate	WTO, FTAA, APEC are in impasse or passé
Trend to regional/global trade pacts	Shift to bilateral FTAs (in north–south trade)
Finance	
Finance capital leads, crisis-prone	Emerging economies hold dollar surpluses
IMF, World Bank discipline developing economies	IMF warns US policies threaten economic stability
US dollar world reserve currency	Multi-currency world
US top destination of FDI	China top destination of FDI
Western financial markets dominate	New financial flows outside the west
IMF blocks Asian monetary fund	Thai Asian Bond Fund; Bank of the South
US investment banks, hedge funds lead	Sovereign wealth funds lead
Institutions	
Convergence IMF–World Bank–WTO	IMF lending down (2003 $70bn, 2006 $20bn)
Social liberalism, poverty reduction	World Bank lost standing
'Wall Street–Treasury–IMF complex'	Weak Treasury, Wall Street in crisis
Washington consensus	'We are all Keynesians now'
Hegemony	
US hegemony solvent and dynamic	US in deficit and cornered in new wars
'Clash of civilizations'	Muslim backlash
US-led security	New security axes (such as Shanghai Cooperation Organization)
Inequality	
Growth and increasing inequality (except East Asia)	Inequality between north and NIEs decreases; inequality in NIEs increases
Deepening rural and urban poverty	Deepening rural and urban poverty
	International migration as flashpoint of global inequality

Turning points

With the onset of the twenty-first century, new trends are the rise of the global south, the growth of south–south relations in trade, energy and politics (UNCTAD speaks of 'a new geography of trade'), and the growing role of the leading emerging societies and sovereign wealth funds.

The tide in south–north relations had begun to turn earlier. The Asian crisis of 1997–98 was a major turning point. The way the IMF handled the crisis was deeply problematic – aggravating the crisis by imposing cuts in government spending even though private spending caused the deficits; vetoing

Japan's bid to establish an Asian monetary fund while mismanaging the crisis. American banks and hedge funds used the crisis to buy distressed assets. This signalled that north–south competition had begun in earnest, not just in agriculture and manufacturing, but also in finance. Since then developing countries have revised their attitude towards the international financial institutions. To safeguard their financial autonomy developing countries began to accumulate hard currency reserves as buffers against financial turbulence, at times sacrificing social investments for the sake of financial security.

The second major turning point in north–south relations came with the WTO ministerial meeting in Cancún in November 2003. Under the slogan 'no deal is better than a bad deal' the global south walked out, with Brazil, South Africa, India and China leading the way, followed by the G22 and, in turn, the G77. This time western divide and rule didn't work, nor did it work during the following years, the repeated attempts to revive the Doha round and the exhortations of western negotiators. This was a major signal of the new weight and cohesion of the global south. Countries that are not part of the global power structure, not part of the G8 or of the UN Security Council (except China), made their global influence felt. The crisis of 2008 is the third major turning point (discussed below).

New development era

As mentioned before, we can identify the following main eras of development. (1) The preludes to development policy from the early 1800s, from classical political economy to Ricardo and Marx. (2) The catch-up policies of the latecomers to industrialization from the mid-nineteenth to the mid-twentieth century. (3) The postwar period of the Keynesian consensus, broadly 1950–1980. (4) The neoliberal era of the Washington consensus, 1980–2000.

Thus, in postwar development policy there have been two major phases, the Keynesian consensus and the Washington consensus. This treatment argues that the twenty-first century has ushered in another development era. That it represents a new phase is clear, though less clear is what its contours are or what its label should be. A tentative characterization might be, in short, the comeback of developmental states.

During 1980–2000, the main rift in the development field was the tension between the Keynesian approach and the Washington consensus; in brief, the state-centred and the market-led approach, rippling through the development field analytically, ideologically and politically. Institutionally the main tension in development policy was the rift between the Washington institutions (the IMF and World Bank, aligned with the WTO) and the human development approach (represented, with oscillations and vacillations, by the UNDP and other UN agencies, development ministries in developing countries and some agencies of international development cooperation). Thérien (1999) refers to the 'Bretton Woods paradigm' and the 'United Nations paradigm'. This rift defines twenty-five years of debate and contestation in development studies, which in recent years has been receding as fast as the Washington model.

Major strands of the twenty-first-century development field include the following. (1) Newly industrializing countries in the global south are increasingly important drivers of the world economy. (2) From 'we develop it' to 'we develop', or a change in the agency of development from metropolitan centres to developing countries. (3) The pendulum swings from market forces back to states. I devote vignettes to each of these trends.

1. *Newly industrializing countries are important drivers of the world economy.* During 1980–2000, the United States was the driver of the world economy with American consumers and the financial sector leading the way. Seventy per cent of the American economy is driven by consumption. Via 'retail therapy' this path led to over-consumption and mounting consumer debt and proved to be unsustainable. Financialization of the economy made Wall Street financial engineering – increasingly arcane and unregulated – the arbiter of the economy. When this reached its apotheosis in 2008, the world economy had already begun to 'decouple' from American consumers for some time.

In the twenty-first century, the driver of world economic growth has gradually been shifting toward newly industrializing countries.[4] This has proved to be a sustainable industrialization, well beyond the 'associated dependent development' diagnosed by Cardoso or the idea that Asian industries are mainly overseas sweatshops of American capitalism. The Asian tiger economies and China have been undertaking a technological upgrading. China has overtaken the United States as the world's leading exporter of technological products and is nearing Japan in research and development spending (though its share in patents remains minuscule). Industrialization in the south is sustainable too in that it outlasts shrinking American consumer demand – which is anticipated and inevitable in view of American indebtedness. Alternative markets for Asian industries have taken shape in growing domestic demand, regional markets, south–south trade and trade with Europe. Whether the new industrialization is sustainable in an ecological sense is a different matter.

The new industrialization is a decisive factor shaping the horizon of the world economy. The early twenty-first century structurally resembles the twentieth-century postwar boom, the 'golden years' of capitalism – except this time the industrialization is occuring in Asia, Latin America and eastern Europe. As before, industrialization as a driver (rather than consumption and FIRE [finance, insurance, real estate]) boosts the demand for commodities, and rising commodities' prices tend to have a relatively equalizing effect between industrial and peripheral economies. A general rule is that when commodity prices are high, the IMF is weak (Petras 2007: 41). High commodity prices enable early repayment of IMF debts and reduce the need for new loans. Accordingly, the influence of the Washington consensus (augmented or not) has been shrinking as rapidly as financial dependence on Washington has been receding.

For some time growth rates in the global south have been much higher than in the developed economies. Even in African countries, the classic basket case of twentieth-century development, growth rates in recent years have been in the order of 6 per cent. These growth rates are achieved without incurring external debt – unlike in the United States where sluggish growth of 1–2 per cent, or recession, is being attained with gargantuan external borrowing ($2 billion per trading day, $700 billion per year) that absorbs 70 per cent of world savings. Third, this growth is not a blip but has been sustained through cycles and shifts in patterns. Fourth, accumulation patterns have changed, as became clear during the 2008 financial crisis when sovereign wealth funds from the global south stepped into the breach. Fifth, as the success model of 1980–2000, Anglo-American capitalism, unravels due to successive crises, accumulation strategies and philosophies have been changing.

Most analyses treat the unravelling of American capitalism as a case of deregulation gone too far and permissive capitalism, producing unprecedented rich–poor polarization and fraud on a massive scale. In contrast, for developing countries the model to emulate has long been East Asia. 'Looking east' has been the norm for almost two decades. That 'the next phase of globalization will most likely have an Asian face' is a cliché.[5] Meanwhile, however, there is no 'Asian model' and, of course, East Asian societies are battlefields and arenas of struggle, so besides a general sense of direction what there is to emulate is not clear.

In the coming years growth in leading emerging markets, even if it is severely curtailed in the wake of the 2008 crisis, will still be in the order of 6 per cent (lower in Latin America and Africa) while growth in the US, Europe and Japan will be 1 per cent at best. Thus, the irony is that developing countries, the erstwhile stepchildren of the world economy, have become its locomotive. This shift is noticeable at many levels, in headlines such as 'BRICs could point the way out of the economic mire', and in reports of sovereign wealth funds in the global south scanning western economies for good deals in a distressed economy.[6]

During the 1990s globalization was welcomed in the west and suspected in the global south; in the twenty-first century it is almost the other way round. According to a recent poll, 57 per cent in G7 countries think that economic globalization is too rapid, whereas the majority in developing countries think the pace is just right.[7] This is reflected in positions on trade. During 1980–2000 the advanced countries pushed for freeing up trade; now in several respects they have retreated to protectionism.[8]

2. *From 'we develop it' to 'we develop'*. Referring to the Growth Commission report that came out in 2008, Dani Rodrik sums up the change in perspective: 'The Spence Commission verdict is that the rulebook for developing countries must be written at home, not in Washington' (2008).

During the Washington era, neoliberal macroeconomics governed development, too, on the premise that there is no need for economic development as a 'special case' and developing economies will benefit from embracing market forces. Thus the 'counterrevolution in development', as Toye called it, meant the termination of development economics. What ensued in practice was that actual development policy was left to international institutions, donors, development agencies and NGOs, consorting with developing country institutions. Indeed, in development studies 'development' usually refers to what is being done, and not done, by the development industry. Thus, implicitly, development is thought of as an external intervention. The root paradigm is not 'we develop' but 'we develop it.' Cowen and Shenton (1996) argue that intrinsic to development thinking is a deep, unresolved friction between development as an immanent process (it grows, we grow, we develop) and as a transcendent process (we grow it, we develop it).

Much post-development thinking is, in effect, a repudiation of development as an external intervention and discipline (as well as a rejection of neoliberalism). 'Indigenous development' is an alternative option but poses different problems (what is indigenous, what is the unit of development?).

The development industry is rife with fads and buzzwords, for buzzwords synchronize diverse actors and stakeholders (Dahl 2008). The turnover of fashions conceals the low success rate of development interventions. The declaration of assorted new development targets – such as the Millennium Development Goals – helps divert attention from the fact that no previous targets have been attained, even remotely. The development industry is, in no small measure, a rhetorical industry, an ideological performance in which discourse production, paradigm maintenance and tweaking the perception of receding horizons are the actual achievement.

The ideological proclivities of Washington used to occupy the front burners – incentives, market forces, good governance, transparency, civil society, and 'participation' and 'empowerment' as ways of sharing the Washington utopia. As states retreated from society, NGOs filled the space. The salience of civil society and NGOs accompanied market forces as an organizational counterpart to the hegemony of business.

Questions of rural livelihoods, urban poverty, ecological changes and democratic struggles, the gritty questions of development, were temporarily outflanked by neoliberal utopianism, the rollback of state oversight and IMF and World Bank regimes; now that the neoliberal era is receding, the development landscape reverts to its 'normal' mode of development struggles and the nitty-gritty of development is coming back on the front burner. Development is again becoming development and no longer a franchise of the 'magic of the marketplace'. The comeback of development means the background becoming foreground. In developing countries, of course, development had never gone away; the developmental state, even if emaciated by structural adjustment programmes, was never quite away. In development debates much energy went into contesting the hegemony of the market and neoliberalism. Now the long-drawn-out critiques of western economic, ideological and cultural hegemonies are gradually becoming superfluous. The major target of criticism of the previous period has become a background issue, still pertinent, but on the back burner. With American capitalism unravelling, who needs a critiquing of American ideologies?

In one account, the new emerging paradigm has been characterized as the 'Beijing consensus' (Ramo 2004). This has a certain historical elegance: the torch passes from one hegemon to the next, whose ethos henceforth is the new rule. But it is also quite misleading. First, what the Beijing consensus is supposed to represent is so general and vague that it is little more than development common sense (such as financial autonomy and cautious and strategic interaction with global forces). Second, it replicates a fundamental fallacy of Washington thinking – that one size fits all, the very idea of a 'model', which is a fallacy before and aside from the contents of the model. Third, it glosses over steep political differences *in* Beijing and China (e.g. Hui 2003, Mittelman 2006, Xin 2003). Fourth, intimating a transition from one hegemon to the next skips over the much likelier and more realistic trend of multipolarity, or, alternatively, nonpolarity (Haass 2008).

The wish for an overarching development paradigm, a master key, is as acute as ever. A colleague in Thailand observes, 'Several "alternative development" concepts are hovering around in Asia including sufficiency economy, human security, engaged Buddhism and gross national happiness. People in the academic world (in our case: Thailand Research Fund) need an overarching framework, a synthesis, to bring things together and/or sort them out in order to make common action and policy advocacy more effective (transformative), less blurred and more inspiring.'[9] Alternatives such as Bhutan's Gross National Happiness approach have been critically examined (e.g. Priesner 1999).

In philosophies of development and the role of government there are major differences in and between developing countries. The idea that there should be a single forward path and development model lies well behind us. The idea of societies in the south not simply waiting for the opportunity to mimic advanced societies but instead shaping their own paths was dominant during the era of decolonization, became faint and distant music in the 1980s and 1990s, and is now becoming more audible. Multiple modernities have been a rising theme. Likewise, the notion of different capitalisms has taken on concrete profiles.

3. *The pendulum swings back towards state capacities*. In advanced societies a new balance is taking shape, a turn away from market fundamentalism and towards re-regulation. Banks have been so leveraged with risk that re-regulation is inevitable. 'I think, therefore I am increasing regulation.'[10] Restructuring Wall Street in the wake of the 2008 crisis might turn banks towards the continental tradition of public service banking – although more likely, in view of the *rapport de forces*, is the socialization of risk combined with business as usual. In the wake of financial crisis, the models of regulation that had been dismissed by the smart set in Wall Street and Washington come back looking good. The mixed economies and coordinated markets of Japan, Germany and Scandinavia suddenly look different – less dynamic, less profitable, but more stable and sustainable, precisely as Michel Albert had argued years ago in his parable of the tortoise and the hare (for Rhineland and American capitalism respectively) and Ronald Dore also argued in

his critiques of shareholder capitalism. As before, in the slipstream of the Enron scandals, the firms and sectors in European economies that have been most vulnerable in 2008 are mostly those that have been closely linked with American branches or financial operations.[11]

The pendulum swings toward greater regulation both in the west and as part of the rising influence of the south. The BRIC economies [Brazil Russia India China] are typically societies with large public sectors. The rise of emerging societies brings back the era of developmental states. Again, development strategies and policies rest primarily with the states of developing countries.

Once the polemic with Washington recedes, other problems show up. Implicit in the discourse of emerging markets is accepting development as a numbers game. Once certain growth thresholds are crossed, they afford an entrée into the global hierarchy. Economic growth begets economic power begets political power begets geopolitical power begets cultural standing. Such is the appeal of this path that the situation is not 'development is for people' but that people serve to achieve development targets, which enable elites to gain that entrée to global echelons, and purchase, for instance, metropolitan real estate or English second division soccer clubs. It is tempting to applaud the arrival of emerging societies and to view it as an emancipation of sorts because we are at a historic juncture, yet their arrival, so far, also implies an extension and institutionalization of present patterns, rather than a transformation. Emerging markets meet with applause because they become an annex of world capitalism, rather than transforming its compulsions. As ratings record the growth of the middle classes in China, India and Latin America, workers and peasants are absent from such accounts.

At the present juncture, state capacities hold the trump cards, including developmental states in emerging societies, energy exporting states and regulatory authorities in developed countries. This is not a return of state capitalism or a rerun of Keynesianism for several reasons. First, the Asian tiger states acted in tandem with market forces – conglomerates in East Asia and multinationals from the west; industrialization in East Asia unfolded in tandem with deindustrialization in the United States – which involves a growing trade and financial imbalance that is not sustainable and not reproducible. Second, the authoritarian character of the East Asian tigers is not an enviable or replicable model. The interest now is in democratic developmental states. Third, the comeback of the state takes place in a context of post-Fordism and concerns state capacities that are responsive and agile in partnering with the private sector and with social forces and able to engage and foster creative economies.

That there has been no development success without a developmental state is the lesson of Japan, East Asia, China and India. Although the World Bank claimed that the 'Asian miracle' was the success of liberalization and export orientation, it would not have materialized without developmental states. Although Thomas Friedman and others cast the rise of China and India as victories of liberalization and unleashing market forces, research shows that the foundations for their economic achievements were laid during the time of Mao and Nehru.[12]

While ample research confirms that states play key roles in development, the pendulum swing-back to the state pivots the spotlight to rest on problems old and new. States typically face problems of capability in designing and implementing policy, local government capacity, and accountability, with further problems in specific cases – such as the delivery of services and job creation in South Africa; uneven development, ecological hazards and product quality control in China; and infrastructure, rural livelihoods, social inequality and education in India. Many of these concern questions of state capability that Gunnar Myrdal, years ago, summed up as the 'soft state'. Yet, behind these loom deeper problems: problems of power, commitment, and the relationship between growth and development.

A recurrent problem is the capture of the state by strategic groups. The state is the expression of a social hierarchy and state power is commonly used to maintain that hierarchy. States from Singapore to the Arab emirates maintain a hierarchy by means of an ethnically stratified division of labour. Development thinking often implicitly assumes a shared social vision of an inclusive society, but this is by no means a given. It is a profound challenge, all the more so in an age of increasing migration and multiculturalism. In societies that make intensive use of migrant labour, such as the Persian Gulf, imaginaries of social development require a sense of regional responsibility and a broadening culture of citizenship. Without an inclusive 'we' there may be pockets of growth but there is no development. An imaginary of social inclusion is a prerequisite without which there is no context or rationale for broad-based development policies. Thus, India's legacy of caste and communalism and its hiatus between state and society hamper development thinking and policy fundamentally. China's social revolution, for all its problems, has inculcated a fundamental sense of social equality into political streams.

A further consideration is that 'stateness' is a variable and not a given; what is understood by the 'state' and how it functions varies widely between different types of society, say between France, Morocco and Pakistan, and between different parts of a society, such as coastal and inland Somalia.

Social imaginaries also shape the understanding of the relationship between growth and development, or, so to speak, the relationship between peaks and valleys. What has been emerging is not a 'flat world' but a world of peaks and valleys, a spiked world, in Richard Florida's (2008) words, and some spikes (in innovation, research and development, productivity, and so forth) have been emerging in the global south – such as the 'new champions' and rising multinationals in emerging societies (Sirkin et al. 2008). The pursuit of peaks (of excellence, competitiveness) is crucial to growth, but maintaining a balance between peaks and valleys is crucial to development. As gradients of accumulation climb in the south, so do gradients of power. Yet, 'it is essential to remember that the well-being of humankind is the essence of development', notes Deepak Nayyar. 'The litmus test for the performance of an economy, hence government, is neither economic growth, nor economic efficiency, indeed not even equity in an abstract sense, but whether or not it meets the basic needs and the growing aspirations of people' (2006: 827). In India there is also a practical rejoinder: 'Even if the share of rural India in national income is less than its share in the population, its share of votes is directly proportional. And rural India decides for the republic at election time' (ibid.: 828).

Such direct praise for democracy seems to match Amartya Sen's formulation of development as freedom, 'as a process of expanding the real freedoms that people enjoy', a process that 'requires the removal of major sources of unfreedom' and entails freedoms such as 'the freedom to enter markets'. In Sen's view, 'freedoms are not only the primary end of development, they are also among its principal means' (Sen 1999: 3, 7, 10). This position short-circuits a lengthy debate in development studies about the relationship between development and democracy, which generally finds that the enabling relationship is first development, then democracy, not the other way round (see Leftwich 1996, Siaroff 1999). Sen's view, by implication, short-circuits the debate about the relative development prospects of China and India, presumably to the advantage of India as a democracy. But this is not a clear-cut matter at all.[13]

The north–south gap has been narrowing, at least with the upper-income developing countries. With newly industrializing countries becoming locomotives of the world economy, the question becomes all the more pressing: what about inequality *in* emerging societies? Here a key question is the nature of accumulation. Is inequality built into the growth path or does it recede with growth; is growth polarizing or is it geared towards inclusive development? Is accumulation based on a narrow track of economic growth or is it geared toward achieving broad-based development?[14]

Fast growth or broad-based development is a classic dilemma. In the 1960s Eisenstadt cautioned that mass mobilization reduces state autonomy in implementing reforms (1966). Part of the discreet subtext of development studies is that modernization is not the same as democratization. In the 1970s World Bank economists advocated a policy of growth and redistribution. By the 1980s this was sidelined by the neoliberal approach of growth plus trickle-down. Then the UNDP took up growth through redistribution and renamed it human development. Thinkers in the human development school – such as Streeten, Jolly, ul Haq, Griffin – argue that viewing growth and distribution as a trade-off is spurious in relation to growth in general and more so if we view human development not as a means but as the end of development.[15]

The fast growth favoured by the World Bank and the Washington consensus during the previous development era was capital and foreign direct investment-intensive and export-oriented. Setting development targets, such as Malaysia's 2020 and India's 2025, may distort priorities. Ratings and rankings turn development into a numbers game. Development becomes the pursuit of growth that is unsustainable – environmentally because of ecological damage, socially because it entails social polarization, economically because it depends on capital inputs and exports and fosters crony capitalism, and politically because it concentrates power.

The growth paths of newly industrializing countries set new standards which are reflected in the report of the Commission on Growth and Development (Growth Report 2008). Drivers of growth, according to the report, are private-sector investment, entrepreneurial activity and innovation responding to market incentives. As a consensus document, the report confirms every major ideological disposition – Schumpeterian leanings, the global economy as an enabling factor, the importance of competition, and anti-state as well as developmental state perspectives. Dani Rodrik notes:

> the report manages to avoid both market fundamentalism and institutional fundamentalism. Rather than offering facile answers such as 'just let markets work' or 'just get governance right,' it rightly emphasises that each country must devise its own mix of remedies. Foreign economists and aid agencies can supply some of the ingredients, but only the country itself can provide the recipe. (2008).

Although it is cast as an augmentation of the Washington consensus, there is little 'Washington' to its leanings. The report's controversial part is the large role it attributes to the public sector in mobilizing and steering growth. The task of the public sector is building a coalition around a growth path, pacing and sequencing development so job destruction is balanced by job creation, and ensuring that growth is inclusive and sustainable. Market forces may generate growth, but it takes the public sector to see to the quality of growth.

Quality growth and sustainable growth have been the Achilles heel of Anglo-American capitalism. As advanced countries are undergoing a transition to high-end service economies, the societies best placed to do so, while sustaining social cohesion and without deepening social inequality, are social market economies with large public sectors and substantial public investments in education, health, social services and technological and green innovation; which is another rationale for adopting a better regulated and more social approach.

Development pluralism

Each type of society and each level of development faces its own choices. Different relations prevail between societies at different levels of development and within societies across gradients of uneven development. Thus, different development horizons prevail in new industrialized countries, in cooperation between NICs, in relations between NICs and commodity-exporting countries, and in north–south relations. The idea of development as a single forward path – 'progress' – or generalizing across developing societies lie well behind us (Schuurman 2000, Slater 2004).

The various transitions taking place at different levels together form the horizon of contemporary development. Heeding the transitions that each developing society, at different levels of development, seeks to undertake is essential to understanding global development. Global development also carries another meaning, in Björn Hettne's words, 'an improvement in the quality of international relations' (2008a: 23–4), and the two are probably related.

As newly industrializing societies seek to develop the service sector, including research and development, education, design, marketing and finance, it calls on different skills, cultural sensibilities and priorities than in the earlier phase of industrialization. For instance, across East Asia knowledge and cultural skills such as English have become crucial.

For the first time in decades sub-Saharan African countries are recognized as major frontiers of business, also by private equity investors. The 2007 report on African Development Indicators notes, 'For the first time in three decades African economies are growing with the rest of the world'. By some assessments Africa is the 'emerging emerging market': 'With the global credit crunch … capital is looking for new places to grow … also to "emerging emerging" markets in Africa … government debt issues in Nigeria and Ghana in 2007 were seven times oversubscribed'.[16] According to another report Africa 'is at the heart of the latest surge of enthusiasm to hit emerging markets'. Private capital flows have tripled since 2003 (at $45 billion in 2006). Factors in this change are the commodities boom, debt relief and improvements in economic policy.[17] Yet, the challenge facing commodity-exporting countries is to convert their export gains into human capital and sustainable development paths. Commodities booms don't last. The 2008 slump has brought prices down. A case in point is the roller-coaster experience of Zambia's copper belt, moving along with the fluctuations in global demand. As copper's fortunes rose during 2002–2007, so did investments in copper mining from India and China, but the global recession since autumn 2008 has more than halved the price of copper. The declining demand for minerals has affected some 11 other African countries and has also affected sub-Saharan Africa's GDP growth.[18]

A major focus of attention is the relations between newly industrializing countries and commodity-exporting countries. China, India and other Asian countries have shown increasing interest in investing in Africa and Latin America. A growing debate concerns the role of China and India in Africa (Kaplinsky and Messner 2008). A budding debate in China concerns the question of how they can develop in a way that is not at the expense of poorer countries.[19]

Converting gains from exports into human capital is a challenge for BRIC societies too. Observers note:

> The fundamental difference between China and India on the one hand and Russia and Brazil on the other is that the former are competing with the west for 'intellectual capital' by seeking to build top-notch universities, investing in high, value-added and technologically intensive industries and utilizing successful diasporas to generate entrepreneurial activity in the mother country. Russia and Brazil are benefiting from high commodity prices but are not attempting to invest their windfall in long-term economic development.[20]

In sum, a challenge for commodity-exporting economies is to cross the thresholds of industry, while the challenge for new industrializing countries is to upgrade into services.

International development cooperation

Another relationship that defines development is that between north and south. What do twenty-first-century trends bode for international development cooperation? One option is a growing awareness of the limited status of development cooperation. The development industry is not as important as it thinks; rather, its sense of self-importance is part of the problem in that it implies the tacit assumption that developed societies are the torchbearers of development. Note, for instance, that remittances of migrants to their home countries at $150 billion in formal flows and another $150 billion in informal flows, at $300 billion a year (2007) far exceed the total disbursements in foreign aid. It follows that supporting policies that ease transnational migration and that recognize its developmental contributions may be a more substantial contribution to international development than most foreign aid.[21]

A core dilemma of development cooperation is, to put it bluntly, how to balance power and emancipation, or how to sustain advanced countries' privileges while promoting or endorsing social justice. The gist of the Washington consensus was, after all, economic management in the interest of the United States and the west, rather than of the world majority.[22] Hence for development cooperation to achieve policy coherence – as discussed in the previous chapter – is not a minor task. Macroeconomics is usually out of synch with development cooperation; development cooperation comes as a benevolent afterthought, which is at times best left to celebrities. The discourse of development cooperation has often been coined in normative and ethical terms. In the introduction to a 1997 White Paper, *Eliminating World Poverty: A Challenge for the 21st Century*, the then British Minister for International Development stated: 'we have a moral duty to reach out to the poor and needy'. Introducing a follow-up White Paper in 2000, Tony Blair defined the elimination of world poverty as the 'greatest moral challenge facing our generation'.[23]

What is troubling about this position is that it takes a shortcut to compartmentalization. 'We should' doesn't mean 'we will.' The gap between ought and shall is a given. Thus the old adage is trade, not aid. But in the WTO industrialized countries have insisted on trade rules that privilege their producers and intellectual property policies that shield their corporations. Does it make sense to pursue the 'free market' with one hand and, with the other, to do damage control? Viewing macroeconomics in a different window from development cooperation produces policy schizophrenia; on the one hand, follow the Washington institutions and, on the other, promote projects and programmes that counterbalance the effects of structural reforms. A two steps backward, one forward, or sideways, kind of policy. While macroeconomics reflects Wall Street–Treasury–IMF clichés, in its margins development cooperation builds on slogans (good governance, civil society, participation, etc.) that now seem tired and compromised. The surfeit of moral exhortation may serve to paper over policy schizophrenia and the realities of what Petras and Veltmeyer call 'reverse aid' (2002), referring to all the ways in which foreign aid greases the wheels of elites and corruption. I'm sidestepping the weary discussions of 'foreign aid' because compartmentalization doesn't make sense, nor does it make sense to discuss aid separately from macroeconomics.[24]

Crisis is also opportunity, including the opportunity of bringing back economics as if people matter. This may involve three moments – in brief, a global we, rebalancing globalization, and social innovations. The deeper challenge is to envision a global 'we' and thus a future that welcomes the world majority and the world's poor. This would imply fundamentally different takes on globalization and development. It is sobering but wise to recognize that this is probably a bridge too far; hence it is appropriate to lower the volume of moral exhortation and to turn to the 'how' of a constructive approach.

According to Stiglitz (2006), what it takes to 'make globalization work' is a different balance of state, market and society. The previous balance was market-led and many states followed market preferences. Were globalization market-led, the world would be headed in the same general direction as Enron, New Orleans and Lehmann Brothers. A new balance is in the making, with a greater role for emerging societies, and smart development cooperation can ease its path. The role of international development cooperation is to assist developing countries and social organizations and movements to see to the quality of growth, that is, on the optimistic assumption that international development cooperation agents would be willing and able to do so. This involves viewing development cooperation not as a tool of a status quo back-up and paradigm maintenance but as a tool for the making of a new balance, a tool for global progressive change. Obviously this is not an easy proposition for there is no consensus on progress, on what is 'progressive', on whether being progressive is desirable, and on whether it is doable at a global level.

Some advantage may be gained from building development cooperation, not around slogans or vague ethical principles but around innovations, whether engineering or social, hardware or software innovations; innovations such as cash-for-trash, mobile phones, rural internet kiosks, new migrant mobility. This may avoid development cooperation getting bogged down in interminable debates on general political economy. Global social policy and a political economy of global social democracy may be desirable but are unlikely to generate a consensus. A global mixed economy approach with many different entrées and exits may be more feasible.

After the crisis

How are these trends holding up in the wake of the 2008 economic crisis? The first major test of the decoupling thesis shows that Asia and other emerging markets are not able to take up the slack, especially if the slowdown affects not just the United States but Europe as well. The decoupling thesis is passé, as Stephen Roach had argued all along. Looking back at 2008 at the onset of 2009, Arun Kumar, economist at Jawaharlal Nehru University, notes:

The year began with policy makers and experts suggesting a decoupling between the Asian and the US and European economies. They suggested that the rapidly growing economies of Asia will provide the boost to the advanced economies so that there would be a soft landing for the world. This was based more on hope and hype rather than on analysis. These economies were already at their peak growth rates and could not double them, which was required to compensate for a decline in the rates of growth in the OECD economies. Further, since China is heavily dependent on exports to these economies and India is much more open than earlier, if anything, their rates of growth were bound to fall. These two economies could not move in a direction opposite to that of the bigger economies, as events have borne out. Clearly, all along, the policy makers and experts have been hoodwinking by denying the reality. (Kumar 2009)

Commodity prices – high from 2002 to 2008 – have come tumbling down. With petrol prices coming down as well, it is a mixed message for developing countries. But since growth in leading emerging societies remains strong, the demand for commodities will swing back to some extent. Migration to the north has slowed and will not easily recover, which in turn affects remittances. The slump enables the IMF to make a comeback, but it does so with a different script – a tad more self-critical, less confident about its prescriptions, refraining from economic micromanagement, and looking over its shoulders for funds. The IMF's capital base has eroded, and to play its role amid financial turmoil its capital stock should include a significant participation of sovereign wealth funds from the global south. This is possible only on the basis of financial power-sharing with emerging economies, which, in turn, signals the passing of the Washington era, not immediately but in time.

In the wake of crisis, financial institutions in the global south have become more careful about acquiring western assets. From South Korea to the Middle East, everyone is cutting back on their US dollar assets. Temasek Holdings, Singapore's main sovereign wealth fund, suffered significant losses on its investments in Merrill Lynch early in 2008. China is cutting back on acquiring US Treasury bonds as part of what looks to be a fundamental realignment.[25]

The economic weakness of the United States is structural and, unlike in the 1990s, not amenable to financial fixes. The financial overhang is too large (for instance, outstanding hedge funds' capital amounts to $71 trillion) and the economic foundations are too weak. The key problem of the American economy is decades' long underinvestment in the private sector, in new technologies generally, and in manufacturing particularly. The industrialization in emerging societies is, in part, a counterpart to the deindustrialization in the US. Financialization of the economy, one of the main ways forward, has only deepened America's economic troubles.[26]

The rise of emerging societies is structural, too, and will outlast the crisis. Although the short-term picture has changed, medium- and long-term trends have not. According to Goldman Sachs' forecasts, 'the Bric countries will be the only source of domestic demand growth globally in 2009'. Thus, 'coming on top of 2008, we project that for three consecutive years we will have seen global demand expansion led by the Bric economies'. A question that comes up is 'are we going to discover that not only can these nations cope better than people in the west think, but that some of their own forms of economic model will be mimicked by developed countries to help them cope with the decline of private sector market systems?'[27]

Crisis may be an opportunity for 'redoing globalization' (Schwenninger 2009) and global social policy and perhaps even global social democracy will emerge on the agenda. This is unlikely to materialize however because the major players are occupied with their own problems. The main significance of crisis is that neoliberalism is past, Keynesianism is back in, financialization will have to be brought under control, and America's lead in the world economy has faded. Clearly, the current era signals a new development epoch, more multipolar, with a much greater role for developing countries and a greater importance to south–south relations.

Notes

1 J. Anderlini, 'China says west's lack of market oversight led to subprime crisis' (*Financial Times*, 28 May 2008: 1). This is part of a pattern; for instance, 'China sovereign wealth group to stop investing in western banks' (*Financial Times*, 4 December 2008); 'Chinese officials lecture Paulson' (*Financial Times*, 5 December 2008).

2 Willem Buiter's blog, *Financial Times*, 18 September 2008. Headline, *Financial Times*, 29 September 2008. J. Authers, *Financial Times*, 21 September 2008: 18.

3 On American hegemony see Nederveen Pieterse 2004, 2008a; on twenty-first-century globalization see Nederveen Pieterse 2008b.

4 'The US' share of global GDP fell to 27.7 per cent in 2006 from 31 per cent in 2000 … the share of the BRICs rose to 11 per cent from 7.8 per cent. China alone accounts for 5.4 per cent … the US continues to play an anchoring, even dominant, role in global financial services, thanks to its deep markets and strong banking systems … in 2007 the BRICs' contribution to global growth was slightly greater than that of the US for the first time. In 2007… US will account for 20 per cent of global growth, compared with about 30 per cent for the BRICs'. D. Gross, 'The U.S. is losing market share, so what?' *New York Times*, 28 January 2007: BU5.

5 Ph. Stephens, *Financial Times*, 3 March 2006: 13.

6 J. O'Neill, *Financial Times*, 23 September 2008: 28.

7 'Poll reveals backlash in wealthy countries against globalisation', *Financial Times*, 23 July 2007: 1.

8 Candidates in the 2008 American presidential election attacked 'unfair' trade deals – Obama attacked Nafta, Cafta and the Clinton administration's establishing regular trade relations with China. According to Hillary Clinton, 'When I'm president, China will be a trade partner, not a trade master' (*New York Times*, 6 April 2008).

9 Hans van Willenswaard 2008 and personal communication. Cf. chapters above on critical holism and world development.

10 J. Authers, *Financial Times*, 21 September 2008: 18.

11 See Albert 1993, Dore 2000, Nederveen Pieterse 2004.

12 See e.g. Gittings 2005, Guthrie 2006, Rodrik 2000. On the developmental state see Chang 2002, 2003; Chang and Grabel 2004.

13 See an interesting critique of Sen by Corbridge 2002.

14 See Krishna and Nederveen Pieterse 2008; Nederveen Pieterse and Rehbein 2009; Thornton and Thornton 2006.

15 For further perspectives on human development see Mkandawire 2004 and Chapter 8 above.

16 A. Mitchell, 'The emerging emerging market', *Wall Street Journal*, 23 October 2007: 13.

17 A. Russell, 'Growth data fuel hopes of new business era in Africa', *Financial Times*, 15 November 2007. J. Chung, 'Investors dive into the heart of Africa's markets', *Financial Times*, 19 November 2007: 19.

18 T. Burgis, 'Copper's fall takes shine off Zambia's ambitions', *Financial Times*, 19 November 2008: 6. On Zambia's copper belt over time, see Ferguson 1999.

19 Personal communication with colleagues at the Chinese Academy of Social Sciences, Beijing.

20 J. Lloyd and A. Turkeltaub, 'India and China are the only real Brics in the wall', *Financial Times*, 4 December 2006: 13. A successor to the BRIC terminology is SICS or 'systemically important countries', which would add Mexico, South Africa, Turkey and South Korea to the group. D. Oakley, 'Different strokes for different folks?' *Financial Times*, 1 December 2008: 17.

21 See the discussion of migration and development in Portes 2009, Nederveen Pieterse 2007.

22 George Soros comments, 'The global financial system as it is currently constituted is characterized by a pernicious asymmetry. The financial authorities of the developed countries are in charge and will do whatever it takes to prevent the system from collapsing. They are, however, less concerned with the fate of countries at the periphery ... This asymmetry explains why the US has been able to run up an ever-increasing current account deficit over the past quarter of a century. The so-called Washington consensus imposed strict market discipline on other countries but the US was exempt from it' ('America must lead a rescue of emerging economies', *Financial Times*, 29 October 2008: 11.) Cf. Soros 2008.

23 Quoted in Slater and Bell, who add, 'This strong sense of moral duty was closely linked to the prioritization of human rights and a more ethical foreign policy' (2002: 342).

24 On foreign aid see e.g. special issues of *Development and Change*, 33 (2), 2002 and 34 (3), 2003.

25 K. Bradsher, 'China losing taste for debt from the U.S.', *New York Times*, 8 January 2009: A1–10.

26 On deindustrialization in the US see Zysman and Cohen 1987; on US economy see Nederveen Pieterse 2008b.

27 J. O'Neill, 'Why it would be wrong to write off the Brics', *Financial Times*, 6 January 2009: 9. See ongoing discussions, e.g. Hutton 2008.

References

Abdel-Malek, A. (1963) 'Orientalism in crisis', *Diogenes*, 44: 109–42.

Abdel-Malek, A. (ed.) (1980/1983) *Contemporary Arab political thought*. London: Zed.

Abraham, R., T. McKenna and R. Sheldrake (1992) *Trialogues at the edge of the West*. Santa Fe, NM: Bear.

Abu-Lughod, L. (1990) 'The romance of resistance: tracing transformation of power through Bedouin women', *American Ethnologist*, 17 (1): 41–55.

Adachi, I. (1996) *The law of undulation*. Tokyo: EVHA.

Addo, H., S. Amin, G. Aseniero, A.G. Frank, M. Friberg, F. Fröbel, J. Heinrichs, B. Hettne, O. Kreye and H. Seki (1985) *Development as social transformation*. London: Hodder and Stoughton.

Adelman, I. and C.T. Morris (1967) *Society, politics and economic development*. Baltimore, MD: Johns Hopkins University Press.

Adelman, I. and S. Robinson (1978) *Income distribution policy in developing countries*. Oxford and Washington, DC: Oxford University Press and World Bank.

African Rights (1994) *Humanitarianism unbound?* Discussion Paper 5. London: African Rights.

Agrawal, A. (1995a) 'Dismantling the divide between indigenous and scientific knowledge', *Development and Change*, 26 (3): 413–40.

Agrawal, A. (1995b) 'Indigenous and scientific knowledge: some critical comments', *Indigenous Knowledge and Development Monitor*, 3 (3): 3–6.

Ahmed, D.S. (1997) 'Women and religion: problems and prospects', in *Women and religion: debates on a search*. Lahore: Heinrich Böll Foundation, pp. 23–58.

Ake, C. (1979) *Social science as imperialism: the theory of political development*. Ibadan: University of Ibadan Press.

Akiwowo, A. (1988) 'Universalism and indigenization in sociological theory: introduction', *International Sociology*, 3 (2): 155–61.

Akiwowo, A. (1999) 'Indigenous sociologies: extending the scope of the argument', special issue, *International Sociology*, 14 (2).

Akyuz, Y. (2000) 'The debate on the international financial architecture: reforming the reformers', *UNCTAD Discussion Paper* 148.

Alavi, H. (1973) 'The state in postcolonial societies: Pakistan and Bangladesh', in K. Gough and H.P. Sharma (eds), *Imperialism and revolution in South Asia*. New York: Monthly Review Press, pp. 145–73.

Albert, M. (1993) *Capitalism against capitalism*. London: Whurr.

Alden, C. (2003) 'Let them eat cyberspace: Africa, the G8 and the digital divide', *Millennium*, 32 (3): 457–76.

Almond, G.A. (1964) 'Comparative political systems', in R.C. Macridis and B.E. Brown (eds), *Comparative politics*, revised edn. Homewood, IL: Dorsey, pp. 50–64.

AlSayyad, N. and A. Roy (2006) 'Medieval modernity: on citizenship and urbanism in a global era', *Space and Polity*, 10 (1): 1–20.

Alvares, C. (1979) *Homo faber*. Bombay: Allied Publishers.

Alvares, C. (1992) *Science, development and violence: the revolt against modernity*. Delhi: Oxford University Press.

Alvesson, M. and K. Skjöldberg (1999) *Reflexive methodology*. London: Sage.

Amin, A. (ed.) (1994a) *Post-Fordism: a reader*. Oxford: Blackwell.

Amin, A. (1994b) 'Post-Fordism: models, fantasies and phantoms of transition', in Amin (ed.), pp. 1–39.

Amin, A. (1997) 'Beyond associative democracy', *New Political Economy*, 3 (1): 309–33.

Amin, A. and N. Thrift (1993) 'Globalization, institutional thickness and local prospects', *Revue d'économie régionale et urbaine*, 3: 405–27.

Amin, A. and N. Thrift (1997) 'Globalisation, socioeconomics, territoriality', in R. Lee and J. Willis (eds), *Society, place, economy*. London: Arnold, pp. 151–61.

Amin, A. and N. Thrift (eds) (2004) *The cultural economy reader*. Oxford: Blackwell.

Amin, S. (1976) *Unequal development*. Sussex: Harvester Press.

Amin, S. (1980) *Class and nation, historically and in the current crisis*. New York: Monthly Review Press (orig. Fr edn 1979).

Amin, S. (1982) 'Crisis, nationalism, and socialism', in S. Amin, G. Arrighi, A.G. Frank and I. Wallerstein, *Dynamics of global crisis*. New York: Monthly Review Press, pp. 167–231.

Amin, S. (1989) *Eurocentrism*. London: Zed (orig. French edn 1988).

Amin, S. (1990a) *Delinking: towards a polycentric world*. London: Zed (orig. French edn 1985).

Amin, S. (1990b) 'Black Athena: la fabrication de la Grèce antique', *Ifda Dossier*, 77: 93–4.

Amin, S. (1990c) *Maldevelopment: anatomy of a global failure*. London: Zed.

Amin, S. (1992) 'The perils of utopia', interview by Monty Narsoo, *Work in Progress*, December: 28–30.

Amin, S. (1997) *Capitalism in the age of globalization*. London: Zed.

Amin, S. (1999) *Spectres of capitalism: a critique of current intellectual fashions*. London: Zed.

Amin, S. (2004) 'Globalism or apartheid on a global scale', in I. Wallerstein (ed.), *The modern world-system in the longue durée*. Boulder, CO: Paradigm, pp. 5–30.

Amin, S. (2006) *Beyond US hegemony?* London: Zed.

Amin, S., D. Chitala and I. Mandaza (eds) (1987) *SADCC: prospects for disengagement and development in Southern Africa*. Tokyo: United Nations University Press.

Anderla, G., A. Dunning and S. Forge (1997) *Chaotics: an agenda for business and society for the 21st century*. London: Adamantine Press.

Anderson, P. (1998) *The origins of postmodernity*. London: Verso.

Antweiler, C. (1993) 'Entwicklungsethnologie und Entwicklungssoziologie', *Entwicklungsethnologie*, 2 (1): 40–60.

Apffel-Marglin, F. and S. Marglin (eds) (1990) *Dominating knowledge: development, culture and resistance*. Oxford: Clarendon.

Apffel-Marglin, F. and S. Marglin (eds) (1996) *Decolonizing knowledge: from development to dialogue*. Oxford: Clarendon.

Appadurai, A. (ed.) (1986) *The social life of things*. Cambridge: Cambridge University Press.

Apter, D.E. (1987) *Rethinking development: modernization, dependency, and postmodern politics*. London: Sage.

Apthorpe, R. and D. Gasper (eds) (1996) *Arguing development policy: frames and discourses*. London: Frank Cass.

Ariansen, P. (1998) 'Anthropocentrism with a human face', *Ecological Economics*, 24 (2–3): 153–62.

Arifa, K. (2002) 'Access to information by the socially disadvantages in developing countries with special reference to India', *Information Studies*, 8 (3): 159–72.

Africa, K. (2002) 'Access to information by the socially disadvantaged in developing countries with special reference to India', *Information Studies*, 8 (3): 159–72.

Aronowitz, S. (1989) *Science as power: discourse and ideology in modern society*. London: Macmillan.

Arrelano-Lopez, S. and J.F. Petras (1994) 'Non-governmental organizations and poverty alleviation in Bolivia', *Development and Change*, 25 (3): 555–68.

Arruda, M. (1994) 'A creative approach to structural adjustment: towards a people-centred development', in Cavanagh et al. (eds), pp. 132–44.

Arruda, M. (1996) *Globalization and civil society: rethinking cooperativism in the context of active citizenship*. Rio de Janeiro: PACS (Alternative Policies for the Southern Cone).

Ashraf, T. (2004) 'Information technology and public policy: a socio-human profile of Indian digital revolution', *International Information & Library Review*, 36 (4): 309–18.

Ashton, J. and R. Laura (1999) *The perils of progress*. London: Zed.

Attali, J. 1997 'The crash of Western civilization: the limits of the market and democracy', *Foreign Policy*, 107: 54–64.

Ayto, J. (1990) *Bloomsbury dictionary of word origins*. London: Bloomsbury.

Badie, B. (1989) 'Comparative analysis in political science: requiem or resurrection?' *Political Studies*, 37 (3): 340–52.

Balasubramaniam, A. (1987) *Participatory action research*. Singapore: Friedrich Naumann Stiftung.

Banuri, T. (1990) 'Modernization and its discontents: a cultural perspective on the theories of development', in Apffel-Marglin and Marglin (eds), pp. 73–101.

Banuri, T. et al. (1993) 'A North–South debate: the meaning of progress', *UNESCO Courier*, 46, December.

Banuri, T., S. Rafi Khan and M. Mahmood (eds) (1997) *Just development: beyond adjustment with a human face*. Karachi: Oxford University Press.

Bauman, Z. (1992) *Intimations of postmodernity*. London: Routledge.

Bayat, A. (1998) *Street politics: poor people's movements in Iran*. Cairo: American University in Cairo Press.

Bazin, M. (1987) 'Tales of underdevelopment', *Race & Class*, 28 (3): 1–12.

Beck, U. (1992) *Risk society: towards a new modernity*. London: Sage.

Beck, U. (1999) *World risk society*. Oxford: Blackwell.

Bell, D. (1978) *The cultural contradictions of capitalism*. New York: Basic Books.

Bello, W. (1992) *People and power in the Pacific*. London: Pluto.

Benedict, R. (1935) *Patterns of culture*. London: Routledge and Kegan Paul.

Berger, P. and T. Luckmann (1967) *The social construction of reality*. London: Allen Lane.

Berman, Marshall (1988) *All that is solid melts into air*. New York: Penguin.

Berman, Morris (1984) *The reenchantment of the world*. New York: Bantam.

Bernal, M. (1987) *Black Athena: Afroasiatic roots of classical civilization: the fabrication of Ancient Greece 1785–1985*. London: Free Association Press.

Bernard, A., H. Helmich and P.B. Lehning (eds) (1998) *Civil society and international cooperation*. Paris: OECD.

Bhabha, H.K. (1994) *The location of culture*. London: Routledge.

Bhaduri, A. and D. Nayyar (1996) *The intelligent person's guide to liberalization*. New Delhi: Penguin.

Bhagwati, J. (1997) *A stream of windows: unsetting reflections on trade, immigration and democracy*. Cambridge, MA: MIT Press.

Bhalla, A. and F. Lapeyre (1997) 'Social exclusion: towards an analytical and operational framework', *Development and Change*, 28 (3): 413–34.

Bharadwaj, K. and S. Kaviraj (1989) 'Introduction', in Bharadwaj and Kaviraj (eds), *Perspectives on capitalism*. New Delhi: Sage, pp. 9–19.

Bhaskar, R. (1991) *Philosophy and the idea of freedom*. Oxford: Blackwell.

Bienefeld, M. (1994) 'The New World Order: echoes of a new imperialism', *Third World Quarterly*, 15 (1): 31–48.

Black, M. (1992) *A cause for our times: Oxfam the first fifty years*. Oxford: Oxford University Press.

Bohm, D. (1980) *Wholeness and the implicate order*. London: Routledge and Kegan Paul.

Boon, J.A. (1990) *Affinities and extremes*. Chicago: University of Chicago Press.

Booth, D. (1993) 'Development research: from impasse to a new agenda', in Schuurman (ed.), pp. 49–76.

Booth, D. (ed.) (1994a) *Rethinking social development*. Harlow: Longman.

Booth, D. (1994b) 'How far beyond the impasse?', in Booth (ed.), pp. 298–311.

Bourdieu, P. (1976) 'Les modes de domination', *Actes de la recherche en sciences sociale*, 2 (2–3): 122–32.

Bourdieu, P. (1988) *Homo academicus*. Stanford, CA: Stanford University Press.

Bourdieu, P. and J.-C. Passeron (1990) *Reproduction in education, society and culture*, 2nd edn. London: Sage.

Bourdieu, P. and L. Wacquant (1992) *An invitation to reflexive sociology*. Chicago: University of Chicago Press.

Boyer, R. and D. Drache (eds) (1996) *States against markets: the limits of globalization*. London: Routledge.

Broad, R. and C. Melhorn Landi (1996) 'Whither the North–South gap?', *Third World Quarterly*, 17 (1): 7–17.

Brohman, J. (1995) 'Economism and critical silences in development studies: a theoretical critique of neoliberalism', *Third World Quarterly*, 16 (2): 297–318.

Brohman, J. (1996) *Popular development: rethinking the theory and practice of development.* Oxford: Blackwell.

Brokensha, D., D. Warren and O. Werner (eds) (1980) *Indigenous knowledge systems and development.* Lanham, MD: University Press of America.

Brookfield, H. (1975) *Interdependent development.* London: Methuen.

Brown, D.L. and D. Ashman (1996) *Participation, social capital, and intersectoral problem-solving: African and Asian cases*, Boston, Institute for Development Research Report 12 (2).

Brown, D.L. and D. Ashman (1999) 'Social capital, mutual influence, and social learning in intersectoral problem solving in Africa and Asia', in Cooperrider and Dutton (eds), pp. 139–67.

Burkey, S. (1992) *People first: a guide to self-reliant participatory rural development.* London: Zed.

Burne, S. (ed.) (1995) *Let the dawn come: social development, looking behind the clichés.* London: Panos.

Buvini, M., C. Gwyn and L.M. Bates (1996) *Investing in women: progress and prospects for the World Bank.* Washington, DC: Overseas Development Council.

Camdessus, M. (1998) 'Camdessus discusses new global architecture', *IMF Survey*, 27 (10): 157, 161–3.

Campbell, D. (2001) 'Can the digital divide be contained?' *International Labour Review*, 140 (2): 119–41.

Capra, F. (1988) *Uncommon wisdom.* London: Century Hutchinson.

Capra, F. (1996) *The web of life.* New York: Doubleday.

Cardoso, F.H. (1993) 'North–South relations in the present context: a new dependency?', in Carnoy et al., pp. 149–60.

Carmen, R. (1996) *Autonomous development: humanizing the landscape.* London: Zed.

Carnoy, M. (1993) 'Multinationals in a changing world economy: whither the nation state?' in Carnoy et al., pp. 45–96.

Carnoy, M., M. Castells, S.S. Cohen and F.H. Cardoso (1993) *The new global economy in the information age.* University Park, PA: Pennsylvania State University Press.

Carr, B. (1999) 'Globalization from below: labour internationalism under NAFTA', *International Social Science Journal*, 159: 49–59.

Castells, M. (1993) 'The informational economy and the new international division of labor', in Carnoy et al., pp. 15–43.

Castells, M. (1996) *The information age*, Vol. 1, *The rise of the network society.* Oxford: Blackwell.

Castells, M. (1997) *The information age*, Vol. 2, *The power of identity.* Oxford: Blackwell.

Cavanagh, J., D. Wysham and M. Arruda (eds) (1994) *Beyond Bretton Woods: alternatives to the global economic order.* London: Pluto.

Center for the Study of the Global South (1994) *Social summit, Copenhagen: expectations of the global South.* Washington, DC: American University.

Chambers, R. (1983) *Rural development: putting the last first.* London: Longman.

Chandra, S. (2002) 'Information in a networked world: the Indian perspective', *International Information & Library Review*, 34 (3): 235–46.

Chang, H.-J. (2002) *Kicking away the ladder: development strategy in historical perspective.* London: Anthem.

Chang, H.-J. (2003) *Globalisation, economic development and the role of the state.* London: zed.

Chang, H.-J. (2004) 'The role of social policy in economic development: some theoretical reflections and lessons from East Asia', in Mkandawire (ed.), pp. 246–61.

Chang, H.-J. and I. Grabel (2004) *Reclaiming development: an alternative economic policy manual.* London: Zed.

Chatterjee, P. (1986) *Nationalist thought and the colonial world.* London/Tokyo: Zed.

Cheah, P. (1998) 'The cosmopolitical – today', in P. Cheah and B. Robbins (eds), *Cosmopolitics: thinking and feeling beyond the nation.* Minneapolis: University of Minnesota Press, pp. 20–43.

Chen, X. (2005) *As borders bend: transnational spaces on the Pacific Rim*. Boulder, CO: Rowman and Littlefield.

Chenery, H. et al. (1974) *Redistribution with growth*. Oxford: Oxford University Press.

Chin, C.B.N. and J.H. Mittelman (2000) 'Conceptualising resistance to globalisation', in B.K. Gills (ed.), *Globalization and the politics of resistance*. London: Macmillan, pp. 29–45.

Chirot, D. (1977) *Social change in the twentieth century*. New York: Harcourt Brace Jovanovich.

Chossudovsky, M. (1997) *The globalization of poverty: impacts of IMF and World Bank reforms*. London: Zed.

Christopherson, S. (1994) 'The fortress city: privatized spaces, consumer citizenship', in A. Amin (1994a), pp. 409–27.

Clark, J. (1991) *Democratizing development: the role of voluntary organizations*. London, Earthscan.

Clarke, G. (1998) 'Non-governmental organizations and politics in the developing world', *Political Studies*, 46: 36–52.

Cleveland, H., H. Henderson and I. Kaul (eds) (1995) *The United Nations: policy and financing alternatives*. New York: Apex Press.

Clifford, J. (1988) *The predicament of culture*. Cambridge, MA: Harvard University Press.

Clifford, J. (1992) 'Travelling cultures', in L. Grossberg, C. Nelson and P. Treichler (eds), *Cultural studies*. London: Routledge, pp. 96–116.

Coco, A. and P. Short (2004) 'History and habit in the mobilization of ICT resources', *Information Society*, 20 (1): 39–51.

Coetzee, J.K. (ed.) (1989) *Development is for people*. Halfway House, South Africa: Southern Book Publishers.

Coleman, J.S. (1988) 'Social capital in the creation of human capital', *American Journal of Sociology*, 94: 95–120.

Collier, P. (2007) *The bottom billion: why the poorest countries are failing and what can be done about it*. Oxford: Oxford University Press.

Collingsworth, T., J.W. Goold and P.J. Harvey (1994) 'Time for a global new deal', *Foreign Affairs*, 73 (1): 8–13.

Colman, D. and F. Nixson (1994) 'Alternative views of development: underdevelopment and dependence', in idem, *Economics of change in less developed countries*, 3rd edn. London: Harvester Wheatsheaf, pp. 48–67.

Comaroff, J. and J.L. Comaroff (eds) (2001) *Millennial capitalism and the culture of neoliberalism*. Durham, NC: Duke University Press.

Comfort, L.K. (1999) *Shared risk: complex systems in seismic response*. Amsterdam: Pergamon.

Commission on Global Governance (1995) *Our global neighbourhood* (report). New York: Oxford University Press.

Conger, L. (1998) 'A fourth way? The Latin American alternative to neoliberalism', *Current History*, November: 380–84.

Connors, M. (1997) *The race to the intelligent state: charting the global information economy in the 21st century*. Oxford: Capstone.

Constantino, R. (1985) *Synthetic culture and development*. Quezon City: Foundation for Nationalist Studies.

Cooke, B. and U. Kothari (eds) (2001) *Participation: the new tyranny?* London: Zed.

Cooperrider, D.L. and J.E. Dutton (eds) (1999) *Organizational dimensions of global change: no limits to cooperation*. London: Sage.

Corbridge, S. (1994) 'Post-Marxism and post-colonialism: the needs and rights of distant strangers', in Booth (1994a), pp. 90–117.

Corbridge, S. (ed.) (1995) *Development studies: a reader*. London: Edward Arnold.

Corbridge, S. (1998) '"Beneath the pavement only soil": the poverty of post-development', *Journal of Development Studies*, 34 (6): 138–48.

Corbridge, S. (2002) 'Development as freedom: the spaces of Amartya Sen', *Progress in Development Studies*, 2 (3): 183–217.

Cornia, G.A. (1999) *Liberalization, globalization and income distribution*. Helsinki: UNU Wider Working Paper 157.

Cowen, M.P. and R.W. Shenton (1996) *Doctrines of development*. London: Routledge.

Cox, R.W. (1991) 'Gramsci, hegemony and international relations: an essay in method', *Millennium*, 12 (2): 162–75.

Craige, Betty Jean (1992) *Laying the ladder down: the emergence of cultural holism*. Amherst, MA: University of Massachusetts Press.

Crehan, K. (1991) 'Structures of meaning and structures of interest: peasants and planners in north-western Zambia', in Kaarsholm (ed.), pp. 185–208.

Crocker, D.A. (1991) 'Insiders and outsiders in international development', *Ethics & International Affairs*, 5: 149–73.

Cross, M. (2005) 'Ethiopia's digital dream', *Guardian Weekly*, 19–25 August: 27.

Crush, J. (ed.) (1996a) *The power of development*. London: Routledge.

Crush, J. (1996b) 'Introduction: imagining development', in idem (ed.), pp. 1–23.

Cullen, R. (2001) 'Addressing the digital divide', *Online Information Review*, 25 (5): 311–20.

Cypher, J.M. (1998) 'The slow death of the Washington Consensus on Latin America', *Latin American Perspectives*, 25 (6): 47–51.

Dag Hammarskjöld Foundation (1975) 'What now? Another development', *Development Dialogue*, 1–2.

Dahl, G. (2008) 'Words as moral badges: a flow of buzzwords in development aid', in B. Hettne (ed.), pp. 172–99.

Dallmayr, F. (1996) 'Global development? Alternative voices from Delhi', *Alternatives*, 21 (2): 259–82.

Daly, H.E. and J.B. Cobb Jr. (1994) *For the common good*, 2nd edn. Boston: Beacon Press.

Dasgupta, P. (1988) 'Trust as a commodity', in D. Gambetta (ed.), *Trust: making and breaking cooperative relations*. Oxford: Blackwell, pp. 49–72.

Dasgupta, S. (1985) *Towards a post-development era*. London: Mittal.

Dasgupta, S. and J. Nederveen Pieterse (eds) (2009) *Politics of globalization*. New Delhi and London: Sage.

Davis, A. (1991) 'Hazardous lives – social work in the 1980s: a view from the left', in M. Loney et al. (eds), *The state or the market: politics and welfare in contemporary Britain*, 2nd edn. London: Sage, pp. 83–93.

Davis, C.M. (2001) 'Information apartheid: an examination of the digital divide and information literacy in the United States', *PNLA Quarterly*, 65 (4): 25–7.

Davis, M. (1990) *City of Quartz*. London: Verso.

Davis, P.J. and R. Hersh (1986) *Descartes' dream: the world according to mathematics*. Boston: Houghton Mifflin.

Deacon, B., M. Hulse and P. Stubbs (1998) *Global social policy*. London: Sage.

Desai, A.R. (ed.) (1971) *Essays on modernization of underdeveloped societies*, 2 vols. Bombay: Thacker.

Dessouki, A.E.H. (1993) 'Globalization and the two spheres of security', *Washington Quarterly*, 16 (4): 109–17.

Development and social diversity — development in practice readers (1996) Oxford: Oxfam.

Dicken, P. (2007) *Global shift: mapping the changing contours of the world economy*, 5th edn. New York: Guilford.

Donaldson, J.A. (2008) 'Growth is good for whom, when, how? Economic growth and poverty reduction in exceptional cases', *World Development*, 36 (11): 2127–43.

Doornbos, M.R. (1989) *The African state in academic debate*, The Hague: Institute of Social Studies.

Dore, R. (1992) 'Goodwill and the spirit of market capitalism', in Granovetter and Swedberg (eds), pp. 159–80.

Dore, R.P. (2000) *Stock market capitalism/welfare capitalism: Japan and Germany versus the Anglo-Saxons*. Oxford: Oxford University Press.

Drabek, A.G. (ed.) (1987) *Development alternatives: the challenge for NGOs in World Development*, 15, Supplement: 1–261.

Drahos, P. (2003) 'The global intellectual property ratchet in the information age: consequences and costs', National University of Singapore.

Drahos, P. and J. Braithwaite (2002) *Information feudalism: who owns the knowledge economy?* New York: New Press.

Drèze, J. and A. Sen (1989) *Hunger and public action*. Oxford: Clarendon Press.

DSE (1994) *Social security in Africa: old age, accident and unemployment*. Berlin: Deutsche Stiftung für Internationale Entwicklung.

DuBois, M. (1991) 'The governance of the Third World: a Foucauldian perspective on power relations in development', *Alternatives*, 16: 1–30.

Duffield, M. (1996) 'The globalisation of public policy: managing the systemic crisis in the South', Birmingham, School of Public Policy, unpublished paper.

Dumont, R. (1965) *Lands alive*. New York: Monthly Review Press.

Dumont, R. (1974) *Utopia or else…* London: André Deutsch.

Dunn, D. (1986) 'Synchronisms: toward a phenomenological science', *International Synergy Journal*, 1: 2–8.

Edwards, M. (1999) *Future positive: international cooperation in the 21st century*. London: Earthscan.

Edwards, M. and D. Hulme (eds) (1992) *Making a difference: NGOs and development in a changing world*. London: Earthscan.

Edwards, M. and G. Sen (1999) 'NGOs, social change and the transformation of human relationships: a 21st century civic agenda', unpublished paper.

Eisenstadt, S.N. (1966) *Modernization: protest and change*. Englewood Cliffs, NJ: Prentice-Hall.

Eisenstadt, S.N. (2000) 'Multiple modernities', *Daedalus*, 129 (1), special issue: 1–30.

Eisenstadt, S.N. (ed.) (2002) *Multiple modernities*. New Brunswick, NJ: Transaction.

Ekins, P. (1992) *A new world order: grassroots movements for global change*. London: Routledge.

Elliott, E. and D. Kiel (1997) 'Nonlinear dynamics, complexity and public policy', in Eve et al. (eds), pp. 64–78.

Elson, D. (1993) 'Gender-aware analysis and development economics', *Journal of International Development*, 5 (2): 237–47.

Elson, D. (2004) 'Social policy and macroeconomic performance: integrating the economic and the social', in Mkandawire (ed.), pp. 63–79.

Enloe, C. (1990) *Bananas, beaches and bases*. Berkeley, CA: University of California Press.

Escobar, A. (1985) 'Discourse and power in development: Michel Foucault and the relevance of his work to the Third World', *Alternatives*, 10: 377–400.

Escobar, A. (1992a) 'Planning', in Sachs (ed.) (1992a), pp. 132–45.

Escobar, A. (1992b) 'Reflections on "Development": grassroots approaches and alternative politics in the Third World', *Futures*, June: 411–36.

Escobar, A. (1995) *Encountering development: the making and unmaking of the Third World*. Princeton, NJ: Princeton University Press.

Escobar, A. (1996) 'Imagining a post-development era', in Crush (ed.) (1996a), pp. 211–27.

Esman, M.J. and N.T. Upton (1984) *Local organizations: intermediaries in rural development*. Ithaca, NY: Cornell University Press.

Esping-Andersen, G. (1994) 'Welfare states and the economy', in Smelser and Swedberg (eds), pp. 711–31.

Esposito, J.L. (1992) *The Islamic threat: myth or reality?* New York: Oxford University Press.

Esteva, G. (1985) 'Beware of participation', and 'Development: metaphor, myth, threat', *Development: Seeds of Change*, 3: 77 and 78–79.

Esteva, G. (1992) 'Development', in Sachs (ed.), pp. 6–25.

Esteva, G. and M.S. Prakash (1998) *Hope at the margins: beyond human rights and development*. London: Zed.

Eve, R.A. (1997) 'Afterword', in Eve et al. (eds), pp. 269–80.

Eve, R.A., S. Horsfall and M.E. Lee (eds) (1997) *Chaos, complexity and sociology*. London: Sage.

Fabian, J. (1983) *Time and the other: how anthropology makes its objects*. New York: Columbia University Press.

Fagan, G.H. (1999) 'Cultural politics and (post) development paradigm(s)', in Munck and O'Hearn (eds), pp. 178–95.

Falk, R. (1994) *On humane governance: towards a new global politics*. Cambridge: Polity.

Fals-Borda, O. (1985) 'Wisdom as power', *Development: Seeds of Change*, 3: 65–7.

Fanon, F. (1967) *The wretched of the earth*. Harmondsworth: Penguin.

Faux, J. (1999) 'Lost on the Third Way', *Dissent*, 46 (2): 67–76.

Fei, J., G. Ranis and S. Kuo (1979) *Growth with equity: the Taiwan case*. Oxford: Oxford University Press.

Femia, J.V. (1981) *Gramsci's political thought*. Oxford: Oxford University Press.

Ferguson, J. (1990) *The anti-politics machine: 'development', depoliticisation and bureaucratic power in Lesotho*. Cambridge: Cambridge University Press.

Ferguson, J. (1999) *Expectations of modernity*. Berkeley: University of California Press.

Fernandes, R.C. (1993) 'Looking for alternatives after the cold war', *Cultures and Development: Quid Pro Quo*, 15: 6–14.

Feyerabend, P. (1975) *Against method*. London: New Left Books.

Fine, B. (1999) 'The developmental state is dead — long live social capital?', *Development and Change*, 30 (1): 1–20.

Fischer, F.G. (1993) 'Emergence of a circumspect society: introducing reflexive institutions', *Futures*, 25 (10): 1077–82.

FitzGerald, E.V.K. (1991) 'Kurt Mandelbaum and the classical tradition in development theory', in K. Martin (ed.), *Strategies of economic development*. London: Macmillan, pp. 3–26.

Florida, R. (2008) *Who's your city?* New York: Basic Books.

Foley, G. (1999) *Learning in social action*. London: Zed.

Fors, M. and A. Moreno (2002) 'The benefits and obstacles of implementing ICTs strategies for development from a bottom-up approach', *Aslib Proceedings*, 54 (3): 198–206.

Foucault, M. (1980) *Power/knowledge*. C. Gordon (ed.). New York: Pantheon.

Foucault, M. (1984) 'Nietzsche, genealogy, history', in P. Rabinow (ed.), *The Foucault reader*. New York: Pantheon, pp. 76–100.

Frank, A.G. (1969) *Latin America: underdevelopment or revolution*. New York: Monthly Review Press.

Frank, A.G. (1971) *Sociology of development and underdevelopment of sociology*. London: Pluto.

Frank, A.G. (1981) *Crisis: in the Third World*. New York and London: Holmes and Meyer.

Frank, A.G. (1996) 'The underdevelopment of development', in S. Chew and R. Denemark (eds), *The underdevelopment of development*. London: Sage, pp. 17–55.

Frank, A.G. (1998) *Re Orient: global economy in the Asian age*. Berkeley, CA: University of California Press.

Friberg, M. and B. Hettne (1985) 'The greening of the world – towards a nondeterministic model of global process', in Addo et al., pp. 204–70.

Friedman, E. (ed.) (1982) *Ascent and decline in the world-system*. London: Sage.

Friedman, T.L. (2000) *The Lexus and the olive tree: understanding globalization*, 2nd edn. New York: Anchor.

Friedman, T.L. (2005) *The world is flat*. New York: Farrar Straus and Giroux.

Friedmann, J. (1992) *Empowerment: the politics of alternative development*. Oxford: Blackwell.

Fukuyama, F. (1995) 'Social capital and the global economy', *Foreign Affairs*, 74 (5): 89–103.

Fukuyama, F. (1996) *Trust: social virtues and the creation of prosperity*. London: Penguin.

Galbraith, J.K. (1996) *The good society*. Boston: Houghton Mifflin.

Gao, Z. (1995) 'Market economy and social development', Beijing and Copenhagen: World Summit for Social Development.

García Canclini, N. (1992) 'Culture and power: the state of research', in P. Scannell, P. Schlesinger and C. Sparks (eds), *Culture and power*. London: Sage.

Gasper, D. (1997) 'Sen's capability approach and Nussbaum's capabilities ethic', *Journal of International Development*, 9 (2): 281–302.

Gasper, D. (2004) *The ethics of development: from economism to human development*. Edinburgh: Edinburgh University Press.

Gaventa, J. (1998) 'Poverty, participation and social exclusion in North and South', *IDS Bulletin*, 29 (1): 50–57.

Gay, P. (1977) *The Enlightenment: an interpretation*. New York: Norton.

Gbotokuma, Z. (1992) 'Cultural identity and under-development in Sub-Saharan Africa', special issue on culture and development, *Voices from Africa* (Geneva, UNNGLS), 4.

George, S. (1992) *The debt boomerang*. London: Pluto.

Gerschenkron, A. (1992) 'Economic backwardness in historical perspective' (1952), in Granovetter and Swedberg (eds), pp. 111–30.

Ghosh, J. (2004) 'Social policy in Indian development', in Mkandawire (ed.), pp. 284–307.

Gibson-Graham, J.K. (1992) 'Waiting for the revolution or, How to smash capitalism while working at home in your spare time', unpublished paper.

Giddens, A. (1984) *The constitution of society: outline of the theory of structuration*. Cambridge: Polity.

Giddens, A. (1991) *Modernity and self-identity: self and society in the late modern age*. Cambridge: Polity.

Giddens, A. (1998) *The Third Way*. Cambridge: Polity.

Gill, S. and J.H. Mittelman (eds) (1997) *Innovation and transformation in international studies*. Cambridge: Cambridge University Press.

Gilligan, C. (1982) *In a different voice*. Cambridge, MA: Harvard University Press.

Gills, B. and G. Philip (1996) 'Editorial: towards a convergence in development policy?' *Third World Quarterly*, 17 (4): 585–91.

Giri, A.K. (1998) *Global transformations: postmodernity and beyond*. Jaipur: Rawat Publications.

Gittings, J. (2005) *The changing face of China: from Mao to market*. Oxford: Oxford University Press.

Gledhill, J. (1994) *Power and its disguises: anthropological perspectives on politics*. London: Pluto.

Gleick, J. (1988) *Chaos: making a new science*. London: Heinemann.

Goetz, E.G. and S.E. Clarke (1993) *The new localism: comparative urban politics in a global era*. Newbury Park, CA: Sage.

Gomez, E.T. (1994) *Political business: corporate involvement of Malaysian political parties*. Townsville: James Cook University of North Queensland.

Goonatilake, S. (1991) *The evolution of information: lineages in gene, culture and artefact*. London: Pinter.

Goonatilake, S. (1999) *Toward a global science*. Bloomington, IN: Indiana University Press.

Gordon, D. (1991) 'Inside and outside the long swing: the endogeneity / exogeneity debate and the social structures of accumulation approach', *Review*, 12 (2): 263–312.

Goulet, D. (1992) 'Development: creator and destroyer of values', *World Development*, 20 (3): 467–75.

Gow, D.D. (1991) 'Collaboration in development consulting: stooges, hired guns, or musketeers?' *Human Organization*, 50 (1).

Granovetter, M. (1992) 'Economic institutions as social constructions', *Acta Sociologica*, 35: 3–11.

Granovetter, M. and R. Swedberg (eds) (1992) *The sociology of economic life*. Boulder, CO: Westview.

Gray, H.P. (1993) 'Globalization versus nationhood: is economic integration a useful compromise?' *Development and International Cooperation*, 9 (16): 35–49.

Green, R. (1995) 'Reflections on attainable trajectories: reforming global economic institutions', in Griesgraber and Gunter (1996a), pp. 38–81.

Greider, W. (1992) *Who will tell the people? The betrayal of American democracy*. New York: Simon and Schuster.

Greider, W. (1997) *One world, ready or not: the manic logic of global capitalism*. New York: Simon and Schuster.

Greig, A., D. Hulme and M. Turner (2007) *Challenging global inequality: development theory and practice in the 21st century*. London: Palgrave.

Griesgraber, M.J. and B.G. Gunter (eds) (1995) *Promoting development: effective global institutions for the 21st century*. London: Pluto.

Griesgraber, M.J. and B.G. Gunter (eds) (1996a) *Development: new paradigms and principles for the 21st century*. London: Pluto.

Griesgraber, M.J. and B.G. Gunter (eds) (1996b) *The World Bank: lending on a global scale*. London: Pluto.

Griffin, K. (1996) 'Culture, human development and economic growth', University of California, Riverside: Working Paper in Economics 96–17.

Griffin, K. (2000a) 'Culture and economic growth: the state and globalization', in Nederveen Pieterse (ed.) (2000a), pp. 189–202.

Griffin, K. (2000b) *Studies in development strategy and systemic transformation*. London: Macmillan.

Griffin, K. and A. Rahman Khan (1992) *Globalization and the developing world*. Geneva: UNRISD.

Griffin, K. and T. McKinley (1994) *Implementing a human development strategy*. London: Macmillan.

Grillo, R.D. and R.L. Stirrat (eds) (1997) *Discourses of development*. Oxford: Berg.

Group of Lisbon (1995) *Limits to competition*. Cambridge, MA: MIT Press.

Growth Report (2008) *Strategies for sustained growth and inclusive development*. Washington, DC: World Bank.

Gupta, A. and J. Ferguson (1992) 'Beyond culture: space, identity, and the politics of difference', *Cultural Anthropology*, 7: 6–23.

Gupta, S. (2005) 'ICTs for the poorest of the rural poor', www.globalatider.nu

Gurstein, M. (2003) 'Effective use: a community informatics strategy beyond the digital divide', *First Monday*, 8 (12), http://www.firstmonday.dk/issues/issue8_12/gurstein/

Guthrie, D. (2006) *China and globalization: the social, economic and political transformation of Chinese society*. New York: Routledge.

Haass, R. (2008) 'U.S. foreign policy in a nonpolar world', *Foreign Affairs*, 87 (3): 44–56.

Habermas, J. (1990) *Moral consciousness and communicative action*. Cambridge: Polity.

Halstead, T. and C. Cobb (1996) 'The need for new measurements of progress', in Mander and Goldsmith (eds), pp. 197–206.

Hamelink, C.J. (2004) 'Did WSIS achieve anything at all?' *Gazette*, 66: 281–90.

Hamilton, G.G. and N. Woolsey Biggart (1992) 'Market, culture and authority: a comparative analysis of management and organization in the Far East', in Granovetter and Swedberg (eds), pp. 181–223.

Hampdon-Turner, C. and F. Trompenaars (1993) *Seven cultures of capitalism*. New York: Doubleday.

Hand, M. and B. Sandywell (2002) 'E-topia as cosmopolis or citadel: on the democratizing and de-democratizing logics of the Internet', *Theory, Culture & Society*, 19 (1–2): 197–225.

Hanloe, M., C.G. Pickvance and J. Urry (eds) (1990) *Place, policy and politics: do localities matter?* London: Unwin Hyman.

Hanlon, J. (1991) *Mozambique: who calls the shots?* London: James Currey.

Harris, N. (1986) *The end of the Third World*. Harmondsworth: Penguin.

Harrison, B. (1992) 'Industrial districts: old wine in new bottles?' *Regional Studies*, 26 (5): 469–83.

Harrison, L.E. and S.P. Huntington (eds) (2000) *Culture matters: how values shape human progress*. New York: Basic Books.

Harriss, J., J. Hunter and C.M. Lewis (eds) (1995) *The new institutional economics and Third World development*. London: Routledge.

Harrod, J. (1997) 'Social forces and international political economy: joining the two IRs', in Gill and Mittelman (eds), pp. 105–14.

Harvey, D. (1989) *The condition of postmodernity*. Oxford: Blackwell.

Harvey, D. (1993) 'From space to place and back again: reflections on the condition of postmodernity', in J. Bird, B. Curtis, T. Putnam, G. Robertson and L. Tickner (eds), *Mapping the futures: local cultures, global change*. London, Routledge, pp. 3–29.

Häusler, S. (1994) 'Alternative development', in R. Braidotti et al., *Women, the environment and sustainable development*. London: Zed, pp. 107–22.

Havel, V. (1985) 'The power of the powerless', in J. Keane (ed.), *The power of the powerless: citizens against the state in Central-Eastern Europe*. London: Hutchinson.

Hearn, J. (1998) 'The 'NGO-isation' of Kenyan society: USAID and the restructuring of health care', *Review of African Political Economy*, 75: 89–100.

Hedley, R.A. (1999) 'The information age: apartheid, cultural imperialism, or global village?' *Social Science Computer Review*, 17 (1): 78–87.

Helleiner, G.K. (1992) 'Conventional foolishness and overall ignorance: current approaches to global transformation and development', in C.K. Wilber and K.P. Jameson (eds), *The political economy of development and underdevelopment*, 5th edn. New York: McGraw-Hill, pp. 36–54.

Henderson, H. (1991) *Paradigms in progress*. Indianopolis, IN: Knowledge Systems.

Henderson, H. (1993) 'Social innovation and citizen movements', *Futures*, 25 (4): 322–38.

Henderson, H. (1996a) *Building a win–win world*. San Francisco: Berrett-Koehler.

Henderson, H. (1996b) 'Changing paradigms and indicators: implementing equitable, sustainable and participatory development', in Griesgraber and Gunter (eds) (1996a), pp. 103–36.

Henwood, D. (1993) 'Global economic integration: the missing Middle East', *Middle East Report*, 184.

Hettne, B. (1990) *Development theory and the three worlds*. London: Longman (2nd edn 1995).

Hettne, B. (1992) 'New trends in development theory', The Hague, Institute of Social Studies, unpublished paper.

Hettne, B. (2008a) 'Development discourses in history', in Hettne (ed.), pp. 6–30.

Hettne, B. (ed.) (2008b) *Sustainable development in a globalized world: studies in development, security and culture*. Vol. 1. London: Palgrave Macmillan.

Hewitt de Alcántara, C. (ed.) (1996) *Social futures, global visions*, special issue of *Development and Change*, 27 (2).

Hill, M. and L. Kwen Fee (1995) *The politics of nation building and citizenship in Singapore*. London: Routledge.

Hirschman, A.O. (1981) *Essays in trespassing*. Cambridge: Cambridge University Press.

Hirst, P.Q. (1993) *Associative democracy*. Cambridge: Polity.

Hirst, P.Q. and G. Thompson (1996) *Globalization in question*. Cambridge: Polity.

Hirst, P.Q. and J. Zeitlin (1991) 'Flexible specialisation versus post-Fordism: theory, evidence and policy implications', *Economy and Society*, 20 (1): 1–56.

Hirtz, F. (1995) *Managing insecurity: state social policy and family networks in the rural Philippines*. Saarbrücken: Verlag für Entwicklungspolitik.

Hobart, M. (ed.) (1993) *An anthropological critique of development: the growth of ignorance?* London: Routledge.

Hobsbawm, E.J. and T. Ranger (eds) (1983) *The invention of tradition*. Cambridge: Cambridge University Press.

Hobson, J.M. (2004) *The eastern origins of western civilisation*. Cambridge: Cambridge University Press.

Hodgen, M.T. (1964) *Early anthropology in the sixteenth and seventeenth centuries*. Philadelphia, PA: University of Pennsylvania Press.

Holcombe, S. (1995) *Managing to empower: the Grameen Bank's experience of poverty allevia- tion*. London: Zed.

Hollingsworth, J.R. and R. Boyer (eds) (1997) *Contemporary capitalism: the embeddedness of institutions*. New York: Cambridge University Press.

Holton, R.J. and B.S. Turner (1986) *Talcott Parsons on economy and society*. London: Routledge.

Hoogvelt, A. (1997) *Globalisation and the postcolonial world: the new political economy of devel- opment*. London: Macmillan.

Hountondji, P.J. (1991) 'African philosophy: myth and reality', in T. Serequeberhan (ed.), *African philosophy*. New York: Paragon, pp. 111–31.

Hoy, D.C. (1986) 'Power, repression, progress: Foucault, Lukes, and the Frankfurt School', in Hoy (ed.), *Foucault: a critical reader*. Oxford: Blackwell, pp. 123–47.

Hui, W. (2003) 'The 1989 movement and the historical origins of neo-liberalism in China', *Asian Exchange: China Reflected*, 18 (2) and 19 (1): 211–23.

Huizer, G. (1993) 'Development anthropology in global perspective', *Entwicklungsethnologie*, 2 (1): 66–82.

Huizer, G. and J. Lava (1989) *Explorations in folk religion and healing*. Manila: Asian Social Institute.

Huntington, S.P. (1976) 'The change to change: modernization, development, and politics', in C.E. Black (ed.), *Comparative modernization*. New York: Free Press.

Huntington, S.P. (1996) *The clash of civilizations and the remaking of world order*. New York: Simon and Schuster.

Hurrell, A. and N. Woods (eds) (1999) *Inequality, globalization, and world politics*. Oxford: Oxford University Press.

Hutton, W. (1995) *The state we're in*. London: Jonathan Cape.

Hutton, W. (2008) 'Don't expect China to get the west out of this mess', *Observer*, 26 October.

Huxley, A. (1946) *The perennial philosophy*. London: Chatto and Windus.

Hyder, S. (2005) 'The information society: measurements biased by capitalism and its intent to control-dependent societies—a critical perspective', *International Information & Library Review*, 37 (1): 25–7.

Ibrahim, A. (1996) *The Asian Renaissance*. Singapore: Times Books.

Ibrahim, S.E. (2008) 'Civil society, faith-based organizations and development in the Arab world', in Hettne (ed.), pp. 200–21.

Inagaki, N. (2007) 'Communicating the impact of communication for development: recent trends in empirical research', World Bank Working Paper No. 120.

Inter-American Development Bank (1995) *Social dimensions in the agenda of the IDB*. Copenhagen.

International Institute for Communication and Development (2004) *The ICT roundtable process*. The Hague: IICD.

Irwan, A. (1996) 'Rent and ethnic Chinese regional business networks: Indonesia's puzzling high economic growth', Kuala Lumpur, unpublished paper.

Isaac, T.M., Th. and M. Tharakan P.K. (1995) 'Kerala: towards a new agenda', *Economic and Political Weekly*, 5–12 August: 1993–2004.

Iwasaki, T., T. Mori and H. Yamaguchi (eds) (1992) *Development strategies for the 21st century*. Tokyo: Institute of Developing Economies.

Jalibi, J. (1984) *Pakistan: the identity of culture*. Karachi: Royal Book Company.

Jessop, B. (1994) 'Post-Fordism and the state', in A. Amin (1994a), pp. 251–79.

Johnson, C. (1982) *MITI and the Japanese miracle*. Stanford, CA: Stanford University Press.

Johnston, D. (1991) 'The deconstruction of development', in C. Murphy (ed.), *The new international political economy*. Basingstoke: Macmillan.

Jolly, R. (1986) 'Adjustment with a human face', in K. Haq and U. Kidar (eds), *Human development: the neglected dimension*. Islamabad: North-South Roundtable, pp. 386–400.

Jolly, R. (ed.) (1996) *Revitalizing African development: an agenda for 21st century reform*, special issue, *Development*, 2.

Jomo, K.S. (ed.) (1995) *Privatizing Malaysia: rents, rhetoric, realities*. Boulder, CO: Westview.

Jones, R.F. (1961) *Ancients and moderns*. New York: Dover.

Jonsson, I. (1999) 'Development, learning processes and institutionalized racism', *Ethnic and Racial Studies*, 22 (1): 113–35.

Judt, T. (1997) 'The social question redivivus', *Foreign Affairs*, 76 (5): 95–117.

Junejo, A.J. and M.Q. Bughio (eds) (1988) *Cultural heritage of Sind*. Jamshoro and Hyderabad, Sindh: Sindhi Adabi Board.

Just World Trust (1995) *Dominance of the West over the rest*. Penang: JUST.

Kaarsholm, P. (ed.) (1991) *Cultural struggle and development in Southern Africa*. Harare, London and Portsmouth: Baobab, James Currey and Heinemann.

Kabeer, N. (1994) *Reversed realities: gender hierarchies in development thought*. London: Verso.

Kandiyoti, D. (1991) 'Identity and its discontents: women and the nation', *Millennium*, 20 (3): 429–44.

Kang, Y.A. (1985) 'Rationality and development in Korea', in C.A. van Peursen and M.C. Doeser (eds), *Development and its rationalities*. Amsterdam: Free University Press, pp. 75–90.

Kaplinsky, R. (1994) *Easternisation: the spread of Japanese management techniques to developing countries*. London: Frank Cass.

Kaplinsky, R. and D. Messner (2008) 'Introduction: the impact of Asian drivers on the developing world', *World Development*, 36 (2): 197–209.

Kaviraj, S. (1992) 'Marxism and the darkness of history', in J. Nederveen Pieterse (ed.), *Emancipations, modern and postmodern*. London: Sage, pp. 79–102.

Kay, C. (1993) 'For a renewal of development studies: Latin American theories and neoliberalism in the era of structural adjustment', *Third World Quarterly*, 14 (4): 691–702.

Kay, C. (1998) *Relevance of structuralist and dependency theories in the neoliberal period: a Latin American perspective*. The Hague: Institute of Social Studies, Working Paper 281.

Keesing, R.M. (1987) 'Anthropology as interpretive quest', *Current Anthropology*, 28 (2): 161–76.

Keohane, R.O. (1984) *After hegemony*. Princeton, NJ: Princeton University Press.

'The Kerala Model of Development: A Debate', *Bulletin of Concerned Asian Scholars*, 30 (3): 25–36.

Khor, M. (1997) 'Effects of globalisation on sustainable development after UNCED', *Third World Resurgence*, 81–2: 5–11.

Kiely, R. (1998) 'Neo liberalism revised? A critical account of World Bank concepts of good governance and market friendly intervention', *Capital & Class*, 64: 63–88.

Kiely, R. (1999) 'The last refuge of the noble savage? A critical account of post-development', *European Journal of Development Research*, 11 (1): 30–55.

Kishimoto, H. (1963) 'Modernization versus westernization in the East', *Cahiers d'histoire mondiale*, 7.

Kissinger, H. (1970) 'The white revolutionary: reflections on Bismarck', in D.A. Rustow (ed.), *Philosophers and kings: studies in leadership*. New York: Braziller, pp. 317–53.

Klauss, R. and D.C. Korten (1984) *People-centered development: contributions toward theory and planning frameworks*. West Hartford, CT: Kumarian Press.

Konrád, G. (1984) *Antipolitics*. London: Quartet Books.

Korten, D.C. (1990) *Getting to the 21st century: voluntary action and the global agenda*. West Hartford, CT: Kumarian Press.

Korten, D.C. (1995) *When corporations rule the world*. London: Earthscan.

Kothari, M.L. and L.A. Mehta (1988) 'Violence in modern medicine', in Nandy (ed.), pp. 167–210.

Kothari, R. (1988) *Rethinking development: in search of humane alternatives*. Delhi: Ajanta.

Kothari, R. (1993a) *Poverty: human consciousness and the amnesia of development*. London: Zed.

Kothari, R. (1993b) 'The yawning vacuum: a world without alternatives', *Alternatives*, 18: 119–39.

Kothari, S. (1994) 'Global economic institutions and democracy: a view from India', in Cavanagh et al. (eds), pp. 39–55.

Kottak, C.P. (1985) 'Dimensions of culture in development', in G.C. Uhlenbeck (ed.), *The cultural dimension of development*. The Hague: Netherlands National Commission for UNESCO, pp. 38–48.

Krishna, A. and J. Nederveen Pieterse (2008) 'Hierarchical integration: the dollar economy and the rupee economy', *Development and Change*, 39 (2): 219–37.

Kuhn, T.S. (1962) *The structure of scientific revolutions*. Chicago: University of Chicago Press.

Kumar, A. (2009) '2008: a difficult year, relief not in sight soon', *The Tribune* (New Delhi), 1 January.

Kuttner, R. (1991) *The end of laissez-faire: national purpose and the global economy after the cold war*. New York: Alfred Knopf.

Laclau, E. (1990) *New reflections on the revolution of our time*. London: Verso.

Laclau, E. and C. Mouffe (1985) *Hegemony and socialist strategy*. London: Verso.

Lal, D. (1983) *The poverty of 'development economics'*. London: Institute of Economic Affairs.

Lal, D. (1995) 'The misconceptions of "development economics"', in Corbridge (ed.), pp. 56–63.

Lal, D. (2004) *In praise of empires: globalization and order*. London: Palgrave.

Lao Tsu (1973) *Tao te Ching*, trans. by Gia-fu Feng and J. English. London: Wildwood House.

Lash, S. and J. Urry (1994) *Economies of signs and space*. London: Sage.

Latouche, S. (1993) *In the wake of the affluent society: an exploration of post-development*. London: Zed (orig. French edn. 1991).

Latour, B. (1993) *We have never been modern*. London: Harvester Wheatsheaf.

Lawson, C. and E. Lorenz (1999) 'Collective learning, tacit knowledge and regional innovative capacity', *Regional Studies*, 33 (4): 305–17.

Lee, M.E. (1997) 'From Enlightenment to chaos: toward nonmodern social theory', in Eve et al. (eds), pp.15–29.

Lee, R.L.M. (1994) 'Modernization, postmodernism and the Third World', *Current Sociology*, 42 (2).

Leftwich, A. (ed.) (1996) *Democracy and development*. Cambridge: Polity.

Leiken, R. (1996) 'Controlling the global corruption epidemic', *Foreign Policy*, 105: 55–73.

Leipziger, D.M. and V. Thomas (1995) *The lessons of East Asia: an overview of country experience*. Washington, DC: World Bank.

Léon, O., S. Burch and E. Tamayo (2005) *Communication in movement*. Quito: Agencia Latino Americana de Información.

Levi, M. (1996) 'Social and unsocial capital: a review essay of Robert Putnam's *Making Democracy Work*', *Politics and Society*, 24 (1): 45–54.

Leys, C. (1996) *The rise and fall of development theory*. London and Nairobi: James Currey and EAEP.

Li Lulu (1989) 'Theoretical theses on "social modernization"', *International Sociology*, 4 (4): 365–77.

Lian, B. and J.R. Oneal (1997) 'Cultural diversity and economic development: a cross-national study of 98 countries, 1960–1985', *Economic Development and Cultural Change*, 46 (1): 61–77.

Light, I. and S. Karageorgis (1994) 'The ethnic economy', in Smelser and Swedberg (eds), pp. 647–71.

Lim, Y. (1995) 'Industrial policy, technological learning and productivity gains theory and evidence from South Korea', The Hague: Institute of Social Studies Industrialization Seminar.

Lindblom, C. (1959) 'The science of "muddling through"', Public Administration Review, 19 (2).

Lipietz, A. (1992) Towards a new economic order: postfordism, ecology and democracy. Cambridge: Polity.

Lipietz, A. (1995) Green hopes: the future of political ecology. Cambridge: Polity.

Lipton, M. (1977) Why poor people stay poor: a study of urban bias in world development. London: Maurice Temple Smith.

Litonjua, M.D. (1994) 'Outside the den of dragons: the Philippines and the NICs of Asia', Studies in Comparative International Development, 28 (4): 3–30.

Lively, J. (1981) 'The Europe of the Enlightenment', History of European Ideas, 1 (2).

Long, N. (1994) 'From paradigm lost to paradigm regained? The case for an actor-oriented sociology of development', in Long and Long (eds), pp. 16–46.

Long, N. and A. Long (eds) (1994) Battlefields of knowledge. London: Routledge.

Long, N. and M. Villarreal (1993) 'Exploring development interfaces: from the transfer of knowledge to the transformation of meaning', in Schuurman (ed.), pp. 140–68.

Lovink, G. (2005) The principle of notworking: concepts in critical Internet culture. Amsterdam: HvA.

Lummis, D. (1991) 'Development against democracy', Alternatives, 16: 31–66.

Lummis, D. (1994) 'The end of development', AMPO, 25 (3): 36–40.

Luyt, B. (2004) 'Who benefits from the digital divide?' First Monday, 9 (8), http://www.firstmonday.org/issues/issue9_8/luyt/index.html

Lynch, M. (2000) 'Against reflexivity as an academic virtue and source of privileged knowledge', Theory, Culture & Society, 17 (3): 26–54.

Mahathir Mohamad and S. Ishihara (1995) The voice of Asia. Tokyo: Kodansha International.

Mair, L. (1965) An introduction to social anthropology. Oxford: Clarendon.

Mander, J. and E. Goldsmith (eds) (1996) The case against the global economy and for a turn toward the local. San Francisco: Sierra Club.

Mann, M. (1986) The sources of social power. Cambridge: Cambridge University Press.

Maquet, J. (1972) Africanity: the cultural unity of Black Africa. London: Oxford University Press.

Marcus, G.E. and M.J. Fischer (1986) Anthropology as cultural critique. Chicago: University of Chicago Press.

Marglin, F.A. and S. Marglin (eds) (1990) Dominating knowledge: development, culture and resistance. Oxford: Clarendon.

Martin, K. (1991) 'Modern development theory', in idem (ed.), Strategies of economic development. London: Macmillan, pp. 27–74.

Martinez-Alier, J. (2000) 'Environmental justice as a force for sustainability', in Nederveen Pieterse (ed.) (2000a), pp. 148–74.

Martinussen, J. (1997) Society, state and market: a guide to competing theories of development. London: Zed.

Massey, D. (1993) 'Power-geometry and a progressive sense of place', in J. Bird, B. Curtis, T. Putnam, G. Robertson and L. Tickner (eds), Mapping the futures: local cultures, global change. London: Routledge, pp. 59–69.

Max-Neef, M.A. (1982) Experiences in barefoot economics. Stockholm: Dag Hammarskjöld Foundation.

Max-Neef, M.A. (1991) Human scale development. New York: Apex Press.

Mazlish, B. and R. Buultjens (eds) (1993) Conceptualizing global history. Boulder, CO: Westview.

McCraw, Th. K. (2007) Prophet of innovation: Joseph Schumpeter and creative destruction. Cambridge, MA: Belknap Press.

McEvilley, T. (1995) 'Here comes everybody', Africus: Johannesburg Biennale. Johannesburg: Exhibition Catalogue, pp. 53–7.

McHale, B. (1992) Constructing postmodernism. London: Routledge.

McLaren, P. (1995) Critical pedagogy and predatory culture. New York: Routledge.

McLaughlin, L. (2005) 'Cisco Systems, the United Nations, and the corporatization of development' (incom-l@communicado.info).

McMichael, P. (1996) *Development and social change: a global perspective.* Thousand Oaks, CA: Pine Forge Press.

Meadows, D.L. and D.H. Meadows et al. (1972) *The limits to growth* (report to the Club of Rome). New York: Universe Books

Mehmet, O. (1995) *Westernizing the Third World: the Eurocentricity of economic development theories.* London: Routledge.

Mehta, P.D. (1989) *Holistic consciousness.* Longmead, Shaftesbury: Element Books.

Mehta, U. (1997) 'Liberal strategies of exclusion', in F. Cooper and Ann L. Stoler (eds), *Tensions of empire: colonial cultures in a bourgeois world.* Berkeley: University of California Press, pp. 59–86.

Melucci, A. (1988) 'Social movements and the democratization of everyday life', in J. Keane (ed.) *Civil society and the state: new European perspectives.* London: Verso.

Melucci, A. (1989) *Nomads of the present.* Ed by J. Keane and P. Mier. London: Hutchinson Radius.

Menou, M.J. (2001) 'The global digital divide: beyond hICTeria', *Aslib Proceedings*, 53 (4): 112–14.

Meppem, T. and R. Gill (1998) 'Planning for sustainability as a learning concept', *Ecological Economics*, 26 (2): 121–38.

Metcalf, T. (1998) *Ideologies of the Raj.* Cambridge: Cambridge University Press.

Meurs, M. van (1997) *J.C. Smuts: staatsman, holist, generaal.* Amsterdam: Suid-Afrikaanse Instituut.

Mhlaba, L. (1991) 'Local cultures and development in Zimbabwe: the case of Matabeleland', in Kaarsholm (ed.), pp. 209–26.

Midgley, J. (1995) *Social development: the developmental perspective in social welfare.* London: Sage.

Mies, M. (1986) *Patriarchy and accumulation on a world scale: women in the international division of labour.* London: Zed.

Migdal, J.S. (1988) *Strong societies and weak states: state-society relations and state capabilities in the Third World.* Princeton, NJ: Princeton University Press.

Miller, C.L. (1990) *Theories of Africans: francophone literature and anthropology in Africa.* Chicago: University of Chicago Press.

Miller, D. (1997) *Capitalism: an ethnographic approach.* Oxford: Berg.

Ministry of Foreign Affairs (1991) *A world of difference.* The Hague: SDU.

Minter, W. (1986) *King Solomon's mines revisited.* New York: Basic Books.

Mishra, R. (1996) 'The welfare of nations', in Boyer and Drache (eds), pp. 316–33.

Mitchell, T. (1988) *Colonising Egypt.* Cambridge: Cambridge University Press.

Mitchell, T. (2002) *Rule of experts: Egypt, techno-politics, modernity.* Berkeley: University of California Press.

Mittelman, J.H. (ed.) (1996) *Globalization: critical reflections.* Boulder, CO: Lynne Riener.

Mittelman, J.H. (2006) 'Globalization and development: learning from debates in China', *Globalizations*, 3 (3): 377–92.

Mkandawire, T. (2004) 'Introduction', in Mkandawire (ed.), pp. 1–33.

Mkandawire, T. (ed.) (2004) *Social policy in a development context.* London: Palgrave.

Mohanty, M. (1989) 'Changing terms of discourse. A poser', *Economic and Political Weekly*, 16 September.

Moll, P., N. Nattrass and L. Loots (eds) (1991) *Redistribution: how can it work in South Africa?* Cape Town: David Philip.

Møller, K. and E. Rasmussen (eds) (1995) *Partnership for new social development: UN World Summit for Social Development.* Copenhagen: Mandag Morgen Strategisk Forum.

Moore Jr, B. (1969) *Social origins of dictatorship and democracy.* Harmondsworth: Penguin.

Moore, T. (1992) *Care of the soul.* London: Judy Piatkus.

Moser, C.O.N. (1991) 'Gender planning in the Third World: meeting practical and strategic needs', in R. Grant and K. Newland (eds), *Gender and international relations.* Buckingham: Open University Press, pp. 83–121.

Mosley, P., J. Harrington and J. Toye (1991) *Aid and power: the World Bank and policy-based lending.* London: Routledge.

Mouzelis, N. (1988) 'Sociology of development: reflections on the present crisis', *Sociology*, 22 (1): 23–44.

Mulgan, G. (1994) *Politics in an antipolitical age.* Cambridge: Polity.

Munck, R. and D. O'Hearn (eds) (1999) *Critical development theory: contributions to a new paradigm.* London: Zed.

Murphy, C.N. (2006) *The United Nations Development Programme: A better way?* Cambridge: Cambridge University Press.

Myrdal, G. (1968) *Asian drama: an inquiry into the poverty of nations.* New York: Twentieth Century Fund.

Mytelka, L.K. (1993) 'Rethinking development: a role for innovation networking in the "other two-thirds"', *Futures*, 25 (6): 694–712.

Naess, A. (1976) *Ecology, community and lifestyle.* Cambridge: Cambridge University Press (1989).

Nandy, A. (ed.) (1988) *Science, hegemony and violence: a requiem for modernity.* New Delhi: Oxford University Press.

Nandy, A. (1989) 'Shamans, savages and the wilderness: on the audibility of dissent and the future of civilizations', *Alternatives*, 14: 263–77.

Nandy, A. (1995) *The savage Freud.* New Delhi: Oxford University Press.

Naqvi, N. (ed.) (1996) *Rethinking security, rethinking development.* Islamabad: Sustainable Development Policy Institute.

Nayyar, D. (2006) 'India's unfinished journey: transforming growth into development', *Modern Asian Studies*, 40 (3): 797–832.

Nederveen Pieterse, J. (1989) *Empire and emancipation: power and liberation on a world scale.* New York: Praeger.

Nederveen Pieterse, J. (1992a) *White on black: images of Africa and blacks in western popular culture.* New Haven and London: Yale University Press.

Nederveen Pieterse, J. (1992b) 'Emancipations, modern and postmodern', in idem (ed.), *Emancipations, modern and postmodern.* London: Sage, pp. 5–43.

Nederveen Pieterse, J. (1994) 'Unpacking the west: how European is Europe?' in A. Rattansi and S. Westwood (eds), *Racism, modernity, identity.* Cambridge: Polity, pp. 129–49.

Nederveen Pieterse, J. (1998a) 'Humanitarian intervention and beyond', in idem (ed.), *World orders in the making: humanitarian intervention and beyond.* London and New York: Macmillan and St Martin's Press, pp. 1–22.

Nederveen Pieterse, J. (1998b) 'Hybrid modernities: mélange modernities in Asia', *Sociological Analysis*, 1 (3): 75–86.

Nederveen Pieterse, J. (ed.) (2000a) *Global futures: shaping globalization.* London: Zed.

Nederveen Pieterse, J. (2000b) 'Collective action and globalization', in H. Lustiger-Thaler, P. Hamel, J. Nederveen Pieterse and S. Roseneil (eds), *Globalization and collective action.* London and New York: Macmillan and St Martin's Press, pp. 21–40.

Nederveen Pieterse, J. (2003) *Globalization and culture: global mélange.* Lanham, MD: Rowman and Littlefield (2nd edn 2009).

Nederveen Pieterse, J. (2004) *Globalization or empire?* New York: Routledge.

Nederveen Pieterse, J. (2005a) 'Digital capitalism and development: the unbearable lightness of ICT4D', in G. Lovink and S. Zehle (eds), *Incommunicado Reader.* Amsterdam: Institute of Network Culture, pp. 11–29 (www.incommunicado.info/reader).

Nederveen Pieterse, J. (2005b) 'Tough liberalism: the Human Development Report and cultural liberty', *Development and Change*, 36 (6): 1267–73.

Nederveen Pieterse, J. (2006) 'Oriental globalization: past and present', in G. Delanty (ed.), *Europe and Asia beyond east and west: towards a new cosmopolitanism.* London: Routledge, pp. 61–73.

Nederveen Pieterse, J. (2007) *Ethnicities and global multiculture: pants for an octopus.* Lanham, MD: Rowman and Littlefield.

Nederveen Pieterse, J. (2008a) 'Globalization the next round: sociological perspectives', *Futures*, 40 (8): 707–20.

Nederveen Pieterse, J. (2008b) *Is there hope for Uncle Sam? Beyond the American bubble.* London: Zed.

Nederveen Pieterse, J. (2009a) 'Introduction: New balance', in Dasgupta and Nederveen Pieterse (eds).

Nederveen Pieterse, J. (2009b) 'Paradigm shifts in development', in P. van Lieshout, M. Kremer and R. Went (eds), *Doing good or doing better: development policies in a globalising world.* Scientific Council for Government Policy, Amsterdam University Press.

Nederveen Pieterse, J. (2009c) 'Media and global divides: representing the rise of the rest as threat', *Global Media and Communication* (forthcoming).

Nederveen Pieterse, J. and B. Parekh (eds) (1995) *The decolonization of imagination*. London: Zed.

Nederveen Pieterse, J. and B. Rehbein (eds) (2009) *Globalization and emerging societies: development and inequality*. London: Palgrave Macmillan.

Needham, J. (1981) 'Attitudes toward time and change as compared with Europe', in *Science in traditional China*. Cambridge, MA: Harvard University Press, pp. 107–32.

Nerfin, M. (ed.) (1977) *Another development: approaches and strategies*. Uppsala: Dag Hammarskjöld Foundation.

Ngenda, A. (2005) 'The nature of the international intellectual property system: universal norms and values or western chauvinism?' *Information & Communications Technology Law*, 14 (1): 59–79.

Nietzsche, F.W. (1976) *Twilight of the idols*, in *The portable Nietzsche*, trans. W. Kaufman. Harmondsworth: Penguin.

Nieuwenhuijze, C.A.O. van (1983) *Culture and development: the prospects of an afterthought*. The Hague: Institute of Social Studies.

Nisbet, R.A. (1969) *Social change and history*. Oxford: Oxford University Press.

Nisbet, R.A. (1980) *History of the idea of progress*. New York: Basic Books.

Niva, S. (1999) 'Alternatives to neoliberalism', *Middle East Report*, 29 (1): 16.

Norberg-Hodge, H. (1995) 'The development hoax', in Just World Trust, pp. 110–23.

Obaid, T. (2008) 'Culture and human rights', in B. Hettne (ed.), pp. 149–71.

O'Connor, S. (1994) *Universal mother*. London: Ensign Records.

Ohmae, K. (1992) *The borderless world: power and strategy in the global marketplace*. London: Collins.

Ohmae, K. (1995) *The end of the nation state: the rise of regional economies*. New York: Free Press.

Ohno, I. (1996) *Beyond the 'East Asian miracle': an Asian view*. New York: UNDP, Office of Development Studies.

Okita, S. (1993) 'Many paths to development', in South Centre (ed.), pp. 272–81.

Okun, A. (1975) *Equality and efficiency: the big trade-off*. Washington, DC: Brookings Institution.

Olowu, B. (1988) *African local governments as instruments of social development*. The Hague, International Union of Local Authorities.

Oman, C. (1993) 'Globalization and regionalization in the 1980s and 1990s', *Development and International Cooperation*, 9 (16): 51–69.

Oman, C. (1994) *Globalisation and regionalisation: the challenge for developing countries*. Paris: OECD.

Oman, P. and G. Wignaraja (1991) *The postwar evolution of development thinking*. London: Macmillan.

Ong, A. (2006) *Neoliberalism as exception: mutations in sovereignty and citizenship*. Durham, NC: Duke University Press.

Oommen, T.K. (1998) 'Changing paradigms of development: the evolving participatory society', *Journal of Social and Economic Development*, 1: 35–45.

Orr, D. (1996) 'Slow knowledge', *Resurgence*, 179: 30–2.

Ottati, G. dei (1994) 'Trust, interlinking transactions and credit in the industrial district', *Cambridge Journal of Economics*, 18 (6): 529–46.

Oxfam (1996) *Development and social diversity*. Oxford: Oxfam.

Palley, T.I. (1999) 'Toward a new international economic order', *Dissent*, 46 (2): 48–53.

Parayil, G. (2005) 'The digital divide and increasing returns: contradictions of informational capitalism', *Information Society*, 21: 41–51.

Parekh, B. (1997) *Gandhi*. Oxford: Oxford University Press.

Parekh, B. (2000) *Rethinking multiculturalism*. London: Macmillan.

Park, D.H. (1985) 'Paradigms of rationality', in C.A. van Peursen and M.C. Doeser (eds), *Development and its rationalities*. Amsterdam: Free University Press, pp. 35–50.

Parker, I. (ed.) (1998) *Social constructionism, discourse and realism*. London: Sage.

Passmore, J. (1978) *Science and its critics*. London: Duckworth.

Patomäki, H. and T. Teivanen (2004) *A possible world: democratic transformation of global institutions*. London: Zed.

Patterson, R. (ed.) (2007) *African brain circulation: beyond the drain-gain debate*. Leiden: Brill.

Peet, R. (1999) *Theories of development*. New York: Guilford.

Peet, R. (with E. Hartwick) (1999) *Theories of development*. New York: Guilford Press.

Peet, R. and M.J. Watts (eds) (1996) *Liberation ecologies: environment, development, social movements*. London: Routledge.

Perkins, P.E. (1998) 'The potential of community-based alternatives to globalization', *Development*, 41 (3): 61–7.

Perri, D., Leat, K. Seltzer and G. Stoker (2001) *Holistic governance*. London: Palgrave.

Petras, J. (1990) 'Retreat of the intellectuals', *Economic and Political Weekly*, 25 (38): 2143–56.

Petras, J. (2007) *Rulers and ruled in the US empire*. Atlanta, GA: Clarity Press.

Petras, J. and H. Brill (1985) 'The tyranny of globalism', *Journal of Contemporary Asia*, 15 (4): 403–20.

Petras, J. and H. Veltmeyer (2002) 'Age of reverse aid: neo-liberalism as a catalyst of regression', *Development and Change*, 33 (2): 281–94.

Petrella, R. (1995) 'Europe between competitive innovation and a new social contract', *International Social Science Journal*, 47 (1 / 143): 11–23.

Pitt, D.C. (ed.) (1976) *Development from below: anthropologists and development situations*. The Hague: Mouton.

Pletsch, C.E. (1981) 'The three worlds, or the division of social scientific labor, circa 1950–1975', *Comparative Studies in Society and History*, 23: 565–90.

Polanyi, K. (1957/1944) *The great transformation*. Boston, MA: Beacon.

Pompa, L. (1990) *Vico: a study of the 'New Science'*, 2nd edn. Cambridge: Cambridge University Press.

Porter, D. (1996) 'Scenes from childhood: the homesickness of development discourses', in Crush (ed.), pp. 63–86.

Portes, A. (1994) 'The informal economy and its paradoxes', in Smelser and Swedberg (eds), pp. 426–50.

Portes, A. (1996) 'Transnational communities: their emergence and significance in the contemporary world-system', in R.P. Korzeniewicz and W.C. Smith (eds), *Latin America in the world economy*. Westport, CT: Greenwood Press, pp. 151–68.

Portes, A. (2009) 'Migration and development: reconciling opposite views', *Ethnic and Racial Studies*, 32 (1): 5–22.

Posey, D.A. (1994) 'Traditional resource rights: de facto self determination for indigenous peoples', in L. van der Vlist (ed.), *Voices of the earth: indigenous peoples, new partners and the right to self-determination in practice*. Amsterdam: Netherlands Centre for Indigenous Peoples, pp. 217–35.

Pradervand, P. (1989) *Listening to Africa: developing Africa from the grassroots*. New York: Praeger.

Pred, A. and M.J. Watts (1992) *Reworking modernity: capitalisms and symbolic discontent*. New Brunswick, NJ: Rutgers University Press.

Preston, P.W. (1996) *Development theory: an introduction*. Oxford: Blackwell.

Prestowitz, C. (2005) *Three billion new capitalists: the great shift of wealth and power to the east*. New York: Basic Books.

Priesner, S. (1999) 'Gross National Happiness: Bhutan's vision of development and its challenges'. Thimphu, Bhutan, bhutanstudies.org.bt.

Prigogine, I. and I. Stengers (1984) *Order out of chaos*. New York: Bantam Books.

Pronk, J. (1990) 'Two worlds in one', in *Solidarity against poverty*. Amsterdam: Evert Vermeer Foundation, pp. 29–42.

Pronk, J. (2000) 'Globalization: a developmental approach', in Nederveen Pieterse (ed.) (2000a), pp. 40–52.

Putnam, R.D. (1993) *Making democracy work: civic traditions in modern Italy*. Princeton, NJ: Princeton University Press.

Quigley, C. (1966) *Tragedy and hope: a history of the world in our time*. New York: Macmillan.

Rahman, M.A. (1993) *People's self-development: perspectives on Participatory Action Research*. London and Dhaka: Zed and Dhaka University Press.

Rahnema, M. (1992) 'Poverty', in Sachs (ed.) (1992a), pp. 158–76.

Rahnema, M. (1997) 'Towards post-development: searching for signposts, a new language and new paradigm', in Rahnema and Bawtree (eds), pp. 377–404.

Rahnema, M. and V. Bawtree (eds) (1997) *The post-development reader*. London: Zed.

Ramo, J.C. (2004) *The Beijing consensus*. London: Foreign Policy Centre.

Rapley, J. (2004) *Globalization and inequality: neoliberalism's downward spiral*. Boulder, CO: Lynne Rienner.

Reich, R.B. (1983) *The next American frontier.* Harmondsworth: Penguin.

Reifer, T.E. (ed.) (2004) *Globalization, hegemony and power.* Boulder, CO: Paradigm.

Rew, A. (1997) 'The donors' discourse: official social development knowledge in the 1980s', in Grillo and Stirrat (eds), pp. 81–106.

Rist, G. (1990a) 'Development as the new religion of the West', *Quid Pro Quo,* 1 (2): 5–8.

Rist, G. (1990b) '"Development" as part of the modern myth: the western socio-economic dimension of "development"', *European Journal of Development Alternatives,* 2 (1): 10.

Rist, G. (1997) *The history of development: from western origins to global faith.* London: Zed.

Rist, G., M. Rahnema and G. Esteva (1992) *Le Nord perdu: repères pour l'après-développement.* Lausanne: Éditions d'en bas.

Robertson, R. (1992) *Globalization.* London: Sage.

Robertson, R. and F. Lechner (1985) 'Modernization, globalization and the problem of culture in world-systems theory', *Theory, Culture & Society,* 2(3): 103–17.

Robin, J. (1992) *Women and wellbeing: how Kerala became a model.* Basingstoke: Macmillan.

Robins, S. (2003) 'Whose modernity? indigenous modernities and land claims after apartheid', *Development and Change,* 34 (2): 265–86.

Rodan, G. (1989) *The political economy of Singapore's industrialization.* Kuala Lumpur: Forum.

Rodrik, D. (2000) 'How far will international economic integration go?' *Journal of Economic Perspectives,* 14 (1): 177–86.

Rodrik, D. (2005) 'Feasible globalizations', in M.M. Weinstein (ed.), *Globalization, what's new?* New York: Columbia University Press, pp. 196–203.

Rodrik, D. (2008) 'Is there a new Washington consensus?' *Business Standard,* Mumbai, 12 June.

Rodrik, D. and R. Hausman (2003) 'Economic development as self discovery', *Journal of Development Economics,* 72: 603–33.

Roe, E. (1995) 'Critical theory, sustainable development and populism', *Telos,* 103: 149–62.

Roe, E. (1998) *Taking complexity seriously: policy analysis, triangulation and sustainable development.* Boston: Kluwer.

Rogaly, B. and C. Roche (1998) *Learning from south–north links in microfinance.* Oxford: Oxfam working paper.

Rorty, R. (1991) *Objectivity, relativism, and truth.* Cambridge: Cambridge University Press.

Rorty, R. (1997) *Achieving our country: leftist thought in 20th century America.* Cambridge, MA: Harvard University Press.

Rosenau, P. (1992) *Postmodernism and the social sciences.* Princeton, NJ: Princeton University Press.

Rostow, W.W. (1960) *The stages of economic growth.* Cambridge: Cambridge University Press.

Rostow, W.W. (1971) *Politics and the stages of growth.* Cambridge: Cambridge University Press.

Roszak, T. (1973) *Where the wasteland ends.* New York: Doubleday.

Roszak, T. (1976) *Unfinished animal.* London: Faber and Faber.

Rowe, W. and V. Schelling (1991) *Memory and modernity: popular culture in Latin America.* London: Verso.

Ryan, A. (1999) 'Britain: recycling the Third Way', *Dissent,* 46 (2): 77–80.

Sabetti, F. (1996) 'Path dependency and civic culture: some lessons from Italy about interpreting social experiments', *Politics and Society,* 24 (1).

Sachs, I. (1972) 'The logic of development', *International Social Science Journal,* 24 (1) (reprinted 1998, 157: 361–5).

Sachs, J. (2008) *Common wealth: economics for a crowded planet.* New York: Penguin.

Sachs, W. (ed.) (1992a) *The development dictionary: a guide to knowledge as power.* London: Zed.

Sachs, W. (1992b) 'Introduction', *The development dictionary.* London: Zed, pp. 1–5.

Sachs, W. (1999) *Planet dialectics: explorations in environment and development.* London: Zed.

Sahlins, M.D. and E.R. Service (eds) (1960) *Evolution and culture.* Ann Arbor: University of Michigan Press.

Said, E.W. (1981) *Covering Islam.* New York: Pantheon.

Said, E.W. (1985) *Orientalism.* Harmondsworth: Penguin (orig. edn 1978).

Said, E.W. (1986) 'Foucault and the imagination of power', in D.C. Hoy (ed.), *Foucault: a critical reader.* Oxford: Blackwell, pp. 149–56.

Said, E.W. (1993) *Culture and imperialism.* New York: Alfred Knopf.

Salmen, L. (1987) *Listen to the people: participant observation evaluation of development projects*. New York: Oxford University Press.

Salmond, A. (1982) 'Theoretical landscapes: on cross-cultural conceptions of knowledge', in D. Parkin (ed.), *Semantic anthropology*. London and New York: Academic Press.

Sampson, A. (1987) *Black and gold: tycoons, revolutionaries and Apartheid*. New York: Pantheon.

Santos, B. de Sousa (1995) *Toward a new common sense*. London: Routledge.

Sanyal, B. (1994) 'Ideas and institutions: why the alternative development paradigm withered away', *Regional Development Dialogue*, 15 (1): 23–35.

Sato, T. and W.E. Smith (1996) 'The new development paradigm: organizing for implementation', in Griesgraber and Gunter (eds) (1996a), pp. 89–102.

Schech, S. and J. Haggis (2000) *Culture and development: a critical introduction*. Oxford: Blackwell.

Schiller, D. (1999) *Digital capitalism: networking the global market system*. Cambridge, MA: MIT Press.

Schiller, D. and V. Mosco (eds) (2001) *Continental order? Integrating North America for cyber-capitalism*. Boulder, CO: Rowman and Littlefield.

Scholte, J.A. (1993) *International relations of social change*. Buckingham: Open University Press.

Scholte, J.A. (1998) *The International Monetary Fund and civil society: an underdeveloped dialogue*. The Hague, Institute of Social Studies, Working Paper 272.

Schudson, M. (1994) 'Culture and the integration of national societies', *Social Science Journal*, 139: 63–82.

Schumacher College (1997) *Course programme 1997–1998*, Dartington, Devon.

Schuurman, F. (ed.) (1993) *Beyond the impasse: new directions in development theory*. London: Zed.

Schuurman, F.J. (2000) 'Paradigms lost, paradigms regained? Development studies in the twenty-first century', *Third World Quarterly*, 21 (1): 7–20.

Schutz, A. (1972) *The phenomenology of the social world*. London: Heinemann (orig. edn 1932).

Schwartzman, K.C. (2004) 'Globalization: the new mechanism of dependency', in Reifer (ed.), pp. 110–30.

Schwenninger, S.R. (2009) 'Redoing globalization', *The Nation*, 12–19 January: 30–32.

Scott, J.C. (1985) *The weapons of the weak*. New Haven, CT: Yale University Press.

Scott, J.C. (1991) *Domination and the arts of resistance*. New Haven, CT: Yale University Press.

Scott, J.C. (1998) *Seeing like a state: how certain schemes to improve the human condition have failed*. New Haven, CT: Yale University Press.

Seabrook, J. (1994) *Victims of development: resistance and alternatives*. London: Verso.

Seagrave, S. (1996) *Lords of the Rim*. London: Corgi Books.

Seers, D. (1979) 'The birth, life and death of development economics', *Development and Change*, 10 (4): 707–19.

Sen, A. (1985) *Commodities and capabilities*. Oxford: Oxford University Press.

Sen, A. (1999) *Development as freedom*. New York: Anchor.

Sen, A. and J.D. Wolfensohn (1999) 'Let's respect both sides of the development coin', *International Herald Tribune*, 5 May.

Sen, G. (1997) 'Globalization in the 21st century: challenges for civil society', Amsterdam: University of Amsterdam.

Senge, P.M. (1990) *The fifth discipline: the art and practice of the learning organization*. New York: Doubleday.

Shack, W.A. and E.P. Skinner (eds) (1979) *Strangers in African societies*. Berkeley: University of California Press.

Shade, L.R. (2003) 'Here comes the Dot Force? The new cavalry for equity!' *Gazette*, 65 (2): 107–20.

Sheffield Group (eds) (1989) *The social economy and the democratic state*. London: Lawrence and Wishart.

Sheth, D.L. (1987) 'Alternative development as political practice', *Alternatives*, 12 (2): 155–71.

Shils, E. (1966) *Political development in the new states*. The Hague: Mouton.

Shiva, V. (1988a) 'Reductionist science as epistemological violence', in Nandy (ed.), pp. 232–56.

Shiva, V. (1988b) *Staying alive: women, ecology and development*. London: Zed.

Shiva, V. (1991) 'Problems with the Enlightenment', in A. Dobson (ed.) *The Green reader*. London: Zed.

Shweder, R.A. (1993) '"Why do men barbecue?" and other postmodern ironies of growing up in the decade of ethnicity', *Daedalus*, Winter: 279–308.

Siaroff, A. (1999) 'Premature democracies, the promotion of development and political-cultural factors', *Third World Quarterly*, 20 (2): 405–19.

Sims, M. (2002) 'A digital dividend?' *Intermedia*, 30 (1): 28–30.

Singer, H.W. (1989) 'When pursuit of surplus ends', *India International Centre Quarterly*, Spring.

Singer, H.W. (1996) 'How relevant is Keynesianism today for understanding problems of development?' Paper presented at EADI conference, Vienna.

Singer, H.W. and R. Jolly (eds) (1995) 'Fifty years on: the UN and economic and social development', *IDS Bulletin*, 26 (4).

Singh, J. (2002) 'From atoms to bits: consequences of the emerging digital divide in India', *International Information & Library Review*, 34 (2): 187–200.

Singh, Y. (1989) *Essays on modernization in India*. New Delhi: Manohar.

Sirkin, H.L., J.W. Hemerling, A.K. Bhattacharya (2008) *Globality: competing with everyone from everywhere for everything*. New York: Business Plus.

Siu, R.G.H. (1957) *The Tao of science: an essay on Western knowledge and Eastern wisdom*. Cambridge, MA: MIT Press.

Skocpol, T. (1979) *States and social revolutions*. Cambridge: Cambridge University Press.

Skocpol, T. (ed.) (1984) *Vision and method in historical sociology*. Cambridge: Cambridge University Press.

Skolimowski, H. (1994) *The participatory mind*. London: Penguin/Arkana.

Slater, D. (1992) 'Theories of development and politics of the post-modern – exploring a border zone', in J. Nederveen Pieterse (ed.), *Emancipations, modern and postmodern*. London: Sage, pp. 283–319.

Slater, D. (1995) 'Challenging western visions of the global', *European Journal of Development Research*, 7 (2): 366–88.

Slater, D. (2004) *Geopolitics and the post-colonial: rethinking north–south relations*. Oxford: Blackwell.

Slater, D. and M. Bell (2002) 'Aid and the geopolitics of the post-colonial: critical reflections on New Labour's overseas development strategy', *Development and Change*, 33 (2): 335–60.

Smelser, N.J. and R. Swedberg (eds) (1994) *The handbook of economic sociology*. Princeton, NJ: Princeton University Press.

Smiers, J. (2000) 'The abolition of copyright: better for artists, Third World countries and the public domain', *Gazette*, 62 (5): 379–406.

Smillie, I. (1997) 'Let them eat paradigms: public attitudes and the long, slow decline of development cooperation', *Development*, 40 (4): 59–65.

Smith, R. (1993) 'The Chinese road to capitalism', *New Left Review*, 199: 55–99.

So, A.Y. (1990) *Social change and development*. London: Sage.

Sobhan, R. (1989) 'The state and development of capitalism: the Third World perspective', in K. Bharadwaj and S. Kaviraj (eds), *Perspectives on capitalism*. New Delhi: Sage, pp. 247–58.

Sogge, D. (ed.) (1996) *Compassion and calculation: the business of private foreign aid*. London: Pluto.

Somjee, A.H. (1991) *Development theory*. London: Macmillan.

Sorj, B. (2003) *Confronting inequality in the information society*. Sao Paolo: UNESCO Brazil (brazil@digitaldivide.com).

Soros, G. (1997) 'The capitalist threat', *Atlantic Monthly*, February.

Soros, G. (1998) *The crisis of global capitalism*. New York: Public Affairs.

Soros, G. (2008) *The new paradigm for financial markets: the credit crisis of 2008 and what it means*. New York: Public Affairs.

Soto, H. de (1989) *The other path: the invisible revolution in the Third World*. New York: Harper and Row.

South Centre (ed.) (1993) *Facing the challenge: responses to the Report of the South Commission*. London: Zed.

Stallings, B. (ed.) (1995) *Global change, regional response: the new international context of development*. Cambridge: Cambridge University Press.

Stansbury, M. (2003) 'Access, skills, economic opportunities, and democratic participation: connecting four facets of the digital divide through research', *Canadian Journal of Information and Library Science*, 27 (3): 142–3.

Stavenhagen, R. (1986) 'Ethnodevelopment: a neglected dimension in development thinking', in R. Apthorpe and A. Kráhl (eds), *Development studies: critique and renewal*. Leiden: Brill.

Stavrianos, L.S. (1981) *Global rift: the Third World comes of age*. New York: Morrow.

Stent, G.S. (1978) *Paradoxes of progress*. San Francisco: W.H. Freeman.

Sternberg, E. (1993) 'Transformations: the eight new ages of capitalism', *Futures*, 25 (10): 1019–40.

Stewart, F. (1996) 'Groups for good or ill', *Oxford Development Studies*, 24 (1): 9–25.

Stewart, F., S. Lall and S. Wangwe (1993) *Alternative development strategies in sub-Saharan Africa*. New York: St Martin's Press.

Stiefel, M. and M. Wolfe (1994) *A voice for the excluded: popular participation in development*. London and Geneva: Zed and UNRISD.

Stiglitz, J. (1998) 'More instruments and broader goals: moving toward the post-Washington Consensus', Helsinki, WIDER annual lecture 2.

Stiglitz, J.E. (2002) *Globalization and its discontents*. New York: Norton.

Stiglitz, J.E. (2006) *Making globalization work*. New York: Norton.

Stocking, G.W. (1987) *Victorian anthropology*. New York: Free Press.

Strange, S. (1996) *The retreat of the state*. Cambridge: Cambridge University Press.

Strange, S. (1996) *The Retreat of the State: the diffusion of power in the world economy*. Cambridge: Cambridge University Press.

Subrahmanyam, K. (1998) 'Nuclear India in global politics', *World Affairs*, 2 (3): 12–40.

Sundaram, K.V. (1994) 'Development from within: a rethinking on an alternative development path', *Asia-Pacific Journal of Rural Development*, 4 (1 & 2): 52–67.

Sugar, D. (2005) 'The free software challenge in Latin America', *Countercurrents.org*, http://www.countercurrents.org/gl-sugar030605.htm

Sunkel, O. (2008) 'The precarious sustainability of democracy in Latin America', in Hettne (ed.), pp. 43–69.

Swaan, A. de (ed.) (1994) *Social policy beyond borders*. Amsterdam: Amsterdam University Press.

Taussig, M. (1980) *The devil and commodity fetishism in South America*. Chapel Hill: University of North Carolina Press.

Taylor, C. (1989) *Sources of the self*. Cambridge, MA: Harvard University Press.

Taylor, L. and U. Pieper (1996) 'Reconciling economic reform and sustainable human development: social consequences of neo-liberalism', New York: UNDP, Office of Development Studies (discussion paper).

Teilhard de Chardin, P. (1955) *Le phénomène humain*. Paris: du Seuil.

Temple, J. and P. Johnson (1996) 'Social capability and economic development', unpublished paper.

Tenkasi, R.V. and S.A. Mohrman (1999) 'Global change as contextual collaborative knowledge creation', in Cooperrider and Dutton (eds), pp. 114–36.

Terhal, P. (1987) *World inequality and evolutionary convergence*. Delft: Eburon.

Tharamangalam, J. (1998) 'The perils of social development without economic growth: the development debacle of Kerala, India', *Bulletin of Concerned Asian Scholars*, 30 (1): 23–34.

Therborn, G. (1995) *European modernity and beyond: the trajectory of European societies 1945–2000*. London: Sage.

Thérien, J.-P. (1999) 'Beyond the north–south divide: two tales of world poverty', *Third World Quarterly*, 20 (4): 723–42.

Thomas, C. and P. Wilkin (eds) (1997) *Globalization and the South*. London: Macmillan.

Thompson, M. (2004) 'Discourse, "development" and the "digital divide": ICT and the World Bank', *Review of African Political Economy*, 31 (99): 103–23.

Thornton, R.J. (1988) 'The rhetoric of ethnographic holism', *Cultural Anthropology*, 3 (3): 285–303.

Thornton, W.H. and S.H. Thornton (2006) 'The price of alignment: India in the new Asian drama', *Journal of Developing Societies*, 22 (4): 401–20.

Thrift, N. and A. Amin (1995) *Holding down the global*. Oxford: Oxford University Press.

Tilly, C. (1984) *Big structures, large processes, huge comparisons*. New York: Russell Sage.

Tipps, D.C. (1973) 'Modernization theory and the comparative study of societies: a critical perspective', *Comparative Studies in Society and History*, 15: 199–226.

Tiryakian, E.A. (1991) 'Modernization: exhumetur in pace (Rethinking macrosociology in the 1990s)', *International Sociology*, 6 (2): 165–80.

Tiryakian, E.A. (1992) 'Pathways to metatheory: rethinking the presuppositions of macrosociology', in G. Ritzer (ed.), *Metatheorizing*. London: Sage, pp. 69–87.

Tiryakian, E.A. (1996) 'Three cultures of modernity: Christian, Gnostic, Chthonic', *Theory, Culture & Society*, 13 (1): 99–118.

Todd, S. (1997) 'Actualizing personal and collective health: questioning how development policy meets innate human needs', MA research paper, The Hague: Institute of Social Studies.

Tomlinson, J. (1991) *Cultural imperialism*. Baltimore, MD: Johns Hopkins University Press.

Toulmin, S. (1990) *Cosmopolis: the hidden agenda of modernity*. Chicago: University of Chicago Press.

Townsend, P. (2004) 'From universalism to safety nets: the rise and fall of Keynesian influence on social development', in Mkandawire (ed.), pp. 37–62.

Toye, J. (1987) *Dilemmas of development: reflections on the counterrevolution in development theory and policy*. Oxford: Blackwell.

Trainer, T. (1989) *Developed to death: rethinking third world development*. London: Green Print.

Truong, T.-D. (1999) 'The underbelly of the tiger: gender and the demystification of the Asian miracle', *Review of International Political Economy*, 6 (2): 133–65.

Tsing, A. (2004) 'Inside the economy of appearances', in Amin and Thrift (eds), pp. 83–100.

Tucker, V. (1996a) 'Critical holism: towards a new health model', Cork: University College.

Tucker, V. (ed.) (1996b) *Cultural perspectives on development*. London: Frank Cass.

Tucker, V. (1996c) 'Health, medicine and development: a field of cultural struggle', in Tucker (ed.), pp. 110–28.

Tucker, V. (1997) 'From biomedicine to holistic health: towards a new health model', in A. Cleary and M.P. Treacy (eds), *The sociology of health and illness in Ireland*. Dublin: University College Dublin Press, pp. 30–50.

Tucker, V. (1999) 'The myth of development: a critique of Eurocentric discourse', in Munck and O'Hearn (eds), pp. 1–26.

Tvedt, T. (1998) *Angels of mercy or development diplomats? NGOs and foreign aid*. Oxford and Trenton, NJ: James Currey and Africa World Press.

ul Haq, M. (1995) *Reflections on human development*. New York: Oxford University Press.

ul Haq, M. and K. Haq (1998) *Human development in South Asia: the education challenge*. Karachi: Oxford University Press.

ul Haq, M., I. Kaul and I. Grunberg (1996) *The Tobin tax: coping with financial volatility*. New York: Oxford University Press.

UNDP (1996) (1997) (1998) *Human development report*. New York: Oxford University Press.

UNDP (2004) *Human Development Report 2004: Cultural liberty in today's diverse world*. New York.

UNRISD (1995) *After the Social Summit: implementing the programme of action*. Geneva: UN Research Institute for Social Development.

Vail, L. (ed.) (1989) *The creation of tribalism in Southern Africa*. London: James Currey.

Vattimo, G. (1988) *The end of modernity*. Cambridge: Polity.

Verhelst, T.G. (1990) *No life without roots: culture and development*. London: Zed.

Verzola, R. (2004) *Towards a political economy of information: studies on the information economy*, 2nd edn. Quezon City: Foundation for Nationalist Studies.

Visvanathan, S. (1988) 'On the annals of the laboratory state', in Nandy (ed.).

Vries, J. de (1963) *Etymologisch woordenboek*. Utrecht: Spectrum.

Wade, R. (1990) *Governing the market: economic theory and the role of government intervention in East Asian industrialization*. Princeton, NJ: Princeton University Press.

Wade, R. (1996) 'Japan, the World Bank and the art of paradigm maintenance: the East Asian Miracle in political perspective', *New Left Review*, 217: 3–36.

Wade, R.H. (2002) 'Bridging the digital divide: new route to development or new form of dependency?' *Global Governance*, 8: 443–66.

Wade, R. and F. Veneroso (1998) 'The Asian crisis: the high debt model versus the Wall Street–Treasury–IMF Complex', *New Left Review*, 228: 3–24.

Waldinger, R. et al. (1990) *Ethnic entrepreneurs: immigrant business in industrial societies.* Newbury Park, CA: Sage.

Wallace, M. (1992) 'Negative images: towards a black feminist cultural criticism', in L. Grossberg, C. Nelson and P. Treichler (eds), *Cultural studies.* London: Routledge, pp. 654–71.

Wallerstein, I. (1979) *The politics of the world economy.* Cambridge: Cambridge University Press.

Wallman, S. (ed.) (1977) *Perceptions of development.* Cambridge: Cambridge University Press.

Warde, I. (1998) 'Crony capitalism in the West: the banking system in turmoil', *Le Monde diplomatique,* November.

Warschauer, M. (2003) 'Dissecting the "digital divide": a case study in Egypt', *The Information Society,* 19 (4): 297–304.

Waters, M. (1995) *Globalization.* London: Routledge.

Watts, M. (2006) 'Culture, development and global neo-liberalism', in S. Radcliffe (ed.), *Culture and development in a globalising world.* London: Routledge, pp. 30–57.

Weber, R. (1982) 'The Tao of Physics revisited: a conversation with Fritjof Capra', in Wilber (ed.), pp. 215–48.

Weber, S. (2004) *The success of open source.* Cambridge, MA: Harvard University Press.

Webster, A. (1984) *Introduction to the sociology of development.* London: Macmillan.

Weerasinghe, S. (2004) 'Revolution within the revolution: the Sri Lankan attempt to bridge the digital divide through e-governance', *International Information & Library Review,* 36 (4): 319–32.

Wei-Ming, T. (1979) *Humanity and self-cultivation: essays in Confucian thought.* Berkeley, CA: Asian Humanities Press.

Weiss, L. (1996) 'Sources of the East Asian advantage: an institutional analysis', in R. Robinson (ed.), *Pathways to Asia: the politics of engagement.* St Leonard's: Allen and Unwin, pp. 171–201.

Wertheim, W.F. (1974) *Evolution and revolution.* Harmondsworth: Penguin.

White, G. (ed.) (1988) *Developmental states in East Asia.* London: Macmillan.

Whitmyer, C. (ed.) (1995) *Mindfulness and meaningful work: explorations in right livelihood.* Berkeley, CA: Parallax Press.

Wicks, D.A. (2003) 'Building bridges for seniors: older adults and the digital divide', *Canadian Journal of Information and Library Science,* 27 (3): 146–57.

Wignaraja, P. (1992) 'People's participation: reconciling growth with equity', in P. Ekins and M. Max-Neef (eds), *Real-life economics: understanding wealth creation.* London: Routledge, pp. 392–401.

Wignaraja, P. (ed.) (1993) *New social movements in the south: empowering the people.* London: Zed.

Wignaraja, P. (2008) 'Towards a new school of thought on development in South Asia', in Hettne (ed.), pp. 70–93.

Wilber, K. (ed.) (1982) *The holographic paradigm and other paradoxes.* Boulder, CO: Shambala.

Wilber, K. (1982) 'Physics, mysticism and the new holographic paradigm: a critical appraisal', in idem (ed.), pp. 157–86.

Willenswaard, H. van (2008) 'A new development paradigm inspired by Gross National Happiness? A contribution to the *Global GDP Debate*'. Paper for GNH Movement workshop, August, Bangkok, Chulalongkorn University.

Willett, C. (1998) 'Introduction', in idem (ed.), *Theorizing multiculturalism.* Oxford: Blackwell.

Williams, R. (1976) *Keywords.* Glasgow: Fontana/Croom Helm.

Wolfe, M. (1981) *Elusive development.* Geneva: UNRISD/ UNECLA.

Wolferen, K. van (1990) *The enigma of Japanese power,* 2nd edn. London: Macmillan.

Wong, P.-K. (2002) 'ICT production and diffusion in Asia: digital dividends or digital divide?' *Information Economics and Policy,* 14 (2): 167–87.

Wood, B. (1984) *E.F. Schumacher: his life and thought.* New York: Harper and Row.

Woost, M. (1997) 'Alternative vocabularies of development? "Community" and "participation" in development discourse in Sri Lanka', in Grillo and Stirrat (eds), pp. 229–54.

World Bank (1995) *Advancing social development.* Washington, DC: World Bank.

World Bank (1996) *The World Bank participation sourcebook.* Washington, DC: World Bank.

World Bank (1997) *The state in a changing world: World Development Report 1997.* New York: Oxford University Press.

World Bank (1998) *Knowledge for development: World Development Report 1998/99*. New York: Oxford University Press.

World Bank Report, *Africa development indicators 2007*. Washington DC: World Bank.

World Commission on Culture and Development (1996) *Our creative diversity* (report). Paris: UNESCO Publishing.

World Commission on Environment and Development (1987) *Our common future* (report). Oxford: Oxford University Press.

Worsley, P. (1984) *The three worlds*. London: Weidenfeld and Nicolson.

Wuyts, M., M. Mackintosh and T. Hewitt (eds) (1992) *Development policy and public action*. Oxford: Oxford University Press.

Xin, C. (2003) 'New development of consumerism in Chinese society in the late 1990s', *Asian Exchange: China Reflected*, 18 (2) and 19 (1): 162–75.

Ya'u, Y.Z. (2004) 'The new imperialism and Africa in the global electronic village', *Review of African Political Economy*, 31 (99): 11–29.

Yoshihara, K. (1988) *The rise of ersatz capitalism in South-East Asia*. Singapore: Oxford University Press.

Young, I.M. (1991) *Justice and the politics of difference*. Princeton, NJ: Princeton University Press.

Young, J. (1999) *The exclusive society: social exclusion, crime and difference in late modernity*. London: Sage.

Yurick, S. (1985) *Behold Metatron the recording angel*. New York: Semiotext(e).

Zachariah, M. and R. Sooryamoorthy (1994) *Science for social revolution? Achievements and dilemmas of a development movement: the case of Kerala*. London: Zed.

Zysman, J. and S. Cohen (1987) *Manufacturing matters: the myth of the post-industrial economy*. New York: Basic Books.

Index

Research Methods Books
from SAGE

Basics of
QUALITATIVE
RESEARCH 3e

Juliet Corbin
Anselm Strauss

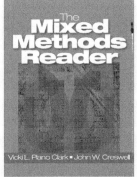

The
**Mixed
Methods
Reader**

Vicki L. Plano Clark ■ John W. Creswell

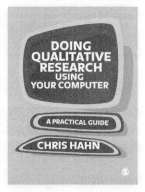

DOING
QUALITATIVE
RESEARCH
USING
YOUR COMPUTER

A PRACTICAL GUIDE

CHRIS HAHN

SECOND EDITION
INTERVIEWS
Learning the Craft of Qualitative Research Interviewing

Steinar Kvale
Svend Brinkmann

DISCOVERING STATISTICS
USING **SPSS** THIRD EDITION

ANDY FIELD

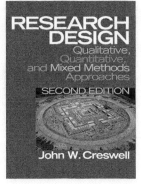

RESEARCH
DESIGN
Qualitative,
Quantitative,
and Mixed Methods
Approaches
SECOND EDITION

John W. Creswell